Lecture Notes in Computer Science   12501

More information about this subseries at http://www.springer.com/series/7410

Sokratis Katsikas · Frédéric Cuppens ·
Nora Cuppens · Costas Lambrinoudakis ·
Christos Kalloniatis · John Mylopoulos ·
Annie Antón · Stefanos Gritzalis ·
Weizhi Meng · Steven Furnell (Eds.)

Computer Security

ESORICS 2020 International Workshops,
CyberICPS, SECPRE, and ADIoT
Guildford, UK, September 14–18, 2020
Revised Selected Papers

 Springer

Editors
Sokratis Katsikas 🆔
Norwegian University of Science
and Technology
Gjøvik, Norway

Nora Cuppens
Polytechnique Montréal
Montréal, QC, Canada

Christos Kalloniatis 🆔
University of the Aegean
Mytilene, Greece

Annie Antón
Georgia Institute of Technology
Atlanta, GA, USA

Weizhi Meng 🆔
Technical University of Denmark
Lyngby, Denmark

Frédéric Cuppens
Polytechnique Montréal
Montréal, QC, Canada

Costas Lambrinoudakis 🆔
University of Piraeus
Piraeus, Greece

John Mylopoulos 🆔
Department of Computer Science
University of Toronto
Toronto, ON, Canada

Stefanos Gritzalis
University of Piraeus
Piraeus, Greece

Steven Furnell 🆔
University of Nottingham
Nottingham, UK

ISSN 0302-9743 ISSN 1611-3349 (electronic)
Lecture Notes in Computer Science
ISBN 978-3-030-64329-4 ISBN 978-3-030-64330-0 (eBook)
https://doi.org/10.1007/978-3-030-64330-0

LNCS Sublibrary: SL4 – Security and Cryptology

This Springer imprint is published by the registered company Springer Nature Switzerland AG
The registered company address is: Gewerbestrasse 11, 6330 Cham, Switzerland

CyberICPS 2020 Preface

This book contains revised versions of the papers presented at the 6th Workshop on Security of Industrial Control Systems and Cyber-Physical Systems (CyberICPS 2020). The workshop was co-located with the 25th European Symposium on Research in Computer Security (ESORICS 2020) and was held online as a virtual event on September 17, 2020.

Cyber-physical systems (CPS) are physical and engineered systems that interact with the physical environment, whose operations are monitored, coordinated, controlled, and integrated by information and communication technologies. These systems exist everywhere around us, and range in size, complexity, and criticality, from embedded systems used in smart vehicles, to SCADA systems in smart grids, to control systems in water distribution systems, to smart transportation systems, to plant control systems, engineering workstations, substation equipment, programmable logic controllers (PLCs), and other Industrial Control Systems (ICS). These systems also include the emerging trend of Industrial Internet of Things (IIoT) that will be the central part of the fourth industrial revolution. As ICS and CPS proliferate, and increasingly interact with us and affect our lives, their security becomes of paramount importance. CyberICPS 2020 brought together researchers, engineers, and governmental actors with an interest in the security of ICS and CPS in the context of their increasing exposure to cyberspace, by offering a forum for discussion on all issues related to their cyber security.

CyberICPS 2020 attracted 21 high-quality submissions, each of which was assigned to 4 referees for review; the review process resulted in 8 papers being accepted to be presented and included in the proceedings. These cover topics related to threats, vulnerabilities, and risks that cyber-physical systems and industrial control systems face; cyber attacks that may be launched against such systems; and ways of detecting and responding to such attacks.

We would like to express our thanks to all those who assisted us in organizing the event and putting together the program. We are very grateful to the members of the Program Committee for their timely and rigorous reviews. Thanks are also due to the event's Organizing Committee and to the ESORICS Organizing Committee. Last, but by no means least, we would like to thank all the authors who submitted their work to the workshop and contributed to an interesting set of proceedings.

October 2020

Sokratis Katsikas
Frédéric Cuppens
Nora Cuppens
Costas Lambrinoudakis

CyberICPS 2020 Organization

General Chairs

Nora Cuppens   Polytechnique Montréal, Canada
Costas Lambrinoudakis   University of Piraeus, Greece

Program Chairs

Sokratis Katsikas   Norwegian University of Science and Technology, Norway
Frédéric Cuppens   Polytechnique Montréal, Canada

Publicity Chair

Vasileios Gkioulos   Norwegian University of Science and Technology, Norway

Program Committee

Cristina Alcaraz   University of Malaga, Spain
Marios Anagnostopoulos   Norwegian University of Science and Technology, Norway
Alvaro Cardenas   University of California Santa Cruz, USA
Mauro Conti   University of Padua, Italy
David Espes   University of Brest, France
Khan Ferdous Wahid   Airbus Group, France
Joaquin Garcia-Alfaro   Telecom SudParis, France
Vasileios Gkioulos   Norwegian University of Science and Technology, Norway
Dieter Gollmann   Hamburg University of Technology, Germany
Youssef Laarouchi   EDF R&D, France
Masahiro Mambo   Kanazawa University, Japan
Michail Maniatakos   NYU Abu Dhabi, UAE
Sjouke Mauw   University of Luxembourg, Luxembourg
Weizhi Meng   Technical University of Denmark, Denmark
Pankaj Pandey   Norwegian University of Science and Technology, Norway
Nikos Pitropakis   Edinburgh Napier University, UK
Indrakshi Ray   Colorado State University, USA
Rodrigo Roman   University of Malaga, Spain
Ayed Samiha   Telecom Bretagne, France
Andrea Saracino   Consiglio Nazionale delle Ricerche, Italy

Houbing Song	Embry-Riddle Aeronautical University, USA
Georgios Spathoulas	Norwegian University of Science and Technology, Norway
Qiang Tang	LIST, Luxembourg
Nils Ole Tippenhauer	CISPA, Germany
Stefano Zanero	Politecnico di Milano, Italy
Jianying Zhou	Singapore University of Technology and Design, Singapore

SECPRE 2020 Preface

This volume contains revised versions of the papers presented at the 4th International Workshop on SECurity and Privacy Requirements Engineering (SECPRE 2020), which was co-located with the 25th European Symposium on Research in Computer Security (ESORICS 2020), and held virtually in Surrey, UK on September 17, 2020.

Data protection regulations, the complexity of modern environments (such as IoT, IoE, Cloud Computing, Big Data, Cyber-Physical Systems, etc.) and the increased level of users awareness in IT have forced software engineers to identify security and privacy as fundamental design aspects, leading to the implementation of more trusted software systems and services. Researchers have addressed the necessity and importance of implementing design methods for security and privacy requirements elicitation, modeling, and implementation in the last decades in various innovative research domains. Today Security by Design (SbD) and Privacy by Design (PbD) are established research areas that focus on these directions. The new GDPR regulation sets even stricter requirements for organizations regarding its applicability. SbD and PbD play a very critical and important role in assisting stakeholders in understanding their needs, complying with the new legal, organizational, and technical requirements, and finally selecting the appropriate measures for fulfilling these requirements. SECPRE aimed to provide researchers and professionals with the opportunity to present novel and cutting-edge research on these topics.

SECPRE 2020 attracted seven high-quality submissions, each of which was assigned to four referees for review; the review process resulted in four papers being selected for presentation and inclusion in these proceedings. The topics covered include: security and privacy requirements and GDPR compliance issues, security and privacy verification on Cyber-Physical Systems, security and privacy in ITS domain, as well as vulnerability analysis though goal modeling.

We would like to express our thanks to all those who assisted us in organizing the events and putting together the programs. We are very grateful to the members of the Program Committee for their timely and rigorous reviews. Thanks are also due to the Organizing Committee of the events. Last, but by no means least, we would like to thank all the authors who submitted their work to the workshop and contributed to an interesting set of proceedings.

October 2020

John Mylopoulos
Christos Kalloniatis
Annie Anton
Stefanos Gritzalis

SECPRE 2020 Organization

General Chairs

Annie Antón — Georgia Institute of Technology, USA
Stefanos Gritzalis — University of Piraeus, Greece

Program Chairs

John Mylopoulos — University of Toronto, Canada
Christos Kalloniatis — University of the Aegean, Greece

Program Committee

Frederic Cuppens — Telecom Bretagne, France
Sabrina De Capitani di Vimercati — Università degli Studi di Milano, Italy
Vasiliki Diamantopoulou — University of the Aegean, Greece
Eric Dubois — Luxembourg Institute of Science and Technology, Luxembourg
Carmen Fernandez-Gago — University of Malaga, Spain
Eduardo Fernandez-Medina — University of Castilla-La Mancha, Spain
Mohamad Gharib — University of Florence, Italy
Paolo Giorgini — University of Trento, Italy
Maritta Heisel — University of Duisburg-Essen, Germany
Jan Juerjens — University of Koblenz-Landau, Germany
Maria Karyda — University of the Aegean, Greece
Costas Lambrinoudakis — University of Piraeus, Greece
Tong Li — Beijing University of Technology, China
Fabio Martinelli — CNR, Italy
Aaron Massey — University of Maryland, USA
Haralambos Mouratidis — University of Brighton, UK
Liliana Pasquale — University College Dublin, Ireland
Michalis Pavlidis — University of Brighton, UK
David Garcia Rosado — University of Castilla-La Manca, Spain
Pierangela Samarati — Università degli Studi di Milano, Italy
Aggeliki Tsohou — Ionian University, Greece
Nicola Zannone — Eindhoven University of Technology, The Netherlands

ADIoT 2020 Preface

This volume contains the papers that were selected for presentation and publication at the Third International Workshop on Attacks and Defenses for Internet-of-Things (ADIoT 2020), which was held virtually online on September 18, 2020. The Internet of Things (IoT) technology is widely adopted by the vast majority of businesses and is impacting every aspect of the world. However, the nature of the Internet, communication, embedded OS, and backend recourses make IoT objects vulnerable to cyber attacks. In addition, most standard security solutions designed for enterprise systems are not applicable to IoT devices. As a result, we are facing a big IoT security and protection challenge, and it is urgent to analyze IoT-specific cyber attacks to design novel and efficient security mechanisms. This workshop focused on IoT attacks and defenses, and sought original submissions that discuss either practical or theoretical solutions to identify IoT vulnerabilities and IoT security mechanisms.

This year, 2 full papers and 2 short papers (extended abstract) out of 12 submissions were selected with an acceptance rate of 33.3%. All papers were reviewed by at least three members of the Program Committee. We would like to extend our thanks to the Program Committee members as well as the additional reviewers who contributed their precious time and expertise to provide professional reviews and feedback to authors in a timely manner. We would also like to express our thanks to all the authors who submitted papers to ADIoT 2020.

October 2020

Weizhi Meng
Steven Furnell

ADIoT 2020 Organization

Steering Committee

Steven Furnell	University of Nottingham, UK
Anthony T. S. Ho	University of Surrey, UK
Sokratis Katsikas	Norwegian University of Science and Technology, Norway
Weizhi Meng (Chair)	Technical University of Denmark, Denmark
Shouhuai Xu	The University of Texas at San Antonio, USA

General Chairs

Anthony T. S. Ho	University of Surrey, UK
Kuan-Ching Li	Providence University, China

Program Co-chairs

Weizhi Meng	Technical University of Denmark, Denmark
Steven Furnell	University of Nottingham, UK

Technical Program Committee

Claudio Ardagna	Università degli Studi di Milano, Italy
Ali Ismail Awad	Luleå University of Technology, Sweden
Alessandro Bruni	IT University of Copenhagen, Denmark
Chao Chen	Swinburne University of Technology, Australia
Nathan Clarke	University of Plymouth, UK
Georgios Kambourakis	University of the Aegean, Greece
Jianming Fu	Wuhan University, China
Linzhi Jiang	University of Surrey, UK
Javier Parra-Arnau	Universitat Rovira i Virgili, Spain
Wenjuan Li	Hong Kong Polytechnic University, China
Jiqiang Lu	Beihang University, China
Xiaobo Ma	Xi'an Jiaotong University, China
Reza Malekian	Malmö University, Sweden
Jianbing Ni	Queen's University, Canada
Meng Shen	Beijing Institute of Technology, China
Kar-Ann Toh	Yonsei University, South Korea
Ding Wang	Peking University, China
Lam Kwok Yan	Nanyang Technological University, Singapore
Xuyun Zhang	Macquarie University, Australia
Peng Zhou	Shanghai University, China

Contents

ADIoT Workshop

CyberICPS Workshop

Integrated Analysis of Safety and Security Hazards in Automotive Systems

Rhea C. Rinaldo$^{(\boxtimes)}$ and Dieter Hutter

German Research Center for Artificial Intelligence (DFKI), Bremen, Germany
{rhea.rinaldo,dieter.hutter}@dfki.de

Abstract. Safety has always been a primary concern in automotive development, but with the growing connectivity requirements due to the increasing demand for autonomous features, security concerns are rising dramatically. Safety and security are partly intertwined, as faults and incidents with one may adversely affect the other. Consequently, evaluating both properties separately is illusive in general, yet still widely adopted in automotive development.

In this paper we introduce an approach to analyze the interaction of the various components in a vehicle with respect to possible safety and security hazards based on the weaknesses of these individual components. We introduce the notion of a dependency graph to specify the interrelation of the components and provide an automated mechanism to transfer these specifications to Markov Decision Processes, which allow us to automatically analyze such systems by using probabilistic model checkers. We describe our approach by means of a simple vehicle example and present parts of its automatic analysis.

Keywords: Safety · Security · Hazard analysis · Threat analysis · Autonomous vehicles · Safety-security interactions · Probabilistic model checking

1 Introduction

The modern vehicle is a historically grown system that combines highly safety-critical modules, such as the engine control unit, with interconnected information devices, like the infotainment system. Due to the increasing connectivity related to the expansion of autonomous features, the risk for security attacks is rising dramatically. According to [22], there are already about 50 million connected vehicles in the U.S. and every major automaker is integrating connectivity features in their vehicles. This trend and the recurring reports of security attacks on cars [6,13,14] clarify the need for appropriate protection. These risks did not remain unrecognized in the automotive industry [22], however, whereas safety

This research is supported by the German Federal Ministry of Education and Research in the project SATiSFy (Timely Validation of Safety and Security Requirements in Autonomous Vehicles) under grant 16KIS0821K.

S. Katsikas et al. (Eds.): CyberICPS 2020/SECPRE 2020/ADIoT 2020, LNCS 12501, pp. 3–18, 2020.
https://doi.org/10.1007/978-3-030-64330-0_1

has always been a priority concern, security is still not targeted satisfyingly. Moreover, the widely adopted separate evaluation of safety and security is illusive, as the two properties are partly intertwined. For instance, on one hand the corruption of a critical component by an attacker endangers the correct operation of other components and on the other hand the failure of a cryptography module increases the vulnerability of a component using this module. Likewise, solutions that merely focus on either safety or security are often contradictory regarding the other. A good example is the highly safety-optimized CAN Bus which employs strong safety features that, however, make it very vulnerable to attacks, as they can easily be exploited by an intruder (see also [3]). The authors of [4] argue that even though this problem has been recognized by the automotive industry, challenges due to "the differing maturity levels, grey areas in law, [and] dissimilarities in content" exist, constraining the integrated evaluation of safety and security. Despite resolving the described challenges, they state that the development of tools that can be used by both, the safety and the security community, would support the integration.

In the present paper we address this issue by developing a methodology that operates on a system design level of composing individual components (e.g. Electronic Control Units (ECUs) in terms of vehicles) that provides an integrated analysis of the safety and security risks of a design with respect to the operativeness of a vehicle. Privacy aspects are not considered in this approach as the corresponding information flow control mechanisms typically require a given implementation of the system.

We represent an automotive system as a graph, called a dependency graph, and formalize the safety and security effects as state changes of components annotated by probabilities for their individual occurrences. For analysis purposes, we formalize a translation from this graph into a probabilistic automaton, which yields a Markov Decision Process (MDP). In order to conquer the complexity yielding from the state explosion problem, we developed a tool called ERIS that helps us with the description of dependency graphs and automatically transfers such an input graph into an MDP, providing for a further analysis with a probabilistic model checker (e.g. PRISM).

The novel contributions of this paper are manifold: 1. To model the system architecture we provide an abstraction level that supports the interplay of security and safety incidents: security issues may be caused by safety failures in components providing security functionalities (or mechanisms) and safety issues may arise due to corruption of safety-critical components. 2. The modeling language allows for the specification of redundant components as well as for different attack probabilities of components depending on the availability of individual security mechanisms in an actual state. 3. The resulting models can be automatically translated and analyzed with the help of a probabilistic model checker to identify weak points of an architecture.

The paper is structured as follows. In Sect. 2 we discuss the related work. Section 3 discusses the chosen abstraction level of our modeling and assumptions about the system in an autonomous vehicle. In Sect. 4 we formalize our abstraction of the vehicle in terms of dependency graphs and in Sect. 4.1 we present their transformation into probabilistic automata to support their analysis by corresponding model checkers. Section 5 provides an illustration of our approach with the help of a small example and a short description of our tool ERIS. Section 6 concludes this paper and discusses further work.

2   Related Work

Inspired by fault tree approaches to analyze potential risks or hazards in the domain of safety (cf. [1]), attack trees (or graphs respectively) have been developed to analyze vulnerabilities in the domain of security (cf. [5,10] for detailed surveys). Attack graphs allow one to model and visualize the combination (or formation) of attack events (or exploits) that enable a successful attack on a given system in order to analyze the vulnerabilities of that system. The nodes of an attack graph are denoting attack events while the subnodes of a node represent the individual (minor) events that contribute to the attack of the node. Preconditions relate these underlying events in a temporal or logical way to formalize situations in which the event of the node can happen while postconditions provide information about the state of system after this event has happened.

Attack graphs allow for the calculation of probabilities of successful attacks if probabilities are assigned to each node in the graph to represent the likelihood of that vulnerability being exposed. Attack graphs or attack trees (see also [19]) represent the combination of multiple vulnerabilities, allowing multiple paths, from the intruder's entry point to a target (root) node. Thereby a condition directly leading to an exploit requires the condition to be satisfied, and the other way round, the execution of the exploit satisfies the condition. Exploits have a probability indicating the relative likelihood that the exploit is executed by an attacker. For example, [20] presents an approach to quantify the probability of network attacks based on attack graphs with a set of vulnerability exploits and a set of security-related conditions that represent the system state and transition relations between these states. Based on this the authors provide a metric for computing the attack probabilities and apply them in their context of network systems, in order to understand and measure the various exploits an attacker could combine to reach his goal. The authors of [16] also developed a method for evaluating attack probabilities based on attack graphs. They focus on the improvement of the risk assessment and mitigation. Therefore they enhance attack graphs with the notion of Bayesian belief networks for enabling the reasoning about causal dependencies. In their approach, precise systems, possible attacks and their consequences are viewed. This approach descriptively shows the calculation of attack-probabilities on realistic scenarios, however, its abstraction level is very low and thus it requires the users to have precise information of the individual components, possible attacks and their specific consequences.

The authors of [11] also use attack trees as a basis as a topology-based risk assessment analysis of automotive systems. They introduce a threat model of the vehicle and extend each step of it by its attack feasibility. To take the underlying network into account, they update these values according to the specific vehicular topology. In the next step, they make use of attack trees to compute the risk and feasibility of each attack, resulting in a report of security-related critical points of the input architecture. Based on these assessment results and empirically-generated constraints the authors produce a security-hardened topology.

In [15] a system-level security analysis regarding automotive architectures is presented. The authors provide a method for establishing exploitability rates of a component, depending on its type (ECUs, Buses and Messages) and the employed security mechanisms (encryption, authentication etc.). Similar to our approach, they transform the architecture into a Markov model (CTMC) to evaluate the risks and find security flaws using the PRISM model checker. Even though this approach is merely focused on security, it shows strong parallels to ours and confirms that this kind of modeling and evaluation technique is suited to analyze automotive architectures on the premise that an appropriate abstraction level is chosen.

Many approaches that target the combination of safety and security exist on a methodological level (cf. e.g. [8]). Frequently, well known safety analyses are combined with established security reasoning such as in [12], where Hazard Analysis and Risk Assessment (HARA) is combined with the STRIDE threat model. [2] integrate fault and attack trees by unifying the notations of safety faults and attack goals as (general) events allowing them to treat such events in a uniform way using an integrated fault and attack tree. As argued in [4], the reason for this rather shallow integration may be that even though engineering processes in safety and security seem to be similar on a high abstraction level, both are entirely different in their nature and thus the combination of existing analyses can be problematic in practice.

Concerning the design of secure systems, John Rushby sketched a general architecture for secure systems in [17] which later on became known as (Multiple Independent Level of Security) MILS-architecture and presented it in more detail in [18]. The idea is to start with a logical decomposition aiming to isolate security critical functionality into components that are as small and as simple as possible to ease the later verification work. This logical decomposition of the system is unconcerned with the later physical realization of the system but is entirely driven by security issues.

3   Modeling

Cars are controlled by an orchestration of numerous distributed components (e.g. ECU), each providing a narrowly defined functionality and communicating with each other with the help of dedicated bus systems (like CAN, FlexRay, or Ethernet). Rather than inspecting the safety and security of particular components, we are interested in the interplay of these components; in how security attacks or safety failures of individual components will propagate to a loss of the entire system. While an outage or a program failure of a component differ in their cause and output behavior, the consequences for a subsequent processing component are identical, as it cannot rely on the data anymore.

Concerning the interaction of safety and security issues, we model both the implications of security faults to safety and the implications of safety failures to security. If the attacker succeeds to capture a component of the vehicle, they obtain the ability to manipulate its internal program. The result is twofold: on the one-hand side the manipulated program may compute wrong output data and cause also a malfunction of the subsequent components relying on the now manipulated output. Furthermore, the attacker may use the captured component as a basis to attack further components in its neighborhood (e.g. residing on the same bus or providing some wireless access, etc.). Residing initially only in the environment of the vehicles, the attacker may step by step capture essential components inside the vehicle. The probability that such an attack succeeds depends on the type of connection (or protocol) used between the components and the strength of the security mechanisms installed and operating in the targeted component. We annotate each component with a probability indicating the feasibility to mount a successful attack, under the presumption that an attacker has some physical access to it. This probability depends in a current state on the active security mechanisms protecting the component. Examples are HW-components like Hardware Security Modules (HSMs) providing a *root of trust* or SW-based cryptographic libraries enabling secured communication. The outage of such components providing these security mechanisms will increase the vulnerability of all components relying on them.

Concerning safety we abstract from the concrete functionality or timing behavior of a component, and consider a component as an abstract computation unit receiving some input, providing some output and executing an internal program. We assume that a component operates correctly if the component executes its designated internal program and all components providing required inputs are operating correctly as well. Verifying the correctness of the internal program is subject to a detailed safety analysis of the (implementation of the) component while typically the probability of failures of a component is determined by the probability of hardware deficits.

In general the outage of a component results in a reduction of functionality or a decrease of redundancy. While in a normal mode the vehicle exposes its full functionality, an emergency mode, for instance, may only allow to bring the vehicle to a safe stop on the hard shoulder of a road. We support the analysis of different modes of operation in our approach. Modes are specified by their extensions, i.e. by the set of all subsets of (operational) components that together have the continuing ability to provide this mode.

4   Formalization

Following the general modeling sketched in the previous section, we formalize the dependencies of the components of an automotive system as a dependency graph. Each node of the graph denotes a particular component of the vehicle (typically ECUs in today's cars or isolated processes running on a central processing unit in future autonomous vehicles). There is a special node Env denoting the environment of the car and we assume that from the start this environment is controlled by the attacker.

The links of the graph refer to various interrelationships between components (or between components and the environment, respectively). First, there are functional dependencies as, for instance, an actor typically relies on the output of some sensors. These are represented by Fct-links. Second, Reach-links represent the connectivity between individual components, i.e. a Reach-link indicates that the source component is (potentially) able to directly communicate to the target component (e.g. via some open port in a client/server solution). A Reach-link from the environment node expresses that the connected system node can be accessed from the outside. Initially, such nodes are the only entry points for an attacker. Finally, Sec-links represent a selective class of functional dependencies as they model the provision of security functionalities to the target component. Failure of the source does not result in a malfunction of the target as a start but raises the probability of a successful attack on it.

Definition 1. *A dependency graph* $\mathcal{G} = \langle \mathcal{N} \cup \{\text{Env}\}, \mathcal{L} \rangle$ *is a finite, directed graph where*

- *$\mathcal{N}$ is a list of nodes representing the individual components of the architecture.*
  - *each node $n \in \mathcal{N}$ is annotated by a probability $p_n^{Safe} \in [0,1]$ and*
  - *each node $n \in \mathcal{N}$ is also annotated by a function $Sec_n : 2^{Src^{Sec}(n)} \to [0,1]$ mapping sets of components providing security mechanisms to a probability of a successful attack on n, where 2^X denotes the powerset of X.*
- *$\mathcal{L} \subseteq (\mathcal{N} \cup \{\text{Env}\}) \times \mathcal{N}$ is a set of links between nodes. Each link $l \in \mathcal{L}$ is annotated by a type $\tau(l) \in \mathcal{T}$ with $\mathcal{T} = \{\text{Fct}, \text{Sec}, \text{Reach}\}$ being the set of link types.*

Let $t \in \mathcal{T}$, $\mathcal{L}^t(n) = \{\langle n', n \rangle \mid \langle n', n \rangle \in \mathcal{L} \wedge \tau(\langle n', n \rangle) = t\}$ denotes all links of $\mathcal{L}$ to n of type t and $Src^t(n) = \{n' \mid \langle n', n \rangle \in \mathcal{L}^t(n)\}$ the set of all their sources.

Concerning security, the vulnerability of a component n depends on the availability of security mechanisms implemented by other components (denoted by Sec-links). Concerning safety, the correct operation of a component depends on the correct input from other components (denoted by Fct-links).

Figure 1 shows the dependency graph of a simplified autonomous vehicle, illustrating the above definition which was designed with our tool ERIS (cf. Sect. 5). The system contains 17 nodes including the environment node. Nodes that are directly connected to the black-drawn environment node by Reach-link, such as the telematics unit ($n1$) and the smartphone ($n2$) may be accessed by the outside and thus may potentially be corrupted by an attacker. Furthermore, outgoing from corrupted nodes, all nodes that are connected via continues Reach-link, e.g. the gateway ($n7$), the Artificial Intelligence (AI) computers ($n9, n10$) etc. may also become corrupted.

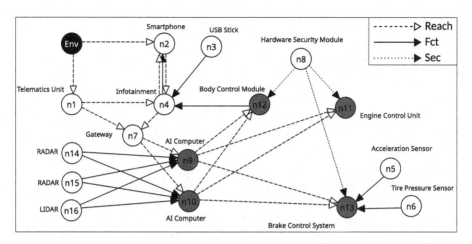

Fig. 1. Dependency graph of an abstracted autonomous vehicle

A state of a dependency graph combines the states of all its nodes. For simplicity, we distinguish three different states of a node. ok denotes a correctly operating component that performs its computations as specified but may receive incorrect input. def means that the component does not work correctly due to internal hardware or software failures. Finally, corr indicates that the attacker has successfully taken over the component. We assume that a corrupted node is no longer working correctly and may be arbitrarily abused by the attacker.

Definition 2. *Let* $\mathcal{G} = \langle \mathcal{N} \cup \{\mathsf{Env}\}, \mathcal{L} \rangle$ *be a dependency graph.* $\Sigma = \{\mathsf{ok}, \mathsf{def}, \mathsf{corr}\}$ *is the set of different node states. A state of the dependency graph* $\mathcal{G}$ *is a mapping* $s : \mathcal{N} \rightarrow \Sigma$. $S_{\mathcal{G}}$ *denotes the set of all states of* $\mathcal{G}$ *(if* $\mathcal{G}$ *is known from the context we simply write* S).

Let $s \in S_{\mathcal{G}}$, $\sigma \in \Sigma$, *and* $n \in \mathcal{N}$ *then* $s[n \leftarrow \sigma]$ *is the state defined by* $s[n \leftarrow \sigma](n) = \sigma$ *and* $\forall n' \in N \setminus \{n\}.\ s[n \leftarrow \sigma](n') = s(n')$.

The functionality that a vehicle offers in a particular state depends on the conditions of its individual components. We distinguish different modes of operations providing different degrees of functionality depending on the remaining operational components. In practice there is, for instance, a mode called *fail to operation* in which the system may have a reduced functionality but is still able to reach a final state in which it can be safely switched off (e.g. in case of an autonomous vehicle to leave the motorway and drive to a parking lane). Formally, a mode of operation is a collection of sets of nodes. Each set represents a set of components which together can guarantee the intended functionality.

Definition 3. *Let* $\mathcal{G} = \langle \mathcal{N} \cup \{\mathsf{Env}\}, \mathcal{L} \rangle$ *be a dependency graph. A set* $Ops \subseteq 2^{\mathcal{N}}$ *of subsets of* $\mathcal{N}$ *is a mode of operation for* $\mathcal{G}$ *iff* Ops *is a upper set i.e.*

$$\forall N, N' \subseteq \mathcal{N}.\ N \subseteq N' \wedge N \in Ops \implies N' \in Ops.$$

A state $s \in S_{\mathcal{G}}$ provides a mode of operation Ops, Ops $\vdash$ s for short, iff $\{n \in \mathcal{N} \mid s(n) = \text{ok}\} \in Ops$.

A mode of operation Ops induces an equivalent relation $\sim_{Ops}$ on S by

$$s \sim_{Ops} s' \text{ iff } s = s' \lor (Ops \nvdash s \land Ops \nvdash s')$$

$S\backslash_{Ops}$ *denotes the set of all equivalence classes of S and* $[s]_{Ops}$ *the equivalence class of a state $s \in S$ w.r.t. $\sim_{Ops}$.* Fail *denotes the equivalence class* $[s]_{Ops}$ *with* $Ops \nvdash s$.

This definition allows for the specification of a redundant design in which a component is included multiple times as separate nodes. Then, a mode of operation *Ops* may demand that in each $N \in Ops$ at least e.g. one copy (i.e. node) of the component occurs. Modes of operations are specified in terms of a boolean formula. In our example given in Fig. 1 we may define a mode of restricted operation by

$$N \in Ops \equiv (n5 \in N \land n6 \in N \land (n9 \in N \lor n10 \in N) \land n11 \in N \land n12 \in N$$
$$\land n13 \in N \land (n14 \in N \lor n15 \in N) \land n16 \in N).$$

The mode is characterized by the redundancy of the two AI-controller ($n9$ and $n10$) responsible for the autonomous driving. Only one of them is needed for the mode. Analogously, the mode demands only the correct operation of one radar sensor from $n14$ and $n15$.

4.1   Markov Decision Processes

In the next step we analyze a dependency graph with respect to the probabilities that the described (distributed) system will fail to satisfy a given mode of operation. Therefore, we translate the dependency graph into a corresponding probabilistic automaton, i.e. a Markov Decision Process, which will allow us to make use of a probabilistic model checker for a thorough analysis of the risks of the system design. Such a *Markov Decision Process* (MDP) is defined as a tuple $\mathcal{D} = (S, s_{init}, Act, P, L)$ consisting of a set of states S with an initial state $s_{init} \in S$, a set of actions Act and discrete probability distributions over S for each action *act* assigning each state s a probability distribution of possible successor states when performing *act*. Finally L is labeling function mapping states to some atomic propositions.

The states of our MDP correlate to the states of the dependency graph. Actions are the failure or the corruption of an individual node. We assume that in one step only one node can change its state, which helps us to reduce the number of possible transitions. Considering the rather low probabilities of failures of components, this interleaving of potentially concurrent events seems to be a realistic assumption.

Considering the probability distributions, our specifications allow for safety and security incidents. A component can fail because of hardware problems which render it ineffectual in its default functionality but also as an operating platform of the attacker. Therefore, we allow transitions which change the state of a component to def regardless whether the previous state was ok or corr. The probability for such a local (hardware) failure is assumed to be fixed and specified by p_n^{Safe}. Second, an operational component may be captured by an attacker provided that the attacker has access to the component and it exposes some weaknesses. This may be caused either by some vulnerability exposed by the component itself or by the failure of some other component that provides necessary security mechanisms. The dependency graph allows for the specification of different probabilities Sec_n for a successful attack of a component depending on which components providing required security mechanisms are operational in the current state.

Definition 4. *Let s be a state of a dependency graph $\mathcal{G} = \langle \mathcal{N} \cup \{\mathsf{Env}\}, \mathcal{L}\rangle$ then the attack probability of n in s is defined as $p_n^{\mathsf{Sec}}(s) = Sec_n(\{n' \in Src^{\mathsf{Sec}}(n) \mid s(n') = \mathsf{ok}\}))$*

In practice it may be difficult to calculate realistic attack probabilities for components. For instance, the attack probability of a component may depend on known vulnerabilities or existing exploits of particular libraries used in the component. Approaches like [7,21] explore entries in Common Vulnerabilities and Exposures (CVE) databases to calculate attack probabilities. Furthermore, metrics as in [15] and risk assessment approaches as in [11] can be used to identify the exploitability of components and topologies, providing a basis for establishing probabilities for security attacks. Rather than encoding the vulnerability of libraries in a fixed attack probability of the components that implement it, our approach also allows one to model a library as a separate component with its own attack vulnerability being a functional requirement for the original component.

The following definition formalizes the Markov Decision Process specified by a dependency graph and a given mode of operation. The MDP operates on the equivalence classes that the mode of operation induces on the states of the dependency graph. Hence, all states that do not satisfy the mode, are considered as a single Fail-state in the MDP.

Definition 5. *Let $\mathcal{G} = \langle \mathcal{N} \cup \{\mathsf{Env}\}, \mathcal{L}\rangle$ be a dependency graph with states S and nodes $\mathcal{N} = \{n_1, \ldots, n_k\}$. An MDP $\mathcal{D} = (\mathbf{S}, \mathbf{s}_{init}, P, L)$ is a Dependency Markov Process (DMP) of $\mathcal{G}$ with respect to a mode of operation Ops iff*

- $\mathbf{S} = S\backslash_{Ops}$ *and* $\mathbf{s}_{init} = [s]_{Ops}$ *with* $\forall n \in \mathcal{N}. \, s(n) = \mathsf{ok}$
- $L(\mathsf{Fail}) = \langle Fail\rangle$ *and* $L([s]_{Ops}) = \langle s(n_1), \ldots s(n_k)\rangle$
- $Act = \mathcal{N} \times \{\mathsf{corr}, \mathsf{def}\}$
- P *is given by (for* $n \in \mathcal{N}, act \in Act, s \in S, \mathbf{s}, \mathbf{s}' \in \mathbf{S})$
  - $P(\mathsf{Fail}, act, \mathsf{Fail}) = 1$
  - $P([s]_{Ops}, \langle n, \mathsf{corr}\rangle, [s[n \leftarrow \mathsf{corr}]]_{Ops}) = p_n^{\mathsf{Sec}}(s)$ *and*
    $P([s]_{Ops}, \langle n, \mathsf{corr}\rangle, [s]_{Ops}) = 1 - p_n^{\mathsf{Sec}}(s)$
    if $Ops \vdash s \wedge s(n) = \mathsf{ok} \wedge \exists \langle n', n\rangle \in \mathcal{L}^{Reach}.(n' = \mathsf{Env} \vee s(n') = \mathsf{corr})$
  - $P([s]_{Ops}, \langle n, \mathsf{def}\rangle, [s[n \leftarrow \mathsf{def}]]_{Ops}) = p_n^{Safe}$ *and*
    $P([s]_{Ops}, \langle n, \mathsf{def}\rangle, [s]_{Ops}) = 1 - p_n^{Safe}$
    if $Ops \vdash s \wedge s(n) \neq \mathsf{def}$
  - *and* $P(\mathbf{s}, act, \mathbf{s}') = 0$ *otherwise*

5   Automating the Risk Analysis

The translation of a dependency graph into an MDP allows us to analyze the probabilities that the specified system will enter particular (undesirable) states. In general, we are interested in the probability that the system will enter the Fail-state in a given period of time (or steps, respectively). Hence, we want to compute the probability for a system loss either by safety problems or by system corruption caused by an attacker within a given number of transition steps. We want to identify whether it is more likely that the system will fail because of some safety problem or that it is successfully corrupted by an attacker. Furthermore, we want to investigate the impact of security mechanisms.

The ultimate goal of our approach is to evaluate possible architectures of automotive IT-systems. Considering admission and standardization processes especially in the automotive industry, we want to evaluate whether risks are within certain bounds that could be given by legal documents in that area, by answering questions such as "is the probability for the corruption of the critical node below 10%?" Furthermore, we want to analyze the interplay-effects of nodes and identify possible weaknesses of systems and components by answering questions such as "is the corruption of node A more probable when node B is defective?".

Our approach is based on known probabilities for safety failures and successful attacks for each individual component of this system. However, in the past it turned out to be rather difficult to specify reliable probability numbers except for hardware deficits. For instance, how should we assess the probability that a component contains some software bug causing a malfunction or the probability that an attacker can find some zero-day exploit to corrupt the component? Hence, we are less interested in computing the absolute (concrete) probability that a specific dependency graph enters the Fail-state depending on the failure probabilities of its components. We are more interested in the impact of the design of the architecture to the overall failure probability, i.e. given two different dependency graphs, which of them is more robust with respect to potential failures (independently of the failure rates of the individual components)? Based on the achieved results, the most suitable architecture between multiple concurrent dependency graphs can be chosen or the modification of the desired dependency graph can be performed and the analysis can be revisited. This would provide for the analysis of the safety and security risk changes of a given architecture modification, such as the addition of a new connection from the telematic unit to an existing component, before it is actually performed. For instance, we can equip critical components with different security mechanisms and compare the impact of these variations to the overall failure probability. Compared to attack tree approaches as described in Sect. 2, this conception adds more flexibility to our approach, since we are not depending on the precise definition of known attacks and their individual probability for occurrence.

In the following we experimentally modify our dependency graph of Sect. 4 and discuss the results. Therefore we define example probability values for all components. Since we are not interested in the value-based results but rather in their relation between different modifications, the values do not need to be realistic, but demonstrative.

The number of states of an MDP grows exponentially with the number of components in the dependency graph that are not part of the underlying mode of operation *Ops* (see also Sect. 5.4), which makes a translation to an MDP by hand very difficult and inefficient. To cope with this complexity we developed a tool called ERIS to support us in the design of dependency graphs and offer an automatic analysis. ERIS is written in C++ and provides a QT[1] GUI which offers great practicality in the designing of the graphs and setting probability values as well as formulating redundancy definitions. For automation, ERIS provides a translation from a given input dependency graph into an MDP in terms of the PRISM language, which allows us to use the probabilistic model checker PRISM [9] for a thorough analysis.

Listing 1 shows an excerpt of the translated vehicle example. We mapped the state of the nodes to numerical values: ok → 0, def → 1 and corr → 2. Firstly, some example probabilities are defined for node $n1$ and $n7$. The formula *Ops* representing the mode of operation as described in Sect. 4, Definition 3.

```
1   const double pn1SEC = 0.2;
2   const double pn1SAFE = 0.25;
3   const double pn7SEC = 0.2;
4   (...)
5   formula operational = (n10=0 & ((n14=0 | n15=0) & n16=0) |
        (n9=0 & ((n14=0 | n15=0) & n16=0))) & (n12=0) & (n11=0) &
        (n13=0 & (n5=0 & n6=0)) ;

7   n1: [0..2] init 0;
8   (...)
9   [] (n1=0) & (operational) -> pn1SAFE : (n1'=1) + 1-pn1SAFE
        : (n1'=0);
10  [] (n1=2) & (operational) -> pn1SAFE : (n1'=1) + 1-pn1SAFE
        : (n1'=2);
11  [] (n1=0) & (operational) -> pn1SEC : (n1'=2) + 1-pn1SEC :
        (n1'=0);
12  [] (n1=2) & (operational) -> pn7SEC : (n7'=2) + 1-(pn7SEC)
        : (n1'=2);
13  (...)
14
```

Listing 1. PRISM code of the vehicle example

In row 7 the node with its three possible states is initialized and subsequently the transitions are defined according to Definition 5: In every state where $n1$ is ok ($n1 = 0$) or corr ($n1 = 2$) and *Ops* holds, there is a probability **pn1SAFE** that a safety incident occurs and $n1$ transitions in the state def ($n1' = 1$) and there is a rest probability that $n1$ stays in the original state. Analogously, whenever $n1$ is ok and *Ops* holds there is a probability **pn1SEC** that $n1$ transitions in the state corr and a rest-probability $n1$ stays in the original state. Given by the architecture, $n1$ can reach $n7$ and thus whenever $n1$ is corr, there is a probability **pn7SEC** that $n7$ is corrupted and that the rest-probability is applied and the state is not changed.

---

[1] The QT Framework, www.qt.io, visited 10.04.2020.

5.1   HSM Integration

Due to the major conflict between component increase, cost-efficiency and safety/security requirements in automotive development, countermeasures for remaining cost-efficient can include the removal or the combination of components. A good example for sparing resources is the HSM. Instead of having one HSM for every critical component, a HSM usually provides security mechanisms for multiple components as pictured in our example vehicle. In order to save more resources, we make use of the unused computing power of the gateway $n7$ by integrating the HSM in it. Thereby we keep the same security mechanisms offered and the same failure probability, however, since the gateway can be reached an attack probability exists. As a result, the probability for attacking one of the critical nodes $n11$, $n12$ or $n13$ rises dramatically which can be observed in the left diagram of Fig. 2, exemplary for the engine control unit $n11$. The reasons for that are, firstly the security mechanisms provided from the gateway cannot even be applied, because whenever either of the legacy components $n11$, $n12$ or $n13$ are about to get intruded, the gateway $n7$ has already been corrupted and thus cannot offer security mechanisms anymore. Secondly, in comparison to the original vehicle, the gateway is more exposed as it can be accessed by Reach-links and, consequently, a probability for an attack on it exists.

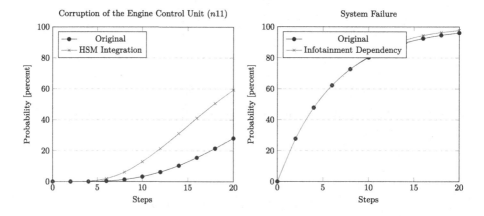

Fig. 2. Diagrams: System failure and corruption of the engine control unit

5.2   Infotainment Dependency

We define an additional dependency so that the body control module requires the infotainment to be operational. This could be a realistic requirement as in certain architectures the BCM may get its user input from the infotainment (e.g. passengers changing the light settings). We expect the failure probability of the system to rise dramatically, since any failure (defect/corruption) of the rather exposed infotainment causes the critical BCM to fail as well. However, quite the contrary is the case; we only detect a slight increase of the system's failure probability, which can only be observed after several steps, as shown in the right diagram of Fig. 2. This effect is explained by the distributed probabilities: the probabilities for the infotainment's failure and corruption are relatively low compared to the probabilities for a system failure. The attack probability, remains unchanged as no Reach-links to from the infotainment to the BCM exists.

5.3   Redundant AI Sensors

In the following scenario we add redundant sensors for both AI computers, meaning that each AI computer has its own two RADARs and one LIDAR that are independent from one another. Thus the failure of the sensors, in the worst-case one RADAR and one LIDAR, leads to failure of one AI Computer, while the other one can still operate normally. The mode of operation still being satisfied, the failure of the sensors does not directly lead to the loss of the system's functionality any-more. Consequently, this modification significantly decreases the failure probability of the AI Computers as shown in Fig. 3.

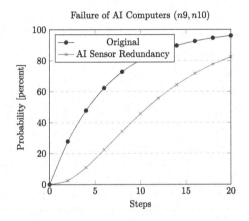

Fig. 3. Redundancy modification and failure of AI computer ($n9$ and $n10$)

5.4   Scalability

The states of our DMP (MDP) increase exponentially, as a state in the DMP is represented by a state-constellation of all nodes of our dependency graph and each node can have three different health states. We reduce the amounts of DMP states by disregarding state-changes originating in the Fail-state and by disregarding impossible transitions such as the corruption of a node, that cannot be reached. However, every node may turn defective independently from the state of the other nodes (except if the Fail-state is already reached). Security mechanisms provided by other nodes are considered depending on the state of the providing node, meaning, a different transition is taken when the node is operational or not, which increases the amount of transitions.

To get a feeling for the time consumption of the analysis we present a small benchmark of the previously described evaluation of the vehicle example and its modifications in Table 1. *Construction* indicates the time needed by PRISM to construct the input model from ERIS to an internal representation of an MDP and *Model Checking* comprises the time needed to evaluate all (10) properties constituting to the individual graph. The tests were run on a Linux machine (Kubuntu 18.04) with an Intel Core i5-8250U CPU 1.60 GHz and 8 GB RAM.

Table 1. Model checking benchmark

Model	Construction	States	Transitions	Model checking
Corruption of $N11$				
Original	0.156 s	32656	146904	0.578 s
HSM integration	0.116 s	16328	71592	0.258 s
System failure				
Original	0.156 s	32656	146904	0.395 s
Infotainment dependency	0.108 s	11808	46572	0.512 s
Failure of AI computers				
Original	0.156 s	32656	146904	0.47 s
AI sensor redundancy	0.607 s	296224	1441648	1.234 s

In the evaluation of the *Failure of AI Computers* a high increase of consumed model checking time can be observed. This is mainly explained by the heavy increase of states and transitions compared to the original example, due to the addition of three more nodes representing the redundant sensors. Furthermore it should be noted that this architectural change, also requires the model checking property to be adjusted to include these three redundant AI sensor, meaning more states are included in the model checking property, which can influence the consumed time as well. However, overall it can be seen that the evaluation can be performed within seconds which confirms that our approach can easily be used for abstracted architectures around the size of our example, or for smaller examples such as fractions and parts of bigger architectures.

In the future, we want to investigate this topic and the limitations of our approach further.

6   Conclusion and Future Work

In this paper we presented a methodology for the integrated evaluation of safety and security risks in automotive systems. We introduced the notion of dependency graphs to specify both, the functional dependencies between components as well as the security impacts of failed components providing security functions (mechanisms) to other components. Furthermore, dependency graphs provide mechanisms to specify the redundancy of components to increase availability. A formalization to transform dependency graphs to a corresponding probabilistic automaton in terms of a Markov Decision Process is defined. For automation, we developed the tool ERIS that supports the design process of dependency graphs and offers an automatic translation into MDPs in order to make use of probabilistic model checkers such as PRISM. Rather than obtaining concrete probabilities for an attack on an individual system architecture, we use the value-based results for the comparison of different alternative architectures with respect to their resistance against possible attacks. This approach reduces the need for precise probability values for the attack resistance of the individual components, which are difficult to compute and changing over time.

In the future, we would like to investigate the scalability of our approach for large system architectures containing more than fifty components and the development of heuristics to avoid potential state explosion. Another aspect is associated with recent developments in the automotive industry. Due to strong fail-safe and fail-operational requirements of autonomous vehicles, recovery strategies such as the reconfiguration, degradation and restoration of components, becomes a necessity.

The integration of these strategies into the present approach could help to analyze the benefits as well as the possible weaknesses of them. Further we want to examine the use of PRISM's reward functions that could add more details to our model such as elapsed time (rather than steps), or required costs for an attack etc. However, this firstly requires to have precise information about these parameters for every component, which is already problematic concerning the probabilities.

Acknowledgments. We thank our colleague Tobias Brandt for his support and constructive feedback.

References

1. Ericson, C.: Fault tree analysis - a history. In: 17th International System Safety Conference
2. Fovino, I.N., Masera, M., Cian, A.D.: Integrating cyber attacks within fault trees. Reliab. Eng. Syst. Safety **94**(9), 1394–1402 (2009). https://doi.org/10.1016/j.ress. 2009.02.020. ISSN 0951-8320
3. Fröschle, S., Stühring, A.: Analyzing the capabilities of the CAN attacker. In: Foley, S.N., Gollmann, D., Snekkenes, E. (eds.) ESORICS 2017. LNCS, vol. 10492, pp. 464–482. Springer, Cham (2017). https://doi.org/10.1007/978-3-319-66402-6_27
4. Glas, B., Gebauer, C., Hänger, J., Heyl, A., Klarmann, J., Kriso, S., Vembar, P., Wörz, P.: Automotive safety and security integration challenges. In: Automotive - Safety & Security 2014, pp. 13–28. GI e.V. (2015)
5. Kordy, B., Piètre-Cambacédès, L., Schweitzer, P.: Dag-based attack and defense modeling: Don't miss the forest for the attack trees. Comput. Sci. Rev. **13–14**, 1–38 (2014). https://doi.org/10.1016/j.cosrev.2014.07.001. ISSN 1574-0137
6. Koscher, K., Czeskis, A., Roesner, F., Patel, S., Kohno, T., Checkoway, S., McCoy, D., Kantor, B., Anderson, D., Shacham, H., Savage, S.: Experimental security analysis of a modern automobile. In: 2010 IEEE Symposium on Security and Privacy, pp. 447–462 (2010). DOI: https://doi.org/10.1109/SP.2010.34
7. Kotenko, I., Chechulin, A.: A cyber attack modeling and impact assessment framework. In: 5th International Conference on Cyber Conflict (2013)

8. Kriaa, S., Pietre-Cambacedes, L., Bouissou, M., Halgand, Y.: A survey of approaches combining safety and security for industrial control systems. Reliab. Eng. Syst. Safety **139**, 156–178 (2015). https://doi.org/10.1016/j.ress.2015.02.008. ISSN 0951-8320

9. Kwiatkowska, M., Norman, G., Parker, D.: PRISM 4.0: verification of probabilistic real-time systems. In: Gopalakrishnan, G., Qadeer, S. (eds.) CAV 2011. LNCS, vol. 6806, pp. 585–591. Springer, Heidelberg (2011). https://doi.org/10.1007/978-3-642-22110-1_47

10. Lallie, H.S., Debattista, K., Bal, J.: A review of attack graph and attack tree visual syntax in cyber security. Comput. Sci. Rev. **35**, 100219 (2020). https://doi.org/10.1016/j.cosrev.2019.100219. ISSN 1574-0137

11. Longari, S., Cannizzo, A., Carminati, M., Zanero, S.: A secure-by-design framework for automotive on-board network risk analysis. In: 2019 IEEE Vehicular Networking Conference (VNC), pp. 1–8 (2019)

12. Macher, G., Höller, A., Sporer, H., Armengaud, E., Kreiner, C.: A combined safety-hazards and security-threat analysis method for automotive systems. In: Koornneef, F., van Gulijk, C. (eds.) SAFECOMP 2015. LNCS, vol. 9338, pp. 237–250. Springer, Cham (2015). https://doi.org/10.1007/978-3-319-24249-1_21

13. Miller, C., Valasek, C.: A survey of remote automotive attack surfaces. http://illmatics.com/remote%20attack%20surfaces.pdf

14. Miller, C., Valasek, C.: Remote exploitation of an unaltered passenger vehicle (2015). http://illmatics.com/Remote%20Car%20Hacking.pdf

15. Mundhenk, P., Steinhorst, S., Lukasiewycz, M., Fahmy, S.A., Chakraborty, S.: Security analysis of automotive architectures using probabilistic model checking. In: 2015 52nd ACM/EDAC/IEEE Design Automation Conference (DAC), pp. 1–6 (2015)

16. Poolsappasit, N., Dewri, R., Ray, I.: Dynamic security risk management using Bayesian attack graphs. IEEE Trans. Depend. Secur. Comput. **9**, 61–74 (2012). https://doi.org/10.1109/TDSC.2011.34

17. Rushby, J.: The design and verification of secure systems. In: 8th ACM Symposium on Operating System Principles. ACM Operating Systems Review, Vol. 15, No. 5 (1981)

18. Rushby, J.: Separation and integration in mils (the mils constitution). Technical report, SRI International (02 2008)

19. Schneier, B.: Attack trees. Dr. Dobb's J. **24**(12) (12 1999). https://www.schneier.com/academic/archives/1999/12/attack_trees.html

20. Wang, L., Islam, T., Long, T., Singhal, A., Jajodia, S.: An attack graph-based probabilistic security metric. In: Atluri, V. (ed.) DBSec 2008. LNCS, vol. 5094, pp. 283–296. Springer, Heidelberg (2008). https://doi.org/10.1007/978-3-540-70567-3_22

21. Wang, L., Jajodia, S., Singhal, A., Noel, S.: k-Zero day safety: measuring the security risk of networks against unknown attacks. In: Gritzalis, D., Preneel, B., Theoharidou, M. (eds.) ESORICS 2010. LNCS, vol. 6345, pp. 573–587. Springer, Heidelberg (2010). https://doi.org/10.1007/978-3-642-15497-3_35

22. Watchdog, C.: Kill switch (2019). https://consumerwatchdog.org/report/kill-switch-why-connected-cars-can-be-killing-machines-and-how-turn-them

Attack Path Analysis for Cyber Physical Systems

Georgios Kavallieratos[1]([✉]) [ID] and Sokratis Katsikas[1,2] [ID]

[1] Department of Information Security and Communications Technology,
Norwegian University of Science and Technology, Gjøvik, Norway
`georgios.kavallieratos@ntnu.no`
[2] Open University of Cyprus, School of Pure and Applied Sciences,
Latsia, Nicosia, Cyprus
`sokratis.katsikas@ouc.ac.cy`

Abstract. The identification and analysis of potential paths that an adversary may exploit to attack Cyber Physical Systems comprising subsystems enables the comprehensive understanding of the attacks and the impact that may have to the overall system, thus facilitating the definition of appropriate countermeasures that will satisfy the pertinent security requirements. To this end, several attack modelling techniques can be employed, the attack graph being the most prevalent among them. Unfortunately, the discovery and analysis of all possible attack paths in an attack graph is not possible in systems even of a moderate size. In this work we propose a novel systematic method for discovering and analyzing attack paths in real-world scale interconnected Cyber Physical Systems. The method considers the criticality of each sub-system in discovering paths and the risk to the overall system that each path presents to analyze and prioritize paths. We illustrate the workings of the method by applying to the navigational Cyber Physical Systems of the Cyber-Enabled Ship to identify and analyze highly critical attack paths originating from the Automatic Identification System (AIS) and targeting the Autonomous Navigation System (ANS).

Keywords: Cyber physical systems · Attack path analysis · Navigational system · Autonomous ships

1 Introduction

Various cyberattacks targeting Cyber Physical Systems (CPSs) have been reported and analyzed in the last decade [1]. Such attacks may have severe impact on both the physical and the cyber parts of the CPS. This is particularly so in autonomous systems, as the higher the level of autonomy, the greater the impact of a cyberattack, due to the extended interconnections and interdependencies among the networked components of such systems [2].

The fourth industrial revolution in shipping is known as cyber-shipping or Shipping 4.0 [3]. This digital transformation increases the cyber risks in the already vulnerable to cyberattacks maritime domain. Various cyberattacks in

© Springer Nature Switzerland AG 2020
S. Katsikas et al. (Eds.): CyberICPS 2020/SECPRE 2020/ADIoT 2020, LNCS 12501, pp. 19–33, 2020.
https://doi.org/10.1007/978-3-030-64330-0_2

this domain have occurred, have been studied and analyzed in the literature [4–6]; the increasing proliferation of interconnected on-board CPSs increases the attack surface of contemporary vessels. The emerging technology of the remotely controlled and autonomous vessels, both variants of the Cyber-Enabled Ship (C-ES) [7], will increase even further the attack surface. Thus, C-ESs of the future will need to be cyber-secure-by-design. The analysis of potential cyberattacks that target CPSs of the C-ES is an important step in this process, as it provides comprehensive insight into possible attacks and facilitates the identification of the necessary mitigation strategies and measures.

Attack models are an important instrument for improving our perception and understanding of cyberattacks; both are fundamental in evaluating the security of a networked system and in subsequently selecting appropriate countermeasures [8]. Attack models are the result of employing attack modelling techniques, that allow the representation of the sequence of events that lead to a successful cyberattack. Such techniques are grouped in three categories, namely (1) techniques that are based on the use case framework; (2) techniques that present a cyberattack from a temporal perspective; and (3) graph based techniques [9]. Among the latter, attack graphs and attack trees are the most commonly used methods for representing cyberattacks.

Attack graphs are conceptual diagrams used to analyze how a target can be attacked, so as to improve its security posture. This is performed in four stages, namely (1) Acquisition of system information; (2) Attack graph generation; (3) Attack graph analysis; and (4) Use of the results. In the first stage, information about the system (e.g. network topology, sub-systems, vulnerabilities, network configuration, connectivity) is collected. This information is subsequently used to generate the attack graph, which is then used for performing the analysis of attacks. Finally, the results of the analysis are used to inform the risk management process.

In a system of networked assets, whereby an asset may well be a system in its own right, an *attack path* is an ordered sequence of assets that can be used as stepping stones by an attacker seeking to attack one or more assets on the path.

The main advantage of an attack graph over other types of attack models is that it helps to identify all possible attacks on a system [10]. Notwithstanding the advantages of graph-based attack models in describing important elements of a cyberattack, these models suffer from a scalability problem if all possible attack paths are considered [11]. This is why, even though the analysis of all attack paths can lead to the identification of the optimal security solutions, techniques that allow the identification of those attack paths that present the most significant risk to the overall system are sought. Examples of such techniques are [12–14].

The analysis of potential attack paths is commonly based only on the *vulnerabilities* of the systems on the attack path. This limits considerably the insight into the possible attack scenarios, and limits the subsequent selection of countermeasures to only those that reduce the vulnerability, excluding countermeasures that reduce the other elements of risk, namely the likelihood of the threats and the extent of the impact, and their combinations.

In this paper we propose a method for cyberattack path discovery and prioritization for CPSs comprising a number of sub-systems. The method is based on the criticality of the sub-systems on each path and on the cyber risk to the overall system that each attack path represents. Thus, we provide a holistic view of the attack, that can be further exploited in designing the necessary and most appropriate mitigation techniques and strategies.

The most vulnerable CPSs on board the C-ES are those comprising the navigational system [7]. We therefore illustrate the workings of our method by applying it to the navigational CPS system of the C-ES.

The contribution of this work is twofold:

- We have developed a novel method for discovering and analyzing attack paths in interconnected CPSs, and
- we have applied it to discover and analyze attack paths for the navigational CPSs in a C-ES.

The remaining of the paper is structured as follows: Sect. 2 reviews the related work. Section 3 describes the proposed method. In Sect. 4 the method is applied to the navigational system of the C-ES. Finally, Sect. 5 summarizes our findings and indicates possible future work.

2 Related Work

Attack graphs find their origins in Dacier's PhD thesis and early papers [15–17], where the concept of the *privilege graph* was introduced. The concept of the *attack graph* was proposed in [18]. Attack graphs are classified into five categories, namely *generic*; *alert correlation*; *vulnerability*; *miscellaneous*; and *dependency* [9]. Several approaches for attack graph generation and analysis have been proposed in the literature. S. Khaitan et al. in [19] surveyed approaches that generate attack graphs in wired and wireless networks, and focused on the limitation of existing approaches to handle complex and scalable networks. Typically, graph construction attempts to identify all possible attacks paths [20]. The process may also be supported by software tools, such as the early tool presented in [21], MulVal [22]; TVA [23]; NuSMV [24]. A survey of attack graph analysis methods can be found in [25].

According to [26], attack graphs face a combinatorial explosion. Thus they can be applied to small network systems only [23]; for large-scale systems it is necessary to reduce the complexity of the attack graph. Methods for doing so include path pruning, network properties compression, and property matching time reducing [25]. Examples of such methods are found in [24], where a Breadth-first search method is used to identify the vulnerabilities and build the attack graph; in [27], that introduces the concept of group reachability to reduce graph complexity; in [28], where the authors propose a multi-agent-based distributed approach to generate the attack graph using Depth-first search; in [29], where the use of a dynamic algorithm that generates an attack graph consisting of the K most probable to be exploited attack paths; in [30], where a a Bayesian-based attack graph generation method is proposed; in [31] that is based on a cut and divide method and a series of division rounds and uses Depth-first search to search the smaller graphs; and in [32], where the authors exploit risk flow within an attack graph for performing security risk assessment. J. H. Castellanos et al. in [33] propose a method to identify attack paths that uses data-flow graphs, and N. Polatidis et al. in [34] propose an attack path discovery method that is used as a component of a maritime risk management system. The method uses constraints and Depth-first search to effectively generate attack graphs and has been used for identifying attack paths and security mechanisms in the maritime domain [34,35].

The main characteristics and goals of attack graph analysis methods for CPSs have been discussed in [36]. Out of the nine methods examined therein, only one considers potential security risks in analyzing and prioritizing potential attack paths, whilst the rest focus on vulnerabilities for performing this analysis; this is also the case with all the methods referenced above.

In the C-ES context, safety-related cyberattacks for autonomous inland ships have been studied in [37]. Cyberattack scenarios against autonomous ships have been analyzed in [7] by leveraging the STRIDE methodology. However, none of these works considered possible paths that an attacker may follow to launch a cyberattack against a C-ES.

3 Discovering and Analyzing Attack Paths

3.1 Problem Formulation

We assume a CPS comprising sub-systems that is described by a directed graph $G(V,E)$ whose nodes respresent the sub-systems and the edges represent interconnections between nodes. The goal is to discover and analyze attack paths between selected *entry* and *target* sub-systems, based on information regarding the criticality of the sub-systems and the overall cyber risk to the overall system that an attack path represents. The results are to be used to inform the risk management process in selecting appropriate countermeasures to reduce the overall cyber risk.

3.2 Components of the Proposed Method

The proposed method integrates a number of components, that are briefly described in this section.

Identifying Critical Components in CPSs: Because of the distributed nature of almost all CPSs, in many cases suffices to destroy or damage only a few influential nodes or links in a system to inflict failure of the entire system. An aggregated index (the Z index) that leverages the characteristics of both nodes and links to rank the components of a CPS according to their criticality, and a method to calculate it by means of a multiple attribute decision making (MADM) method was proposed in [38]. The method involves the use of novel graph metrics, namely the *Tacit Input Centrality (TIC)* and the *Tacit Output Centrality (TOC)* that measure how frequently each link in a system is utilized and reflect the importance of a link in relation to the nodes it connects. It also involves the *Closeness Centrality (CC)* of a node that measures how close the node is to all other nodes, by calculating the shortest path length from the node to every other node in the network.

Estimating the Risk of Each CPS Component: The DREAD method was developed by Microsoft as a complement to STRIDE [39], to provide a quantitative estimate of the risk in a software system [40]. DREAD stands for *Damage, Reproducibility, Exploitability, Affected users*, and *Discoverability*. *Damage* represents the damage that a cyber-attack may inflict to the system; together with *Affected Users/Systems* they reflect the *Impact* of the attack. *Reproducibility* reflects the ability of the attacker to reproduce the attack, and *Exploitability* represents the ability to exploit the system's vulnerabilities and perform the attack. *Discoverability* reflects the capacity of the adversary to identify system vulnerabilities. The sum of *Reproducibility, Exploitability*, and *Discoverability* reflects the *Likelihood* of the cyberattack [41].

Table 1. DREAD criteria

	High (3)	Medium (2)	Low (1)
D	The adversary is able to bypass security mechanisms; get administrator access; upload/modify the CPS content	Leakage of confidential information of the CPS (functions/source code); inflict partial malfunction/disruption to the system	Leaking non-sensitive information; the attack is not possible to be extended over other CPSs
R	The cyberattack can be reproduced anytime to the targeted CPS	The adversary is able to reproduce the attack but under specific risk conditions	Although they know CPS's vulnerabilities/faults, the attacker is not able to perform the cyberattack
E	The cyberattack can be performed by a novice adversary in a short time	A skilled adversary could launch the attack	The attack requires an extremely skilled person and in-depth knowledge of the targeted CPS
A	All CPSs are affected	Partial users/systems, non-default configuration	The attack affects only the targeted CPS
D	The CPS's vulnerabilities are well known and the attacker is able to get access to the relevant information to exploit the vulnerabilities	The CPS's vulnerabilities/faults are not well known and the adversary needs to get access to the CPS	The threat has been identified and the vulnerabilities have been patched

Each of the DREAD variables accepts an integer value in [0,3], the value being assigned by considering the criteria listed in Table 1 that is adapted from [40] to capture also aspects of CPSs.

The DREAD score is calculated as follows [41]:

$$\frac{\sum(Damage, Affectedsystems)}{2} = Impact \tag{1}$$

$$\frac{\sum(Reproducibility, Exploitability, Discoverability)}{3} = Likelihood \tag{2}$$

$$DREADscore = \frac{(Impact + Likelihood)}{2} \tag{3}$$

The DREAD risk level is determined as follows:

- **If** *DREAD score* ≤ 1 **then** *DREAD risk level* := Low
- **If** 1 < *DREAD score* ≤ 2 **then** *DREAD risk level* := Medium
- **If**: 2 < *DREAD score* ≤ 3 **then** *DREAD risk level* := High

Integrating the Stakeholders' Views: The assessment of the importance of each possible attack path is based upon the combination of two values, namely the risk of each CPS component on the path (as estimated by e.g. the DREAD method); and the effect that a failure of each such component would have to the operation of the overall system, as seen from the perspective of the system stakeholders; this is captured by the *CPSImp* metric. *CPSImp* is assigned to each CPS by the administrator/designer/operator/relevant stakeholder of the system to reflect the importance of each sub-system to the overall system. It can take one of three distinct values as follows:

- 1: Low importance (potential system damage or disruption cannot inflict any significant damage to the overall system);
- 2: Medium importance (if the system is damaged or disrupted, overall system malfunctions may occur, but no crucial deviation from normal operation);
- 3: High importance (if the system is damaged or disrupted, the operation of the overall system will be severely affected).

The importance of the overall attack path taking into account both the risk level and the stakeholders' view is calculated according to the following equation [35]:

$$AttackPathImportance = 0.6 * CPSImp + 0.4 * Risk \tag{4}$$

3.3   Input Data

The proposed method operates on the following input data:

1. A directed graph $G(V,E)$ representing the CPS under study, as defined in Sect. 3.1. Such a graph can be generated using automated tools such as the CASOS ORA tool from Carnegie Mellon University [42].
2. The entry CPS (e) and the targeted CPS (t) in G.
3. The profile of the assumed adversary. One of the novel features of the proposed approach is that it is both risk driven (as opposed to only vulnerability driven) and is intended to in turn drive the subsequent risk management process. Thus, the adversary model must also be considered when discovering and analyzing attack paths, following the suggestion in NIST SP800-30 [43]. The adversary is profiled by means of the following attributes, adapted from [35]:
   - *Accessibility* is a measure of the adversary's logical and physical accessibility of the adversary to the attack surface of each entry sub-system. It assumes a "yes" or "no" value.
   - *Capability* represents the ability of the adversary to access the necessary resources (technical, physical, and logical) to perform an attack against each entry sub-system. It is measured in a qualitative scale ranging from "Low" to "Medium" to "High".
   - *Motivation* represents the determination of the adversary to carry out the attack. It is measured in a qualitative scale ranging from "Low" to "Medium" to "High".

When the adversary does not have the required levels of accessibility, capability, and motivation, there are no possible attack paths.

3.4   The Proposed Method

As shown in Fig. 1 the proposed method is structured in six steps. These are described below.

1. **Step 1 - Load input data:** All input data as specified in Fig. 1 are loaded.
2. **Step 2 - Check adversary profile:** The profile of the adversary is checked against threshold values. If the adversary is deemed incapable of launching an attack against e, no possible attack paths exist and the method terminates.
3. **Step 3 - Determine the criticality of the nodes in G:** The method in [38] is applied to G to determine the criticality of each node. The result of this step is a list of all nodes in G sorted according to their Z value in ascending order[1] (the L list). The reader is referred to [38] for the detailed workings of the method that are hereby omitted in the interest of saving space.
4. **Step 4 - Discover attack paths:** By performing a depth-first search, all non-circular paths starting at e and terminating at t that include at least one of the top n nodes in L are discovered.

---

[1] The lower the Z value of a sub-system the more critical the sub-system is.

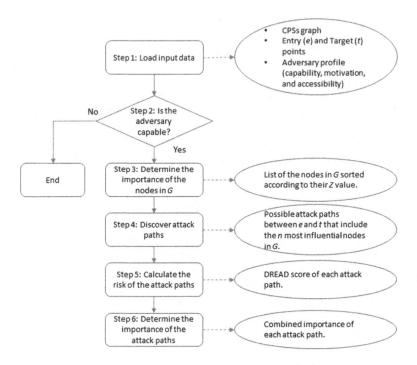

Fig. 1. Process

5. **Step 5 - Calculate the risk of the attack paths:** The risk to the overall system that each attack path among those discovered in Step 4 represents is calculated, by applying the DREAD method [39] on each of the nodes on each path. The risk of the path equals the maximum risk of its nodes.
6. **Step 6 - Determine the importance of the attack paths:** The importance of each attack path among those discovered in Step 4 is calculated by means of equation (4), and the list of attack paths is prioritized.

3.5   Characteristics of the Method

The proposed method enjoys some desirable characteristics that are not always shared with alternative methods for discovering and analyzing attack paths in CPSs:

- The proposed method allows the analysis of attack paths against *composite CPSs* i.e. cyber-physical systems that comprise subsystems; it thus constitutes a step towards attack path analysis against systems-of-systems.
- The proposed method incorporates a component that allows the *identification of critical subsystems* in a composite CPS. This is particularly useful when designing the set of countermeasures, as the protection of critical subsystems would be prioritized.

- The proposed method analyzes attack paths by considering *all the elements of risk* rather than simply vulnerabilities. This is also particularly useful when designing the set of countermeasures, as it allows the informed selection of controls that may reduce more than one of the elements of risk.
- The proposed method incorporates a component that *involves the stakeholders* to determine the importance of the discovered attack paths, thus enabling the extraction of realistic results, particularly in complex environments where multiple stakeholders exist.
- The proposed method *scales well* with the number of subsystems of the composite CPS.
- The proposed method is *domain-agnostic*; it can be applied in any CPS domain.

4   Attacks Against the Navigational CPSs of the C-ES

The generic ICT architecture of the Cyber-Enabled Ship in the form of a hierarchical tree structure was proposed in [7]. The detailed interconnections, dependencies and interdependencies among the CPSs of the C-ES, including those in the navigational system were determined in [2]. The latter, along with their interconnections are depicted in Fig. 2. According to [7, 44], the three most vulnerable systems on board the C-ES are the Automatic Identification System (AIS), the Electronic Chart Display Information System (ECDIS), and the Global Maritime Distress and Safety System (GMDSS); among these, the Automatic Identification System (AIS) is the most vulnerable. On the other hand, a potential failure of the Autonomous Navigation System (ANS) or the Autonomous Ship Controller (ASC) can result in a cascade failure effect among the CPSs of the C-ES, with significant impact [2]. Accordingly, in order to illustrate the workings of the proposed method, we selected to analyze attack paths for the navigational system of the C-ES that have as entry point the AIS and as target system the ANS.

Assuming that the adversary is deemed capable of launching the attack, Step 3 of the proposed method returns the *Tacit Input Centrality - TIC, Tacit Output Centrality - TOC, Closness Centrality - CC,* and *Aggregated index - Z* values for the systems in Fig. 2 as depicted in Table 2.

Table 2. Navigational CPSs metrics

	ANS	AIS	ECDIS	RADAR	GPS	ASC	C.A.	ASM	AP	VDR	Gyro	GMDSS	Satellite
TIC	0.772	0.590	0.545	0.409	0.50	1	0.590	0.636	0.545	0.545	0.409	0.590	0.5
TOC	0.727	0.590	0.545	0.409	0.50	1	0.590	0.636	0.545	0.545	0.409	0.181	0.045
CC	0.767	0.697	0.676	0.657	0.657	0.920	0.719	0.719	0.697	0.657	0.622	0.697	0.657
Z	**0.538**	**0.851**	0.940	1.193	1.116	0	**0.843**	**0.736**	0.933	0.803	0.984	1.034	1.53

Assuming that we are interested in analyzing attack paths that include the five most critical components, we set n equal to 5 in Step 4 of the proposed

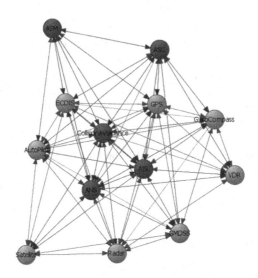

Fig. 2. Navigational CPSs of the C-ES

Table 3. Attack paths from AIS to ANS

Path ID	Cyber-attack path
1	AIS, ANS
2	AIS, ASC, ANS
3	AIS, ASC, ASM, ANS
4	AIS, ASC, ASM, C.A., ANS
5	AIS, ASC, C.A., ANS
6	AIS, ASC, C.A., ASM, ANS
7	AIS, ASM, ANS
8	AIS, ASM, ASC, ANS
9	AIS, ASM, ASC, CA, ANS
10	AIS, ASM, C.A., ANS
11	AIS, ASM, C.A., ASC, ANS
12	AIS, C.A., ANS
13	AIS, C.A., ASC, ANS
14	AIS, C.A., ASC, ASM, ANS
15	AIS, C.A., ASM, ANS
16	AIS, C.A., ASM, ASC, ANS

method. The five systems with the lowest Z values are shown as red nodes in Fig. 2. Step 4 then results in identifying sixteen attack paths having as entry system the AIS and as target system the ANS. These are depicted in Table 3.

Table 4 presents the *CPSImp* values assigned to the sub-systems involved in the discovered attack paths. Note that the *CPSImp* of the AIS, Advanced Sensor Module (ASM), and Collision Avoidance (C.A.) sub-systems is set to *2*, while the *CPSImp* of the Autonomous Navigation System (ANS) and the Autonomous Ship Controller (ASC) sub-systems is set to *3*. This is because the former are navigational systems that provide voyage, dynamic, and static data; the redundancy of such data is sufficient since other on-board systems generate and transmit dynamic and voyage data respectively. Therefore, potential malfunction in any of the AIS, Advanced Sensor Module (ASM), or Collision Avoidance (C.A.) sub-systems cannot cause significant damage to the overall system. On the other hand, the *CPSImp* of the Autonomous Navigation System (ANS) and of the Autonomous Ship Controller (ASC) is *3* since both systems

Table 4. Importance of navigational CPSs

CPS	CPSImp
AIS	2
ANS	3
ASM	2
CA	2
ASC	3

Table 5. Prioritized list of attack paths

Path ID	Affected CPSs	Attack Path Importance
6	AIS, ASC, C.A., ASM, ANS	**8.08**
9	AIS, ASM, ASC, CA, ANS	**8.08**
11	AIS, ASM, C.A., ASC, ANS	**8.08**
14	AIS, C.A., ASC, ASM, ANS	**8.08**
4	AIS, ASC, ASM, C.A., ANS	**8.08**
16	AIS, C.A., ASM, ASC, ANS	8.08
5	AIS, ASC, C.A., ANS	6.88
8	AIS, ASM, ASC, ANS	6.88
13	AIS, C.A., ASC, ANS	6.88
3	AIS, ASC, ASM, ANS	6.88
10	AIS, ASM, C.A., ANS	6.28
15	AIS, C.A., ASM, ANS	6.28
2	AIS, ASC, ANS	5.68
7	AIS, ASM, ANS	5.08
12	AIS, C.A., ANS	5.08
1	AIS, ANS	3.88

control other navigational systems, and they also have attained the highest TIC and TOC values, as shown in Table 2.

The application of Steps 5 and 6 of the proposed method on the attack paths of Step 4 yields the prioritized list of attack paths shown in Table 5.

5   Conclusions

In this work we proposed a novel systematic method for analyzing attack paths in interconnected CPSs. Contrary to existing alternatives, the method handles the scalability problem of attack graphs by considering highly critical nodes and analyzes the resulting paths by considering the cyber risk that each of these represents to the overall system rather than only considering vulnerabilities. We illustrated the workings of the method by applying it to the navigational CPSs of the C-ES, to analyze the possible attack paths that start at the AIS and target the ANS. Five highly critical attack paths have been identified. The results of this analysis can then be fed back to the risk-based process of identifying appropriate countermeasures to satisfy the relevant security requirements and check whether indeed the selected countermeasures alter the possible attack paths and decrease the risk. One pathway for future work is to apply the method as part of an holistic process to identify and analyze cyberattack paths for all the on-board CPSs of the C-ES, so as to propose a complete system security architecture for the C-ES.

References

1. Al-Mhiqani, M.N., Ahmad, R., Yassin, W., Hassan, A., Abidin, Z.Z., Ali, N.S., Abdulkareem, K.H.: Cyber-security incidents: a review cases in cyber-physical systems. Int. J. Adv. Comput. Sci. Appl. **9**(1), 499–508 (2018)
2. Kavallieratos, G., Katsikas, S., Gkioulos, V.: Modelling shipping 4.0: a reference architecture for the cyber-enabled ship. In: Nguyen, N.T., Jearanaitanakij, K., Selamat, A., Trawiński, B., Chittayasothorn, S. (eds.) ACIIDS 2020. LNCS (LNAI), vol. 12034, pp. 202–217. Springer, Cham (2020). https://doi.org/10.1007/978-3-030-42058-1_17
3. Emad, G.R., Khabir, M., Shahbakhsh, M.: Shipping 4.0 and training seafarers for the future autonomous and unmanned ships. In: Proceedings of the 21th Marine Industries Conference (MIC 2019), pp. 202–217(2020)
4. Chang, C.H., Wenming, S., Wei, Z., Changki, P., Kontovas, C.A.: Evaluating cybersecurity risks in the maritime industry: a literature review. In: Proceedings of the International Association of Maritime Universities (IAMU) Conference (2019)
5. Silgado, D.M.: Cyber-attacks: a digital threat reality affecting the maritime industry (2018)
6. Hassani, V., Crasta, N., Pascoal, A.M.: Cyber security issues in navigation systems of marine vessels from a control perspective. In: Proceedings of the ASME: 36th International Conference on Ocean, p. 2017. American Society of Mechanical Engineers Digital Collection, Offshore and Arctic Engineering (2017)
7. Kavallieratos, G., Katsikas, S., Gkioulos, V.: Cyber-attacks against the autonomous ship. In: Katsikas, S.K., Cuppens, F., Cuppens, N., Lambrinoudakis, C., Antón,

A., Gritzalis, S., Mylopoulos, J., Kalloniatis, C. (eds.) SECPRE/CyberICPS -2018. LNCS, vol. 11387, pp. 20–36. Springer, Cham (2019). https://doi.org/10.1007/978-3-030-12786-2_2

8. Chen, Y.C., Mooney, V., Grijalva, S.: A survey of attack models for cyber-physical security assessment in electricity grid. In: Proceedings of the 2019 IFIP/IEEE 27th International Conference on Very Large Scale Integration (VLSI-SoC), pp. 242–243. IEEE (2019)

9. Lallie, H.S., Debattista, K., Bal, J.: A review of attack graph and attack tree visual syntax in cyber security. Comput. Sci. Rev. **35**, 100219 (2020)

10. Al-Mohannadi, H., Mirza, Q., Namanya, A., Awan, I., Cullen, A., Disso, J.: Cyber-attack modeling analysis techniques: an overview. In: Proceedings of the 2016 IEEE 4th International Conference on Future Internet of Things and Cloud Workshops (FiCloudW), pp. 69–76. IEEE (2016)

11. Hong, J.B., Kim, D.S.: Performance analysis of scalable attack representation models. In: Janczewski, L.J., Wolfe, H.B., Shenoi, S. (eds.) SEC 2013. IAICT, vol. 405, pp. 330–343. Springer, Heidelberg (2013). https://doi.org/10.1007/978-3-642-39218-4_25

12. Xie, A., Cai, Z., Tang, C., Hu, J., Chen, Z.: Evaluating network security with two-layer attack graphs. In: Proceedings of the 2009 Annual Computer Security Applications Conference, pp. 127–136 (2009)

13. Ou, X., Boyer, W.F., McQueen, M.A.: A scalable approach to attack graph generation. In: Proceedings of the 13th ACM Conference on Computer and Communications Security, CCS 2006, pp. 336–345. Association for Computing Machinery, New York, NY, USA (2006)

14. Sheyner, O., Haines, J., Jha, S., Lippmann, R., Wing, J.M.: Automated generation and analysis of attack graphs. In: Proceedings 2002 IEEE Symposium on Security and Privacy, pp. 273–284 (2002)

15. Dacier, M., Deswarte, Y., Kaâniche, M.: Models and tools for quantitative assessment of operational security. SEC 1996. IAICT, pp. 177–186. Springer, Boston, MA (1996). https://doi.org/10.1007/978-1-5041-2919-0_15

16. Dacier, M.: Towards Quantitative Evaluation of Computer Security. Ph.D. thesis, Institut National Polytechnique de Toulouse (1994)

17. Dacier, M., Deswarte, Y.: Privilege graph: an extension to the typed access matrix model. In: Gollmann, D. (ed.) ESORICS 1994. LNCS, vol. 875, pp. 319–334. Springer, Heidelberg (1994). https://doi.org/10.1007/3-540-58618-0_72

18. Phillips, C., Swiler, L.P.: A graph-based system for network-vulnerability analysis. In Proceedings of the 1998 Workshop on New Security Paradigms, NSPW 1998, pp. 71–79. Association for Computing Machinery, New York, NY, USA (1998)

19. Khaitan, S., Raheja, S.: Finding optimal attack path using attack graphs: a survey. Int. J. Soft Comput. Eng. **1**(3), 2231–2307 (2011)

20. Ou, X., Singhal, A.: Quantitative security risk assessment of enterprise networks. In: Ou, X., Singhal, A. (eds.) Attack Graph Techniques, pp. 5–8. Springer, New York (2011)

21. Swiler, L.P., Phillips, C., Ellis, D., Chakerian, S.: Computer-attack graph generation tool. In: Proceedings DARPA Information Survivability Conference and Exposition II. DISCEX 2001, Vol. 2, pp. 307–321 (2001)

22. Ou, X., Govindavajhala, S., Appel, A.: MulVAL: a logic-based network security analyzer. In: Proceedings of the USENIX Security Symposium 2005, pp. 113–127 (2005)

23. Jajodia, S., Noel, S., O'Berry, B.: Topological analysis of network attack vulnerability. In: Kumar, V., Srivastava, J., Lazarevic, A. (eds.) Managing Cyber Threats Massive Computing, pp. 244–266. Springer, Boston, MA (2005)

24. Ammann, P., Wijesekera, D., Kaushik, S.: Scalable, graph-based network vulnerability analysis. In: Proceedings of the 9th ACM Conference on Computer and Communications Security, CCS 2002, pp. 217–224. Association for Computing Machinery, New York, NY, USA (2002)

25. Zeng, J., Wu, S., Chen, Y., Zeng, R., Wu, C.: Survey of attack graph analysis methods from the perspective of data and knowledge processing. Secur. Commun. Netw. **2019**, 1–17 (2019)

26. Hsu, L.H., Lin, C.K.: Graph Theory and Interconnection Networks. CRC Press, Boca Raton (2019)

27. Ingols, K., Lippmann, R., Piwowarski, K.: Practical attack graph generation for network defense. In: Proceedings of the 22nd Annual Computer Security Applications Conference (ACSAC2006), pp. 121–130 (2006)

28. Kaynar, K., Sivrikaya, F.: Distributed attack graph generation. IEEE Trans. Depend. Secur. Comput. **13**(5), 519–532 (2016)

29. Bi, K., Han, D., Jun, W.: K maximum probability attack paths dynamic generation algorithm. Comput. Sci. Inform. Syst. **13**(2), 677–689 (2016)

30. Poolsappasit, N., Dewri, R., Ray, I.: Dynamic security risk management using Bayesian attack graphs. IEEE Trans. Depend. Secur. Comput. **9**(1), 61–74 (2012)

31. Jehyun L., Heejo L., Peter, H.: Scalable attack graph for risk assessment. In: Proceedings of the International Conference on Information Networking, pp. 1–5 (2009)

32. Dai, F., Hu, Y., Zheng, K., Wu, B.: Exploring risk flow attack graph for security risk assessment. IET Inform. Secur. **9**(6), 344–353 (2015)

33. Castellanos, J.H., Ochoa, M., Zhou, J.: Finding dependencies between cyber-physical domains for security testing of industrial control systems. In: Proceedings of the 34th Annual Computer Security Applications Conference, pp. 582–594 (2018)

34. Polatidis, N., Pavlidis, M., Mouratidis, H.: Cyber-attack path discovery in a dynamic supply chain maritime risk management system. Comput. Stand. Interf. **56**, 74–82 (2018)

35. Mouratidis, H., Diamantopoulou, V.: A security analysis method for industrial internet of things. IEEE Trans. Indust. Inform. **14**(9), 4093–4100 (2018)

36. Ibrahim, M., Al-Hindawi, Q., Elhafiz, R., Alsheikh, A., Alquq, O.: Attack graph implementation and visualization for cyber physical systems. Processes **8**(1), 12 (2020)

37. Bolbot, V., Theotokatos, G., Boulougouris, E., Vassalos, D.: Safety related cyber-attacks identification and assessment for autonomous inland ships. In: Proceedings of the International Seminar on Safety and Security of Autonomous Vessels (ISSAV) (2019)

38. Akbarzadeh, A., Katsikas, S.: Identifying critical components in large scale cyber physical systems. In: Proceedings of the 1st International Workshop on Engineering and Cybersecurity of Critical Systems (EnCyCriS) (2020)

39. Shostack, A.: Threat modeling: Designing for security. John Wiley & Sons, New Jersey (2014)

40. Microsoft. Chapter 3 - Threat modeling (2010). https://docs.microsoft.com/en-us/previous-versions/msp-n-p/ff648644(v=pandp.10)?redirectedfrom=MSDN. Accessed 26 May 2020

41. Zinsmaier, S.D., Langweg, H., Waldvogel, M.: A practical approach to stakeholder-driven determination of security requirements based on the GDPR and common criteria. In: Proceedings of the International Conference on Information Systems Security and Privacy ICISSP, pp. 473–480 (2020)
42. CASOS. http://www.casos.cs.cmu.edu/index.php. Accessed 09 Dec 2019
43. Guide for conducting risk assessments. NIST SP 800–30 Rev. 1, National Institute of Standards and Technology, Gaithersburg MD, USA (2012)
44. Kavallieratos, G., Diamantopoulou, V., Katsikas, S.K.: Shipping 4.0: Security requirements for the cyber-enabled ship. IEEE Trans. Indust. Inform. **16**(10), 6617–6625 (2020)

Identifying and Analyzing Implicit Interactions in a Wastewater Dechlorination System

Jason Jaskolka$^{(\boxtimes)}$ ⓘ

Systems and Computer Engineering, Carleton University, Ottawa, ON, Canada
`jason.jaskolka@carleton.ca`

Abstract. Critical infrastructures consist of numerous components, and even more interactions, many of which may not be expected or foreseen by the system designers. The existence of these so-called implicit interactions indicates design flaws that, if not mitigated, could result in losses of system stability, safety, and security. In this paper, we apply a formal methods-based approach for identifying and analyzing implicit interactions in a real-world Wastewater Dechlorination System provided by a municipal wastewater treatment facility. A system model is developed using the C^2KA modeling framework and the analysis is automated using a software prototype. The analysis results include a summary of the identified implicit interactions and a calculation of their severity and exploitability, which helps to inform mitigation efforts at early stages of system design. We validate the results with a questionnaire which shows that the rigorous, practical approaches applied in this case study have the potential to improve overall system security and resilience.

Keywords: Implicit interactions · Critical infrastructure · Industrial control systems · Wastewater systems · Formal methods

1 Introduction

Critical infrastructures, including water and wastewater distribution systems, transportation systems, communications networks, manufacturing facilities, and energy systems often consist of numerous components linked in complex ways. This can lead to unforeseen interactions among components that may not be expected or intended by the designers and operators of the system. Such interactions have come to be known as *implicit interactions* [11,12]. The presence of implicit interactions in a system can indicate unforeseen flaws that, if not mitigated, could result in the loss of system stability, safety, and security.

In previous work, we developed a rigorous, formal methods-based approach for identifying the existence of implicit interactions in critical infrastructures and industrial control systems [11,12]. We also developed an approach for analyzing

---

Supported by U.S. Department of Homeland Security Grant 2015-ST-061-CIRC01.

S. Katsikas et al. (Eds.): CyberICPS 2020/SECPRE 2020/ADIoT 2020, LNCS 12501, pp. 34–51, 2020.
https://doi.org/10.1007/978-3-030-64330-0_3

the identified implicit interactions to determine how they can be exploited to directly or indirectly influence the behavior of critical system components [8].

In this paper, we describe our recent experience in applying, testing, and validating the developed approaches to identify and analyze the existence of implicit interactions in a real-world Wastewater Dechlorination System (WDS) provided by a municipal wastewater treatment facility. In particular, we model the system using the Communicating Concurrent Kleene Algebra (C^2KA) modeling framework and automate the analysis using a software prototype. We report our experimental findings demonstrating the existence, severity, and exploitability of implicit interactions in the system. Furthermore, we validate the applicability, value, and usefulness of the approaches for identifying and analyzing implicit interactions in critical infrastructure and industrial control systems.

This paper is organized as follows. Section 2 provides a short overview of the system modeling and analysis approaches applied in this paper. Section 3 briefly describes a real-world WDS and specifies the system model using C^2KA. Section 4 presents the experimental results of our implicit interactions analysis on the WDS. Section 5 describes the validation of our approaches and results through a stakeholder questionnaire. Section 6 highlights the lessons learned from our experience and the feedback obtained from the stakeholder questionnaire. Section 7 discusses related work and lastly, Sect. 8 concludes.

2   Modeling and Analysis Approaches

2.1   System Modeling Approach

We use the algebraic modeling framework known as Communicating Concurrent Kleene Algebra (C^2KA) [7,10] for system modeling. A C^2KA is a mathematical system $(\mathcal{S}, \mathcal{K})$ that characterizes the response invoked by a stimulus on a system behavior as a next behavior mapping (denoted by $\circ$) and a next stimulus mapping (denoted by λ). $\mathcal{K} = (K, +, *, ;, 0, 1)$ forms a concurrent semiring where K is a set of agent[1] behaviors, $+$ is a choice between behaviors, and $;$ and $*$ denote a sequential and parallel composition of behaviors, respectively. The *inactive* behavior 0 is neutral with respect to $+$ and the idle behavior 1 is neutral with respect to $;$ and $*$. Similarly, $\mathcal{S} = (S, \oplus, \odot, \eth, \mathfrak{n})$ forms an idempotent semiring where S is a set of stimuli, $\oplus$ is a choice between stimuli, and $\odot$ is a sequential composition of stimuli. The *deactivation stimulus* $\eth$ influences all agents to become inactive. The *neutral stimulus* $\mathfrak{n}$ has no influence on agent behavior. We refer the reader to [7] for a detailed presentation of C^2KA.

C^2KA provides three levels of specification for agent behaviors. The *stimulus-response specification* specifies the next behavior mapping $\circ$ and next stimulus mapping λ for each agent. The *abstract behavior specification* represents each agent behavior as an algebraic term restricting the agent to its desired behaviors in the system. Lastly, the *concrete behavior specification* provides the state-level

---

[1] An *agent* refers to any component, combination of components, or process which can execute a discrete set of actions [14].

specification wherein the concrete programs for each agent behavior are given using any suitable programming or specification language.

2.2 Approach for Identifying Implicit Interactions

Systems typically have intended sequences of communication and interaction to perform their operations. Let $\mathcal{P}_{\text{intended}}$ be the set of intended interactions for a given system. $\mathcal{P}_{\text{intended}}$ can be derived from the system description and requirements. An *implicit interaction* is any potential for communication [9] that is unfamiliar, unplanned, or unexpected, and is either not visible or not immediately comprehensible by the system designers. Implicit interactions represent previously unknown linkages among system components. Because system designers are generally unaware of such linkages, they indicate vulnerabilities that can be exploited to impact system stability, safety, and security [11].

To identify the implicit interactions in a system modeled using C^2KA, we first identify all of the possible interactions (direct and indirect) among each pair of agents by performing an analysis of the potential for communication of the given system specification. Then, we verify whether each possible interaction exists as part of a characterization of the intended system interactions resulting from the system design. Any interaction that deviates from this intended behavior is an implicit interaction. The full details of the approach can be found in [11,12].

2.3 Approach for Analyzing Implicit Interactions

In a system formed by a set $\mathcal{A}$ of agents, an *interaction*[2] is represented as: $p_n^{\mathcal{T}_n} \overset{\text{def}}{=} A_n \rightarrow_{\mathcal{T}_n} A_{n-1} \rightarrow_{\mathcal{T}_{n-1}} \cdots \rightarrow_{\mathcal{T}_2} A_1 \rightarrow_{\mathcal{T}_1} A_0$ where each $A_i \in \mathcal{A}$ for all $0 \leq i \leq n$, and each $\mathcal{T}_j \in \{\mathcal{S}, \mathcal{E}\}$ for all $1 \leq j \leq n$. In an interaction $p_n^{\mathcal{T}_n}$, A_n is called the *source agent* and A_0 is called the *sink agent*. Furthermore, $\rightarrow_{\mathcal{S}}$ denotes communication via stimuli (e.g., message passing) and $\rightarrow_{\mathcal{E}}$ denotes communication via shared environments (e.g., shared variables). We refer the reader to [7] for more details about communication via stimuli and shared environments.

Severity Analysis. The *severity* of an implicit interaction is a measure indicating how much of the interaction is unexpected in the system. The severity measure is interpreted as the relative non-overlap between a given interaction and the intended interactions of a system. Intuitively, the less that an interaction overlaps with the intended system interactions, the more unexpected that interaction is. In this way, an interaction with a high severity measure indicates that the interaction can pose a higher threat to the system in which it exists and therefore should be granted higher priority for mitigation. Formally, this intuition is captured in Definition 1.

---

[2] When the context is clear, we also refer to an interaction simply as p.

Definition 1. (Severity Measure [11]) *Let p be a possible interaction in a system with intended interactions* $\mathcal{P}_{\text{intended}}$. *The severity of p is computed by:*

$$\sigma(p) = 1 - \max_{q \in \mathcal{P}_{\text{intended}}} \left\{ \frac{|\text{lcs}(p, q)|}{|p|} \right\}$$

where $\text{lcs}(p, q)$ *denotes the longest common substring of interactions p and q.*

The severity measure of an interaction p is a numeric value $\sigma(p)$ such that $0 \le \sigma(p) \le 1$. Any intended, or expected, interaction in a given system has a severity measure of 0, and conversely any implicit interaction has a severity measure greater than 0. This means that intended interactions present no (additional) threat to the system because they are known and expected by the system designers and it is assumed that the designers are aware of any risks inherently present with the behavior associated with these interactions. The full details of the derivation of the severity measure can be found in [11].

Exploitability Analysis. The *exploitability* of an implicit interaction measures the percentage of ways in which a source agent can influence its neighboring agent's behavior in a way that propagates the influence along the implicit interaction to eventually influence the sink agent's behavior. Formally, this intuition is captured in Definition 2.

Definition 2. (Exploitability Measure [8]) *The exploitability of an implicit interaction* $p_n^{\mathcal{T}_n}$ *is computed recursively by:*

$$\xi(p_n^{\mathcal{T}_n}) = \begin{cases} \xi(p_{n-1}^{\mathcal{T}_{n-1}}) \dfrac{|\text{Infl}(A_{n-1}) \cap \text{attack}(p_n^{\mathcal{T}_n})|}{|\text{Infl}(A_{n-1})|} & \text{if } \mathcal{T}_n = \mathcal{S} \wedge n > 1 \\[3mm] \xi(p_{n-1}^{\mathcal{T}_{n-1}}) \dfrac{|\text{Ref}(A_{n-1}) \cap \text{attack}(p_n^{\mathcal{T}_n})|}{|\text{Ref}(A_{n-1})|} & \text{if } \mathcal{T}_n = \mathcal{E} \wedge n > 1 \\[3mm] 1 & \text{otherwise} \end{cases}$$

where for any agent $A \in \mathcal{A}$, $\text{Infl}(A)$ *is the set of stimuli that can influence (i.e., cause an observable change) the behavior of* A, $\text{Ref}(A)$ *is the set of referenced variables for* A, *and* $\text{attack}(p_n^{\mathcal{T}_n})$ *is the set of possible ways in which a compromised[3] source agent of* $p_n^{\mathcal{T}_n}$ *can influence the behavior of the sink agent.*

The exploitability of an implicit interaction $p_n^{\mathcal{T}_n}$ is a numeric value $\xi(p_n^{\mathcal{T}_n})$ such that $0 \le \xi(p_n^{\mathcal{T}_n}) \le 1$. Intuitively, the fewer possibilities that each agent in an implicit interaction has to cause a "chain reaction" of influence in its neighboring agents, the lower the exploitability of interaction, and therefore the lower the priority for mitigation. The full details of the derivation of the exploitability measure can be found in [8].

---

[3] A *compromised agent* can issue any stimulus and/or alter or define any program variable in a way that is not consistent with its original or intended specification [8].

2.4   Tool Support

To automate the approaches described above, we use a prototype software tool, first described in [7]. The tool is implemented in the *Haskell* programming language and uses the *Maude* term rewriting system [2]. It allows for the specification of systems using C^{2}KA and automatically identifies the implicit interactions in a given system. The prototype also computes the severity and exploitability measures for each identified implicit interaction. Example usage of the software prototype for identifying and analyzing implicit interactions can be found in [11].

3   System Modeling and Specification

3.1   Wastewater Dechlorination System Description

The WDS described in this section was provided by the supervisory control and data acquisition (SCADA) system operators at a municipal wastewater treatment facility. The objective of the system is to reduce the total residual chlorine in the plant's final effluent to comply with the Federal Government's regulated level. The general operation of the system is summarized in Fig. 1.

When the process is ready to begin, a *start* event[4] is triggered. A Sample Pump (SAP) feeds the effluent (*eff*, effluent) to a sulfite (SO$_3$) Analyzer (SO3) and a Sample Flow Meter (SFM). The SO$_3$ Analyzer (SO3) measures the residual Sodium Bisulfite (SBS) in the effluent and sends its results (*res*, residual) to the Programmable Logic Controller (PLC). Simultaneously, the Sample Flow Meter measures the flow rate from the Sample Pump and sends its results (*rate*, flowRate) to the PLC. The PLC controls the chemical feed pumps which are in a lead-lag configuration. The PLC's proportional-integral-derivative (PID) control algorithm calculates the SBS flow (in L/h), demanded by the Chlorine Contact Tank (CCT), and determines if the SBS flow should be increased or decreased based on the SBS residual feedback received from the SO$_3$ Analyzer; residual is the process variable for the PID control. If the SBS feedback is decreasing

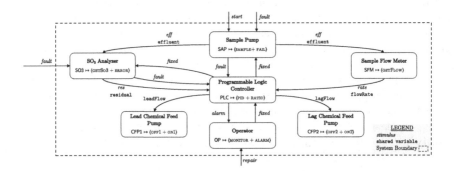

Fig. 1. Summary of the Wastewater Dechlorination System operation

---

[4] Because this is a continuous process, the *start* event can be viewed as a time triggered event which is sent infinitely often to discretize the continuous process.

below the set-point, then the CCT demand for SBS increases. The PLC always runs the Lead Pump (CFP1) to match the SBS flow demanded by the CCT (leadFlow), up to a maximum flow of 75 L/h. When the SBS flow, demanded by the CCT, exceeds the Lead Pump maximum flow, the PLC stages on the Lag Pump (CFP2); both the Lead and Lag Pumps will then be controlled by the PLC to satisfy the SBS flow demand (leadFlow and lagFlow). When the SBS flow, demanded by the CCT, falls below 70 L/h (minus a satisfactory 5 L/h dead-band), the PLC turns off the Lag Pump. Alternatively, if the SBS feedback is increasing above the set-point, the CCT demand for SBS decreases.

The Sample Pump is located downstream of the dechlorination zone and continuously draws a sample of the final effluent for analysis by the SO_3 Analyzer. The analysis takes about 20 s to send an SBS residual value to the PLC. The PLC verifies that the Sample Pump is providing a continuous flow of final effluent to the SO_3 Analyzer greater than 2 L/s, otherwise an *alarm* is sent to the Operator (OP) to notify them of a Sample Pump failure.

The Operator has an option to select from one of two dosing methods: (1) PID control or (2) Ratio control. PID control is more efficient and cost effective than Ratio control. However, if PID control fails, for example, due to SO_3 Analyzer or Sample Pump failure[5], as determined by the PLC, the Operator will be notified. In this case, the Operator will switch the CCT dosing method from PID to Ratio control until maintenance can get the SO_3 Analyzer or Sample Pump back online (*repair*). SBS dosing is always required to satisfy the government regulations.

3.2   C²KA Specification of the WDS

The system consists of seven agents as shown in Fig. 1: {SAP, SO3, SFM, PLC, CFP1, CFP2, OP}. The set of agents is derived from the system description (see Sect. 3.1) and represents the primary components involved in the system operation. For the C²KA specification, let the set of all agent behaviors K be generated using the operations of the structure $\mathcal{K}$ and the set of basic behaviors given by: {SAMPLE, FAIL, GETSO3, ERROR, GETFLOW, PID, RATIO, OFF1, ON1, OFF2, ON2, MONITOR, ALARM}. The basic behaviors correspond to the operations that each system agent can perform. Similarly, let the set of all stimuli S be generated using the operations of the structure $\mathcal{S}$ and the set of basic stimuli given by: {*start*, *fault*, *eff*, *res*, *rate*, *off1*, *on1*, *off2*, *on2*, *alarm*, *fixed*, *repair*}. The basic stimuli correspond to messages that are passed between agents that will trigger the execution of their behaviors.

Assumptions. To simplify the modeling and specification of the WDS, we assume that valves are incorporated as part of the pump system, so they are controlled internally by the PLC. We also assume that system faults causing failures in the SO_3 Analyzer or Sample Pump, and repairs to system faults are external events outside of the control of the WDS. As such these events are propagated to the PLC to be handled. These assumptions have been validated by the SCADA operators that provided the WDS description for this case study.

---

[5] SO_3 Analyzer or Sample Pump failure can be caused by an external *fault*.

Abstract Behavior Specification. The abstract behavior of each agent is represented as shown in Fig. 1. For example, the abstract behavior specification of the Sample Pump is given as SAP $\mapsto \langle$ SAMPLE $+$ FAIL $\rangle$ which shows that, at any given time, SAP can exhibit any of the two behaviors SAMPLE or FAIL which represent the normal continuous sampling of final effluent and the failure of the Sample Pump, respectively. This is reflected in the use of the choice operator $+$ in the term representing the Sample Pump behavior. Similarly, the abstract behavior specification of the PLC (i.e., PLC $\mapsto \langle$ PID $+$ RATIO $\rangle$) shows that it can be in its PID control mode or in its Ratio control mode.

Stimulus-Response Specification. The stimulus-response specification of the WDS agents is compactly specified as shown in Fig. 2. In each table, the row header shows the basic behaviors that the agent can perform in the system, and the column header shows the basic stimuli to which the agent may be subjected in the system. These sets of basic behaviors and stimuli are dictated by the sets K and S of the C^{2}KA structure described above. Each table grid shows the next behavior or next stimulus (respective to the operator shown in the top left cell) that results when the stimulus in the column header is applied to the behavior in the row header. For example, in the stimulus-response specification of SAP, when a *fault* event occurs while it is operating in its normal SAMPLE behavior, the response is to change SAP to its failure behavior FAIL and to broadcast the *fault* so that it can be handled by another agent (namely PLC). Alternatively, when an *alarm*, event occurs while SAP is operating in its normal SAMPLE, behavior because SAP does not respond to an *alarm* event, it remains operating in its normal SAMPLE behavior, and it does not provide any output stimulus (denoted by the neutral stimulus n).

Sample Pump (SAP):

o	start	fault	eff	res	rate	off1	on1	off2	on2	alarm	fixed	repair
SAMPLE	SAMPLE	FAIL	SAMPLE	SAMPLE	SAMPLE	SAMPLE	SAMPLE	SAMPLE	SAMPLE	SAMPLE	SAMPLE	SAMPLE
FAIL	FAIL	FAIL	FAIL	FAIL	FAIL	FAIL	FAIL	FAIL	FAIL	FAIL	SAMPLE	FAIL

λ	start	fault	eff	res	rate	off1	on1	off2	on2	alarm	fixed	repair
SAMPLE	eff	n	n	n	n	n	n	n	n	n	n	n
FAIL	n	fault	n	n	n	n	n	n	n	n	n	n

SO$_3$ Analyzer (SO3):

o	start	fault	eff	res	rate	off1	on1	off2	on2	alarm	fixed	repair
GETSO3	GETSO3	ERROR	GETSO3	GETSO3	GETSO3	GETSO3	GETSO3	GETSO3	GETSO3	GETSO3	GETSO3	GETSO3
ERROR	ERROR	ERROR	ERROR	ERROR	ERROR	ERROR	ERROR	ERROR	ERROR	ERROR	GETSO3	ERROR

λ	start	fault	eff	res	rate	off1	on1	off2	on2	alarm	fixed	repair
GETSO3	n	fault	n	n	n	n	n	n	n	n	n	n
ERROR	n	n	n	n	n	n	n	n	n	n	n	n

Sample Flow Meter (SFM):

o	start	fault	eff	res	rate	off1	on1	off2	on2	alarm	fixed	repair
GETFLOW	GETFLOW	GETFLOW	GETFLOW	GETFLOW	GETFLOW	GETFLOW	GETFLOW	GETFLOW	GETFLOW	GETFLOW	GETFLOW	GETFLOW

λ	start	fault	eff	res	rate	off1	on1	off2	on2	alarm	fixed	repair
GETFLOW	n	n	rate	n	n	n	n	n	n	n	n	n

Programmable Logic Controller (PLC):

o	start	fault	eff	res	rate	off1	on1	off2	on2	alarm	fixed	repair
PID	PID	RATIO	PID	PID	PID	PID	PID	PID	PID	PID	PID	PID
RATIO	RATIO	RATIO	RATIO	RATIO	RATIO	RATIO	RATIO	RATIO	RATIO	RATIO	PID	RATIO

λ	start	fault	eff	res	rate	off1	on1	off2	on2	alarm	fixed	repair
PID	n	alarm	n	n	n	n	n	n	n	n	n	n
RATIO	n	n	n	n	n	n	n	n	n	n	fixed	n

Lead Chemical Feed Pump (CFP1):

o	start	fault	eff	res	rate	off1	on1	off2	on2	alarm	fixed	repair
OFF1	OFF1	OFF1	OFF1	OFF1	OFF1	OFF1	ON1	OFF1	OFF1	OFF1	OFF1	OFF1
ON1	ON1	ON1	ON1	ON1	ON1	OFF1	ON1	ON1	ON1	ON1	ON1	ON1

λ	start	fault	eff	res	rate	off1	on1	off2	on2	alarm	fixed	repair
OFF1	n	n	n	n	n	n	n	n	n	n	n	n
ON1	n	n	n	n	n	n	n	n	n	n	n	n

Lag Chemical Feed Pump (CFP2):

o	start	fault	eff	res	rate	off1	on1	off2	on2	alarm	fixed	repair
OFF2	OFF2	OFF2	OFF2	OFF2	OFF2	OFF2	OFF2	OFF2	ON2	OFF2	OFF2	OFF2
ON2	ON2	ON2	ON2	ON2	ON2	ON2	ON2	OFF2	ON2	ON2	ON2	ON2

λ	start	fault	eff	res	rate	off1	on1	off2	on2	alarm	fixed	repair
OFF2	n	n	n	n	n	n	n	n	n	n	n	n
ON2	n	n	n	n	n	n	n	n	n	n	n	n

Operator (OP):

o	start	fault	eff	res	rate	off1	on1	off2	on2	alarm	fixed	repair
MONITOR	MONITOR	MONITOR	MONITOR	MONITOR	MONITOR	MONITOR	MONITOR	MONITOR	MONITOR	ALARM	MONITOR	MONITOR
ALARM	ALARM	ALARM	ALARM	ALARM	ALARM	ALARM	ALARM	ALARM	ALARM	ALARM	ALARM	MONITOR

λ	start	fault	eff	res	rate	off1	on1	off2	on2	alarm	fixed	repair
MONITOR	n	n	n	n	n	n	n	n	n	n	n	n
ALARM	n	n	n	n	n	n	n	n	n	n	n	fixed

Fig. 2. Stimulus-response specification of the Wastewater Dechlorination System

Concrete Behavior Specification. We use a fragment of Dijkstra's guarded command language [3] for the concrete behavior specification of the WDS agents as shown in Fig. 3. For example, the concrete behavior specification of SO3 shows that in its normal measuring behavior GETSO3, it computes the SBS residual of the effluent from the Sample Pump (MEASURE_SBS_RESIDUAL(effluent)) and assigns it to a control variable residual. Alternatively, in its error behavior ERROR, because of the error, SO3 is unable to effectively compute the SBS residual of the effluent received from the Sample Pump and instead has an undefined control variable residual (represented by NULL).

$$\text{SAP} \mapsto \begin{cases} \text{SAMPLE} \stackrel{\text{def}}{=} \texttt{effluent} := \texttt{SAMPLE()} \\ \text{FAIL} \stackrel{\text{def}}{=} \texttt{effluent} := \texttt{SAMPLE()} \end{cases}$$

$$\text{SO3} \mapsto \begin{cases} \text{GETSO3} \stackrel{\text{def}}{=} \texttt{residual} := \texttt{MEASURE\_SBS\_RESIDUAL(effluent)} \\ \text{ERROR} \stackrel{\text{def}}{=} \texttt{residual} := \texttt{NULL} \end{cases}$$

$$\text{SFM} \mapsto \left\{ \text{GETFLOW} \stackrel{\text{def}}{=} \texttt{flowRate} := \texttt{MEASURE\_FLOW\_RATE(effluent)} \right.$$

$$\text{PLC} \mapsto \begin{cases} \text{PID} \stackrel{\text{def}}{=} \text{if} \quad \texttt{flowRate} >= \texttt{FLOW\_SETPOINT} \longrightarrow \text{skip} \\ \qquad [] \quad \texttt{flowRate} < \texttt{FLOW\_SETPOINT} \longrightarrow \text{send } \textit{alarm} \\ \quad \text{fi}; \\ \quad \texttt{targetFlow} := \texttt{COMPUTE\_FLOW(residual)}; \\ \quad \text{if} \quad \texttt{targetFlow} > \texttt{MAX\_PUMP\_FLOW} \longrightarrow \text{send } \textit{on2}; \texttt{leadFlow} := \texttt{MAX\_PUMP\_FLOW}; \\ \qquad\qquad \texttt{lagFlow} := \texttt{targetFlow} - \texttt{MAX\_PUMP\_FLOW} \\ \qquad [] \quad \texttt{targetFlow} \leq \texttt{MAX\_PUMP\_FLOW} \wedge \texttt{targetFlow} \geq \texttt{DEADBAND} \longrightarrow \texttt{leadFlow} := \texttt{targetFlow} \\ \qquad [] \quad \texttt{targetFlow} < \texttt{DEADBAND} \longrightarrow \text{send } \textit{off2}; \texttt{leadFlow} := \texttt{targetFlow} \\ \quad \text{fi} \\ \text{RATIO} \stackrel{\text{def}}{=} \text{skip} \quad /\!/ \textit{ details not provided as part of the system description} \end{cases}$$

$$\text{CFP1} \mapsto \begin{cases} \text{OFF1} \stackrel{\text{def}}{=} \texttt{leadPumpOn} := \texttt{FALSE}; \texttt{pumpRate} := 0 \\ \text{ON1} \stackrel{\text{def}}{=} \texttt{leadPumpOn} := \texttt{TRUE}; \texttt{pumpRate} := \texttt{leadFlow} \end{cases}$$

$$\text{CFP2} \mapsto \begin{cases} \text{OFF1} \stackrel{\text{def}}{=} \texttt{lagPumpOn} := \texttt{FALSE}; \texttt{pumpRate} := 0 \\ \text{ON1} \stackrel{\text{def}}{=} \texttt{lagPumpOn} := \texttt{TRUE}; \texttt{pumpRate} := \texttt{lagFlow} \end{cases}$$

$$\text{OP} \mapsto \begin{cases} \text{MONITOR} \stackrel{\text{def}}{=} \texttt{mode} := \texttt{PID} \\ \text{ALARM} \stackrel{\text{def}}{=} \texttt{mode} := \texttt{RATIO} \end{cases}$$

Fig. 3. Concrete behavior specification of the Wastewater Dechlorination System

3.3   Intended System Interactions

We use the visualization of the WDS system operation in Fig. 1 to derive the sequence of control or data transferred among the system agents as shown in Fig. 4, where solid arrows denote communication via stimuli and dashed arrows denote communication via shared environments. Since some agents in the system respond to the same stimulus at the same time, the expansion of the concurrent interaction of the agents is captured by branches in its execution trace. This concurrent interaction is translated and embodied as a set of possible walks of the system's underlying communication graph. In other words, the set of intended system interactions characterizes the possible execution traces representing the interleavings of the concurrent behaviors of the system agents.

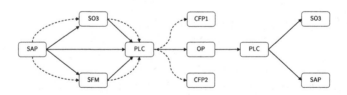

Fig. 4. Execution trace of the Wastewater Dechlorination System intended interactions

4 Identification and Analysis of Implicit Interactions

4.1 Identification of Implicit Interactions

After using the software prototype to apply the approach for identifying implicit interactions on the WDS model, we found that 74 out of 141 possible interactions ($\approx$ 52%) are implicit interactions. The identification is summarized in Fig. 5 and Table 1. The summary shows that, with respect to the system specification, some agents do not have the potential to communicate at all. For example, CFP1 cannot communicate with CFP2 and vice versa. Intuitively, this makes sense because these chemical feed pumps are controlled by PLC and therefore should not be able to influence one another's behavior. Instead, we see that there is exactly one interaction from PLC to CFP1 and CFP2, respectively. Alternatively, the summary shows that of the six possible interactions between PLC and SO3, five are implicit. This means that these five interactions deviate from the intended control flow (or sequence of interaction) among the system agents. Similarly, all interactions between SFM and SO3 are implicit, showing that these two agents which normally should not interact with one another, do in fact have the potenial to interact in the system which can lead to unexpected or undesirable system behaviors affecting system stability, safety, and security.

The existence of implicit interactions indicates that there is an aspect of the system design (whether accidental or intentional, innocuous or malicious) allowing for this kind of interaction to be present. For example, referring to Table 1, implicit interaction x_{43} (PLC $\rightarrow_S$ OP $\rightarrow_S$ SAP $\rightarrow_\varepsilon$ SO3) shows that it is possible for PLC to influence the behavior of OP with a stimulus communication (denoted $\rightarrow_S$), which will cause OP to influence the behavior of SAP with another stimulus communication, which in turn will cause SAP to write a shared variable (denoted $\rightarrow_\varepsilon$) which will be read by, and ultimately influence the behavior of, SO3. One such scenario may involve an attacker causing a false *alarm* in the PLC, triggering the Operator to waste time finding and fixing a *fault*, which can affect how the Sample Pump feeds `effluent` to the SO$_3$ Analyzer, which may then compute incorrect SBS residual readings, potentially impacting system safety and stability. Considering the set of intended system interactions shown in Fig. 4, it

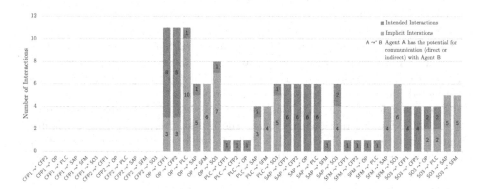

Fig. 5. Implicit interactions identified in the Wastewater Dechlorination System

is easy to see that there is no subpath matching the implicit interaction x_{43}. It is important to note that these implicit interactions are not easily found without the rigorous analysis of the system based on its C^2KA specification.

4.2 Severity Analysis of Implicit Interactions

After having identified the implicit interactions present in the WDS, we used the software prototype to compute their severity. The severity analysis is summarized in Table 1. The summary shows that the severity of the implicit interaction x_{43}, for example, is 0.67. This indicates that this implicit interaction is rather unexpected and may provide a more "stealthy" way for an attacker to cause unintended system behaviors if they can compromise the source agent of the interaction (i.e., PLC). When comparing the severities of the implicit interactions provided in Table 1, some interactions are more severe than others because they involve more intermediate agent interactions that are not expected or foreseen as part of the intended system behavior. Therefore, these interactions present a greater risk because the system designers are generally more unaware of such potential communication sequences.

4.3 Exploitability Analysis of Implicit Interactions

We also used the software prototype to compute the exploitability of the implicit interactions in the WDS. The exploitability analysis is summarized in Table 1.

Of particular note is that, for some interactions, we computed an exploitability of 1.00 (e.g., x_{11}, x_{12}, etc.). Consider x_{43} which has an exploitability of 1.00. According to the specification of PLC (i.e., the source agent), of all of the possible ways in which PLC can influence the behavior of OP to cause it to influence the behavior of SAP to cause it to influence the behavior of SO3, any of them will have the desired effect. Examining the C^2KA system specification more closely, we can see that if PLC is compromised such that an attacker is able to force it to send an *alarm* stimulus or a *repair* stimulus, it can indirectly influence the behavior of SO3. This indicates that implicit interactions with an exploitability of 1.00 are *maximally exploitable*, meaning that as long as a compromised source agent influences the behavior of its neighboring agent, then it will ultimately influence the behavior of the sink agent. This makes the compromised source agent very powerful in its ability to cause unintended or expected system behaviors. Consequently, these particular implicit interactions present the most serious threat to the safety, security, and reliability of the system and ought to be assigned the highest priority for mitigation.

Conversely, for some interactions, we computed an exploitability of 0.00 (e.g., x_3, x_6, etc.). For interactions p_n^S, where the initial interaction from the source agent is via stimuli (i.e., $\rightarrow_S$), this indicates that these implicit interactions can only be *exploited trivially* by having the compromised source agent issue a *deactivation stimulus* $\mathfrak{d}$ which will cause all other agents in the system to fail. In this way, these interactions pose little threat to the system since this very

Table 1. Summary of the implicit interaction analysis for the Wastewater Dechlorination System

ID	Implicit Interaction	Severity $0 \leq \sigma(x_i) \leq 1$	Exploitability $0 \leq \xi(x_i) \leq 1$
x_1	OP $\rightarrow_S$ PLC $\rightarrow_\varepsilon$ CFP1	0.50	0.50
x_2	OP $\rightarrow_S$ SO3 $\rightarrow_\varepsilon$ PLC $\rightarrow_\varepsilon$ CFP1	0.33	1.00
x_3	OP $\rightarrow_S$ SO3 $\rightarrow_S$ PLC $\rightarrow_\varepsilon$ CFP1	0.33	0.00
x_4	OP $\rightarrow_S$ PLC $\rightarrow_\varepsilon$ CFP2	0.50	0.50
x_5	OP $\rightarrow_S$ SO3 $\rightarrow_\varepsilon$ PLC $\rightarrow_\varepsilon$ CFP2	0.33	1.00
x_6	OP $\rightarrow_S$ SO3 $\rightarrow_S$ PLC $\rightarrow_\varepsilon$ CFP2	0.33	0.00
x_7	OP $\rightarrow_S$ SAP $\rightarrow_S$ PLC	0.50	0.00
x_8	OP $\rightarrow_S$ SO3 $\rightarrow_S$ SAP $\rightarrow_S$ PLC	0.50	0.00
x_9	OP $\rightarrow_S$ SAP $\rightarrow_\varepsilon$ SFM $\rightarrow_\varepsilon$ PLC	0.33	0.00
x_{10}	OP $\rightarrow_S$ SO3 $\rightarrow_S$ SAP $\rightarrow_\varepsilon$ SFM $\rightarrow_\varepsilon$ PLC	0.33	0.00
x_{11}	OP $\rightarrow_S$ SO3 $\rightarrow_\varepsilon$ PLC	0.50	1.00
x_{12}	OP $\rightarrow_S$ SAP $\rightarrow_\varepsilon$ SO3 $\rightarrow_\varepsilon$ PLC	0.33	1.00
x_{13}	OP $\rightarrow_S$ SAP $\rightarrow_S$ SO3 $\rightarrow_\varepsilon$ PLC	0.33	0.00
x_{14}	OP $\rightarrow_S$ SO3 $\rightarrow_S$ PLC	0.50	0.00
x_{15}	OP $\rightarrow_S$ SAP $\rightarrow_\varepsilon$ SO3 $\rightarrow_S$ PLC	0.33	0.00
x_{16}	OP $\rightarrow_S$ SAP $\rightarrow_S$ SO3 $\rightarrow_S$ PLC	0.33	0.00
x_{17}	OP $\rightarrow_S$ SAP	1.00	1.00
x_{18}	OP $\rightarrow_S$ SO3 $\rightarrow_\varepsilon$ PLC $\rightarrow_S$ SAP	0.67	0.00
x_{19}	OP $\rightarrow_S$ SO3 $\rightarrow_S$ PLC $\rightarrow_S$ SAP	0.67	0.00
x_{20}	OP $\rightarrow_S$ SO3 $\rightarrow_S$ SAP	1.00	0.00
x_{21}	OP $\rightarrow_S$ PLC $\rightarrow_S$ SO3 $\rightarrow_S$ SAP	0.33	0.00
x_{22}	OP $\rightarrow_S$ SAP $\rightarrow_\varepsilon$ SFM	0.50	1.00
x_{23}	OP $\rightarrow_S$ PLC $\rightarrow_S$ SAP $\rightarrow_\varepsilon$ SFM	0.33	0.50
x_{24}	OP $\rightarrow_S$ SO3 $\rightarrow_\varepsilon$ PLC $\rightarrow_S$ SAP $\rightarrow_\varepsilon$ SFM	0.67	0.00
x_{25}	OP $\rightarrow_S$ SO3 $\rightarrow_S$ PLC $\rightarrow_S$ SAP $\rightarrow_\varepsilon$ SFM	0.67	0.00
x_{26}	OP $\rightarrow_S$ SO3 $\rightarrow_S$ SAP $\rightarrow_\varepsilon$ SFM	0.67	0.00
x_{27}	OP $\rightarrow_S$ PLC $\rightarrow_S$ SO3 $\rightarrow_S$ SAP $\rightarrow_\varepsilon$ SFM	0.50	0.00
x_{28}	OP $\rightarrow_S$ SO3	1.00	1.00
x_{29}	OP $\rightarrow_S$ SAP $\rightarrow_S$ PLC $\rightarrow_S$ SO3	0.67	0.00
x_{30}	OP $\rightarrow_S$ SAP $\rightarrow_\varepsilon$ SFM $\rightarrow_\varepsilon$ PLC $\rightarrow_S$ SO3	0.50	0.00
x_{31}	OP $\rightarrow_S$ SAP $\rightarrow_\varepsilon$ SO3	0.50	1.00
x_{32}	OP $\rightarrow_S$ PLC $\rightarrow_S$ SAP $\rightarrow_\varepsilon$ SO3	0.33	0.50
x_{33}	OP $\rightarrow_S$ SAP $\rightarrow_S$ SO3	0.50	0.00
x_{34}	OP $\rightarrow_S$ PLC $\rightarrow_S$ SAP $\rightarrow_S$ SO3	0.33	0.00
x_{35}	PLC $\rightarrow_S$ OP $\rightarrow_S$ SAP	0.50	1.00
x_{36}	PLC $\rightarrow_S$ OP $\rightarrow_S$ SO3 $\rightarrow_S$ SAP	0.67	0.00
x_{37}	PLC $\rightarrow_S$ SO3 $\rightarrow_S$ SAP	0.50	0.00

(continued)

Table 1. (*continued*)

ID	Implicit Interaction	Severity $0 \leq \sigma(x_i) \leq 1$	Exploitability $0 \leq \xi(x_i) \leq 1$
x_{38}	PLC $\rightarrow_{\mathcal{S}}$ OP $\rightarrow_{\mathcal{S}}$ SAP $\rightarrow_{\varepsilon}$ SFM	0.67	1.00
x_{39}	PLC $\rightarrow_{\mathcal{S}}$ SAP $\rightarrow_{\varepsilon}$ SFM	0.50	1.00
x_{40}	PLC $\rightarrow_{\mathcal{S}}$ OP $\rightarrow_{\mathcal{S}}$ SO3 $\rightarrow_{\mathcal{S}}$ SAP $\rightarrow_{\varepsilon}$ SFM	0.67	0.00
x_{41}	PLC $\rightarrow_{\mathcal{S}}$ SO3 $\rightarrow_{\mathcal{S}}$ SAP $\rightarrow_{\varepsilon}$ SFM	0.67	0.00
x_{42}	PLC $\rightarrow_{\mathcal{S}}$ OP $\rightarrow_{\mathcal{S}}$ SO3	0.50	1.00
x_{43}	PLC $\rightarrow_{\mathcal{S}}$ OP $\rightarrow_{\mathcal{S}}$ SAP $\rightarrow_{\varepsilon}$ SO3	0.67	1.00
x_{44}	PLC $\rightarrow_{\mathcal{S}}$ SAP $\rightarrow_{\varepsilon}$ SO3	0.50	1.00
x_{45}	PLC $\rightarrow_{\mathcal{S}}$ OP $\rightarrow_{\mathcal{S}}$ SAP $\rightarrow_{\mathcal{S}}$ SO3	0.67	0.00
x_{46}	PLC $\rightarrow_{\mathcal{S}}$ SAP $\rightarrow_{\mathcal{S}}$ SO3	0.50	0.00
x_{47}	SAP $\rightarrow_{\mathcal{S}}$ PLC $\rightarrow_{\mathcal{S}}$ OP $\rightarrow_{\mathcal{S}}$ SO3	0.33	0.50
x_{48}	SAP $\rightarrow_{\varepsilon}$ SFM $\rightarrow_{\varepsilon}$ PLC $\rightarrow_{\mathcal{S}}$ OP $\rightarrow_{\mathcal{S}}$ SO3	0.25	0.00
x_{49}	SAP $\rightarrow_{\mathcal{S}}$ PLC $\rightarrow_{\mathcal{S}}$ SO3	0.50	0.50
x_{50}	SAP $\rightarrow_{\varepsilon}$ SFM $\rightarrow_{\varepsilon}$ PLC $\rightarrow_{\mathcal{S}}$ SO3	0.33	0.00
x_{51}	SFM $\rightarrow_{\varepsilon}$ PLC $\rightarrow_{\mathcal{S}}$ OP $\rightarrow_{\mathcal{S}}$ SAP	0.33	1.00
x_{52}	SFM $\rightarrow_{\varepsilon}$ PLC $\rightarrow_{\mathcal{S}}$ SAP	0.50	0.00
x_{53}	SFM $\rightarrow_{\varepsilon}$ PLC $\rightarrow_{\mathcal{S}}$ OP $\rightarrow_{\mathcal{S}}$ SO3 $\rightarrow_{\mathcal{S}}$ SAP	0.50	0.00
x_{54}	SFM $\rightarrow_{\varepsilon}$ PLC $\rightarrow_{\mathcal{S}}$ SO3 $\rightarrow_{\mathcal{S}}$ SAP	0.67	0.00
x_{55}	SFM $\rightarrow_{\varepsilon}$ PLC $\rightarrow_{\mathcal{S}}$ OP $\rightarrow_{\mathcal{S}}$ SO3	0.33	1.00
x_{56}	SFM $\rightarrow_{\varepsilon}$ PLC $\rightarrow_{\mathcal{S}}$ SO3	0.50	0.00
x_{57}	SFM $\rightarrow_{\varepsilon}$ PLC $\rightarrow_{\mathcal{S}}$ OP $\rightarrow_{\mathcal{S}}$ SAP $\rightarrow_{\varepsilon}$ SO3	0.50	1.00
x_{58}	SFM $\rightarrow_{\varepsilon}$ PLC $\rightarrow_{\mathcal{S}}$ SAP $\rightarrow_{\varepsilon}$ SO3	0.67	0.00
x_{59}	SFM $\rightarrow_{\varepsilon}$ PLC $\rightarrow_{\mathcal{S}}$ OP $\rightarrow_{\mathcal{S}}$ SAP $\rightarrow_{\mathcal{S}}$ SO3	0.50	0.00
x_{60}	SFM $\rightarrow_{\varepsilon}$ PLC $\rightarrow_{\mathcal{S}}$ SAP $\rightarrow_{\mathcal{S}}$ SO3	0.67	0.00
x_{61}	SO3 $\rightarrow_{\mathcal{S}}$ SAP $\rightarrow_{\mathcal{S}}$ PLC $\rightarrow_{\mathcal{S}}$ OP	0.33	0.00
x_{62}	SO3 $\rightarrow_{\mathcal{S}}$ SAP $\rightarrow_{\varepsilon}$ SFM $\rightarrow_{\varepsilon}$ PLC $\rightarrow_{\mathcal{S}}$ OP	0.25	0.00
x_{63}	SO3 $\rightarrow_{\mathcal{S}}$ SAP $\rightarrow_{\mathcal{S}}$ PLC	0.50	0.00
x_{64}	SO3 $\rightarrow_{\mathcal{S}}$ SAP $\rightarrow_{\varepsilon}$ SFM $\rightarrow_{\varepsilon}$ PLC	0.33	0.00
x_{65}	SO3 $\rightarrow_{\varepsilon}$ PLC $\rightarrow_{\mathcal{S}}$ OP $\rightarrow_{\mathcal{S}}$ SAP	0.33	1.00
x_{66}	SO3 $\rightarrow_{\mathcal{S}}$ PLC $\rightarrow_{\mathcal{S}}$ OP $\rightarrow_{\mathcal{S}}$ SAP	0.33	0.50
x_{67}	SO3 $\rightarrow_{\varepsilon}$ PLC $\rightarrow_{\mathcal{S}}$ SAP	0.50	0.00
x_{68}	SO3 $\rightarrow_{\mathcal{S}}$ PLC $\rightarrow_{\mathcal{S}}$ SAP	0.50	0.50
x_{69}	SO3 $\rightarrow_{\mathcal{S}}$ SAP	1.00	1.00
x_{70}	SO3 $\rightarrow_{\varepsilon}$ PLC $\rightarrow_{\mathcal{S}}$ OP $\rightarrow_{\mathcal{S}}$ SAP $\rightarrow_{\varepsilon}$ SFM	0.50	1.00
x_{71}	SO3 $\rightarrow_{\mathcal{S}}$ PLC $\rightarrow_{\mathcal{S}}$ OP $\rightarrow_{\mathcal{S}}$ SAP $\rightarrow_{\varepsilon}$ SFM	0.50	0.50
x_{72}	SO3 $\rightarrow_{\varepsilon}$ PLC $\rightarrow_{\mathcal{S}}$ SAP $\rightarrow_{\varepsilon}$ SFM	0.67	0.00
x_{73}	SO3 $\rightarrow_{\mathcal{S}}$ PLC $\rightarrow_{\mathcal{S}}$ SAP $\rightarrow_{\varepsilon}$ SFM	0.67	0.50
x_{74}	SO3 $\rightarrow_{\mathcal{S}}$ SAP $\rightarrow_{\varepsilon}$ SFM	0.50	1.00

specific and trivial way to exploit the interaction is straightforward to monitor and mitigate. Alternatively, for interactions $p_n^{\mathcal{E}}$, where the initial interaction from the source agent is via shared environments (i.e., $\rightarrow_{\mathcal{E}}$), this indicates that these implicit interactions cannot be exploited in the given system. Therefore, these interactions can be considered *benign*, which is very useful when we need to determine where and how to spend valuable resources in mitigation efforts.

In addition to the special cases discussed above, Table 1 also shows there are a number of implicit interactions with exploitability measures that fall in between the two extremes of benign or trivially exploitable and maximally exploitable. For example, the exploitability of x_1 is 0.50. This indicates that if an attacker compromises OP (i.e., the source agent) and chooses at random to send a stimulus to influence PLC, there is only a 50% chance that they will be successful in influencing the behavior of CFP1 (i.e., the sink agent).

Further analysis of the exploitability of the identified implicit interactions for the WDS indicates that **43** implicit interactions are *benign*, **21** are *maximally exploitable*, and **10** have an intermediate exploitability. This means that a significant proportion ($43/74 \approx 58\%$) of the identified implicit interactions do not present a significant risk to the system. This leaves notably fewer implicit interactions which require our attention.

4.4   Additional Observations

By further studying the implicit interactions, we can identify potential mitigations to ensure that such interactions are either not possible in the system, or that they are detectable. For instance, many of the identified implicit interactions (especially those that are exploitable) involve PLC, OP, and SO3. This indicates that these agents are somehow problematic in terms of enabling implicit interactions in the system. With this information, analysts can focus their attention on identifying and implementing countermeasures to prevent these implicit interactions from being realized. The automated analysis generated here intends to simplify and facilite this kind of reasoning and decision-making.

5   Validation of the Model and Analysis Results

5.1   Model Validation

We worked very closely with the SCADA operators at the municipal waster water treatment facility that provided the WDS case study to validate the system model and obtained analysis results. The SCADA operators received and reviewed documents including background papers on the developed methods and approaches for identifying and analyzing implicit interactions, and detailed reports of the specifications and analysis results of the provided WDS. Among these reports was the informal system description (Sect. 3.1), the C^2KA system model (Sect. 3.2), and the system analysis results generated by the software prototype (Table 1). Each of these artifacts were reviewed, validated (by domain expert inspection), and approved by the Senior Control Systems Engineer and the team responsible for the WDS, confirming that the system model and analysis results are valid in real-world contexts and scenarios.

5.2 Domain Expert Questionnaire

We developed a simple questionnaire to further validate and measure the applicability, value, and usefulness of the approaches and the analysis results presented in Sect. 4. We aimed to better understand the perceptions of potential end-users, practitioners, and stakeholders regarding the ability to utilize the analysis results in conducting cybersecurity assurance activities and assessments.

The questionnaire was divided into two parts. Part I, which consisted of Q1–Q3 as shown below, was concerned with the modeling and analysis of the WDS as described in Sects. 3 and 4. Part II, which consisted of Q4–Q9 as shown below, was concerned with the overall approach for identifying and analyzing implicit interactions as described in [8, 11, 12] and summarized in Sect. 2. Q1–Q6 had a possible response of *Yes*, *No*, or *Maybe*. Respondents were also asked to provide an explanation of their response for each question in a free-form text field. Q7–Q9 were free-form text fields giving respondents an opportunity to provide additional comments and feedback.

Q1 *Did the obtained and presented analysis results match your expectations based on your understanding of the WDS?*

Q2 *Are the obtained and presented analysis results understandable?*

Q3 *Are the obtained and presented analysis results valuable to you, your team, and/or your organization/others?*

Q4 *Do you believe that the approach for identifying and analyzing implicit interactions has value?*

Q5 *If you had a tool to perform the analysis offered by the approach for identifying and analyzing implicit interactions, would it benefit your activities?*

Q6 *If you had a tool to perform the analysis offered by the approach for identifying and analyzing implicit interactions, would you use it?*

Q7 *In your opinion, what are the strengths of the approach for identifying and analyzing implicit interactions?*

Q8 *In your opinion, what are the weaknesses of the approach for identifying and analyzing implicit interactions?*

Q9 *Please provide any other comments/feedback about the approach for identifying and analyzing implicit interactions?*

5.3 Questionnaire Results

The questionnaire was distributed to relevant stakeholders at the municipal wastewater treatment facility that provided the WDS for this study. It was completed by six respondents, each of which were involved in SCADA operations.

In Part I, there was consensus (100% *Yes* for Q1–Q3) that the analysis results *exceeded expectations* and were *understandable* and *valuable* to their operations. More specifically, several respondents commented that the analysis results "provided an alternative perspective on the analysis of the dechlorination process" and that they "highlight subtle weaknesses of certain interactions in the process."

In Part II, again there was consensus (100% *Yes* for Q4) that found the overall approach for identifying and analyzing implicit interactions to be *valuable* because it is capable of "identifying some weaknesses in the process." Additionally, it was found that a tool to perform the implicit interaction analysis would not benefit the activities of the respondents and that there was only a chance that they would use such a tool (100% *No* for Q5, and 100% *Maybe* for Q6). This is because each of the respondents were involved in SCADA operations. The respondents pointed out that such a tool "should be used by the integrator or developer in the early stages of the design" and that the SCADA operators could use such a tool "to verify the integrator's or developer's design."

The responses for Q7 highlighted that "the analysis is good at pointing to the source of problem areas in the system" and "the value of the approach is in finding issues early in the engineering design of systems." One respondent stated "the analysis may also find a use as part of the internal continuous improvement processes, especially, if it is easy to perform with good tool support."

The responses for Q8 pointed to some challenges of the approach including the fact that it "requires end-user expertise on the subject matter." In addition, the responses highlight some areas for improvement that can be addressed in future work. It was suggested that "it would be nice if in addition to showing the implicit interactions, some advice on mitigations for the identified interactions could be provided" and that "a summary of problematic areas would be helpful as part of the reporting of the results." Finally, the responses again indicated that "the analysis may be more useful for system integrators rather than system operators; as operators, this kind of analysis would be nice to have included in proposals from integrators that are contracted to upgrade the system, etc."

The responses to Q9 summarized that "if used in the early stages of system development, the approach can identify hidden problems and perhaps provide cost savings and time."

6   Lessons Learned

First and foremost, the results of our questionnaire indicate that the approaches for identifying an analyzing implicit interactions are useful for identifying potential issues early in the design of the system. There is promise for the approaches to find adoption and use among system integrators in support of their security assurance efforts. By incorporating such a formal and rigorous analysis early in the system development lifecycle, evidence that systems have been designed to be resilient to cyber-threats as part of the proposal for system upgrades can be useful to owners and operators making important contracting decisions. Moving forward, we will turn our attention to this important group of potential end-users to further validate the developed approaches to ensure transition to practice.

Based on our experience in applying the approach for identifying and analyzing implicit interactions in the WDS, we found that the approach scaled reasonably well, but that it could be improved. Using the software prototype on a 2.7 GHz Intel Core i5 processor and 8 GB RAM, the analysis results reported in Table 1 were obtained in 01:06:04. The WDS is of moderate size and complexity, but many industrial control systems that are part of critical infrastructures are larger and more complex than the system studied in this paper. Thus, more effort in developing appropriate tool support capable of more efficiently applying these approaches to conduct the analysis will help to reduce the barriers of adoption of the proposed approaches in practical settings.

Finally, while the approaches have been applied in the context of a wastewater treatment process, the analogous communication and dependencies are found in nearly all industrial control systems, meaning the approaches can be applied in other contexts as well including energy, utility, chemical, transportation, manufacturing, and other industrial and critical infrastructure sectors.

7   Related Work

Many approaches for studying component interactions in complex systems by analyzing information flows [4] have been proposed using formalisms such as state machines (e.g., [15]), Petri nets (e.g., [16]), process algebras (e.g., [4]), and typing systems (e.g., [5]). However, information flow analyses are often conducted at later stages of system development, such as the implementation stage. Instead, our approach helps to identify implicit interactions at earlier stages of system development. A similar idea has been carried out with the proposal of FlowUML [1]. Similarly, a number of risk formulations and analysis approaches for critical systems have been proposed. Many of these are based on network analysis and fault trees (e.g., [13]) and anomaly detection (e.g., [6]). However, probabilistic risk assessments typically focus on identifying and dealing with failure events, with design errors only being considered indirectly through the probability of the failure event. Problems resulting from unwanted or unexpected component interactions and systemic factors are often not considered. By contrast, we described an alternative approach meant to aid designers in systematically examining the interactions of system components by analyzing the potential communication paths that arise from the system design and specification.

8   Concluding Remarks

Identifying and analyzing implicit interactions in critical infrastructures and industrial control systems provides a step towards uncovering potential cybersecurity vulnerabilities that can help to improve system stability, safety, and security. In this paper, we demonstrated that the approaches for identifying and analyzing implicit interactions described in [8,11,12] are applicable in a real-world context. We described our experience in modeling and analyzing a WDS provided by a municipal wastewater treatment facility and we reported our experimental analysis results. The value and usefulness of the approaches and results in practice were validated by domain experts operating within the wastewater treatment facility that provided the WDS description.

This case study has shown that the approaches for identifying and analyzing implicit interactions can enable system designers and integrators to systematically analyze their designs to uncover potential vulnerabilities early in the system development life-cycle. In turn, this gives them an enhanced understanding of the hidden complexity and coupling in the systems that they design and build. The analysis results can be used to inform mitigation efforts at early stages of the system design, including prioritization when there are limited resources available to address safety, security, and reliability concerns for such systems.

Disclaimer. The views and conclusions contained in this document are those of the authors and should not be interpreted as necessarily representing the official policies, either expressed or implied, of the U.S. Department of Homeland Security.

References

1. Alghathbar, K., Farkas, C., Wijesekera, D.: Securing UML information flow using FlowUML. J. Res. Pract. Inf. Tech. **38**(1), 111–120 (2006)
2. Clavel, M., et al.: The maude 2.0 system. In: Nieuwenhuis, R. (ed.) RTA 2003. LNCS, vol. 2706, pp. 76–87. Springer, Heidelberg (2003). https://doi.org/10.1007/3-540-44881-0_7
3. Dijkstra, E.W.: Guarded commands, nondeterminacy and formal derivation of programs. Commun. ACM **18**(8), 453–457 (1975)
4. Focardi, R., Gorrieri, R., Martinelli, F.: Real-time information flow analysis. IEEE J. Sel. Areas Commun. **21**(1), 20–35 (2003)
5. Hristova, K., Rothamel, T., Liu, Y.A., Stoller, S.D.: Efficient type inference for secure information flow. In: PLAS 2006, pp. 85–94 (October 2006)
6. Iturbe, M., Garitano, I., Zurutuza, U., Uribeetxeberri, R.: Visualizing network flows and related anomalies in industrial networks using chord diagrams and whitelisting. In: 11th Joint Conference on Computer Vision, Imaging and Computer Graphics Theory and Applications, vol. 2, pp. 99–106 (2016)
7. Jaskolka, J.: On the Modelling, Analysis, and Mitigation of Distributed Covert Channels. Ph.D. thesis, McMaster University, Hamilton, ON, Canada (March 2015)
8. Jaskolka, J.: Evaluating the exploitability of implicit interactions in distributed systems. arXiv:2006.06045 [cs.CR] (June 2020). https://arxiv.org/abs/2006.06045
9. Jaskolka, J., Khedri, R.: A formulation of the potential for communication condition using C^2KA. In: Peron, A., Piazza, C. (eds.) GandALF 2014, EPTCS, vol. 161, pp. 161–174. Verona, Italy (September 2014)
10. Jaskolka, J., Khedri, R., Zhang, Q.: Endowing concurrent kleene algebra with communication actions. In: Höfner, P., Jipsen, P., Kahl, W., Müller, M.E. (eds.) RAMICS 2014. LNCS, vol. 8428, pp. 19–36. Springer, Cham (2014). https://doi.org/10.1007/978-3-319-06251-8_2
11. Jaskolka, J., Villasenor, J.: An approach for identifying and analyzing implicit interactions in distributed systems. IEEE Trans Reliab. **66**(2), 529–546 (2017)
12. Jaskolka, J., Villasenor, J.: Identifying implicit component interactions in distributed cyber-physical systems. In: HICSS-50, pp. 5988–5997 (January 2017)
13. Lewis, T.G.: Critical Infrastructure Protection in Homeland Security: Defending a Networked Nation. John Wiley & Sons Inc., New Jersey (2006)
14. Milner, R.: Communication and Concurrency. Prentice-Hall International Series in Computer Science. Prentice Hall, New Jersey (1989)
15. Shen, J., Qing, S.: A dynamic information flow model of secure systems. In: ASIACCS 2007, pp. 341–343. ACM, Singapore (2007)
16. Varadharajan, V.: Petri net based modelling of information flow security requirements. In: Computer Security Foundations Workshop III, pp. 51–61 (1990)

A Survey of Cryptography-Based Authentication for Smart Grid Communication

Nabin Chowdhury[✉]

NTNU, Teknologivegen 22, 2815, Gjøvik, Norway
nabin.chowdhury@ntnu.no
https://www.ntnu.no/

Abstract. The adoption of new means of communication in the form of internet-based communication, power line communication, wireless communication and other communication protocols have allowed smart grids many additional functionalities over traditional power grid systems. Nonetheless, The many downsides of using these communication protocols have also started to affect smart grids. Smart grids are now vulnerable to cyber-attacks and more specifically attacks that try to intercept, alter or damage data that is communicated through the various networks of smart grids. With the essential role that these grids play in daily life activity and the functioning of industrial systems, protecting the grids against attacks that may compromise their communication channels is crucial. To safeguard communication channels and networks, many authentication schemes have been established and adopted in smart grid network communication. Due to the properties and requirements of smart grid, finding a suitable authentication scheme can be a challenging task. In this paper, we survey different cryptographic-based authentication schemes adopted in smart grids, including both traditional authentication schemes and also more recent proposals. We analyse the attributes of each scheme, to list their advantages and disadvantages. After establishing what are the required attributes for smart grid communication, we try to determine which cryptography algorithms are best suited for smart grid network security.

Keywords: Survey · Authentication scheme · Elliptic curve · Cryptography · Smart Grid

1 Introduction

Smart grids rely on internal means of communication to process real-time data regarding customer consumption and then satisfy the demands by distributing the sufficient amount of power [29]. This and other additional functionalities have been the contributing factors that allowed smart grids to significantly cut the

Supported by the Norwegian University of Science and Technology (NTNU).

costs associated to power distribution. Smart grids have integrated many widely used communication protocols, including the ethernet protocol, TCP/IP [31] and other popular wireless and wired communication technologies [11] for their internal communication and for data exchange with external parties. Unfortunately, many of the protocols used in smart grid network communication do not prioritize guaranteeing high levels of security [8]. In fact, the adoption of new communication protocols has brought a slew of vulnerabilities to cyber-attacks and threats that exposed the security of the grids. Due to the highly confidential nature of the data that is transmitted in smart grid communication and the importance of keeping the grids to function properly and uninterruptedly, securing the communication channels is one of the highest priority tasks when it comes to smart grid security. To protect the transmitted data, a reliable authentication scheme should always be integrated to the communication system. Unfortunately, designing an authentication protocol that is optimal for smart grid systems have been proven to be challenging. This is due to not only having to ensure that the authentication protocol is secure against the various attacks that could be run on the grid, but also to assure that transmission of data is fast and efficient, which makes computation-intensive algorithms not suitable for smart grid authentication [30]. A number of authentication schemes have been proposed and adopted by smart grids over the years [19]. Ideally, an authentication scheme should be able to balance the need for lightweight computation to diminish delay with reliability and protection against the highest number of possible attacks, although requirements may vary depending on the specific needs of the grid and compatibility with the communication systems. In recent years, due to their properties, authentication schemes based elliptic curve cryptography have been one the focus areas of research on authentication protocols for smart grid [29]. In this work we conduct a research on authentication schemes that are currently available or that have been recently proposed for smart grids. For this purpose, we selected articles dating from January 2015 to January 2020, in order to focus on more advanced proposals, often built on the strengths and requirements of older models. We try to analyse the properties that allow each scheme to offer reduced overhead on the system's hardware and communication, but also provide the most comprehensive security capabilities. These properties are later compared to establish which solution can best leverage security and performance needs.

2 Related Work

To the best of the author's knowledge, there has been only one survey [4] that has been conducted in recent years to discuss cryptographic-based authentication algorithms for communication in smart grid systems. Abood et al. (2017) [4] survey and compare some of the most established algorithms for smart grid secure communication. The parameters that are object of comparison are the following: effectiveness, key size, complexity and time required between those algorithms. The comparison is conducted between the following symmetric key algorithms:

AES, DES, TDES, E-DES, and BLOWFISH. RSA, one of the more popular asymmetric encoding systems is also added to the comparison. The comparison conducted by the authors consisted in calculating encryption and decryption time for different plain text lines and also the time required to break the algorithm, to evaluate the security of the algorithms. Unsurprisingly, the symmetric algorithms have showed to have better overall performance than the asymmetric counterparts. This is due to the much larger size of key used in asymmetric exchange. All the symmetric algorithms have shown to have competitively similar encryption and decryption times. What differentiate them is the time to break, which sees AES having an exponentially superior security capability over the DES variants and BLOWFISH. For this reason, the authors conclude that AES should be the algorithm adopted in smart grid secure communication and that research should be conducted in enhancing the algorithm with DNA computing, to increase its complexity and security capabilities. The authors fail to conduct a more detailed security analysis of the algorithms to identify which attacks each algorithm is secure or not secure against, which could be useful to show their performance against specific types of attacks. Additionally, the survey also fails to review many other alternative authentication schemes and a significant amount of schemes has also been proposed since the time of this survey.

In addition to this this work, a number of surveys and reviews have been conducted to detail security challenges in smart grids and various solutions to these challenges. Ferrag et al. (2016) [9] present a survey of privacy-preserving schemes for smart grid communications. they classify schemes in five categories and for each scheme they describe attacks of leaking privacy and countermeasures, including game theoretic approaches. Additionally they also survey recent articles that discuss smart grids communications, applications, standardization, and security. The authors conclude that while the development of security measures and privacy-preserving schemes for smart grids have advanced in the last years, there are still challenging research areas that should be target of future research.

Wang and Lu (2013) [27] present a survey on cyber-security issues in Smart Grids. The authors discuss network vulnerabilities that may compromise the security of the system and review security requirements, attack countermeasures, secure communication protocols and architectures in the Smart Grid. While a general overview of both security attacks and security measures is presented, the lack of detail in their work limits its applicability in providing useful insight in the domain of smart grid communication security. Mrabet et al. (2018) [24] also provide a survey of possible attacks against the smart grid and their countermeasures and security strategies to detect and counter these attacks. The author focus on describing global solutions to smart grid security in addition to specific counter-measures to individual cyber-attacks. Similarly to [27], this work also lack in depth and more focused analysis.

Baumeister (2010) [6] conducted a literature review on smart grid cybersecurity. The author identifies five categories that make up different components of the smart grid, one of them being smart grid communication protocol security. The author discusses the design principles for these communication protocols and also the cryptographic security measures that should be implemented in these protocols. Although the author discusses the main attributes that should be incorporated in these protocols, he fails to identify and discuss the most significant protocols currently adopted or in development for smart grid communication and the associated cryptography-based authentication methods.

3   Smart Grid Cryptography

When it comes to cyber security for smart grids, the main objectives that are pursued are *availability, confidentiality* and *integrity*. [15] Availability must be ensured to allow users to receive uninterrupted power supply. User information, which is collected to efficiently provide the required amount of energy and facilitate both communication and transmission, must be secured to guarantee the confidentiality of sensitive data. To ensure integrity, messages received from the user should be authenticated and the information should be checked to detect any signs of tampering. The processing, communication and storage of digital information in Smart Grids is often done by supervisory control and data acquisition (SCADA) systems [15]. Scada systems are composed of multiple blocks, each with their own communication network. To assure that the data exchanged in these networks is secure, multiple cryptographic schemes and algorithms have been developed.

3.1   Overview of Cryptography Schemes

The majority of cryptography algorithms can be divided in two groups:

- Symmetric algorithms: Symmetric algorithms use the same key for encryption and decryption purposes In most cases, they are used for plain-text encryption. The key is shared with cipher text on the network for decryption. [17] Some of the most well-known symmetric algorithms include: Advanced encryption standards (AESs), triple data encryption algorithm (TDEA), or triple data encryption standard (TDES)
- Asymmetric algorithms: In asymmetric algorithms, different keys are used for encryption and decryption purposes. Their use is often reserved for authentication purposes. [17] Common asymmetric algorithms include Digital signature standard (DSS), digital signature algorithm (DSA), RSA digital signature algorithm (RSA), elliptic curve digital signature algorithm (ECDSA), Elliptic Curve Diffie-Hellman (ECDH) .

When designing smart grid cryptography algorithms, two main objectives need to be achieved: guaranteeing the highest level of protection against security attacks and avoiding overloading memory and computational capacity of single devices, to ensure no delay or other communication issues are raised. In order to achieve this, a number of considerations have been suggested in the design of cryptography schemes for smart grid [15]:

- robust and flaw free design;
- use of cryptography modules that allow for updates;
- guarantees availability;
- allows for alternatives for authentication in case of issues in connecting to a system;
- key length sufficient for high level security and safe from unauthorized access or device tampering;
- algorithm should not have a very high complexity overhead to avoid computational ;

4   Literature Overview

In this section we will discuss some of the standard cryptography solutions for smart grid, as well as recently developed solutions. Alohali et al. [5] conduct a detailed investigation of cryptography algorithms used for Smart Grid security that takes into account not only the security challenges of smart grids, but also smart grid architecture. They survey key management schemes for each network in the smart grid, including: smart meters, AMI, sensors, IED and SCADA. The authors note that the functional topology of the smart grid segment where the devices are deployed is a determining factor to the suitability of a specific key management scheme. Limitations to sensor and smart meter devices also should be taken into account when determining the most well-suited scheme. Overall, the authors note that while there are shared properties that are preferred and chosen when developing a cryptography algorithm for smart grid (such as symmetric key over asymmetric key), there is not a general scheme that is best suited for all type of smart grid communication. Instead, the single requirements of the network and of the physical devices should be taken into consideration when choosing the ideal scheme and multiple scheme should be adopted to satisfy specific requirements over using one general scheme. The authors note that their survey does not take into consideration the various attacks that can be conducted on smart grids. It is fundamental to weight this factor when choosing a cryptography key management scheme, as certain attacks can compromise large portions of the grid and multiple stakeholders. It should also be noted that many current schemes and proposals have not been taken into consideration, such as multiple elliptic curve cryptography schemes. The many advantages of these schemes should justify the necessity for comparison to many traditional counterparts [13].

He et al. (2017) [13] discuss a Privacy-preserving data aggregation (P2DA) that is also secure against internal attackers or can provide data integrity. The proposed scheme uses Boneh-Goh-Nissim public key cryptography, to increase computational efficiency. Key generation and decryption are executed by the user, while encryption is done by the sender. The algorithm is composed of three phases: initialization, registration and aggregation. The authors demonstrate that the algorithm is both more efficient and more secure than previous data aggregation schemes. Nonetheless, they do note that algorithms based on elliptic curve cryptography provide similar level of security for a much smaller key size and consequent lower computational overhead. Kumar et al. (2019) [18] propose a cryptography scheme which employs hybrid cryptography to facilitate mutual trust, dynamic session key, integrity, and anonymity. The proposed schemes involves communication between the smart meter and the NAN gateway. The protocol consists of three phases: system set-up phase, registration phase, authentication and key establishment phase. Security analysis of the algorithms show that it is safer than previously discussed proposals. Its performance analysis also reveals that it is faster and lighter than the previous algorithms. In addition to these algorithms, a significant amount of research has been conducted to develop Elliptic curve cryptography(ECC)-based security algorithms.

4.1 Elliptic Curve Cryptography

Elliptic curve cryptography falls into the category of lightweight asymmetric (or public key) cryptography. Public key cryptography has been widely used in digital security to provide confidentiality, integrity, authentication, non-repudiation, availability and access control services [20]. One of the main disadvantages of public key cryptography is its high operational cost due to complex group operations, which makes it sub-optimal for constrained devices and networks that need to be optimized against delays. Lightweight cryptography and more specifically ECC tries to provide security to constrained environments by using low-cost cryptographic algorithms [20]. To achieve this, a trade-off between implementation size, performance and security is usually needed, but this often allows ECC to be more efficient than many conventional cryptography schemes [21]. In ECC the curve equation of the form is used:

$$Y^2 = x^3 + ax + b;$$ (1)

Eq. 1 is known as Weierstrass equation, where a and b are the constant with

$$4a^3 + 27b^2 \neq 0;$$ (2)

ECC defined over a finite field F_q, denoted as $E(F_q)$, contains the affine points $(x; y) \in F_q x F_q$ so that it satisfy the Weierstrass equation

$$y^2 + a_1xy + a_3y = x^3 + a_2x^2 + a_4x + a_6 \ where(a_1 \in F_q);$$ (3)

. E(Fq) together with a special point named the point at infinity O form an abelian group. t. O serves as the neutral element in the group operation. The security of ECC is based on exponential difficulty of solving the Discrete Logarithm Problem ECDLP over the abelian group formed by $E(F_q)$ and a special point O, It is not an easy task to find a group E(Fq) with the required properties that make the ECDLP difficult to solve [20]. The more recent proposals for elliptic curves seek to achieve both high security levels and also reduce operational costs and hardware resources required to perform computations efficiently [20].

4.2 Literature Overview of ECC Algorithms for Smart Grid

Due to the advantages that ECC brings to Smart Grid, a significant amount of research has been conducted in recent years to develop secure and lightweight cryptography ECC-based algorithms. In this section we review some of the more recent ECC-based proposals for smart grid authentication, published between 2016 to 2019, analyze their characteristics and performances. Zhang et al. (2016) [29] propose a two-phase elliptic curve cryptographic scheme, based on the El-Gamal asymmetric encryption protocol [12]. An interesting feature of the protocol proposed by the author is identity protection, including the identity of smart appliances and substations. The protocol has an initial initialization phase, followed by an authentication phase. An adopted version of Gong-Needham-Yahalom (GNY) logic [2] is used to analyse the completeness of the protocol. The performance of the protocol is also compared to other tamper-resistant protocols. The storage overhead is demonstrated to be lower than other protocols.

He et al. (2017) [14] propose a three-phase elliptic curve cryptographic algorithm. The algorithm consists in three phases. Initialization , registration and aggregation. The aggregation phase consists on having the data collected by the smart meter and sends it to the aggregation scheme. Overall, the performance of their scheme is evaluated to be higher than previously proposed schemes, due to the adaptations made to incorporate smart meter computational memory. Their security analysis also proves safety of the algorithm against most common attack vectors. The increase in performance and security guarantee is discussed to be more relevant at the moment due to the projected capabilities of quantum computing, which will be able to solve traditional mathematical problems in polynomial time, rendering current aggregation schemes insecure.

Mohammadali et al. (2018) [23] propose a novel identity-based key establishment protocol which also employs elliptic curves. The authors claim that their model has the lowest computational overhead among current secure protocols, at the smart meter side. The proposed model has two variations, referred to as NIKE and $NIKE^+$. The model itself is an identity-based key establishment protocol for AMI which does not rely on pairing and version that shifts the load to the advanced metering infrastructure head end. Both variations consist of three steps: setup, installation, and key agreement. When it comes to smart grid communication, the computational cost should be reduced at the meter's side. The variant of the protocol ($NIKE^+$) allows to shift the processing load from one side to the other, shifting almost half of the costly multiplications from the meter to AHE. Security analysis and performance analysis of these protocols show that they allow for secure communication, resistant to most security attacks, for a comparatively low computational costs. The protocols that had a lower performance overhead are other lightweight cryptographic operations that are demonstrated to not be resistant to many attacks that their proposed scheme is secure against [23].

Mahmood et al. (2018) [21] proposes an elliptic curve based lightweight authentication scheme, composed of three phases: Initialization, registration and authentication During the initialization phase, the Trusted Third Party (TTP) assembles the preliminary parameters. Afterwards, the user communicates his ID to the TTP for registration. Finally, Authentication can happen using a three-step procedure. The proposed algorithm is evaluated by the authors through automated protocol verifier tool ProVerif [1]. The scheme is proven to have a lower computation cost and lower memory overhead than analogous schemes. This makes it better suited for Smart Grid communication than other schemes. The analysis of adversarial attacks is conducted only informally.

More recently, an evaluation conducted by Kumar et al. (2020) [19] has shown that the solution proposed by [22] contained many security flaws. In particular, they noted that the authentication scheme was vulnerable against a wide range of attacks, including: session key, guessing identity attack, insider attack, user anonymity, impersonation attack, stolen device attack, lack of login phase, lack of password information, and clock synchronization problem. Abbas et al. (2018) [3] designed an elliptic curve scheme that tried to solve known issues with previously proposed schemes, including the schem proposed by [21], such as vulnerability to well-known attacks and overhead of the PKI maintenance. The Canetti-Krawczyk adversarial model [25] has been adopted by the authors. This selection was based on the fact that many of the schemes investigated by the authors were shown to be vulnerable to it. The authentication scheme proposed by the authors consists in three steps: initialization, registration and authentication. The security analysis conducted by the authors showed that the scheme was resistance to many of the attacks that were found to be effective on other schemes. The escrow issue and forward security were two particular issues that affected many of the other schemes that were solved by the authors' proposal. Formal verification was also conducted using ProVerif. When it comes to performance analysis, the scheme was shown to be the second-fastest, after the one proposed by Xia and Wang [28]. Compared to Xia and Wang's scheme, Abbasinezhad's scheme offers a vast array of increased protection, out-weighting the low difference in performance.

A further study conducted by Garg et al. (2019) [10] proposed a mutual authentication-based key exchange mechanism which employs the features of Fully Hashed Menezes-Qu-Vanstone (FHMQV) key agreement protocol [7]. FHMQVkey was selected for its security, efficiency, and resiliency against the ephemeral secret exponent leakage and its capability to store/protect the secret keys [10]. The scheme proposed by the authors tries to leverage the advantages of ECC and FHMQV. The scheme designed by the authors has three phases: system initialization, registration and mutual authentication and key agreement. Assessment of the protocol was conducted using the AVISPA tool [26], which established its safeness on different back-ends under the most realistic threat models. The protocol also revealed to be lightweight compared to the state-of-the-art. The authors also conducted energy consumption analysis, which demonstrated that the energy consumption of the protocol was also lower compared to others. As the authors note, the protocol is still open to further enhancement, which could allow for improved robustness and lightweight.

Khan et al. (2019) [16] propose an ECC-based mutual authentication protocol for smart grid communication using biometric approach. The biometric data
is transformed by a fuzzy extractor into a uniformly random string, making it
feasible to apply the cryptographic approach for biometric security. As previously discussed protocols, the proposed scheme is composed of three phases:
initialization, registration and login and authentication. Security analysis comparison shows that the protocol has strong security properties compared to older
proposed schemes in the Smart Grid environment. The computation and communication costs of the protocols were also found to be much lower compared
to other existing protocols, although the comparative analysis conducted by the
authors was only against a few older schemes.

5   Comparison of Cryptography Schemes for Smart Grids

In this section we compare the algorithms discussed based on their security
properties and their performance analysis.

5.1   Comparison of Security Properties of Cryptography Schemes

The security analysis is based on formal and informal evaluation conducted by
the authors regarding the security of the schemes against attacks and their ability
to provide integrity, confidentiality, authentication, non-repudiation, availability
and other security properties to network communication.

Table 1 shows the result of the informal evaluation conducted by the authors
regarding the security of the cryptography schemes against common attacks.
The schemes were considered to be safe against the

Table 1. Security Attacks captions: MITM: Man in the middle, Imp.: Impersonation,
FWS: Forward security , MA: Message authentication, SK: Session key, MI: Message
integrity, DoS: Denial of Service, Imp.: Impersonation

Work	Replay	MITM	Imp	FWS	MA	SK	MI	DoS	Ins
[13]		X			X		X		
[18]	X	X	X	X	X	X	X	X	X
[30]	X	X	X		X		X		X
[14]	X	X	X						
[21]	X	X	X	X	X		X		X
[3]	X	X	X	X	X	X	X		X
[23]	X	X	X		X		X		
[10]	X	X	X	X	X	X	X	X	X
[16]	X	X	X	X	X	X	X		X

Security of a number of the schemes is also proved formally by using certified tools and methods. These, together with other formal strategies are used to demonstrate the security properties of the algorithms, as show in Table 2. [30] uses GNY logic to demonstrate security of their algorithm. [18] and [10] use AVISPA [26] tool to conduct security analysis of their schemes. [10] also

Table 2. Strategies used by the authors to demonstrate the security properties of the proposed algorithms.

Work	Confidentiality	Authentication	Integrity	Anonymity
D. He et al.	Indistinguishability under a chosen plain-text attack is guaranteed by showing that the Boneh-Goh-Nissim public key cryptography is secure against it.	Ciphertext unforgeability under the adaptive chosen message attack is guaranteed by showing how discrete logarithm problem is hard under the scheme. is hard	No adversary can produce a valid digital signature. Thus, any modification of the message can be detected by checking the legality of the digital signature	Demonstrated by showing how the private key cannot be accessed by an attacker, thus making consumption data of users safe from attackers
Kumar et al.	Use of symmetric cryptosystems that provide confidentiality.	Mutual authentication verified using LAKA.	Proposed scheme prevents message alteration during the transit.	When a smart meter connects to the NAN gateway, the ID is hidden in a message, thus providing privacy
Zhang et al.		Proved using GNY logic		
He et al.	Use of same proof strategy as D. He et al.	Use of same proof strategy as D. He et al.	Proved by showing how the Computational Diffie-Hellman is hard under the scheme	
Mahmood et al.	Proved using the tool ProVerif	Proved using the tool ProVerif	Proved using Burrows-Abadi-Needham (BAN) Logic	Proved using the tool ProVerif
Abbasinezhad-Mood et al.	Proved using the tool ProVerif	Proved using the tool ProVerif	Proved using the tool ProVerif	Proved using the tool ProVerif
Mohammadali et al.	Proved using the AVISPA tool	Proved using the AVISPA tool	Proved using the AVISPA tool	Proved using the AVISPA tool
Garg et al.	Proved using the AVISPA tool	Proved using the AVISPA tool and support of mutual authentication between the SMs and the NAN gateways.	Proved using the AVISPA tool	The designed protocol supports anonymity of SMs and NAN gateways. This is because random numbers and timestamps are used in all the message exchanges
Khan et al.	By providing non-traceability and other security properties, confidentiality is guaranteed	Messages secure within verifying conditions, and hash values which is not essay to guess for any adversary. Hence, the proposed scheme stand with message authentication.		Attackers can not get original identity of users in the presence of anonymous identity. Hence, the proposed protocol stand with user anonymity

demonstrates the security of their schemes against eavesdropping attacks and how anonymity of communication is guaranteed. Security of the algorithms used by [21] and [3] is proven with the use of ProVerif. From 1, it can be seen that the algorithms proposed by [18] and [10] protect against the highest number of security attacks. [16] also is demonstrated to protect against a wide range of attacks, although DoS attack protection is not guaranteed. Also, formal security analysis of the algorithm was not conducted, in contrast to the other two proposals.

5.2   Performance Analysis of Cryptography Schemes

The performance analysis is based on two attributes:

– Computation cost: Calculated as the runtime of executing the scheme.
– Communication cost: Calculated as the sum of size of messages transmitted during the communication .

The computation cost of each algorithm can be calculated as the sum of operational times of each operation needed during communication. The design and complexity of each scheme affects the number of messages and operations needed by each algorithm during each communication exchange. The following equations represent the computational times for each scheme:

– [13]: $T_{DB} + T_{EB} + n \times T_{MG} + (n+1) \times T_{ED} + n \times T_{ES} + (2n-1) \times T_{MD} + (n+1) \times T_H$
– [18]: $6T_{PM} + 9T_H + 4T_{MAC} + 4T_{ED}$
– [30]: $T_{A_E} + T_{A_D} + 2T_H + 2T_E + 2T_{S_E} + 2T_{S_D}$
– [14]: $(3n+2) \times T_{PM} + 2n \times T_{PA} + 3n \times T_H$
– [21]: $10T_{PM} + 4T_{PA} + 8T_H$
– [3]: $8T_{PM} + 4T_{PA} + 8T_H$
– [23]: $2T_{RN} + 5T_{PM} + 7T_H$
– [10]: $4T_{PM} + 8T_H$
– [16]: $4T_{PM} + 7T_H$

With: T_{DB} = Boneh-Goh-Nissim [13] public key decryption operation, T_{EB} = Boneh-Goh-Nissim public key encryption operation, T_{MG}= multiplication operation of G_T, T_{ED}= Exponentiation operation of the DL problem [13], T_{ES} = exponentiation operation with short exponent of the DL problem, T_{MD} = multiplication operation of the DL problem, T_H = hash function operation, T_{PM} = point multiplication T_{MAC} = message authentication, T_{ED} = encryption decryption operation, T_{PA} = point addition operation, T_{AE} and T_{AD} asymmetric encryption and decryption respectively, T_{SE} and T_{SD} symmetric encryption and decryption operations respectively, T_E = Time for executing a scalar multiplication operation. [10] and [16] need the least amount of operations, with [16] needing one less hash operation than [10].

Table 3 confirms that [16] has the least computation overhead, as its computation time is lower than that of any other algorithm. When it comes to communication cost [10] performs much better than the competition, requiring less

Table 3. Computation cost, calculated as runtime (in milliseconds) and communication cost (in bits), calculated as sum of operation size of the reviewed algorithms. N is equal to the number of hash operations

Work	Computation Cost	Communication Cost
[13]	1.433 x n +13.436 ms	2272 bits
[18]	17.965 ms	1088 bits
[30]	19.8658 ms	3808 bits
[14]	17.751 ms	2240 bits
[21]	22.4 ms	1790 bits
[3]	17.9 ms	1790 bits
[23]	4910(NIKE) 2460($NIKE^+$) ms	NA
[10]	11.912 ms	509 bits
[16]	8.9201 ms	1152 bits

than half the amount of bits than the next two best solutions. Combining this performance analysis with the security properties shown in Sect. 5.1, we could conclude that the solution proposed by [10] provides the best combination of security and lightweight communication. [16] and [18] also provide competitive performances and similar level of security, with [16] outperforming [10] when it comes to computation time and [18] proving the amount of protection of [10] with only slightly higher overhead. It is also interesting to note that more recent authentication schemes based on ECC provide better performances and better security than many other proposals, especially when combined with advantageous properties of other protocols, as it is the case with [10].

6   Limitations

A number of research limitations have been noted during the completion of this work, which are described in this section:

- Informal security analysis: the findings relative to the security performance of the different schemes are based on formal and informal security analysis conducted by the authors. Formal analysis of all algorithms should be conducted, using the same methodology and evaluation tools. This should be done to correct any inaccuracies reported by the authors or discover possible vulnerabilities of the schemes not reported in the findings.
- Hardware non-equivalence: the results of the performance analysis extracted in this work are based on the values reported by the authors from their own performance analysis. These analysis have been conducted using different hardware systems, albeit very similar in specifications. To eliminate possible hardware-based differences in computation cost evaluation, performance evaluation of the algorithms should be re-conducted using one unique system for all schemes.

7   Conclusion and Future Work

In this work we discussed and reviewed both traditional and recent proposals of cryptography authentication schemes for smart grid security. Based on the physical properties of smart grids, their requirement when it comes to security and hardware and communication overhead, it has been agreed that an ideal authentication scheme should try to leverage the most comprehensive security features against common attacks that occur on smart grid and providing lightweight communication. ECC-based authentication schemes have been demonstrated to satisfy these requirements, with many of the recent proposals outperforming traditional schemes, while at the same time providing higher levels of security. The scheme proposed by Garg et al. [10] has been found to provide some of the most optimal performances, while also ensuring protection against a wider range of attacks than most of the other reviewed schemes. Their scheme is unique in how it tries to leverage the advantages of ECC and FHMQV, to provide the benefits of both protocols. As the authors note in their work, further improvement in both performance and security capability are possible, which would suggest that further research should be conducted in how to optimize authentication schemes by using properties of different models. Further studies should also be conducted to formally compare the security and performance attributes of the state-of-the-art in cryptographic authentication schemes for smart grid, to identify other possible algorithms that may outperform currently adopted schemes.

References

1. Abadi, M., Blanchet, B., Comon-Lundh, H.: Models and proofs of protocol security: a progress report. In: Bouajjani, A., Maler, O. (eds.) CAV 2009. LNCS, vol. 5643, pp. 35–49. Springer, Heidelberg (2009). https://doi.org/10.1007/978-3-642-02658-4_5

2. Abadi, M., Tuttle, M.R.: A logic of authentication. In: ACM Transactions on Computer Systems. Citeseer (1990)

3. Abbasinezhad-Mood, D., Nikooghadam, M.: Design and hardware implementation of a security-enhanced elliptic curve cryptography based lightweight authentication scheme for smart grid communications. Future Gener. Comput. Syst. **84**, 47–57 (2018)

4. Abood, O.G., Elsadd, M.A., Guirguis, S.K.: Investigation of cryptography algorithms used for security and privacy protection in smart grid. In: 2017 Nineteenth International Middle East Power Systems Conference (MEPCON), pp. 644–649 (2017)

5. Alohali, B., Kifayat, K., Shi, Q., Hurst, W.: A survey on cryptography key management schemes for smart grid. J. Comput. Scie. Appli. Sci. Educ. Spec. Issue Big Data Analytics Intelli. Syst. **3**, 27–39 (2015)

6. Baumeister, T.: Literature review on smart grid cyber security. Collaborative Software Development Laboratory at the University of Hawaii (2010)

7. Capossele, A., Petrioli, C., Saturni, G., Spaccini, D., Venturi, D.: Securing underwater communications: Key agreement based on fully hashed MQV. In: Proceedings of the International Conference on Underwater Networks & Systems. WUWNET 2017, Association for Computing Machinery, New York, NY, USA (2017). https://doi.org/10.1145/3148675.3152760, https://doi.org/10.1145/3148675.3152760

8. Dzung, D., Naedele, M., Von Hoff, T.P., Crevatin, M.: Security for industrial communication systems. Proc. IEEE **93**(6), 1152–1177 (2005)

9. Ferrag, M.A., Maglaras, L.A., Janicke, H., Jiang, J.: A survey on privacy-preserving schemes for smart grid communications (2016)

10. Garg, S., Kaur, K., Kaddoum, G., Rodrigues, J.J.P.C., Guizani, M.: Secure and lightweight authentication scheme for smart metering infrastructure in smart grid. IEEE Trans. Industr. Inf. **16**(5), 3548–3557 (2020)

11. Gungor, V.C., et al.: Smart grid technologies: communication technologies and standards. IEEE Trans. Industr. Inf. **7**(4), 529–539 (2011). https://doi.org/10.1109/TII.2011.2166794

12. Hankerson, D., Menezes, A.J., Vanstone, S.: Guide to Elliptic Curve Cryptography. Springer Science & Business Media, Berlin (2006)

13. He, D., Kumar, N., Zeadally, S., Vinel, A., Yang, L.T.: Efficient and privacy-preserving data aggregation scheme for smart grid against internal adversaries. IEEE Trans. Smart Grid **8**(5), 2411–2419 (2017)

14. He, D., Zeadally, S., Wang, H., Liu, Q.: Lightweight data aggregation scheme against internal attackers in smart grid using elliptic curve cryptography. Wireless Commun. Mobile Comput. **2017**, 1–11 (2017)

15. Iyer, S.: Cyber security for smart grid, cryptography, and privacy. Int. J. Digit. Multimedia Broadcast. **2011**, 1687–7578 (2011)

16. Khan, A.A., Kumar, V., Ahmad, M.: An elliptic curve cryptography based mutual authentication scheme for smart grid communications using biometric approach. J. King Saud Univ. - Comput. Inf. Sci. (2019). https://doi.org/10.1016/j.jksuci.2019.04.013, http://www.sciencedirect.com/science/article/pii/S1319157819301193

17. Kumar, A., Agarwal, A.: Research issues related to cryptography algorithms and key generation for smart grid: a survey. In: 2016 7th India International Conference on Power Electronics (IICPE), pp. 1–5. IEEE (2016)

18. Kumar, P., Gurtov, A., Sain, M., Martin, A., Ha, P.H.: Lightweight authentication and key agreement for smart metering in smart energy networks. IEEE Trans. Smart Grid **10**(4), 4349–4359 (2019)

19. Kumar, V., Khan, A.A., Ahmad, M.: Design flaws and cryptanalysis of elliptic curve cryptography-based lightweight authentication scheme for smart grid communication. In: Jain, V., Chaudhary, G., Taplamacioglu, M.C., Agarwal, M.S. (eds.) Advances in Data Sciences, Security and Applications. LNEE, vol. 612, pp. 169–179. Springer, Singapore (2020). https://doi.org/10.1007/978-981-15-0372-6_13

20. Lara-Nino, C., Díaz-Pérez, A., Morales-Sandoval, M.: Elliptic curve lightweight cryptography: a survey. IEEE Access **6**, 72514–72550 (2018). https://doi.org/10.1109/ACCESS.2018.2881444

21. Mahmood, K., Chaudhry, S.A., Naqvi, H., Kumari, S., Li, X., Sangaiah, A.K.: An elliptic curve cryptography based lightweight authentication scheme for smart grid communication. Future Gener. Comput. Syst. **81**, 557–565 (2018)

22. Mahmood, K., Chaudhry, S.A., Naqvi, H., Kumari, S., Li, X., Sangaiah, A.K.: An elliptic curve cryptography based lightweight authentication scheme for smart grid communication. Future Gener. Comput. Syst. **81**, 557–565 (2018). https://doi. org/10.1016/j.future.2017.05.002. http://www.sciencedirect.com/science/article/ pii/S0167739X17309263

23. Mohammadali, A., Sayad Haghighi, M., Tadayon, M.H., Mohammadi-Nodooshan, A.: A novel identity-based key establishment method for advanced metering infrastructure in smart grid. IEEE Trans. Smart Grid **9**(4), 2834–2842 (2018)

24. Mrabet, Z.E., Kaabouch, N., Ghazi, H.E., Ghazi, H.E.: Cyber-security in smart grid: survey and challenges. Comput. Electr. Eng. **67**, 469–482 (2018). https://doi.org/10.1016/j.compeleceng.2018.01.015. http://www. sciencedirect.com/science/article/pii/S0045790617313423

25. Tin, Y.S.T., Boyd, C., Nieto, J.M.G.: Provably secure mobile key exchange: applying the canetti-krawczyk approach. In: Safavi-Naini, R., Seberry, J. (eds.) Information Security and Privacy, pp. 166–179. Springer, Berlin Heidelberg, Berlin, Heidelberg (2003)

26. Viganó, L.: Automated security protocol analysis with the avispa tool. Electron. Notes Theoret. Comput. Scie. **155**, 61–86 (2006). https://doi.org/10. 1016/j.entcs.2005.11.052, http://www.sciencedirect.com/science/article/pii/ S1571066106001897, Proceedings of the 21st Annual Conference on Mathematical Foundations of Programming Semantics (MFPS XXI)

27. Wang, W., Lu, Z.: Cyber security in the smart grid: Survey and challenges. Comput. Netw. **57**(5), 1344–1371 (2013). https://doi.org/10.1016/j.comnet.2012.12. 017. http://www.sciencedirect.com/science/article/pii/S1389128613000042

28. Xia, J., Wang, Y.: Secure key distribution for the smart grid. IEEE Trans. Smart Grid **3**(3), 1437–1443 (2012)

29. Zhang, L., Tang, S., Luo, H.: Elliptic curve cryptography-based authentication with identity protection for smart grids. PloS one **11**(3), e0151253 (2016)

30. Zhang, L., Tang, S., Luo, H.: Elliptic curve cryptography-based authentication with identity protection for smart grids. PLOS ONE **11**(3), 1–15 (2016). https://doi. org/10.1371/journal.pone.0151253. https://doi.org/10.1371/journal.pone.0151253

31. Zhou, C., Hassanein, H., Qiu, R., Samarati, P.: Communications and networking for smart grid: technology and practice. Int. J. Digit. Multim. Broadcast. **2011**, 617624:1–617624:2 (2011). https://doi.org/10.1155/2011/617624

Cybersecurity Awareness Platform with Virtual Coach and Automated Challenge Assessment

Tiago Gasiba[1,2]([✉]) [ID], Ulrike Lechner[2] [ID], Maria Pinto-Albuquerque[3] [ID],
and Anmoal Porwal[1] [ID]

[1] Siemens AG, Munich, Germany
{tiago.gasiba,anmoal.porwal}@siemens.com
[2] Universität der Bundeswehr München, Munich, Germany
{ulrike.lechner,tiago.gasiba}@unibw.de
[3] Instituto Universitário de Lisboa (ISCTE-IUL), ISTAR-IUL, Lisboa, Portugal
maria.albuquerque@iscte-iul.pt

Abstract. Over the last years, the number of cyber-attacks on industrial control systems has been steadily increasing. Among several factors, proper software development plays a vital role in keeping these systems secure. To achieve secure software, developers need to be aware of secure coding guidelines and secure coding best practices. This work presents a platform geared towards software developers in the industry that aims to increase awareness of secure software development. The authors also introduce an interactive game component, a virtual coach, which implements a simple artificial intelligence engine based on the laddering technique for interviews. Through a survey, a preliminary evaluation of the implemented artifact with real-world players (from academia and industry) shows a positive acceptance of the developed platform. Furthermore, the players agree that the platform is adequate for training their secure coding skills. The impact of our work is to introduce a new automatic challenge evaluation method together with a virtual coach to improve existing cybersecurity awareness training programs. These training workshops can be easily held remotely or off-line.

Keywords: Cybersecurity · Awareness · Training · Artificial intelligence · Serious games · Secure coding · Static Application Security Testing · Capture-the-Flag

1 Introduction

Errors and vulnerabilities in software development, if not solved early, can end up in a final product. These problems can result in serious consequences for the customer and the company that produced the software. This work aims to improve the situation through a serious game to raise awareness on secure coding and software development best practices of software developer – thus addressing the issues at early stages in software development, i.e., when it is being written.

© Springer Nature Switzerland AG 2020
S. Katsikas et al. (Eds.): CyberICPS 2020/SECPRE 2020/ADIoT 2020, LNCS 12501, pp. 67–83, 2020.
https://doi.org/10.1007/978-3-030-64330-0_5

In the next sub-sections, we present the problem at hand in more detail. We give a brief overview of standardization bodies, industry-led efforts, and academic efforts that were started to address the current situation. Finally, we describe our proposed methodology and our contributions to scientific knowledge.

1.1 The Need for Secure Coding Awareness

The number of security advisories issued per year by the Industrial Control System - Computer Emergency Response Team (ICS-CERT) has been steadily increasing. While before 2014 the number of advisories per year was less than 100, from 2017 to 2019 more than 200 advisories have been issued per year. These facts correlate well with the observed increase in the number and sophistication of cyber-attacks to industrial control systems (ICS).

The ransomware WannyCry, released by the "The Shadow Brocker" hacker group in 2017, which exploits a vulnerability in the Server Message Block (SMB) protocol, dubbed EternalBlue, has affected numerous industrial control systems. It has caused a financial impact exceeding 4 billion USD in more than 140 countries. The vulnerability exploited by EternalBlue is a buffer overflow caused by an integer overflow; exploitation of buffer overflows is not new - this is known since the late '70s.

While not everything (e.g., attacks and vulnerabilities) can be traced back directly to a specific software vulnerability, an increasing number of such vulnerabilities (i.e., related with secure coding) have also been observed. Software security and secure software development play a fundamental role in industrial cybersecurity, particularly in critical infrastructures. According to a recent survey with more than 4000 software developers [14], *"less than half of developers can spot security holes"* [18]. This lack of awareness causes a severe issue in terms of cybersecurity of industrial control systems and critical infrastructures. The present work focuses on C and C++ programming languages. This is motivated by a recent study by Whitehat [23], which has shown that C and C++ are among the most used programming languages for industrial environments, but they are also among the most vulnerable in terms of cybersecurity vulnerabilities. This study also implies that the majority of vulnerabilities are created in these programming languages.

1.2 Standards, Industry, and Academic Efforts

In recognition of the importance of secure products and a consequence of the current move towards digitalization and higher connectivity, several large industrial players have joined together and committed to a document called the charter of trust [19]. The charter of trust outlines ten fundamental principles that the partners vow to obey to address the issues inherent with cybersecurity. ICS relevant standards such as IEC 62443-4-1 [12] or ISO 27001 [13] mandate the implementation of secure software development life-cycle processes and awareness training. These standards address security from a high-level perspective and are not specific enough about recommendations, policies, and best practices to be followed in software development. Towards this goal, an industry-led effort was created, the Software Assurance Forum for Excellence in Code (SAFECode), with the aim of *identifying and promoting best practices for developing and delivering more secure and reliable software, hardware and services.*

Serious Games designed to train developers and raise their awareness for cybersecurity and secure coding is our approach to ameliorate the situation, and other approaches are [5,6,15,16]. We designed a game to raise awareness for cybersecurity among programmers and for secure coding guidelines and secure coding best practices. Our approach is an adoption of the popular format of Capture-the-Flag. CTF is a serious game genre in the domain of cybersecurity popular in the penetration-test community as a means to practice offensive skills. In this kind of game, the game participants aim to gather the highest amount of awarded by solving cybersecurity challenges, e.g., breaking into systems. In [6], Gasiba et al. study the requirements that a game designer should follow to target the game to software developers in the industry. In a further work [8], the authors provide six concrete and different challenge types to be used in this kind of CTF event. One of these is the "code entry" challenge type, where the proposed idea is that player interacts through a web interface with a backend by modifying vulnerable code until all the coding guidelines are fulfilled, thus solving the challenge.

1.3 Automatic Challenge Evaluation

This paper extends the previous work, particularly the "code entry" challenge type, by describing the architecture of a platform, which the authors call Sifu, that was constructed to implement the game backend. The goal of this platform is to: 1) automatically analyze the solution submitted by the participant to the backend, 2) determine if this solution contains vulnerabilities and fulfills the required functionality, 3) generate hints to the player if the solution does not achieve a pre-determined goal and finally 4) provide a flag (i.e., a unique code) which the player can use to gather points in the game. The correctness of the solution depends on it following established secure coding guidelines and secure programming best practices.

The generated hints are provided by a virtual coach, which assists the player in solving the challenge. These hints are created using a simple artificial intelligence (AI) engine that provides automatic pre-programmed interactions with the player when the submitted solution fails to meet the secure coding criteria. These hints generated by the AI Engine (i.e., the virtual coach) assist the player in solving the challenge in a playful way and help lower the frustration, increase the fun, and improve the learning effect during gameplay.

The core of the present work is to describe the virtual coach platform. Nevertheless, to validate its suitability as a means to raise secure coding awareness, a small survey was performed with real players. Our preliminary results show that the participants have fun using the platform and also find it adequate for learning secure coding guidelines and secure software development best practices.

1.4 Contributions of This Work

This work seeks to provide the following impact in the research community:

- introduce a novel method to automatically analyze player code submission in terms of secure coding guidelines and software development best practices,
- introduce a virtual coach based on the laddering interview AI technique, and
- provide a preliminary analysis of the suitability of the proposed architecture in terms of adequacy to raise secure coding awareness of software developers.

Although we intend to use the Sifu platform in a CTF environment, it can also be used stand-alone in remote and offline training scenarios. This can be especially important if the players are spread over a large geographic area or have inherent restrictions on a face-to-face workshop.

1.5 Paper Outline

This work is organized as follows. In Sect. 2 we present previous related scientific work. Section 3 presents details on the architecture and implementation of the Sifu platform. This section also introduces the virtual coach and gives details on the implemented artificial intelligence algorithm. In Sect. 4, preliminary results from a short survey to 15 participants in a pilot are presented. Finally, Sect. 5 presents the conclusions and further work.

2 Related Work

Playing cybersecurity games is gaining more and more attention in the research community. In [5], Frey et al. show both the potential impact that playing cyber-security games can have on the participants and also show the importance of playing games as means of cybersecurity awareness. They conclude that cyberse-curity games can be useful to *build a common understanding of security issues*.

A serious game [4] is a game that is designed with a primary goal and purpose other than entertainment. Typically these games are developed to address a specific need such as learning or improving a skill. A Capture-the-Flag (CTF) game is one possible instance of a serious game. Votipka et al. [22] argue in their work that CTF events can be used as a means to improve security software development. In particular, their work shows that the participants of such events experience positive effects on improving their security mindset. Davis et al., in [2], discuss the benefits of CTF for software developers. In their work, they argue that CTFs can be used to teach computer security and conclude that playing CTFs is a fun and engaging activity.

In their work, Graziotin et al. [9] argue that *happy developers are better coders*. They show that developers that are happy at work tend to be more focused, adhering to software development processes, and following best prac-tices. This improvement in software development leads to the conclusion that happy developers can produce higher quality and more secure code than unhappy developers. The authors believe that CTF events since they are experienced as fun events, can foster higher code quality and adherence to secure development principles.

However, CTF events need to be properly designed to achieve this goal. Gasiba et al., in [6], perform requirements elicitation employing systematic literature review, interview of security experts, and also CTF participants from industry. Their work details the requirements for CTF events to raise secure coding awareness of software developers in the industry. In particular, they conclude that CTF challenges for software developers should focus on the defensive perspective instead of offensive.

In their work, Simoes et al. [20] present several programming exercises for teaching software programming in academia. Their design includes nine exercises that can be presented to students to foster student motivation and engagement in academic classes and increase learning outcomes. Their approach uses gamification and automatic assessment tools. However, their work focus on the correct solution (implementation) of the programming exercise and not on the secure programming and security best practices aspects.

Gasiba et al. [8] propose, in a similar work, six different challenge types. These challenges, which are also a form of programming exercises, are executed in the context of a serious game of the type CTF and target software developers in the industry. One of the challenge types is a so-called code-entry challenge, where the CTF participant is given a project (e.g., in C or C++) that contains software vulnerabilities. The challenge aims to have the participants fix the security vulnerabilities by applying secure coding guidelines and software development best practices. In this previous work, the challenge type was only derived conceptually and lacked implementation and practical evaluation aspects.

Vasconcelos et al. [21] have recently shown a method to evaluate programming challenges automatically. In their work, the authors use Haskell and the QuickCheck library to perform automated functional unit tests of challenges submitted by students. Their goal is to evaluate if the solutions presented by the students comply with the programming challenge in terms of desired functionality. One of the main limitations of this work is that the code to be tested should be free from side effects. The authors also focus on functional testing of single functions and do not address the topic of cybersecurity.

In [1,3], Dobrovsky et al. describe an interactive reinforcement learning framework for serious games with complex environments where a non-player character is modeled using human guidance. They argue that interactive reinforcement learning can be used to improve learning and the quality of learning. However, their work aims to train an algorithm better to recreate human behavior by means of machine learning techniques. In our work, we aim at training humans to write better and more secure code. Due to this fact, machine learning techniques are not applicable. Nonetheless, we draw inspiration from the conceptual framework, which we adapt to our scenario.

Rietz et al. [17], show how to apply the principles of the laddering interview technique for requirements elicitation. The laddering technique consists of issuing a series of questions that are based on previous system states (i.e., previous answers and previous questions). The questions generated are refined versions of previously issued questions as if the participant is climbing up a ladder containing more specific questions. Although this previous work applies in the field of requirements elicitation and does not focus on cybersecurity, the laddering technique principle can be adapted to a step-wise hint system.

In the present work, we also make use of the concept of awareness or IT-security awareness as defined by Haensch et al. in [11], in order to evaluate our artifact. In their work, they define awareness as having the following three dimensions: perception, protection, and behavior. The perception dimension is related to the knowledge of existing software vulnerabilities. The protection dimension is related to knowing the existing mechanisms (best practices) that avoid software vulnerabilities. Finally, the behavior dimension relates to the knowledge and intention to write secure code. We collect data from participants based on the three dimensions of awareness through a small survey. We use best practices in the design, collection, and processing of survey information given by Grooves et al. [10].

3   Sifu Platform

In following sub-sections we present the research problem in terms of research questions and present a possible solution. Additionally, we describe the setup of a small survey that was performed to evaluate our result.

3.1   Problem Statement

In [8], the authors present a type of challenge for CTFs in the industry, which is called code-entry challenge (CEC). The main idea of this type of challenge is for the Player to be given a software development project that contains code that does not follow secure coding guidelines (SCG) and secure software development best practices (BP) and contains security vulnerabilities. In this work, we target specifically ICS by using SCG and BP, which are specific for this field. The task of the Player is to fix the vulnerabilities and to follow SCG and BP. The Player should do this so that the original intended functionality is still fulfilled in the new version of the code. The present work aims to solve these requirements by means of a platform that performs an automatic evaluation of the code submitted by the participant and guides the participant towards the final solution. Considering these requirements, the following research questions are then raised:

RQ1: how to automatically assess the challenges in terms of SCG and BP?
RQ2: how to aid the software developer when solving the challenges?

This work proposes to address RQ1 through a specialized architecture to automatically assess the level of compliance to SCG and BP by combining several state-of-the-art security testing frameworks, namely Static Application Security Testing (SAST), Dynamic Application Security Testing (DAST), and Runtime

Application Security Protection (RASP). The functional correctness of the provided solution by the Player is evaluated using state-of-the-art Unit Testing (UT). To address RQ2, the authors propose to combine the output of the security testing tools with an AI algorithm to generate hints based on the laddering technique, thus implementing a virtual coach. The task of the virtual coach is to lower the frustration of the participant during gameplay and to aid in the participant to improve the code.

The proposed solution herein described makes a contribution towards answering these research questions. To validate the assumption of the suitability of our proposal as a means to address the research questions, a small survey was conducted.

3.2   Code-Entry Challenge Platform Architecture

Figure 1 shows the top-level view of the Sifu architecture. In this figure, the "Player" represents the game participant (a human) and the "Project" represents a software project that contains vulnerabilities to be fixed by the Player. The "Analysis & Hints" (AH) component performs the core functionality: 1) evaluates the submitted code (Project) in terms SCG and BP, 2) indicates if the challenge is solved or not and, if not solved, 3) generates hints to send back to the participant. The "State" component stores previous interactions and generated hints. During gameplay, the Player reads the Project and modifies the code by interacting with a web editor interface. When the changes in the code are done, the Player submits the code to the AH component for analysis.

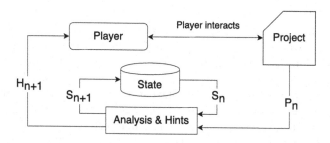

Fig. 1. Conceptual game overview: interaction and components

A possible realization of the conceptual architecture is shown in Fig. 2. Interaction takes place between the Player and a web interface, which connects to a web backend. The web backend is responsible for triggering the automated security assessment, collecting the answer from the AI engine, and sending the answer back to the participant. To realize this, the Project submitted by the participant is first saved into a temporary folder after a pre-processing step (e.g. to inject code necessary for unit tests). After the addition of auxiliary files (e.g. C/C++ include files) to the temporary project directory, the Project is compiled, and a functional test and security assessment is performed. All these results are then made available to an AI engine, which determines if the challenge is solved and generates hints. This feedback is collected by the web backend and stored in an internal database and forwarded as the answer back to the participant's web browser.

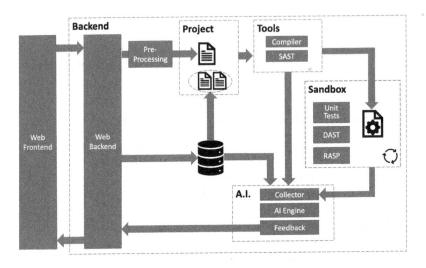

Fig. 2. Detailed architecture: the Sifu Platform

Automatic Security Assessment. The security assessment which is performed to the Project is composed of the following steps: 1) Compilation, 2) Static Application Security Testing, 3) Unit Testing, 4) Dynamic Application Security Testing, and 5) Runtime Application Security Testing. In step 1, the Project is compiled; if there are compilation errors, these are reported to the AI component, and no further analysis takes place. Step 2 performs static code analysis. Note that in this step, the code does not need to be executed. Since the steps 3, 4 and 5 involve executing untrusted (and potentially dangerous) code, these are performed in a time-limited sandbox. The sandbox is very restrictive, e.g., it only contains the project executable and drops security-relevant capabilities (e.g., debugging and network connections are not allowed). Additionally, the executable is only allowed to run for a certain amount of time inside the sandbox. If this time is exceeded, the process will be automatically terminated. This avoids denial-of-service attacks by means of high CPU usage. Two types of Unit tests are executed: 1) functional testing - in order to guarantee that the provided code is working as intended (e.g., in the challenge description), and 2) security testing - in order to guarantee that typical vulnerabilities are not present in the code (e.g., buffer overflow). Security testing is done using self-developed tests and also using state-of-the-art fuzzing tools. Steps 4 and 5 perform several dynamic security tests. Table 1 lists the tools that the authors have used in each of these components. In this table, the open-source components used in the Sifu platform are marked with "OS".

Table 1. Security assessment tools

Component	Tools
Compiler	GCC v10.1 (OS), Clang 9.0.0 (OS)
SAST	SonarQube, Pc Lint, cppchecker (OS), fbinfer (OS), semgrep (OS)
DAST	Valgrind (OS), Helgrind (OS)
RASP	Address Sanitizer (OS), Leak Sanitizer (OS), Thread Sanitizer (OS)
Unit test	ATF (OS), Kyua (OS), AFL (OS)

Virtual Coach with AI Technique. The AI component shown in Fig. 2 collects the results of the previous analysis steps, runs an AI engine based on the laddering technique, and generates the feedback to be sent back to the participant. Figure 3 shows the implementation of the AI engine using the laddering technique.

As previously detailed, the automated assessment tools perform several tests that are used to determine the existing software vulnerabilities present in the Project. These are collected in textual form (e.g., JSON and XML) and normalized to be processed by the AI engine. The two most essential test results from the security assessment components are related to compilation errors (e.g., syntax errors) and functional unit testing. The participant's solution will be rejected if the code does not compile or is not working (functioning) as intended. When both these tests pass, the artificial engine uses the security tests, SAST, DAST, and RASP tools to generate hints to send to the participant.

A combination of findings from these tools forms a vulnerability. These findings and vulnerabilities are then mapped to SCG and BP. In Fig. 3, each horizontal path (ith row) corresponds to a ladder and also to a specific combination of vulnerabilities or static events found in the source code. Each path is also assigned a priority $p(i)$ based on the criticality of the SCG and vulnerabilities. These priorities are assigned according to the ranking of secure coding guidelines, as presented in Gasiba et al. (see [7]). Higher-ranked secure coding guidelines are given higher priorities, and lower-ranked secure coding guidelines are given lower priorities. The AI engine to selects the corresponding path (corresponding to one ladder) which based on the finding with the highest rank.

The chosen hint H_{n+1} depends on the ladder and on the previous hint level sent to the participant on the ladder, as given by the system state. If there are no more hints in the ladder, no additional hint is sent to the Player.

Table 2 shows an example of hints provided by the virtual coach's AI engine corresponding to an "undefined behavior" path. The lower level hints are generic

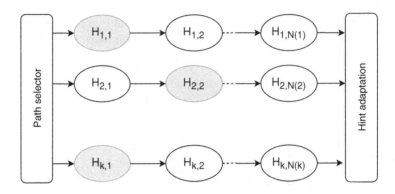

Fig. 3. Laddering technique to generate hints

Table 2. Example of hint ladder with six levels

Level	Hint text
1	The following links contain information that might be helpful: <link>, <link>
2	The compiler is free to optimize the compiled code assuming that there is no undefined behavior in the code
3	Look at the variable 'i'
4	Read carefully the following secure coding guideline: <link>
5	The code accesses the variable "Values" - check carefully the bounds
6	Since undefined behavior is not allowed, and the variable "Values" must be indexed within the bounds, the check i < 4 is removed by the compiler!

and give background information for the participant. The highest level hint contains exact information on how to solve the problem, thus revealing the solution.

Finally, the Feedback component formats and enriches the selected hint by the AI Engine with project-specific information and sends it to the Web Back-End component to present to the Player. To foster critical thinking, the authors have also implemented a hint back-off (i.e., no hint will be given to the Player who is brute-forcing the hint system). This back-off system implements the following rule: 1) no hint is provided to the Player during 4 min after the backend has sent a hint to the Player, and 2) no hint is given until the number of code submissions since the previous hint sent to the Player by the backend is equal to 3 submissions.

Note that the feedback component not only fosters critical thinking by the Player, but can also be used to train the Player with the usage of static code analysis tools. However, further investigation of this aspect is needed in the future.

Real-World Artifact. Figure 4 shows the web interface of a real-world implementation of the Sifu platform. The machine where the Sifu platform was deployed was an AWS instance of type T3.Medium (2 CPUs with 4 Gb RAM and network connection up to 5 Gb/s). In order to install the required tools, a hard-disk of 40 Gb was selected. The Sifu platform itself is developed in Python 3.8 using Flask.

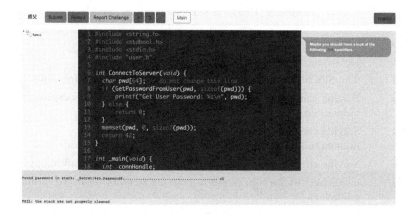

Fig. 4. Sifu web interface

On the left, the Player can browse the Project and select a file to edit; the file editor is in the center, and on the right are the hints that the Player receives from the backend. The upper part contains buttons which include the following functionality: *Submit* - to submit the Project for analysis, *Reload* - to reload the Project from scratch, *Report Challenge* - to report problems with the challenge to the developers. Note that, when a player finishes a challenge successfully, it is taken to an additional page with discussions on the impact of the vulnerability and additional closing questions (e.g., on which secure coding guidelines have not been taken into consideration).

Evaluation of Real-World Artifact. The platform containing five different challenges was made available for experimentation to 15 participants in Germany in June 2020. Participants' ages ranged between 20 and 50 years old, with an average of 28.3. The participants' background was: 7 computer science students, 7 professional software developers, and 1 assistant professor. Participants were allowed to try the platform for as long as they liked; this resulted in a range from 15 min to 45 min. When successfully solving a challenge, the participants were asked (through the web interface) to rate the challenge based on the questions presented in Table 3. Additionally, upon completing the experiment, when the participants were asked to fill out a small online survey. The questions asked in this survey are presented in Table 4. Both the challenge rating and the platform survey questions were based on a 5-point Likert scale.

Table 3. Challenge rating questions

Number	Question
Q1	Please give an overall rating to the challenge
Q2	How well could you recognize the vulnerability in the code?
Q3	How well can you fix this problem in production code?

Table 4. Platform survey questions

Number	Feedback question
F1	My overall experience with the platform was positive
F2	The Sifu platform helps me to improve my secure coding skills
F3	Solving challenges in the Sifu platform helps me in recognizing vulnerable code
F4	Solving challenges in the Sifu platform helps me in understanding consequences of exploiting vulnerable code
F5	Solving challenges in the Sifu platform makes me overall happy
F6	Challenges in the Sifu platform help me to practice secure coding guidelines
F7	I find the Sifu platform adequate as a means to raise awareness on secure coding
F8	The examples in the Sifu platform are clearly presented
F9	It is fun to solve challenges in the Sifu platform

4 Results

In this section, we present the results of the challenge feedback questions and the participants' survey. The results were processed using RStudio version 1.2.5019. Additionally, we briefly discuss the threats to validity.

4.1 Challenge Feedback

Figure 5 shows the results of the challenge rating questions. The average values and standard deviation are the following: Q3 3.92 ($\sigma = 1.19$), Q1 3.76 ($\sigma = 1.30$), Q2 3.72 ($\sigma = 1.21$). In order of agreement: the participants are confident to be able to fix the problem in production code, have rated positively the presented challenges and would be able to recognize the vulnerability in (production) code.

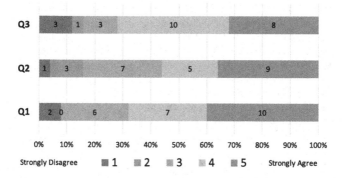

Fig. 5. Evaluation of challenges in Sifu platform

4.2 Sifu Survey

Figure 6 shows the survey results. The average values and standard deviation are the following: F6 4.33 ($\sigma = 0.49$), F2 4.00 ($\sigma = 0.38$), F9 3.93 ($\sigma = 1.03$), F7 3.80 ($\sigma = 0.86$), F8 3.80 ($\sigma = 0.94$), F1 3.73 ($\sigma = 0.70$), F3 3.67 ($\sigma = 0.62$), F5 3.67 ($\sigma = 1.35$), and F4 3.33 ($\sigma = 0.82$). In general, the overall positive feedback gathered through the survey shows that the Sifu platform helps to raise awareness on software developers on the topic of secure coding and secure software development best practices. In particular, the Sifu platform helps software developers to practice secure coding guidelines (F6) and helps software developers to improve their secure coding skills (F2). Furthermore, using the platform is fun and adequate as a means to raise secure coding awareness (F9 and F7). In terms of awareness (perception - F3, protection - F2, and behavior - F6), as defined by Hänsch et al. [11], the platform is also seen as adequate to improve awareness. Another important aspect is that the participants find that the programming examples are clearly presented in the platform (F8). Finally, the participants also tend to agree that using the platform can be fun (F9) and improve happiness (F5) and is an overall positive experience (F1). The results can be split into three clusters, according to the level of agreement as follows: *medium agreement* (3.33–3.67), *higher agreement* (3.73–3.8) and *highest agreement* (3.80–4.33). Using these clusters, the results can be interpreted in the following way (from highest agreement to medium agreement):

- *highest agreement:* helps to practice and improve secure coding, is fun and adequate to raise secure coding awareness
- *higher agreement:* challenges are clearly presented and the experience is positive
- *medium agreement:* helps to recognize vulnerable code and understand consequences and makes happy.

The results hereby presented give an indication towards the suitability of the herein proposed solution to address RQ1 and RQ2, as stated in the problem statement of Sect. 3.

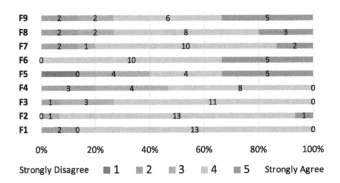

Fig. 6. Survey results

4.3   Threats to Validity

The main aim of this work is to present an architecture of a serious game geared towards improving the secure coding skills of software developers. To validate the platform's usefulness, the authors have gathered feedback from 15 participants in a trial experiment. Possible sources of threat to the validity of the results and conclusions presented in the previous section include:

- *low number of participants*: although the gathered feedback shows a clear tendency towards positive feedback, the number of participants was low, making the standard deviations relatively high,
- *participants' background*: while the serious game is designed for industrial environments, a large portion of the participants were computer science students. Although the authors do not believe that this causes a significant change in the results, further studies with industry players is required,
- *survey design*: the survey administered at the end of the experiment was guided by survey best practices; however, it lacks a formal and thorough design, e.g., based on existing theories and existing questions database,
- *external validity*: although the goal of the present work is to propose a new method to raise secure coding awareness of software developers, our study did not contain a comparison of the methodology against existing and established methods.

5   Conclusions

Secure coding guidelines, secure software development best practices, and secure coding policies form an essential aspect of secure software development for industrial control and cybersystems. Motivated by cybersecurity standards and industry needs on raising awareness about secure coding guidelines, this work presents a novel method where software developers learn these secure coding best practices in an online environment in the context of a serious game - Capture-the-Flag, while being assisted through a virtual coach. In particular, this work addresses and details an architecture that can scale (e.g., through online training) and is based on an interview laddering technique to generate helpful hints. Another source of inspiration for the current work is reinforcement learning techniques; however, the trainee is a human being, not a machine.

Our proposed solution uses existing open source components to perform unit-testing, static, dynamic, and run-time security analyses of the project code, which the participants need to change to eliminate software vulnerabilities. We also briefly discuss implemented mechanisms that prevent cheating by the players and mechanisms that do not allow them to attack the system back-end.

Finally, we obtain feedback on the produced artifact through evaluation questions upon completing different challenges and a small survey at the end of the experiment. Preliminary results show that the participants have fun using the platform and find it an adequate means to raise awareness on secure coding best practices. The developed platform will be made available in the future, after the internal software clearing process.

In future work, the authors would like to investigate additional factors that lead software developers to understand better the consequences of exploiting vulnerable code. Furthermore, the authors would like to investigate additional means to implement a more robust artificial engine for the virtual coach through systematic literature research. Furthermore, in a future publication, the authors will perform a large-scale comparative study with existing and established cybersecurity teaching methods. Finally, the quality of the virtual coach engine depends heavily on the quality and number of input sources. In this aspect, the authors intend to investigate further possible sources and the quality (e.g., false positive, false negative) of the existing and future input sources.

Acknowledgments. The authors would like to thank the participants of the survey for their time and their valuable answers. This work is financed by portuguese national funds through FCT - Fundacão para a Ciência e Tecnologia, I.P., under the project FCT UIDB/04466/2020. Furthermore, the third author thanks the Instituto Universitário de Lisboa and ISTAR-IUL, for their support.

References

1. Brisson, A., et al.: Artificial intelligence and personalization opportunities for serious games. In: 8th Artificial Intelligence and Interactive Digital Entertainment Conference, pp. 51–57 (October 2012)
2. Davis, A., Leek, T., Zhivich, M., Gwinnup, K., Leonard, W.: The fun and future of CTF. In: 2014 USENIX Summit on Gaming, Games, and Gamification in Security Education, 3GSE 2014, pp. 1–9 (2014). https://www.usenix.org/conference/3gse14/summit-program/presentation/davis
3. Dobrovsky, A., Borghoff, U.M., Hofmann, M.: An approach to interactive deep reinforcement learning for serious games. In: 2016 7th IEEE International Conference on Cognitive Infocommunications (CogInfoCom), pp. 85–90. IEEE (2016)
4. Dörner, R., Göbel, S., Effelsberg, W., Wiemeyer, J. (eds.): Serious Games. Foundations, Concepts and Practice, vol. 1, p. 421. Springer, Cham (2016). https://doi.org/10.1007/978-3-319-40612-1

5. Frey, S., Rashid, A., Anthonysamy, P., Pinto-Albuquerque, M., Naqvi, S.A.: The good, the bad and the ugly: a study of security decisions in a cyber-physical systems game. IEEE Trans. Softw. Eng. **45**(5), 521–536 (2019)

6. Gasiba, T., Beckers, K., Suppan, S., Rezabek, F.: On the requirements for serious games geared towards software developers in the industry. In: Damian, D.E., Perini, A., Lee, S. (eds.) 27th IEEE International Requirements Engineering Conference, RE 2019, Jeju Island, South Korea, 23–27 September 2019. IEEE (2019). https:// ieeexplore.ieee.org/xpl/conhome/8910334/proceeding

7. Gasiba, T., Lechner, U., Cuellar, J., Zouitni, A.: Ranking secure coding guidelines for software developer awareness training in the industry (June 2020)

8. Gasiba, T., Lechner, U., Pinto-Albuquerque, M., Zouitni, A.: Design of secure coding challenges for cybersecurity education in the industry. In: Shepperd, M., Brito e Abreu, F., Rodrigues da Silva, A., Pérez-Castillo, R. (eds.) QUATIC 2020. CCIS, vol. 1266, pp. 223–237. Springer, Cham (2020). https://doi.org/10.1007/ 978-3-030-58793-2_18

9. Graziotin, D., Fagerholm, F., Wang, X., Abrahamsson, P.: What happens when software developers are (un)happy. J. Syst. Softw. **140**, 32–47 (2018)

10. Groves, R.M., Fowler, F., Couper, M., Lepkowski, J., Singer, E.: Survey Methodology, 2nd edn. Wiley, Hoboken (2009)

11. Hänsch, N., Benenson, Z.: Specifying IT security awareness. In: 25th International Workshop on Database and Expert Systems Applications, Munich, Germany, pp. 326–330 (September 2014). https://doi.org/10.1109/DEXA.2014.71

12. IEC 62443-4-1: Security for industrial automation and control systems - part 4-1: Secure product development lifecycle requirements. Standard, International Electrotechnical Commission (January 2018)

13. ISO 27001: Information technology - Security techniques - Information security management systems - Requirements. Standard, International Standard Organization, Geneva, CH (October 2013)

14. Patel, S.: 2019 Global Developer Report: DevSecOps finds security roadblocks divide teams (July 2020). https://about.gitlab.com/blog/2019/07/15/ global-developer-report/ (posted on 15 July 2019)

15. Rieb, A.: IT-Sicherheit: Cyberabwehr mit hohem Spaßfaktor. In: kma - Das Gesundheitswirtschaftsmagazin, vol. 23, pp. 66–69 (July 2018)

16. Rieb, A., Gurschler, T., Lechner, U.: A gamified approach to explore techniques of neutralization of threat actors in cybercrime. In: Schweighofer, E., Leitold, H., Mitrakas, A., Rannenberg, K. (eds.) APF 2017. LNCS, vol. 10518, pp. 87–103. Springer, Cham (2017). https://doi.org/10.1007/978-3-319-67280-9_5

17. Rietz, T., Maedche, A.: LadderBot: a requirements self-elicitation system. In: 2019 IEEE 27th International Requirements Engineering Conference (RE), pp. 357–362. IEEE (2019)

18. Schneier, B.: Software Developers and Security (July 2020). https://www.schneier. com/blog/archives/2019/07/software_develo.html

19. Siemens AG: Charter of Trust (July 2020). https://www.charteroftrust.com/

20. Simoes, A., Queirós, R.: On the nature of programming exercises. In: 1st International Computer Programming Education Conference, ICPEC, vol. 81, pp. 251–259 (June 2020). Virtual Conference

21. Vasconcelos, P., Ribeiro, R.P.: Using property-based testing to generate feedback for C programming exercises. In: 1st International Computer Programming Education Conference, ICPEC, vol. 81, pp. 285–294 (June 2020). Virtual Conference

22. Votipka, D., Mazurek, M.L., Hu, H., Eastes, B.: Toward a field study on the impact of hacking competitions on secure development. In: Workshop on Security Information Workers (WSIW), Marriott Waterfront, Baltimore, MD, USA (August 2018)
23. WhiteSource: What are the Most Secure Programming Languages? (March 2019). https://www.whitesourcesoftware.com/most-secure-programming-languages/

IoT Vulnerability Scanning: A State of the Art

Ahmed Amro[✉]

Norwegian University of Science and Technology, Gjøvik, Norway
ahmed.amro@ntnu.no

Abstract. Our modern life becomes more and more dependent on technology and services provided through an increasing number of deployed devices "Things" which are connected over networks that can sometimes be accessed remotely via the Internet. Although this Internet of Things (IoT) has led to innovations and improvements to our way of life, it has created many issues, especially related to cybersecurity. Ensuring the security of the IoT ecosystem can be achieved using pro-active security processes, including vulnerability scanning. In this paper, we capture the state of the art of the process that is IoT vulnerability scanning to determine its popularity and maturity. We have captured the different motivations for vulnerability scanning, the scanning space, process, and faced challenges. A Systematic Literature Review (SLR) has been conducted to achieve this goal, and the results are presented hereof. Moreover, we conducted a group of experiments to assess the status of IoT services and their associated vulnerabilities in the Nordic countries and found that additional work is needed to improve the security of the IoT ecosystem.

Keywords: IoT · IIoT · Vulnerability scanning · Shodan

1 Introduction

Innovations are being witnessed every day that affect every aspect of our daily lives. You can start your day by waking up to a smart alarm that knows your schedule, use a smart toaster to perfect your breakfast, go to your work where you are surrounded with connected devices, printers that know what documents you print, video cameras capturing your movement, sensors, and controllers that control critical industrial operations and so on. These innovations led to the creation of the paradigm known as the Internet of Things (IoT) and its emerging sub-domain the Industrial IoT (IIoT).

The number of connected devices to the Internet is increasing at an incredible rate. According to statistics published in May 2019, 22 Billion devices were connected in 2018, expected to reach 50 Billion by 2030 [4]. The advantages of IoT devices are clear to many. They improve the quality of life at home by providing features such as entertainment, smart monitoring, and security. They

ⓒ Springer Nature Switzerland AG 2020
S. Katsikas et al. (Eds.): CyberICPS 2020/SECPRE 2020/ADIoT 2020, LNCS 12501, pp. 84–99, 2020.
https://doi.org/10.1007/978-3-030-64330-0_6

also facilitate daily business operations, such as printing, perimeter monitoring, etc. IoT has found its way also to industrial facilities to improve the overall production process using IIoT. These advantages are related to the nature of IoT devices which can be characterized by connectivity to networks and the Internet, cheap, simple to install, and many others. These characteristics aided in the widespread and increased adoption of this technology. However, the advantages to the users and market investors are what make IoT security worrisome due to their susceptibility to cyber threats.

An enormous amount of resources exists discussing attacks against the IoT ecosystem. Types of attacks differ based on the characteristics of the targeted IoT devices. Some attacks target short-range communication technology such as Bluetooth which requires proximity to targeted devices [28]. Others target networked devices that are connected to home, industrial, corporate, or university networks while others target devices that are connected to the Internet. To mention a few, in 2019, an attack was discovered that makes two million IoT devices discoverable and susceptible to hijacking with no solution at the time of writing the article [20]. Another attack targeted internet connectivity in a specific geographical area through carrying a Distributed Denial of Service (DDoS) attack against 900,000 routers, blocking their owners from online access [23].

Due to the connectivity nature of IoT, it makes compromised devices a threat not only to the functionality of the devices themselves, to their owners or their operating environment but the threat can extend to any Internet-connected device, its owner, and its environment. This was the case for the Mirai botnet, where a group of compromised IoT devices all over the globe was leveraged to launch attacks against hosts in other geographical areas including disrupting DNS providers affecting groups of web servers which consequently affected millions of users [2].

What makes IoT devices a preferable target to attackers; other than their connectivity nature, is the broad availability of vulnerabilities [18]. Moreover, other characteristics regarding IoT devices such as being cheap and simple to install complicates the integration of proper security functions into these devices, which in turn deepens the hole that is called IoT security.

A major factor in improving the posture of the IoT security domain is the proposal of recent IoT standardized communication protocols that integrates security features or suggest guidelines for the manufacturers and users. Nevertheless, the adoption of such standards is not optimal due to implementation flaws [17]. Moreover, the fast deployment (quick-to-market) of IoT due to their cost, simplicity, and functionality makes security assessment a limitation to the market[17]. Thus comes the need to capture the security status of already connected devices, even with their adoption of new security-enhanced standards and after-deployment security assessment. A growing direction to bridge the gap between the rapid deployment of IoT devices and improving the security posture of the Internet and private networks against them is by performing proactive security assessment, including IoT vulnerability scanning. Security researchers are challenged and generously rewarded for hacking an IoT operating system called Azure Sphere to improve its security [26]. Moreover, Bureau Veritas, a leading certification company, has recently targeted the certification of IoT devices by performing security assessments using IoT vulnerability scanning techniques to improve the market value of their customers' products [17]. In addition to that, proactive vulnerability scanning has been utilized to improve the security posture of the TLS certificate ecosystem [25].

This paper aims to capture the state-of-the-art of IoT vulnerability scanning in the literature to comprehend the popularity and maturity of such an approach in improving the security posture in the IoT domain. For this sake, a Systematic Literature Review (SLR) has been conducted, and its results are presented in this paper. The SLR methodology applies the guidelines proposed by Okoli and Schabram (2010) [22], which is the most relevant to the domain of this study. Three digital libraries were searched for articles containing the phrases "IoT" AND scan AND "vulnerability" in their metadata section, the libraries are Scopus, IEEE, and Science Direct. In total, 25 unique works were found relevant to the scope of this paper in the initial selection phase. After a deeper study of the results, two major work categories were discovered, five works focused on IoT device scanning without a focus on vulnerability scanning, and the remaining 20 focused mainly on vulnerability scanning which is relevant to the scope of this paper. Moreover, due to time limitations, only half of the remaining works were thoroughly studied based on prioritization criteria favoring recent works with higher research impact measured by their citation count. Overall, the freshness of the research filed is indicated by the low amount of literature, but, the growing interest in it is clearly witnessed and can be seen in Fig. 1. The contributions of this paper are summarized below:

1. The promising research direction of IoT vulnerability scanning is highlighted by the results of the conducted SLR.
2. A vulnerability scanning process is proposed based on the observed literature.
3. A vulnerability scanning space is proposed which is useful for visualizing the different scanning processes and can be used as basis for measuring expected time and complexity requirements.
4. The status of the most relevant vulnerabilities in the Nordic countries are assessed which is useful to shape cyber security solutions that are more relevant to the market as well as direct research directions.

2 Vulnerability Scanning: State-of-the-Art

2.1 Scanning Goals

Among the studied literature, the main observed goal for performing vulnerability scanning is to investigate security and privacy issues with some works aiming to enforce security rules [21]. Secondary goals are related to developing security solutions for IoT and IIoT [3,9,10,17,21], certification of IoT and IIoT devices to improve their market value [17], while others aim to provide platform for threat information sharing in IoT [10].

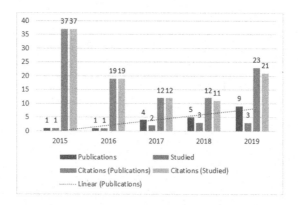

Fig. 1. Number of publications in the field of IoT vulnerability scanning, the number of studied works in this paper and the citation count of both categories

2.2 Scanning Space

From the studied scanning processes, we were able to identify an IoT vulnerability scanning space in which all the observed scanning processes reside. The scanning space as shown in Fig. 2 consists of three dimensions, the x-axis represents the IPv4 address space reflecting the scanned hosts, the y-axis represents the port numbers reflecting scanned services, and the z-axis represents the scanned vulnerabilities. We also captured the effect on the scanning process from time and complexity perspectives when attempting to cover more areas in each axis. It was observed that scanning more hosts and more ports are relatively simple but time-consuming. For instance, scanning 3.702 Billion IP addresses consumes on average 1 h and 8 min for each protocol in a specific port with a limited time difference between the different protocols [10]. On the other hand, detecting vulnerabilities requires additional processing and more complicated logic. The Figure also reflects the most observed scanned ports and IoT vulnerabilities.

IPv4 Addresses (x-Axis): Regarding Internet Protocols (IP), only IPv4 scanning has been observed. To the best of our knowledge, no work has yet accomplished a full scan for IPv6 addresses due to its large space. Nevertheless, *Shodan* [16], an IoT search engine (more in Sect. 2.4) collects IPv6 addresses during the IPv4-based scanning [12]. The coverage of IPv4 scanning differs from work to work. Table 1 depicts the different types of networks targeted for coverage in the studied literature. Note that some works performed or discussed several scanning processes with different network types; therefore, they appear in multiple categories. Some works have scanned the entire IPv4 in search of specif vulnerabilities in specific ports, others scanned small and home networks, others scanned large networks while others focused on a country level.

Another aspect that has been discussed regarding IPv4 scanning is related to address randomization. Some works proposed algorithms to generate random IPv4 addresses for the scanning process in an attempt to avoid the detection

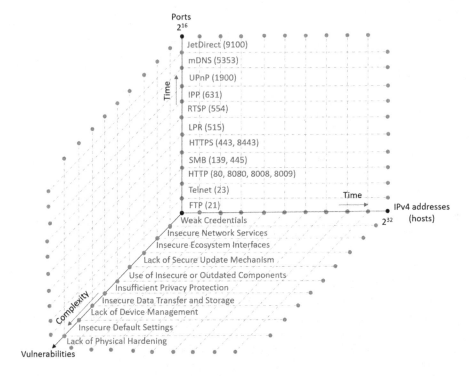

Fig. 2. IoT vulnerability scanning space

and scanning prevention by security solutions such as firewalls which can easily detect sequential IPv4 scanning [9].

Table 1. Observed Network types in the literature

Internet-wide			
[9, 10, 25]			
Country			
[1]			
Testing Environment	Local Active Network	Industrial Network	SDN Network
[3, 21, 27]	[1, 3, 11, 17, 25]	[1, 3, 17, 25]	[21]

Port Numbers (y-Axis): Scanning processes differ in their coverage of ports. Most works scan the entire port numbers looking for open ports to perform banner grabbing to fingerprint device type and infer additional details to be utilized in further vulnerability scanning and analysis. However, some works only target specific vulnerabilities associated with a specific protocol, thus covering only a subset of the port number space. Kumar et al. [11] analyzed scanning data collected from 83 million IoT devices in 16 million homes aiming to reflect the current status of the IoT domain. In their work, they were able to identify the most popular open IoT services and their ports (y-axis in Fig. 2).

Vulnerabilities (z-Axis): As mentioned before, the number of discovered IoT vulnerabilities is increasing. In 2018, the Open Web Application Security Project (OWASP) published the top 10 IoT vulnerability categories (z-axis in Fig. 2) as part of a dedicated project targeting IoT security [18]. Ogunnaike and Lagesse [21] proposed that systematic vulnerability scanning should be according to the OWASP IoT vulnerability category, and we agree with this notion.

2.3   Scanning Challenges

There are several challenges associated with IoT vulnerability scanning related to the device type identification, visibility, and management of legacy devices as well as some ethical aspects that should be considered but would limit the scanning results.

Device Type and Operating System Identification: As mentioned before, the amount of IoT devices is immense; their types and operating systems as well are increasing with innovations every day. Only in the home environment, 14 categories of devices have been observed based on their functionality (network node, mobile device, work appliance, game consoles, etc.) produced by 14,3 thousand manufacturers [11]. Machine learning techniques have been applied to improve the identification of device types [11] and operating systems [9]. Communicating with these devices to scan them and identifying their associated vulnerabilities require varying levels of scrutiny, especially since most of them do not adhere to certain standards.

Legacy Devices: Industrial environments rely on a wide range of devices, and some of them are relatively old. Such devices mostly apply proprietary or legacy software with out-of-business providers, and some of these devices cannot be discovered using traditional scanners [3]. Even scanners that are tweaked to discover such devices do not usually account for many devices due to the large variety of them [3]. Therefore, scanning such devices constitutes a great challenge that has been addressed in the literature by several works [1,3,17,25].

Ethical Considerations: Vulnerability scanning could reveal information that might be utilized during malicious activities such as revealing personal information or harming the reputation of some companies. Therefore, some works have addressed this issue and argued that this might have affected the value and validity of the results [1,11]. The validity can be affected when only passive scanning of previously available scanning data has been performed without active scanning to validate, leading to uncertainty regarding the current status of the scanned devices. On the other hand, the value of the scan can be reduced when some users request that their network should not be scanned or choose not to share the scanning results which could lead to reduced data collection.

Some works claimed that they had acquired permission before scanning the network [14]. Others provided home users with clarified request to approve the collection of user-triggered vulnerability scanning data [11]. Other works claimed that they only queried (Passive scanning) *Shodan* and *Censys* without performing any active scanning [1,25]. The rest of the studied works either used their equipment in their networks or did not mention ethical considerations.

2.4 Scanning Process

After studying the different scanning methods in the different works, an overview of the observed steps in the scanning processes has been identified and presented in Fig. 3.

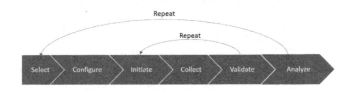

Fig. 3. Overview of IoT device and vulnerability scanning process

A brief description of each step is mentioned below:

– **Select:** The first step is determining what tool or platform to utilize for scanning. The most reference tools are *Shodan* [16], *Censys* [5], *Masscan* [6], and *Nmap* [13]. *Shodan* and *Censys* are both online search engines that perform periodic scanning of the IPv4 address space, store results, index them, and make them available for searching. Both platforms can be used for free or with a subscription for advanced functionalities such as on-demand scanning. Other tools that can be selected that are not necessarily vulnerability scanners are network traffic capturing tools such as *Wireshark* [24], which captures network traffics and stores them for later analysis. We categorize the scanning process that utilizes such platforms as a "Passive Scanning" process. *Masscan* and *Nmap*, on the other hand, are open-source tools used mainly for active port scanning and relatively limited vulnerability scanning capabilities. We categorize the scanning process that utilizes such tools as an "Active Scanning" process. A simplified scanning model that combines active and passive scanning is shown in Fig. 4, this model is followed by *Censys* and *Shodan*. Furthermore, some works have proposed their own platforms for Active and/or Passive vulnerability scanning with improvements over available tools in aspects such as IP address randomization, OS fingerprinting,

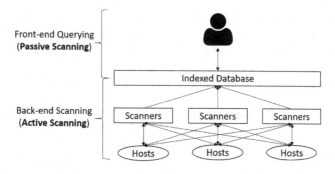

Fig. 4. Simplified scanning model combining active and passive scanning

device type identification, and advanced vulnerability identification and management.

- **Configure:** The determination of the scanning scope by tuning the parameters for active scanning directly influences the scanning time and is dependent on the goal of the scanning process. Time for passive scanning, on the other hand, is not influenced by the configuration but the configuration influence the amount of returned results. The configurable parameters are mainly related to the three dimensions captured in the scanning space (Sect. 2.2). Figure 5 shows a visualization of different types of scanning determined by different

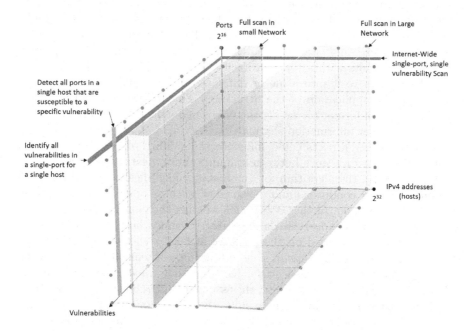

Fig. 5. Visualizing examples of scanning processes in the scanning space

configurations and how they would look in the defined scanning space. The increased area suggests increased time or/and complexity. Some scanning processes target the discovery of specific vulnerability (e.g. Heartbleed) in the entire IPv4 space, others aim to identify all vulnerabilities in a home, corporate or industrial network, and many other scanning processes have been observed.

- **Initiate:** There is a difference between the initiation of the scanning process (active scanning) and the initiation of the search process (passive scanning). This difference should be considered in evaluating the freshness of the identified vulnerabilities. For instance, an active scan could uncover a vulnerability and record it at a certain time. After a while, when this vulnerability is searched and found, it will not necessarily mean that the vulnerability still exists, maybe it was fixed during the time difference between the active scan and the passive scan. Another aspect has been identified regarding the initiation step; some tools initiate the scanning process automatically and periodically such as *Shodan* and *Censys* in the back-end while others require a human to initiate the scanning process by invoking the selected tools, such as Wi-Fi Inspector [11].

- **Collect:** Different tools collect different types of data. Some works grab service banners (e.g. FTP) when establishing a connection with devices. Others collect protocol headers and responses (e.g. HTTP) while others utilize crafted requests to trigger informative responses. On the other hand, some relay on capturing the communicated packets and massages. *Shodan* and *Censys* both perform a group of collection methods including banner grabbing and capturing of protocol headers. Then they index and host the results of the back-end scanning in an online database available for querying. On the other hand, other tools, especially the ones that perform active scanning, return the results within the tool itself (Command Line Interface (CLI) or graphical) or save it into a file or database for later analysis. Some works proposed the application of the Structured Threat Information Expression (STIX) [8] as a format for saving the discovered vulnerabilities which can be useful for threat information sharing [10].

- **Validate:** Many aspects could influence the validity of the search results. Other than the difference between scanning times mentioned before (in the initiation step), the algorithm for vulnerability identification could be based upon high-level conditions and parameters, such as open port, or protocol header value without further verification whether the vulnerability is actually exploitable. For instance, Al-Alami et al. [1] scanned hosts on *Shodan* with default credentials based on the presence of FTP response code 230 which means successful login; *Shodan* suggests this after attempting to log in using a list of most common credentials. Knowing that *Shodan* scans the entire IPv4 at least once each month [9], the assumed vulnerability could have been resolved but still appears in the results, therefore should be validated using active scanning, bearing in mind the associated ethical considerations.

Some processes utilize additional tools to validate the results of the scanning tools. For instance, the results of *Shodan* discovered open ports have been validated using *Nmap* [14]. Other processes perform in-tool validation as part of the scanning process by invoking certain modules able to communicate with the target devices and actively validate the discovered vulnerabilities [3,11,17,21].

- **Analyze:** The amount and format of the results can be overwhelming. Therefore, post-processing and analysis are usually where most of the work is required. Additional tools are usually utilized for additional analysis such as using *binwalk* [7] for analysis of the identified firmware looking for vulnerabilities. Moreover, some works targeted the assessment of the identified vulnerabilities through the analysis of related information and metrics such as Common Vulnerabilities and Exposures (CVE), the Common Vulnerability Scoring System (CVSS) and others. Overall, this step should determine if the scanning process has accomplished the goal it was intended for. The observed targets for analysis include TLS certificates, weak cryptographic algorithms (hashing, encryption, and digital signatures), open ports, CVE's associated with discovered device type or operating systems, and their CVSS scores, devices' firmware, weak credentials, clear images, and video and many others.

- **Repeat:** IoT vulnerability scanning is goal-oriented, utilizing the available tools, techniques, and information to reach a conclusion. Usually, the process is iterative either entirely or partially. For instance, some works use the same selected tools, same configurations but initiate the process at different times to capture the difference in the state of certain vulnerabilities over a period of time, such as capturing the security state of the TLS ecosystem by performing the same scan process twice over three years [25]. Other works have conducted multiple scanning processes using different tools, configurations, analysis, etc., in order to detect different vulnerabilities in different devices.

3   Nordic IoT and IIoT Telescope: Empirical Study

In this section, we present our conducted experiments to capture the connectivity status of IoT and IIoT devices and some of their associated vulnerabilities in the Nordic countries. Due to the location of NTNU in Norway and considering the cultural, economic, and industrial ties between Norway and its neighboring Nordic countries, we decided to focus our study on them. The Nordic countries are considered globally influential and residing in a stable geographical region consisting of Norway, Sweden, Denmark, Finland, and Iceland [19]. Two experiments were conducted, the first experiment aimed to capture the discoverability of devices listening to the most common observed ports. The second experiment aimed to uncover the status of certain vulnerabilities in the discovered devices. Such experiments shed some light over IoT connectivity in the Nordic region to direct the market toward more relevant solutions as well as focus research directions toward the most relevant protocols. Moreover, similar experiments can be conducted as a source of threat intelligence.

Both experiments followed the scanning process presented in Sect. 2.4. We **selected** Shodan as our scan tool to avoid any legal and ethical issues associated with active scanning. Then, we **configured** the search parameters for each performed experiment specifying the elements of the proposed scanning space. The IP addresses were specified by choosing the country, ports chosen by specifying the port numbers, and the vulnerabilities specified by their CVE or signature strings. We **initiated** the scans using Shodan's CLI tool in Linux and **Collected** the results by saving them into files. We **validated** the scan results by repeating the scanning several times and documenting the latest results. Finally, we **analyzed** the collected results and presented our analysis in this paper.

3.1   Nordic Connectivity

In this experiment, we captured the status of IoT and IIoT connectivity in the Nordic countries. We utilized Shodan to query the number of discovered connections in the most common IoT services and their observed ports, namely, JetDirect (9100), mDNS (5353), UPnP (1900), IPP (631), RTSP (554), LPR (515), HTTPS (443,8443), SMB (139 and 445), HTTP (80, 8080, 8008 and 8009), Telnet (23) and FTP (21). In addition to the most common IIoT services, namely, Modbus (502), DNP3 (20000), and RPC (135 and 102). Firstly, we aimed to assess the Nordic connectivity with these services on a global level. It can be observed from Fig. 6 that Sweden has relatively higher connections as the number of connections in these ports constitutes 0,53% of the global connections and ranking as the 25th globally.

Secondly, we aimed to assess the connectivity for each of these services. The highest numbers of connections were associated with HTTP and HTTPS services constituting 88,96% (51,29% and 37,57% for HTTP and HTTPS respectively) of the total connections among the services under analysis. It can be observed from Fig. 7 that the less secure service that is HTTP is more dominantly implemented across the Nordic countries with a relative balance in Denmark between HTTP and HTTPS.

Then, the connectivity status of the remaining IoT services is captured in Fig. 8. It can be observed that the FTP service is the most deployed across all countries except Norway in which telnet is the most common.

Finally, we aimed to assess the connectivity status of most common IIoT services. As shown in Fig. 9, Distributed Network Protocol 3 (DNP3) protocol is the most common across all countries except Sweden, where Modbus protocol stands higher. In fact, we discovered that Sweden ranks as the 7th globally in the number of Modbus connections discovered by Shodan. It is worth mentioning that the DNP3 protocol has much higher connections globally than Modbus (260888 and 15543, respectively). We argue that these numbers are alarming and reflect a high degree of connectivity for IIoT devices using protocols that are known for their security issues.

Having in mind the connectivity status presented previously, we aimed to assess the security status of the analyzed services. By utilizing the Shodan Exploits database [15] we searched for the exploits associated with these services.

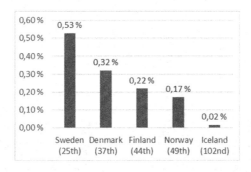

Fig. 6. The Nordic shares and rankings in the global connectivity with IoT and IIoT Services

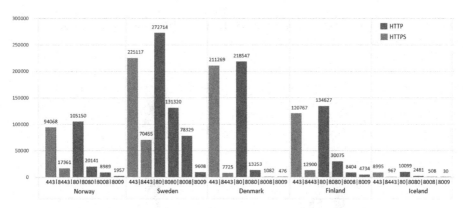

Fig. 7. The number of HTTP and HTTPS connections in the Nordic countries at different service ports

HTTP and HTTPS have the largest amount (2151 and 115 respectively) then, FTP (157), SMB (33), Telnet (17), and RPC (15) with many available exploits. Considering the relatively large number of FTP exploits, and the relatively large number of discovered devices running FTP (Fig. 8) we argue that FTP service is the most exposed service in the Nordic region which makes it a candidate enabler for launching a wide range of cyberattacks. Similar concerns are drawn for the Telnet and SMB services.

3.2   Vulnerability Scanning

We searched Shodan for a group of vulnerabilities observed in the literature, namely, in the work of Al-Alami [1] in which the authors searched for these vulnerabilities in Jordan. The searched vulnerabilities are Heartbleed (CVE-2014-0160), TicketBleed (CVE-2016-9244), SMB anonymous login, and FTP weak authentication. Heartbleed vulnerability allows for the stealing of information by exploiting the OpenSSL cryptographic library. As shown in Fig. 10a Sweden is the Nordic country with the highest number of devices vulnerable to Heartbleed

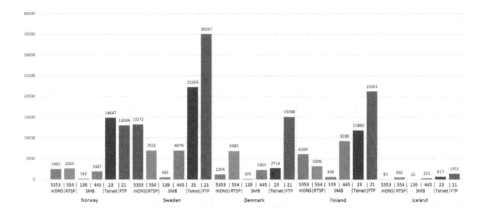

Fig. 8. Number of connections with mDNS, RTSP, SMB, Telnet and FTP services in the Nordic countries

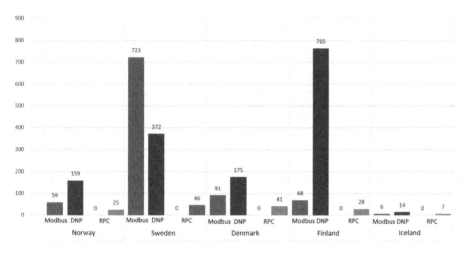

Fig. 9. Number of connections with IIoT services in the Nordic countries

and hosts 0,46% of the vulnerable devices globally. TicketBleed vulnerability is similar to Heartbleed but allows for steeling less amount of information and affects proprietary TLS stack [1]. It can be observed from Fig. 10b that the vulnerability affects very few devices in the Nordic countries. As a matter of fact, our search revealed that TicketBleed is less exiting globally than Heartbleed, with only 404 vulnerable devices compared to 78414 for Heartbleed. Moreover, the SMB anonymous login vulnerability allows the exposure of folders, files, and printers. Figure 10c depicts the number of vulnerable devices in the Nordic countries and Finland hosting the majority of these devices. Finally, the FTP weak credentials vulnerability points to the devices with easy and guessable credentials brute-forced by Shodan. As shown in Fig. 10d, Sweden is hosting the most vulnerable devices.

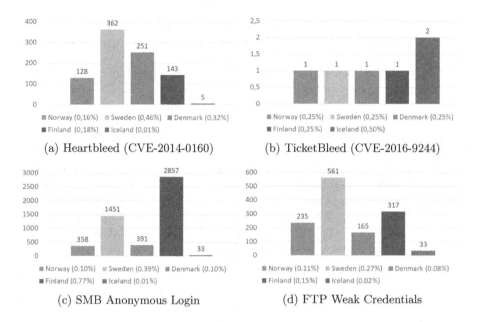

(a) Heartbleed (CVE-2014-0160)   (b) TicketBleed (CVE-2016-9244)

(c) SMB Anonymous Login   (d) FTP Weak Credentials

Fig. 10. Status of certain vulnerabilities in the Nordic Countries

4   Conclusion

In this paper, we have conducted a Systematic Literature Review (SLR) to capture the state of the art of vulnerability scanning in the Internet of things (IoT). We have observed a growing interest in the field indicated by the growing amount of literature and research impact.

The main goal for performing vulnerability scanning as observed in the literature is to investigate security and privacy issues in the connected "things". Additional goals could be related to developing security solutions, usage as a source of information for threat sharing as well as certification of IoT products. The main challenges faced during scanning for vulnerabilities are related to the large number of devices provided by different manufacturers with functionalities not adhering to certain standards.

An overview of the observed vulnerability scanning process is presented in this paper. The process consists of 6 main iterative steps, select, configure, initiate, collect, validate, and analyze. All the studied works apply in one way or another each of the identified steps in the presented process. A scanning space has also been identified in which all the observed scanning processes reside. The indicated space can be used to visualize the scanning process and assess its coverage, complexity, and time requirements.

Moreover, the availability of accessible tools to perform scanning at a varying degree of detail is observed. But, improvements are yet to be made in the aspects of supporting new and legacy device types and their operating systems as well as the discovery of new vulnerabilities which is a continuous operation in the field of IoT. Furthermore, the availability of such tools allows for different unexplored use cases to capture the state of IoT and their security in many domains which could pave the way for future research.

Finally, an empirical study was conducted in this paper, following the proposed scanning process and using the available scanning tools. The study aimed to capture the status of the connectivity and exposure of vulnerabilities in the Nordic countries. Among the observations is the relatively high exposure of IIoT protocols especially Modbus and DNP in Sweden and Finland considering their associated insecurities. In addition to that, although Heartbleed vulnerability has been around for a while, it still exists in the Nordic Countries accumulating a total of 889 vulnerable devices. Finally, the number of vulnerable devices due to insecure implementation of FTP and SMB protocols is also high (1311 and 5090 respectively). We argue that the total number of vulnerable devices considering only the scanned 4 vulnerabilities (7295) could establish a sufficient base for launching a large-scale attack such as the one originating from the Mirai botnet.

References

1. Al-Alami, H., Hadi, A., Al-Bahadili, H.: Vulnerability scanning of IoT devices in Jordan using Shodan. In: 2017 2nd International Conference on the Applications of Information Technology in Developing Renewable Energy Processes & Systems (IT-DREPS), pp. 1–6. IEEE (2017)
2. Antonakakis, M., et al.: Understanding the Mirai botnet. In: 26th USENIX Security Symposium, USENIX Security 17, pp. 1093–1110 (2017)
3. Antrobus, R., Green, B., Frey, S., Rashid, A.: The forgotten I in IIoT: a vulnerability scanner for industrial Internet of Things (2019)
4. Statista Research Department: Number of connected devices worldwide 2030 (February 2020). https://bit.ly/Statista-IoTConnectivity
5. Durumeric, Z., Adrian, D., Mirian, A., Bailey, M., Halderman, J.A.: A search engine backed by internet-wide scanning. In: Proceedings of the 22nd ACM SIGSAC Conference on Computer and Communications Security, pp. 542–553 (2015)
6. Graham, R.D.: Masscan: Mass IP port scanner (2014). https://github.com/robertdavidgraham/masscan
7. Heffner, C.: Binwalk: Firmware analysis tool (2013). https://code.google.com/p/binwalk/. Accessed 3 Mar 2013
8. Cyber Threat Intelligence Technical Committee: Structured threat information expression (stix) (2017)
9. Kim, H., Kim, T., Jang, D.: An intelligent improvement of internet-wide scan engine for fast discovery of vulnerable IoT devices. Symmetry 10(5), 151 (2018)
10. Ko, Eunhye, Kim, Taeeun, Kim, Hwankuk: Management platform of threats information in IoT environment. J. Ambient Intell. Humaniz. Comput. 9(4), 1167–1176 (2017). https://doi.org/10.1007/s12652-017-0581-6
11. Kumar, D., et al.: All things considered: an analysis of IoT devices on home networks. In: 28th USENIX Security Symposium, USENIX Security 19, pp. 1169–1185 (2019)

12. ManXmachina LLC: How to hack a self-driving car with low tech paint and other serious artificial intelligence Safety Issues (May 2019). https://bit.ly/IPv6Scanning
13. Lyon, G.F.: Nmap network scanning: The official Nmap project guide to network discovery and security scanning. Insecure (2009)
14. Markowsky, L., Markowsky, G.: Scanning for vulnerable devices in the internet of things. In: 2015 IEEE 8th International Conference on Intelligent Data Acquisition and Advanced Computing Systems: Technology and Applications (IDAACS), vol. 1, pp. 463–467. IEEE (2015)
15. Matherly, J.: Shodan exploits (2015). Accessed Apr 2017
16. Matherly, J.: Complete Guide to Shodan. Shodan, LLC (25 February 2016)
17. Maurin, T., Ducreux, L.F., Caraiman, G., Sissoko, P.: Iot security assessment through the interfaces p-scan test bench platform. In: 2018 Design, Automation & Test in Europe Conference & Exhibition (DATE). pp. 1007–1008. IEEE (2018)
18. Miessler, D., Smith, C.: OWASP Internet of Things project. OWASP Internet of Things Project-OWASP (2018)
19. NUPI: The Nordic countries - landing page. https://bit.ly/Nordic-C0ntries
20. O'Donnell, L.: 2 million IoT devices vulnerable to complete takeover (April 2019). https://threatpost.com/iot-devices-vulnerable-takeover/144167/
21. Ogunnaike, R.M., Lagesse, B.: Toward consumer-friendly security in smart environments. In: 2017 IEEE International Conference on Pervasive Computing and Communications Workshops (PerCom Workshops), pp. 612–617. IEEE (2017)
22. Okoli, C., Schabram, K.: A guide to conducting a systematic literature review of information systems research (2010)
23. Oltermann, P.: Briton admits to cyber-attack on Deutsche Telekom (July 2017). https://bit.ly/Guardian-DeutscheTelekom
24. Orebaugh, A., Ramirez, G., Beale, J.: Wireshark & Ethereal Network Protocol Analyzer Toolkit. Elsevier, Amsterdam (2006)
25. Samarasinghe, N., Mannan, M.: Another look at TLS ecosystems in networked devices vs. web servers. Comput. Secur. **80**, 1–13 (2019)
26. Sheridan, K.: Microsoft challenges security researchers to hack Azure sphere (May 2020). https://bit.ly/Microsoft-Challenge
27. Tekeoglu, A., Tosun, A.Ş.: A testbed for security and privacy analysis of IoT devices. In: 2016 IEEE 13th International Conference on Mobile Ad Hoc and Sensor Systems (MASS), pp. 343–348. IEEE (2016)
28. Vijayan, J.: Most Bluetooth devices vulnerable to impersonation attacks (May 2020). https://bit.ly/VulnerableBluetooth

Learning from Vulnerabilities - Categorising, Understanding and Detecting Weaknesses in Industrial Control Systems

Richard J. Thomas$^{(\boxtimes)}$ and Tom Chothia

School of Computer Science, University of Birmingham, Birmingham, UK
{R.J.Thomas,T.P.Chothia}@cs.bham.ac.uk

Abstract. Compared to many other areas of cyber security, vulnerabilities in industrial control systems (ICS) can be poorly understood. These systems form part of critical national infrastructure, where asset owners may not understand the security landscape and have potentially incorrect security assumptions for these closed source, operational technology (OT) systems. ICS vulnerability reports give useful information about single vulnerabilities, but there is a lack of guidance telling ICS owners what to look for next, or how to find these. In this paper, we analyse 9 years of ICS Advisory vulnerability announcements and we recategorise the vulnerabilities based on the detection methods and tools that could be used to find these weaknesses. We find that 8 categories are enough to cover 95% of the vulnerabilities in the dataset. This provides a guide for ICS owners to the most likely new vulnerabilities they may find in their systems and the best ways to detect them. We validate our proposed vulnerability categories by analysing a further 6 months of ICS Advisory reports, which shows that our categories continue to dominate the reported weaknesses. We further validate our proposed detection methods by applying them to a range of ICS equipment and finding four new critical security vulnerabilities.

1 Introduction

Industrial Control Systems (ICS) form a key part of the critical national infrastructure and industrial environments. Attacks against ICS devices, such as Stuxnet [9], BlackEnergy [18] and Triton [16], have aim to cause disruption and damage ICS equipment. Many ICS environments were segregated from IT networks, however most now exist on the same, heterogeneous network, opening them up to a wide range of attacks.

In recognition of the importance of ICS cybersecurity, the European Union Network and Information Systems (NIS) Directive came into force in May 2018. Member states are required to define essential services and improve infrastructure security and resilience in identified sectors. The NIS Directive shifted

© Springer Nature Switzerland AG 2020
S. Katsikas et al. (Eds.): CyberICPS 2020/SECPRE 2020/ADIoT 2020, LNCS 12501, pp. 100–116, 2020.
https://doi.org/10.1007/978-3-030-64330-0_7

responsibility for assurance onto asset owners, who may lack cybersecurity under-standing of what vulnerabilities and issues exist in the ICS space. IT Security is considered a well-understood problem, with insights available to OT opera-tors. However, there are different assumptions and requirements placed on OT devices, for example operational lifespan measured in the order of decades, not years, and safety which may not exist in IT environments. By reviewing what vulnerabilities exist in the industrial space, we can define what priorities for asset owners and the supply chain should be and how they can be addressed and detected to improve industrial security.

ICS environments are typically made up of Programmable Logic Controllers (PLCs), automating a process given a set of inputs, controlling outputs. PLCs may be connected to sensors, actuators and Human Machine Interfaces (HMIs), operator control panels displaying the state of the system and allow an operator to interface with the process. Other components, such as Supervisory Control and Data Acquisition (SCADA) may be integrated for logging, analytics and con-trol purposes, and Remote Terminal Units (RTUs), enable remote management for devices. The exception of some SCADA systems that run on standard PCs is that these are usually provided to the ICS owner as proprietorial, closed source software running on unidentified hardware. Sometimes, the security assumptions made by the designers of this equipment are not clear, and there is no easy way for ICS owners to inspect and run their own software on the ICS equipment. This makes the security controls and issues for ICS equipment quite different from, e.g., securing desktop machines and servers in a company setting. There-fore, general work on common vulnerability categories and detection methods does not carry over to the ICS domain.

To provide insight into vulnerabilities in ICS environments, this paper car-ries out a detailed review of nine years of ICS-CERT Advisories and related data. This tells us the kinds of vulnerabilities that commonly occur in ICS envi-ronments. We analyse this data, identifying trends and what kind of detection methods could find the vulnerabilities. Based on this analysis, we suggest eight categories for the vulnerabilities based on concrete detection methods. These categories cover 95% of all vulnerabilities in our dataset and give the ICS owner clear steps they can follow to find the weaknesses, and advise vendors on priority areas to resolve. It is important to note that our analysis is purely concerned with the kind of vulnerability in ICS systems that leads to an ICS advisory, i.e., a new flaw in the security of a system. There are many other weaknesses which might be exploited to attack an ICS systems, such as phishing e-mails, or the use of unpatched systems with known vulnerabilities. Most of these issues are well addressed by existing IT security methods and practices. This gives ICS owners an understanding of the types of vulnerabilities that exist in an accessible way, where current information is ambiguous and, as a result, not actionable. Our categories enable an asset owner to act, with appropriate tooling and techniques such that they can be confident in the security of their infrastructures.

To validate the categories and trends we identify, we look at an extra six months of ICS advisory reports. We find that our eight categories continue to dominate the advisories (accounting for 96% of the new vulnerabilities) and each category is well represented. To validate the category detection methods we apply the automated methods to three PLCs and two HMIs from major ICS manufacturers. As a result we find six new attacks against the ICS equipment four of which would be ranked as critical: two denial of service attacks, an open redirect on a web control panel, and an authentication bypass. Responsible disclosure for these vulnerabilities is ongoing and we will make the information public once ICS advisories have been released.

Our contributions are as follows:

- combining a number of data sources together, we present a detailed analysis of ICS vulnerabilities and trends,
- suggesting new eight categories for classifying ICS vulnerabilities that are based on detection methods,
- validating the trends and categories against 6 months of new vulnerability reports, and our detection methods by applying them to five pieces of ICS equipment finding 4 new critical vulnerabilities.

In Sect. 2, we outline our process for connecting sources of data, outlining key statistics and priority areas. We go further to define detectable vulnerability classes to test for such vulnerabilities in Sect. 3 and predict future ICS vulnerabilities and validate these predictions in Sect. 4, concluding in Sect. 5.

Related Work: ICS security research is an active field, where most research focuses on vulnerability research in specific devices and implementations [4,5, 13,20] which highlight particular flaws and are aimed towards finding new flaws and proposing resolutions to improve collective ICS security. These however do not consider the security of ICS as a whole and what common types of vulnerability exist. On the other hand, a chronology of ICS security incidents provides a thorough analysis of high-profile incidents [12], but some commercially-led research papers [1,7,8,17,19] have carried out ICS vulnerability analysis and provide highlights of some of the vulnerability categories that exist, but do not consider all vulnerabilities, or show only a few categories. The last assessment report from ICS-CERT highlighting the top weakness categories in ICS was published in 2016, where no authoritative report has since replaced it [14]. More recently, the authors in [10] review ICS vulnerability reports to determine how many resulted from architectural design decisions, but simply state common root causes. In [15], the authors propose a linked and correlated database for ICS vulnerabilities, to support security operations centres, but additionally categorise vulnerabilities into 6 categories, which do not lend themselves towards detecting such vulnerability categories, and do not provide the level of detail required for ICS owners and supply chain to improve their respective security models. Similar work as part of the OpenCTI project[1] has attempted to make vulnerability information accessible, however, it requires significant expert efforts to integrate for ICS vulnerability reports, and again, informs the ICS owner and vendor what has happened, but not how it can be resolved, or detected.

---

[1] https://opencti.io.

2 Connecting Sources of Data for Vulnerability Insights

Data Sources and Building the Dataset: ICS vulnerabilities are reported
and published in a number of places, for example vendor websites, CVE listings
and ICS-CERT. For ICS owners and vendors, it is not clear which source is
authoritative and provides the best whole-of-sector coverage. A number of vendors individually publish advisories, however in a survey of a number of common
ICS vendors, we found that some required a support contract/approval to gain
access to security reports, which limits this coverage if vendors were used as the
primary source. Our ICS vulnerability dataset is therefore built up from three
sources: ICS-CERT advisories, MITRE and the National Vulnerability Database
(NVD). ICS-CERT advisories are the root source of information, where references to MITRE and the NVD are used to extract further information. A workflow which imports these sources is given in Fig. 1.

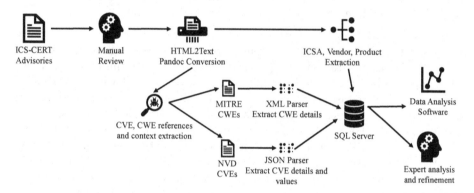

Fig. 1. Parsing and Processing Workflow to create our Dataset. ICS Advisories are
parsed, and when a CWE/CVE ID is found, the corresponding record is parsed and
the information brought together before being committed into the database.

ICS-CERT Advisories: These are published by the USA Cybersecurity and
Infrastructure Security Agency (CISA), providing authoritative vulnerability
information to the ICS community. To the best of our knowledge, it is the most
comprehensive source of ICS vulnerability information. These reports are in
HTML format[2], which we convert into plaintext and markdown to flatten all
formatting, making it easier to extract reference fields for CWEs and CVE numbers. When we find these we retrieve the corresponding record and import some
fields from those sources to provide context to the vulnerability information.

MITRE CWEs: The MITRE Corporation is responsible for two schemes used
within our dataset; Common Weakness Enumeration (CWE) and Common Vulnerability and Exposure (CVE). While MITRE provides CVE information in a

---

[2] An example is available at https://us-cert.cisa.gov/ics/advisories/ICSA-17-157-01.

machine-readable format, it is not as full-featured as the National Vulnerability Database's input to CVE information, for example appraisals of the impact and criticality of that vulnerability in addition to further analysis, such as listing affected products.

The CWE or root cause identifier stated in ICS advisories, however, is used in our analysis. These are unique, distinct vulnerability patterns and anti-patterns in software development, which can express the type of vulnerability that exists. One benefit of CWEs is that they can be grouped together to give types of vulnerability, e.g. memory or web vulnerabilities [21].

National Vulnerability Database (NVD) CVEs: The NVD, provided by NIST, takes the CVE information, analyses and assesses the vulnerability. This assessment allocates the CVSS score, used to define the criticality and impact of the vulnerability, how it may be exploited and under what conditions the system was exploitable. NIST CVEs are provided in JSON files, which we parse. When a CVE reference is found, the corresponding CVE record is retrieved, tagged with the CWE referenced in the ICS advisory and is imported.

The Combined Dataset. Our dataset[3] is built from 1,114 ICS vulnerability reports, with 283 distinct CWE references, and 2,232 CVEs, collected from 2011, when ICS Advisories started to be published to August 2019 (this cut-off was chosen to allow sufficient new vulnerabilities to be produced, allowing validation of our results). The dataset contains the ICS advisory number, release and update dates, the name of the vendor affected and a short description which includes the product affected. For CWEs found in the ICS advisory, we include the CWE ID, the name of the CWE, a brief description and contextual background details, and the CWE status (e.g. if it has been deprecated). CVEs stated in the ICS advisory include the number, description, base, impact[4] and exploitability (see Footnote 4) scores, CVSS vector, severity, access vector, complexity to exploit, availability, integrity and confidentiality impact, the list of privileges required, the impact on system privileges and whether user interaction is required for the exploit to be successful.

Limitations of Existing Data Sources. In isolation, these sources provide little contextual information and means to identify trends and types of vulnerabilities that exist in ICS systems. By connecting ICS advisories to CWE-specific information, we can categorise the type of vulnerabilities that arise in the ICS domain, identify patterns and follow trends. With CVSS, we do not use the assigned scores, where the vector components provide concrete information about the impact of the vulnerability, as the impact scores does not exist in CVSS v2, but all have a defined vector, where 791 of 2,232 CVEs in our dataset do not have these numerical scores. Other fields and content are also not imported, e.g. acknowledgements, researchers or URLs as these are not relevant in our analysis.

Accuracy of the data being used is critical, where a survey of ICS vulnerability data quality showed that in 2018, 32% of ICS CVEs had the wrong

---

[3] Available at https://github.com/uob-ritics/esorics2020-dataset.

[4] Exists only in CVSS v3.

CVSS score assigned [7], improving to 19% [8] in 2019. The combination of these sources mitigates the risk, where we use the most current version of the record, rather than its first instance. Out of 1097 ICS Advisories surveyed up to August 2019, 197 had been updated, which may include additional products affected, new vulnerabilities identified, or new mitigations, for example patch availability. Without using the most current information, these additional vulnerabilities may have been overlooked. These, however, generally do not require further analysis, unless some new, unclustered CWEs were introduced.

3 Understanding and Classifying Vulnerabilities

Understanding the Type of ICS Vulnerabilities: In order to categorise all ICS vulnerabilities and define detection strategies, we must first understand the ICS vulnerability landscape. In order to categorise these vulnerabilities, as we explain later in this section, we must consider existing groupings.

MITRE offers a number of groupings of CWEs, for example based on the OWASP Top 10 and the CWE Top 25 Most Dangerous Software Errors. In Table 1, we map our dataset onto existing clusters (groupings) based on prevalence, and the number of CVEs that had a high impact on the integrity or availability of the system. We note that firstly, these mappings are not mutually exclusive; one CWE may exist in more than one SFP cluster. Secondly, these mappings do not capture the majority of the dataset, where the CWE Top 25 leaves over 50% unclassified.

Table 1. Coverage of ICS Vulnerabilities for existing mappings. For the number of ICS vulnerabilities which have a *'COMPLETE'* or *'HIGH'* impact value.

Grouping	Prevalence	Availability	Integrity
CWE/SANS Top 25 (2011)	24%	11%	10%
CWE Weaknesses on the Cusp (2011)	2%	1%	1%
CWE Top 25 (2019)	48%	28%	18%

The CWE contains clusters defined around the concept of software fault patterns (SFPs), which contains most of the CWEs specified in ICS advisories with no overlap between clusters. These CWEs are mapped to a specific cluster, e.g. memory access (CWE-890) and cryptography (CWE-903). Out of the 2,232 CVEs in our dataset, 1,801 could be mapped directly to a SFP cluster. For the remaining 431 CVEs, we manually assigned them to a respective cluster based on the stated issue (e.g. buffer overflow or cross-site scripting attack) in the ICS Advisory and CVE description. As an example, Cross-Site Request Forgery attacks (CWE-352) have no mapping, but are web-based attacks which are exploited through malicious input, and thus, we categorise it as 'Tainted Input', where other web-based weaknesses sit. This manual expert analysis ensures that

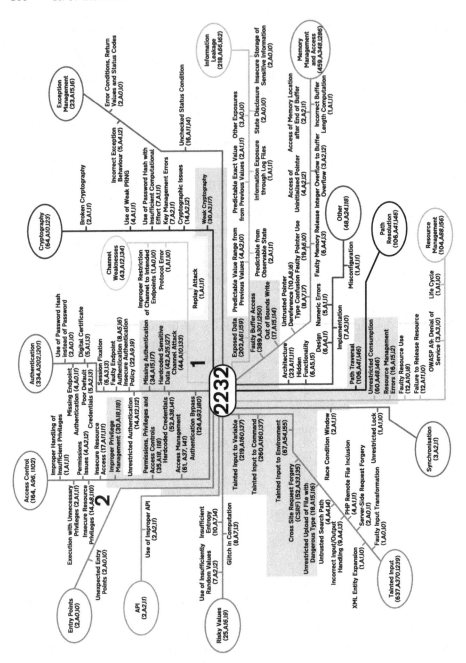

Fig. 2. A map of vulnerabilities from our dataset where each subclass (mark) is ranked based on the prevalence, availability (A) and integrity (I), and subclasses with a higher number of CVEs with critical impact rank higher. Each line represents a MITRE CWE Grouping, and each 'station' represents a subclass within that grouping. Zone 1 subclasses where ≥15 CVEs has a critical availability/integrity impact, and Zone 2 has ≥10 CVEs with a critical impact.

all CWEs are represented within the correct categories rather than 'Other'. The result of this classification is shown in Fig. 2, where we group the vulnerability subclasses, highlight the types of vulnerability that exist within the category and rank vulnerabilities based on the number of CVEs with a 'high' or 'complete' (critical) CVSS availability and integrity impact. The objective of introducing a 'Zone 1' and 'Zone 2' is to highlight priority areas, where it is expected that, as these vulnerability classes are investigated and resolved, the next class can be addressed, where classes with 15 or more critical impact CVEs are in 'Zone 1' and those with 10 or more are in 'Zone 2'.

Defining a Better Classification for ICS Vulnerabilities: While the groupings and subclasses provided in Fig. 2 have distinct types of ICS vulnerabilities, they do not guide ICS owners and vendors in their detection, and contain some ambiguity. This means that, for a given grouping, many detection methods may apply but have different outcomes. Such examples include 'Tainted Input to Variable' and 'Information Leakage' where it may not be clear to an ICS owner what the effect was or how it may be detected.

We propose 8 new detectable, evidence-driven, vulnerability categories, defined below, which categorise vulnerabilities based on the detection method and techniques that can be used by ICS owners and vendors. These categories enable vendors and asset owners to understand the type of vulnerabilities that exist, where the current information is vague and lacks an application context. Our categories capture 95%[5] of all vulnerabilities within our dataset with a clear definition and specific detection methods. An overview of these methods is given in Table 2.

By classifying vulnerabilities in this way, ICS owners and vendors are able to identify techniques in which such classes of vulnerability can be found, how such vulnerabilities are manifested, and furthermore, aids in the validation of ICS device security. In Fig. 3, we show the flow of ICS CVEs from their CWE groupings to our new categories. These flows are built by tagging each CVE in the dataset with its old grouping and its new detectable category and mapping changes from the old tag to the new one, where we clustered like CWEs together under a common name, based on their detectable method. For the purposes of legibility, where the count of CVEs flowing from one grouping to a category was less than 10, we exclude it from the figure (137 of 2,232 CVEs).[6]

For each of our detectable vulnerability categories, we give a precise definition and an example where a prominent ICS attack fits into that category.

Web-Based Weaknesses: These vulnerabilities represent flaws and weaknesses that exist in web-based applications, for example path traversal, cross-site scripting (XSS), and cross-site request forgery (CSRF), which can be detected through conventional web scanners.

---

[5] Of all CVEs categorised, 94% with high availability and integrity impacts were categorised.

[6] A full Figure including these individual flows is given in our longer version of this paper.

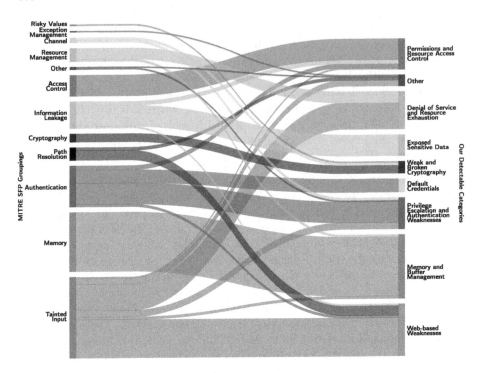

Fig. 3. Flow of CVEs from their original CWE groupings to our detectable classes.

Example: The BlackEnergy [18] malware campaign, which targeted the Ukrainian power grid in 2015, used a vulnerability (CVE-2014-0751) in a GE SCADA web interface that allowed the attack to execute shell code.

Default Credentials: The use of default and hardcoded sensitive credentials has a distinct detection method, where this category has a clear proportion of vulnerabilities over time as shown in Fig. 4. Vulnerabilities in this category consider a system, as delivered, having hardcoded credentials or sensitive data (e.g. SSH keys) which an adversary can recover and use.

Example: Stuxnet [9] targeted and damaged Iranian nuclear centrifuges. In the case of the Siemens system affected by Stuxnet, it contained hard-coded passwords, allowing the adversary to gain access to privileged functions (CVE-2010-2772).

Denial of Service and Resource Exhaustion: These vulnerabilities result in the loss of availability given a non-standard input which does not trigger some memory-related flaw in the system.

Example: CRASHOVERRIDE [6] was an attack which affected a Ukrainian power transmission system, forcing the circuit breakers to remain in an open

Table 2. Comparison of detection methods for our proposed categories.

Category	Easy to use (new vulnerabilities)	Expert tooling (new vulnerabilities)	Tools to find existing vulnerabilities
Permissions and resource access control	Access Control Policy Tooling (NIST ACPT), testing functions as a non-privileged user	Nothing Recommended	Attack Frameworks (e.g. ISF)
Privilege escalation and authentication weaknesses	Check for no authentication	Network Capture and Replay tools (e.g. Wireshark)	Device-specific tools (e.g. PLC Inject, Project Basecamp)
Weak and broken cryptography	Source Code Scanner (SonarQube), Read Papers, Crypto Implementation Scanners (Crypto Detector)	Reverse Engineering (e.g. IDA, GHIDRA, dnspy), Manual Cryptanalysis	Device-specific tools (e.g. s7cracker, ISF)
Default credentials	Use stated default credentials (e.g. from manuals)	Firmware Analysis (e.g. Binwalk) and search for specific artefacts, e.g. keys, shadow files	SCADA StrangeLove Default Password CSV
Denial of service and resource exhaustion	Packet Storm simulators (Low Orbit Ion Cannon)	Fuzzing (e.g. AEGIS Protocol Fuzzer, Codenomicon)	Device-specific tools (e.g. EtherSploit-IP)
Exposed sensitive data	Simple Packet Captures (Wireshark) and search for artefacts	Manual Expert Analysis (detailed packet captures and protocol reverse engineering)	Device-specific tools (e.g. ISF, Metasploit modules, Project Basecamp)
Memory and buffer management	Source Code Scanner (SonarQube, Veracode)	Memory Assessment Tools (e.g. VALGRIND)	Device-specific tooling (e.g. EtherSploit-IP, ics_mem_collect)
Web-based weaknesses	Source Code Scanner (SonarQube), Web Application Scanners (OWASP ZAP, Burpsuite)	Manual Expert Analysis (e.g. using Burpsuite)	Nothing recommended

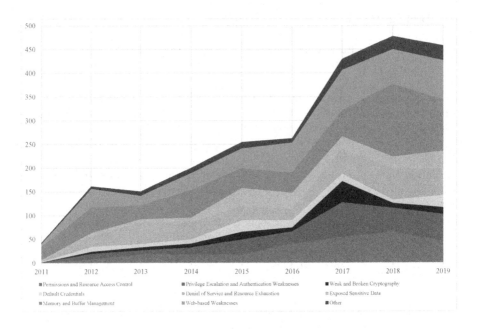

Fig. 4. ICS Vulnerabilities mapped against our new detectable classes

position, even if override commands were issued. The Siemens SIPROTEC protection relay was vulnerable to a denial of service attack (CVE-2015-5374).

Exposed Sensitive Data: Vulnerabilities in this category allow unauthenticated users to access sensitive information. Such information could be leaked via log and debug messages or stored in an openly accessible location. From our dataset, most vulnerabilities classed as information leakage either leaked user credentials or some other sensitive information.

Example: Of the 202 vulnerabilities classed using the SFP clusters as 'Exposed Data' in Fig. 2, only 143 were cases of sensitive information leakage, specifically around the insecure storage of data. One of the high impact vulnerabilities in our dataset affected a Kunbus Modbus gateway, where credentials were stored in plain-text XML configurations, accessible via an FTP server on the device (CVE-2019-6549). Another vulnerability, from a LOYTEC industrial router, allowed password hashes to be read from the device and then recovered (CVE-2015-7906).

Weak and Broken Cryptography: In this category we include cryptography that is weak by design (e.g. proprietorial crypto), as well as strong cryptography that is used incorrectly, allowing it to be broken. This extends the definition of Cryptography in the SFP cluster with e.g. weak PRNGs, use of low entropy keys and certificate misuse.

Example: In the case of Rogue7 [5], the MAC scheme implemented to guarantee integrity and authenticity of data between an engineering workstation (TIA Portal) and a Siemens PLC was weak, allowing an adversary to impersonate a genuine workstation to program the PLC (CVE-2019-10929). In another example using weak cryptography is the use of MD5 highlighted by CVE-2019-6563, this allows an adversary to recover passwords and gain full access to a Moxa industrial switch.

Memory and Buffer Management: Vulnerabilities which specifically relate to memory and buffer implementation flaws, for example buffer overflows, allowing an adversary to influence functionality by manipulating the memory of a system.

Example: Two example CVEs arising out of the Triton attack [16], targeting Schneider Electric safety management systems and modifying their configurations to modify, or in some cases disable the fail-safe protocols, are CVE-2018-8872 and CVE-2018-7522. In the first, memory was read directly from addresses without any verification and attacker-controlled data could be written anywhere in memory. In the case of CVE-2018-8872, the system registers were located in fixed areas of memory where modifying these registers would allow the adversary to control the system state.

Permissions and Resource Access Control: These vulnerabilities allow a user to carry out arbitrary actions on a system using standard interfaces with the privilege of another user. This could, for instance, be due to incorrect assignment of privileges, functions being executed with excessive permissions, or a lack of access control for a given resource.

Example: On an Emerson SCADA system, an authenticated user's actions were not restricted, allowing executables and library files to be changed (CVE-2018-14791), potentially affecting the integrity of the system configuration and its availability. In another case, by using standard interfaces on a Schneider Electric PLC, an unauthenticated adversary could overwrite the password which protects the running program (CVE-2018-7791).

Privilege Escalation and Authentication Weaknesses: These vulnerabilities allow a user, privileged or not, to change their state of privilege in the system through non-standard means. The most prevalent type of vulnerability in this category is 'Authentication Bypass', where an unauthenticated user can become privileged by interacting with the system via an alternative entry point.

Example: Stuxnet, one of the first prominent attacks against an ICS system, used a vulnerability in the Siemens programming software that allowed adversaries to gain privileges by using a trojan DLL (CVE-2012-3015). This would give the adversary full control of the system state.

Discussion: 5% of vulnerabilities held in our dataset do not map directly into these distinct categories, shown in Fig. 3. These vulnerabilities do not have high levels of prevalence or critical impact and require more manual, case-by-case inspection by an expert.

To demonstrate the continued prevalence of these categories over time, Fig. 4 shows these remain largely within proportion over time. We also note that the distribution of detectable categories against a sample of CVEs is even, where the same detectable categories exist across most ICS device types as well as vendors, as shown in Figs. 5 and 6. It is important, however, to note that in Fig. 5, we show the top 6 vendors by CVE prevalence, and this should not be interpreted such that one vendor is considered more vulnerable than another, as different vendors have very different market shares.

Table 2 shows tooling that can be used to detect vulnerabilities for our 8 categories. Other tooling can be used by ICS owners to discover assets (e.g. GRASSMARLIN) and identify whether their product is vulnerable to existing, known, CVEs (e.g. Simaticscan [3], PIVoT [2], Modscan [11] and Nessus).

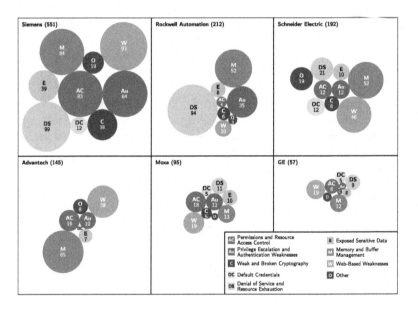

Fig. 5. The prevalence of detectable categories for the top 6 vendors by CVE count.

4   Validating Our Categories and Detection Methods

Assessing Our Categories Against New Data: For our categories to be useful for detecting new vulnerabilities we must be sure that future vulnerabilities follow the same trends as those in our dataset. At some point it is likely that industry will improve its practices, for instance, fixing the use of default passwords or carefully checking the security of all web interfaces, meaning that categories we have identified may no longer be relevant.

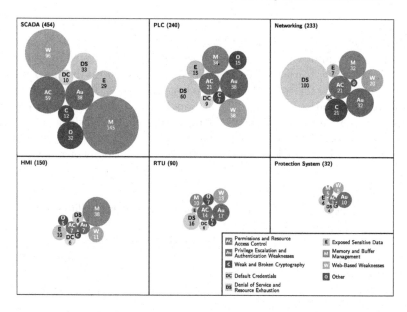

Fig. 6. The prevalence of detectable categories across different product types from a sample of 1199 CVEs.

To test this we compared our finding to the ICS advisories issued between September 2019 and March 2020 (which were not included in our original dataset). In this period, 126 new ICS advisories were published with 334 CVE references, which were parsed into our database and the same process to automatically classify the CVEs based on their CWE ID was taken, with final manual refinements for some CVEs that had previously unmapped CWE references.

Of the 334 CVEs parsed, 322 were directly mapped into our vulnerability classes, and 12 were not classified, an accuracy of 96%. Of the 12 vulnerabilities which were not classified, 3 related to vulnerabilities affecting 'Path Traversal' within software, a different type of vulnerability to web path traversal, 2 related to input validation, and 7 individual vulnerabilities, two of which occurred in the same product.

What this level of accuracy shows is that, with 6 months of new data, we are able to predict with high confidence which of 8 possible categories new ICS CVEs will map to, with specific tooling to support validation and verification activities. There is no sign of industry having seriously addressed any of the categories we identify. However, by using this data-driven approach and the tools we identified which support the identification of issues within our detectable categories, there is an opportunity to reduce the vulnerability space.

Validating Security Tooling and Techniques for ICS. In order to validate our suggested detection methods, and to provide evidence that our categorisation does assist in finding new vulnerabilities, we applied our "easy to use" detection methods listed in Table 2 to five ICS devices - two HMIs (Phoenix Contact and Siemens) and three PLCs (two Siemens PLCs and one ABB PLC). Neither HMI had a web server, whereas all PLCs have web-servers enabled, two of which required some form of authentication to gain access to privileged functions. We did not have access to the source code of the devices, so we did not run tools which required this, or tools that required paid licenses. These results of our analysis are summarised in Table 3. It is important to note that using our categories, we are able to use the most appropriate tooling, and demonstrate how they can be taken from an IT environment and applied to OT systems. Some devices remain anonymised as the disclosure and resolution is ongoing with the vendors.

Table 3. Results from our tooling validation, ✓ = new vulnerabilities discovered

	PLC1	PLC2	PLC3	HMI1	HMI2	Result
Default credentials (from user manual)				✓		Manual updated
NMAP (authentication bypass)	✓					Discussed in text
Wireshark (information leakage)					✓	CVE-2020-7592 issued
Low Orbit Ion Cannon (denial of service)			✓	✓		CVE due to be released
OWASP ZAP (web vulnerabilities)		✓				Update to be issued

In one PLC, a previous CVE for denial of service was issued where long inputs to the web server would cause the device to enter 'Stop' mode and crashing. In our testing using Low Orbit Ion Cannon[7], we found that in the patched version, the web server would stop responding during and after a packet flood, but unlike the CVE (where the PLC would also crash), we found the PLC would continue running in this patched version. This new vulnerability would cause the ICS owner to lose visibility of the PLC via the web portal. Using the same tool on a HMI, we found that it would become unresponsive during a flood, resuming some time after the flood stopped. On that same HMI, we found default credentials in an online manual which would provide access to change its configuration, where no credentials are given with the device. For the HMI DoS, a CVE will be issued, and for the default password, the manual will be revised to state this risk.

Using standard web-scanners as unauthenticated/authenticated users, OWASP ZAP found that the Siemens S7-1200 web portal was found to have

---

[7] https://github.com/NewEraCracker/LOIC.

a high-criticality Open Redirect (CWE-601), which, given a malicious URL, the PLC would redirect users to an arbitrary website. We manually validated the scanner's findings for each identified weakness as part of a validation exercise. Burpsuite, however, did not find this vulnerability due to the implementation of the login form, where ZAP was able to follow the login process without any issues. Siemens confirmed this was an related issue to CVE-2015-1048 and will be patched.

For HMI2 (Siemens KTP700), which was unaffected by the Denial of Service tests, we found that part of its configuration was sent in the clear using Wireshark to capture the configuration process, leaking content which would be displayed on the screen. Siemens confirmed this as an issue, issuing CVE-2020-7592 in response to our disclosure. Finally, on the PLC which was not vulnerable to Web and Denial of Service issues, we found that where the web server requires authentication, an alternative entry point (found by using nmap) was found, where reverse engineering the app commands and submitting them to this entry point would give the user access to the same functionality without using a web portal. The vendor said the device should only be used on trusted networks. The vector was valid, but users should use the PLC in a secure environment.

Discussion: Using these techniques, we find six new vulnerabilities in ICS devices for which we are completing responsible disclosure with the respective vendors. All are CVE-worthy but have differing severity. For PLC1, an adversary could control the PLC state, and the web interface of PLC2 could redirect the user to a malicious website with more serious consequences. In PLC3, the visibility of the PLC is lost via the web portal, but its logic continues to run, which we believe not to be critical. For HMI1, the default credentials is not a critical issue, with the denial of service a more critical issue, as the operator may not be able to interact with the system. In the case of HMI2, the cleartext data issue is not critical, as more sensitive information, e.g. credentials, are encrypted.

5   Conclusion

ICS security has important differences to standard IT, such as vulnerability classes and detection. By analysing nine years of ICS vulnerability reports, identifying trends and suggesting eight new categories for classifying ICS vulnerabilities based on detection methods, we can better inform ICS owners and vendors on the types of ICS vulnerabilities, how they can be detected and prioritised for resolution. We discuss easy automated and in-depth testing methods for ICS owners and experts, validating our results on six months of new reports and analysing five pieces of ICS equipment, finding four new critical vulnerabilities.

Acknowledgements. Funding for this paper was provided by the National Cyber Security Centre UK (NCSC UK), Research Institute in Trustworthy Inter-Connected Cyber-Physical Systems (RITICS) and the UK Rail Research and Innovation Network (UKRRIN). We thank the Bristol Cyber Security Group for providing access to an additional device for testing.

References

1. Andreeva, O., et al.: Industrial Control Systems Vulnerabilities Statistics. Kaspersky Lab, Report (2016)
2. Antrobus, R., Green, B., Frey, S., Rashid, A.: The forgotten I in IIoT: a vulnerability scanner for industrial internet of things. IET (2019)
3. Antrobus, R., Frey, S., Green, B., Rashid, A.: SimaticScan: towards a specialised vulnerability scanner for industrial control systems. In: 4th International Symposium for ICS & SCADA Cyber Security Research (2016)
4. Beresford, D.: Exploiting Siemens Simatic S7 PLCs. Black Hat USA (2011)
5. Biham, E., Bitan, S., Carmel, A., Dankner, A., Malin, U., Wool, A.: Rogue7: Rogue Engineering-Station attacks on S7 Simatic PLCs. Black Hat USA (2019)
6. Dragos: CRASHOVERRIDE: Analysis of Threat to Electric Grid Operations (2017)
7. Dragos: 2018 Year in Review - Industrial Controls System Vulnerabilities (2018)
8. Dragos: 2019 Year in Review - ICS Vulnerabilities (2019)
9. Falliere, N., Murchu, L.O., Chien, E.: W32. stuxnet dossier. White paper, Symantec Corp., Security Response (2011)
10. Gonzalez, D., Alhenaki, F., Mirakhorli, M.: Architectural security weaknesses in industrial control systems (ics) an empirical study based on disclosed software vulnerabilities. In: 2019 IEEE International Conference on Software Architecture (ICSA) (2019)
11. Hankin, C., Chothia, T., M3, P., Popov, P., Rashid, A., Sezer, S.: Availability of Open Source Tool-Sets for CNI-ICS (2018)
12. Hemsley, K.E., Fisher, E., et al.: History of Industrial Control System Cyber Incidents. Technical report (2018)
13. Hui, H., McLaughlin, K.: Investigating current PLC security issues regarding Siemens S7 communications and TIA portal. In: 5th International Symposium for ICS & SCADA Cyber Security Research (2018)
14. Industrial Control Systems Cyber Emergency Response Team: ICS-CERT Annual Assessment Report FY 2016 (2016)
15. Jiang, Y., Atif, Y., Ding, J.: Cyber-physical systems security based on a cross-linked and correlated vulnerability database. In: Nadjm-Tehrani, S. (ed.) CRITIS 2019. LNCS, vol. 11777, pp. 71–82. Springer, Cham (2020). https://doi.org/10.1007/978-3-030-37670-3_6
16. Johnson, B., Caban, D., Krotofil, M., Scali, D., Brubaker, N., Glyer, C.: Attackers Deploy New ICS Attack Framework "TRITON" and Cause Operational Disruptionto Critical Infrastructure (2017)
17. Kaspersky ICS CERT: Threat Landscape for Industrial Automation Systems (2019)
18. Khan, R., Maynard, P., McLaughlin, K., Laverty, D., Sezer, S.: Threat analysis of blackenergy malware for synchrophasor based real-time control and monitoring in smart grid. In: 4th International Symposium for ICS & SCADA Cyber Security Research (2016)
19. Nelson, T., Chaffin, M.: Common cybersecurity vulnerabilities in industrial control systems. Control Systems Security Program (2011)
20. Niedermaier, M., et al.: You snooze, you lose: measuring PLC cycle times under attacks. In: 12th USENIX Workshop on Offensive Technologies (WOOT) (2018)
21. OWASP: OWASP Top 10–2017: The Ten Most Critical Web Application Security Risks (2017)

Self Adaptive Privacy in Cloud Computing Environments: Identifying the Major Socio-Technical Concepts

Angeliki Kitsiou[1]([✉]), Eleni Tzortzaki[2], Christos Kalloniatis[1], and Stefanos Gritzalis[3]

[1] Privacy Engineering and Social Informatics Laboratory, Department of Cultural Technology and Communication, University of the Aegean, GR 81100 Lesvos, Greece
{a.kitsiou,chkallon}@aegean.gr
[2] Information and Communication Systems Security Laboratory, Department of Information and Communications Systems Engineering, University of the Aegean, GR 83200 Samos, Greece
etzortzaki@aegean.gr
[3] Laboratory of Systems Security, Department of Digital Systems, University of Piraeus, GR 18532 Piraeus, Greece
sgritz@unipi.gr

Abstract. Privacy protection within Cloud Computing Environments (CCE) is extremely complex to be realized, due to multiple stakeholders' interactions that lead to several privacy risks and leaks. Therefore, the necessity for self-adaptive privacy preserving schemes, in order to safeguard users' privacy by considering their social and technological context within CCE is highlighted. Our analysis has indicated that a group of criteria should be satisfied in order to support this aim. However, it is pointed out that the criteria concerning the identification of users' social needs and stakeholders' technical privacy needs are not sufficiently satisfied, failing to determine which stakeholders' privacy aspects should be examined and how. Towards this, the paper points out that Self Adaptive Privacy within CCE should be addressed as an emerged interdisciplinary research area, since the identified criteria concern both users' social norms and technical privacy artifacts. Based on these criteria, the social and technical privacy aspects that should be considered from both users' and developers' perspective are discussed, leading to the identification of the socio-technical concepts and their interdependencies that should be taken into account. It proposes that a proper research design regarding Self Adaptive Privacy within CCE should be built, based on an interrelated three-layered examination that concerns users', developers' and CCE context, aiming to lay the ground for the identification of the Self-Adaptive Privacy related requirements within CCE.

Keywords: Self adaptive privacy · Cloud computing environments · Users' social norms · Developers' perceptions · Privacy risks

© Springer Nature Switzerland AG 2020
S. Katsikas et al. (Eds.): CyberICPS 2020/SECPRE 2020/ADIoT 2020, LNCS 12501, pp. 117–132, 2020.
https://doi.org/10.1007/978-3-030-64330-0_8

1 Introduction

Privacy, as a socially constructed phenomenon, is differentiated across diverse social and technical contexts and frames becoming even more perplexed within Cloud Computing Environments (CCE) [1–4]. CCE, whose services are usually developed either in-house or built by third-party providers [5], provide multidimensional capabilities and flexibility, enhancing multiple interactions and dependences among social actors and service providers [6]. Thus, these interactions result in a huge amount of information disclosure that alters users' personal information management [7]. For instance, CCE for e-commerce or medical care domains require a great amount of users' analyzed personal and sensitive information (e.g. name, social security number), so as for their services to be provided. This ubiquitous data analysis impacts on users' privacy protection either due to misuse or disclosure of such information without users' consent, raising consequently plenty of privacy leaks [8]. Particularly, with regard to Social Network Sites (SNS), as the most widespread CCE, a large body of previous research has indicated users' and systems' inability to manage privacy issues [9–11]. Towards this, Self-Adaptive Privacy approaches have been developed. Self-Adaptive privacy aims at safeguarding users' privacy by providing holistic user models, considering their socio-cultural and technological context [12]. Although several self-adaptive privacy models and mechanisms have been introduced, these are limited to piecemeal analyses, focusing either on users' fragmented socio-contextual characteristics exploration that impact on their privacy management or solely on privacy software and CCE artifacts [8]. However, rethinking about privacy protection in CCE with focus on both users' social norms and software engineering is immense [1, 3, 13, 14]. This emergence is even more crucial due to the General Data Protection Regulation (GDPR) enforcement in Europe, which brought significant changes on citizens' privacy rights, as well as new obligations for data controllers and processors [15]. Thus, previous literature – to our best knowledge-has not yet provided a structured framework that incorporates both social and technical privacy prerequisites for an adequate self adaptive privacy approach within CCE to be developed, while it is not still clear, which social and technical aspects of privacy should be explored and how.

Towards this, by examining previous works, we point out that Self Adaptive Privacy within CCE should be addressed as an emerged interdisciplinary research area, due to the identification of a group of criteria that should be satisfied in order for self-adaptive privacy protections schemes to be effectively designed. These criteria concern both users' social norms and technical privacy artifacts. Based on these identified criteria, we discuss which social and technical privacy aspects should be considered from both users' and developers' perspective. Gradually, the elicited aspects assist on capturing the socio-technical concepts that a research design regarding Self-Adaptive Privacy within CCE should include under an integrated spectrum. In this regard, our work proposes that a research design regarding Self-Adaptive Privacy within CCE should be built, based on an interrelated three-layered examination. This examination focuses on: a) a more thoroughly investigation of users' social attributes based on sociological identity and capital theories, b) the role of the developers' perceptions regarding the proper technical privacy requirements in CCE and c) the influencing CCE factors, indicating their independences. Therefore, our work aims at laying the ground for the identification of the Self-Adaptive Privacy related requirements within CCE and at providing researchers with a further insight for this research area.

The rest of the paper is organized as follows. Section 2 analyses the emerging of Self Adaptive Privacy Aware Systems within CCE. In Sect. 3.1. we present which social aspects of privacy should be considered, drawing on social identity and social capital, in order for the users' social privacy norms to be indicated, while in Sect. 3.2. the importance of developers' perceptions regarding technical privacy challenges and affordances within CCE is indicated. In Sect. 4 our proposed examination in which a research design for Self Adaptive Privacy within CCE should be based, is demonstrated. Finally, Sect. 5 concludes our work and suggests future research aims.

2 Self-adaptive Privacy Within Cloud Computing Environments (CCE)

Since CCE are gradually developing, new challenges for both providers and users are posed especially as far as privacy protection concerns [7]. These challenges derive from the potential dynamic changes and combination of cloud services, as well as due to the different privacy features utilized in each cloud service distribution and deployment model [16]. Furthermore, the provision of these services includes the access, collection, storage and disclosure of personal information, often by third parties as well, while data loss and data breaches have been acknowledged as the most essential risks that should be addressed [17]. The loss of direct control from local to remote cloud servers, the virtualization that brings new risks to users' authentication and authorization, the non-technical issues related to the technical solutions [17], the low degree of transparency and privacy assurance provided into customers operations [18], the sharing of platforms among users and the non-compliance with enterprise policies and legislation leading to the loss of reputation and credibility [16], are some of the most important issues that raise privacy risks within CCE. Additional reasons, from users' perspective, concern the association of these privacy risks with users' personalization in social and spatial level and the delineation of their behavior within CCE [19], the users' personal information disclosure willingly or not [20], the users' failure to read or understand privacy policies or to anticipate downstream data uses [21], the stationary and complexity of privacy protection software that make the adoption and applicability by users a hard case [22].

These rapid privacy risks within CCE, due to users' social norms and technology affordances on information collection, storage, disclosure and analysis [23], require more sophisticated and targeted privacy services according to their needs [7, 24] in order for their privacy to be effectively protected. To meet this need, the design of Self Adaptive Privacy Aware Systems [6, 25, 26] is highlighted. Self-Adaptive privacy aims at safeguarding users' privacy by providing holistic user models, considering their sociocultural and technological context [12]. In this regard, self-adaptive privacy systems should have the ability to maintain users' privacy in changing contexts, either by providing users with recommendations or by proceeding to automated actions based on users' decisions for personal information disclosure or not, within their context [27]. In order for the Systems to meet these needs, standards of specific functions should be satisfied, as those briefly outlined as follows. According to [28], classified interaction strategies concerning users' privacy protection should be applied, which facilitate the connection of the system (through three phases: a) privacy awareness, b) justification & privacy decision, c) control capabilities with users' cognitive processes for their privacy settings. Users should be provided with adequate opportunities to express preferences and give feedback in relation to the justification and the findings of privacy settings adjustment. What is more, according to [9], users should be offered with the possibility of selective information disclosure, by providing the context and the control level over the information they want to reveal. To employ that, four operations should be performed: a) monitoring, b) analysis, c) design d) implementation, utilizing framework models-identifying user's environment and interconnections as well as their role in the system- and behavioral models, in order to identify features to control, detect threats before data disclosure and calculate users' benefit in comparison to data disclosure cost. Finally, according to [24], the systems should be adapted to the interoperability of technologies, to the structure of the systems and the behavior within users' natural environment. They should also be capable of determining privacy requirements and the values of the involved groups, of diagnosing threats based on these values and of determining users' sensitive information so as to balance between privacy choices automation and users' choices, demanding short time investment regarding their operation training. The aforementioned analysis reveals a number of criteria that should be considered in order to reason about privacy under a socio-technical view.

Figure 1 proposes a grouping of the identified criteria, concerning: a) the identification of users' privacy social needs in each context, b) the identification of all stakeholders' privacy technical needs, c) the identification of privacy risks and threats, d) the indication of users' sensitive information in each context, e) the systems' adaption to the interoperability of technologies, f) the assessment of the best options among users' and systems' privacy choices and g) an effective decision-making procedure to be followed, which balances users' social and privacy needs.

Following these criteria, it is indicated that for the successful design of the Self Adaptive Privacy Systems in CCE, it is essential to consider empirical data related to users' social characteristics within their interacting frameworks in and out of the information systems [28]. However, despite the fact that many self-adaptive privacy solutions under the differential privacy scheme [29] or under the context-adaptive privacy scheme [30–32], have been suggested, they were subsequent to many limitations. These works satisfied only specific parameters, such as: anonymity, systems' access control architecture, noise insertion, sensitive ratings based on social recommendation or streams data aggregation in real time, users' personal privacy risks contrary to their disclosure benefits within pervasive scenarios, the location parameter. Kumar and Naik [33] proposed an Adaptive Privacy Policy framework to protect users' pictures within cloud, taking into consideration users' social settings and the content of their pictures, while other studies related to the deployment of self adaptive privacy systems in SNSs [34–36] considered users' social characteristics. However, they specified these social aspects only on the basis of the systems' usage. In this regard, several challenges could not be addressed, since only static data were considered, while most of them did not consider real-time aggregated data with high accuracy and furthermore users' socio-contextual attributes

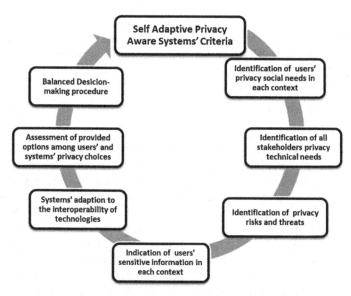

Fig. 1. Self Adaptive Privacy Aware Systems' Satisfaction Criteria

were examined fragmentally, focalizing separately either on space or time. Especially, the lack of the proper identification of users' social context and the failure of correlating users' privacy concerns with the privacy infrastructural choices provided by the system have led respectively to the dissatisfaction of the privacy technical requirements as well [9].

3   Exploring Socio-technical Aspects

Given the above analysis, it is clear that a number of criteria should be satisfied in order for efficient self-adaptive privacy solutions to be provided within CCE. However, the analysis brought to the forefront that previous self-adaptive privacy schemes do not efficiently address the satisfaction of those criteria, which require an adequate bridging of stakeholders' privacy social and technical aspects. In particular, it is indicated that a great emphasis is required regarding the identification of users' social needs in each context. The satisfaction of this criterion is of great importance, since this identification will provide the self-adaptive privacy system with the proper information in order for the system to offer privacy choices that balance between users' will for preserving personal information or disclosing them. However, little attention has been given in previous literature on how to identify effectively these social needs. Therefore, in order for this criterion to be satisfied, it is immense to understand which social parameters affect users' interpretations and values about privacy, so as to indicate their social privacy norms. Furthermore, the criterion of the identification of all stakeholders' privacy technical needs is also crucial. Sufficient self-adaptive privacy systems should have the ability to address the technological possibilities and limitations deriving from CCE, satisfying all stakeholders' needs. Consequently, the identification of which technical privacy requirements should be prioritized and be chosen and how this procedure is realized, is also required. The determination of the social and technical aspects that influence these criteria is a critical step so that the elicitation of the functional and non-functional Self-Adaptive Privacy related requirements within CCE to be achieved.

3.1 Users' Social Aspects

Privacy has been recognized as a fundamental individual and social principle in contemporary societies, without, though, reflecting a standard social reality [22] and consequently it is defined as multifaceted. Within CCE, a solid and clear definition of privacy becomes an even more complex procedure. For instance, within SNS, in order for users to utilize their services, several information disclosures are required due to system's privacy settings, making this a common practice within SNS [37]. SNS's structure puts in question the notion of privacy within socio-technical contexts, making indistinguishable the boundaries among public and private sphere [1]. The technical features and software of SNS not only alter users' constructs for their functioning and purpose, but they also alter how users actually employ these features for sharing information and managing privacy, while interacting with other users [8, 11, 13]. In this regard, individuals' personal interpretations and values about privacy are respectively formatted according to users' whole context [38] both online and offline. Therefore, privacy in SNSs is not just a personal matter, which depends on users' options, but it constitutes a social dynamic and ongoing process [4], by which users balance among their social needs and their needs for privacy. Despite the fact that these social needs have been acknowledged to regulate the concept of privacy [1, 3, 14, 23], they have not been thoroughly examined, identified or correlated, especially in ways that could help researchers to provide adequate adaptive privacy solutions that satisfies users' social needs [2, 13, 23]. One of the most important social factors, which has been indicated by privacy literature [10, 37, 39] to determine users' social and privacy needs, is social capital. Nevertheless, the complex interrelation between social capital and privacy has not been explored adequately [2, 37], due to fragmentary users' social capital benefits examination, which is not related with their specific social context both online and offline. Furthermore, users' social norms reflect also the reciprocal arrangements of the community they belong, depending on their specific context [1, 14]. Therefore, to gain a further understanding of how social capital mediates the balance between users' social and privacy needs, the examination of a variety of users' social attributes under a specific context is required. Thus, users' social attributes have been also fragmentary explored, irrespective of social capital benefits. Previous literature has highlighted the importance of identity theories to examine these and how they affect privacy management within SNS [4, 40]. Social identity indicates how users define their behaviour, based on social attributes that express their self-inclusive social categories and their personal idiosyncratic attitudes [41], while it impacts on social capital creation [29]. However, previous research focuses only on users' digital identity, despite the fact that several works indicate that many privacy breaches within SNS derive from the disclosure of users' real identity information, reflecting both their online and offline reality. Additionally, social identity, as a dynamic and ongoing process [42], leads often to multiple and overlapping identities that respectively define users' different behaviours within each different context [41]. Although privacy managing issues arise from users' multiple identities or due to the influence of the other members of their groups [4, 43], still these users' complex social contexts have been overlooked. The following Fig. 2 represents the current literature state regarding the exploration of the social aspects of privacy, indicating its limitations.

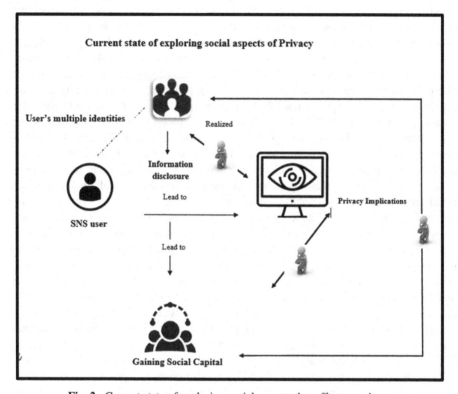

Fig. 2. Current state of exploring social aspects that affect on privacy

Therefore, the research question posed is RQ1: *how to capture efficiently users' social attributes in and out of informational systems that affect their privacy management within CCE, in order to develop the proper behavioral models, which will enable an optimal design for self-adaptive privacy preserving schemes.*

3.2   Exploring Technical Privacy Aspects

On the other side, the non-correspondence of privacy software to integration and inter-operability challenges in CCE, in order for the users' digital and social needs to be satisfied, has been recognized [24]. Furthermore, it is still not clear the process in which privacy is introduced into software and in cyber-physical systems in general, and how its requirements are understood [44]. Usually, it is solely dealt by the developers as a technical set of requirements that are satisfied after the implementation of the respective functional requirements of the system to be [45]. Thus, little attention has been given to the role that developers play during privacy engineering and the ways that developers understand and apply privacy [44]. In particular, within CCE, privacy design and its implementation are still major issues due to the Cloud technical complexities, but also due to the heterogeneity of the whole system [46], while the role of developers is also unclear. Nonetheless, privacy requirements within CCE have not been developed efficiently in order to identify their distinctive features [47], established encryption methods are not adequate to address the needs of privacy protection, while privacy leaks may be widely differentiated according to the CCE that is utilized [16]. In this regard, an accurate methodology that will provide software developers with the ability to determine which technical requirements should be prioritized accordingly to the proper cloud service provider pursuant to these, is lacking [44, 46], while users' social requirements are usually ignored [13]. Several reasons have been highlighted for this, concerning: the insufficient system design [9], the challenges which cloud providers face, such as the sheer volume of big data residing in cloud data centers that require time and cost to be accessed, the fact that data and resources distribution to users in cloud environments needs to be improved because it complicates resource segregation, the severe lack of policies, procedures and techniques for addressing malware in virtual machines, which cloud services utilize, in order to facilitate an investigation for a user's privacy breach in cloud forensics, as well as the limited privacy choices offered by cloud providers to users [7, 48, 49]. Additionally, the different legal jurisdiction of each country in which cloud services are hosted, results in various definitions of privacy protection and in multiple frameworks for privacy applicability. This complicates even more the way developers understand and apply privacy. For instance, GDPR has practically recognized the need to ensure users' data technical privacy protection in accordance with the legal prerequisites, aiming to provide developers with guidelines. Towards this, it has introduced in its framework the principle of Privacy by Design (PbD), as the most appropriate approach to fulfil the adequate technical privacy requirements [50]. Privacy by design approaches include privacy aspects as part of the requirements analysis along with the functional requirements, addressing more holistically privacy-aware systems and services' design [46]. Several PbD goal-oriented privacy requirements engineering methodologies have been introduced to support privacy design from its early stage, e.g. PRIPARE [51], the RBAC methodology, PROPAN methodology, the i* method, the STRAP method, the LINDDUN method [52], while Islam, Mouratidis & Weippl in [48] proposed a framework, focusing on CCE, by which security and privacy risks are analyzed as a decision-making procedure. However, plenty of criticism has been raised for the PbD approaches, focusing on the ways that they can be applied by the developers during engineering [44]. Some of them are either generic enough to address the proper requirements within the broad range of CCE or they focus on individual agents' goals rather than examining the system under a holistic view. Additionally, others were more security than privacy oriented.

An interested approach concerns the extended version of PriS methodology, an established PbD approach, which focused on cloud computing [46]. PriS introduced nine cloud-based privacy concepts, namely: *Isolation, Provenanceability, Traceability, Interveanability, CSA Accountability, Anonymity, Pseudonymity, Unlinkability, Undetectability and Unobservability*, which are considered as systems' organisational goals (privacy goals). These goals constraint the causal transformation of organisational goals into processes, and, by using privacy-process patterns, they describe the impact of privacy goals to the affected organisational processes in order to cover the gap between CCE system design and privacy implementation phase. The applicability of these cloud-based concepts, presented through a conceptual meta-model, has been tested on a real case study, where it was founded to be usable by all stakeholders. However, in order for a PbD approach to be applied in a viable way, it is essential to understand developers' point of view [44]. Previous literature has indicated the necessity to understand how developers interpret and apply privacy, since in many cases developers were willing to trade off the level of privacy offered to end users in order to achieve better usability of the system [44]. In this regard, the question posed concerns on RQ2: *how developers define the optimal identification of technical requirements within CCE, in order to meet efficiently both users' social requirements and systems' technical ones before performing adaptive privacy mechanisms.*

4 Self Adaptive Privacy Concepts Within CCE

Our analysis on previous works regarding self-adaptive privacy within CCE has indicated that a group of criteria should be satisfied in order to support its aim for safeguarding users' privacy by considering their social and technological context. However, by examining previous literature, we pointed out that, among these criteria, the identification of users' social needs and the identification of all stakeholders' technical privacy needs are not sufficiently satisfied. This highlights the need for the thoroughly investigation of users' social norms intertwined with the appropriate technical privacy affordances, so as privacy preservation to be achieved in a self-adaptive user-centric way within CCE. Consequently, our analysis has shown the emerge of determining users' social attributes in and out of informational systems (RQ1) and of defining the developers' perceptions regarding the proper privacy technical requirements within CCE (RQ2).

To address that issue from a starting point of view, we argue that a targeted research design in this area should examine these research questions under an integrated interdisciplinary spectrum, in order to indicate and capture all the relevant concepts of self-adaptive privacy within CCE. In this regard, and inspired from [53] work in holistic security requirements analysis for socio-technical systems, we propose that a proper research design should be built, based on a high level structured examination, which aims to indicate the aspects that derive not only from stakeholders' social and technical privacy parameters, but also from CCE infrastructural ones that impact on privacy management. In this sense, our proposed examination, illustrated in Fig. 3, incorporates all systems stakeholders' privacy contexts, suggesting which concepts should be examined, deriving from both sociological and privacy literature. It also contemplates, as a main concept to be investigated, the privacy risks due to CCE structure. Therefore, it is based on the determination of three Layers that represent the stakeholders' privacy contexts, namely: the Social, the Software and the Infrastructure Layer. Each layer includes the proposed concepts that should be considered and investigated, in order for specific tasks to be implemented, leading to the identification, for each Layer separately, of the respectively three-dimensional Self Adaptive privacy related requirements.

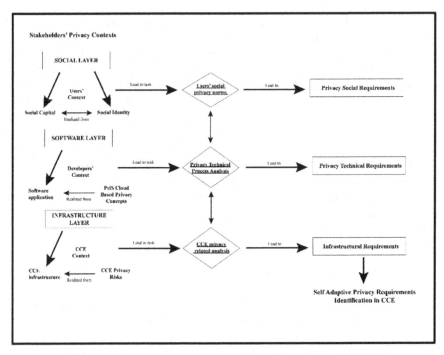

Fig. 3. Identifying the concepts of Self Adaptive Privacy within CCE

4.1 Social Layer:

Social Layer concerns the users' context determination. Aiming to address the question of how users' social attributes should be captured, the Social identity and Social capital concepts, as the central social factors indicated by previous literature to affect privacy management within CCE [4, 37], are considered to be examined. Social identity can be an important interpretative tool, indicating users' different identities and their overlapping degree in and out of the CCE, as well as users' belonging to several social groups that influence their privacy attitudes and behaviours. Social capital affects the balance among users' social interaction and privacy needs, indicating why users are willing to disclosure personal information within CCE. Contrary to previous privacy literature, the two concepts are suggested to be not only considered separately, but in combination as well, since they constitute interactive concepts that reinforce one another. The interrelation of these concepts and their thoroughly investigation will provide valuable insight for users' context, and it will lead to the task of users' social privacy norms analysis, in order for the respective social requirements to be identified. By this way, not only users' social privacy norms can be reflected, but also the ones that derive from the communities' in which they belong to, related to the CCE they utilize.

4.2 Software Layer:

Software Layer concerns the developers' context. In order to meet the question of how developers define the optimal identification of technical requirements within CCE, the

Cloud based Privacy Concepts proposed and applied by PriS method [45] are considered to be under examination. Developers' perceptions should be examined in order to identify if the extended version of PriS methodology is able, according to them, to provide the effective means for analyzing privacy requirements in frequently changing contexts, such as CCE. Since researchers' understanding is quite limited regarding the ways that developers understand and attend privacy [44], developers' perceptions should be examined regarding the suitability of the Isolation, Provenanceability, Traceabillity, Interveanability, CSA Accountability, Anonymity, Pseudonymity, Unlinkability, Undetectability and Unobservability concepts, indicating which of these cloud- based privacy properties can be included as part of the self-adaptive privacy requirements analysis. This examination will enable the technical privacy process task to be realized, highlighting the fitted technical self-adaptive privacy requirements' identification related to CCE openness and fluidity.

4.3 Infrastructure Layer:

This Layer concerns the determination of CCE context and of its impact on users' and developers' privacy implications, since previous literature has shown the failure of CCE provided privacy features, resulting in the dissatisfaction of both social and privacy technical requirements. The privacy risks are introduced as the main concept that should be examined. Privacy risks derive from the CCE technical features and the resources that support users' privacy preferences and software deployment. Its examination will lead to the task of CCE infrastructure' privacy analysis, which respectively will contribute to the identification of the infrastructural requirements of each cloud service distribution and deployment model.

4.4 Layers' Interrelation:

Besides the separate examination of the main concepts in each Layer, the interactive relationships among the three of them are also indicated, supporting that the examination of all stakeholders' privacy contexts should be elaborated under an integrated view. Their interdependencies affect the whole research procedure that will contribute to the identification of all self-adaptive privacy related requirements. Therefore, despite the fact that each one of the three Layers leads to its own set of tasks, so as for each category of privacy related requirements' identification to be realized, the interdependencies among Layers are also reflected on, indicating that the examination phase should be elaborated throughout of all the three layers, in an interdisciplinary way, utilizing research methodologies from both social and privacy literature. The Layers' bilateral interactions present the effects to each other, indicating respectively the impact of social on technical requirements identification phase and the technical on the infrastructural one and vice versa. In this regard, considering that "privacy within CCE cannot be protected in isolation for a system, but the interdependencies among users and systems should be also analysed" [7, p. 21]., the proposed by the developers privacy cloud-based concepts can be extended, including properties that derive from users' social norms and CCE infrastructure, so as to satisfy the criteria for self-adaptive privacy. Consequently, our proposal aims at making visible the significant interrelation of these centric social, technical and structural variables that affect privacy management in a self-adaptive way.

Furthermore, it, not only, indicates the necessity for an interdisciplinary examination for the Self-adaptive privacy related requirements identification to be realized, but to our best knowledge, is the first one which suggests the capturing of its dynamical concepts regarding all stakeholders' context. It also proposes a novel identification for users' context under the interrelated exploration of social identity and social capital concepts. Therefore, our proposed examination provides the ground for the development of targeted research models on self-adaptive privacy within CCE and the construction of relative measurement instruments, while it allows a further understanding of how the self adaptive related requirements can be identified, in order for suitable self-adaptive privacy schemes to the openness and the fluidity of these environments, to be designed [54]. This approach will also enhance the development of Cyber Physical Systems and Industrial Internet of Things, by facing certain difficulties related to privacy. Since their development is based on communication protocols and massive datasets, the formulation of efficient design privacy patterns is required, so as for these systems to be advance and autonomous [55].

5   Conclusion and the Future

CCE cause new privacy challenges and risks for both providers and users, while privacy safeguards within several cloud services and applications are not adequately underpinned and do not fulfill all stakeholders' complex privacy needs in different contexts [7]. Up to this, the necessity for the deployment of dynamic self-adaptive privacy schemes is indicated, as a more proper way to support users' privacy needs during their interactions within the systems [27]. Despite the fact that several self-adaptive privacy approaches have been proposed, CCE structures related to users' social norms and software deployment by the developers make hard to provide effective privacy solutions in a users' self adaptive way [1, 7, 12] and to satisfy several required criteria that derived from our analysis. Among these criteria, the identification of users' social needs and the identification of all stakeholders' technical privacy needs are inadequately addressed. Therefore, capturing the users' social attributes that impact on their privacy management and the developers' perceptions regarding privacy deployment in CCE in a self-adaptive way, is of great importance. In this regard, this paper proposes that an interdisciplinary examination should be elaborated that expands the research area of Self Adaptive Privacy within CCE, while proposing which socio-technical and infrastructural concepts should be included in a research design, so as an integrated self-adaptive privacy related requirements' identification to be achieved. The examination is presented in a three-layered visualization (Social, Software and Infrastructure Layer), indicating all stakeholders' privacy contexts and highlighting their interdependencies. Therefore, in order for users' social attributes to be adequately captured, the investigation of the social identity correlated with the social capital concept is proposed, in order for users' social privacy norms to be identified. This examination will contribute researchers to design the proper measurement instruments in order to provide insight for the development of the behavioral models that will enhance the optimal design of self-adaptive privacy preserving schemes.

Furthermore, developers' perceptions investigation regarding the appropriateness of the PriS cloud based concepts is suggested. This examination will provide researchers with further insight on developers' privacy considerations fit into software design decisions, in order to innovate and design self- adaptive privacy-preserving solutions in CCE, in contrast to traditional existing privacy methodologies. Finally, our proposed examination will enable researchers to capture the continuing privacy challenges within CCE, which affect the functional and applicable privacy software, by examining the concept of Privacy Risks within CCE. In this regard, future research aims concern the conceptualization of a Self-Adaptive Privacy cloud-based Requirements Analysis model, which can be translated in specific social and technical privacy patterns in order for the operationalization of Self-Adaptive Privacy Systems to be achieved.

Acknowledgments. This research is co-financed by Greece and the European Union *(European Social Fund- ESF)* through the Operational Programme "Human Resources Development, Education and Lifelong Learning 2014-2020" in the context of the project "Adaptive Privacy-aware Cloud-based Systems: Socio-technical requirements" (MIS:5047231)".

References

1. Martin, K.: Understanding privacy online: development of a social contract approach to privacy. J. Bus. Ethics **137**(3), 551–569 (2016)
2. Kitsiou, A., Tzortzaki, E., Kalloniatis, C., Gritzalis, S.: Towards an integrated socio-technical approach for designing adaptive privacy aware services in cloud computing. In: Benson, V. (ed.) Cyber Influence and Cognitive Threats, pp. 9–32. Elsevier (2020)
3. Sujon, Z.: The triumph of social privacy: understanding the privacy logics of sharing behaviors across social media. Int. J. Commun. **12**, 3751–3771 (2018)
4. Marwick, A.E., Boyd, D.: Networked privacy: how teenagers negotiate context in social media. New Media Soc. **16**(7), 1051–1067 (2014)
5. Badidi, E., Atif, Y., Sheng, Q.Z., Maheswaran, Muthucumaru: On personalized cloud service provisioning for mobile users using adaptive and context-aware service composition. Computing **101**(4), 291–318 (2018). https://doi.org/10.1007/s00607-018-0631-8
6. Abowd, G.D.: Beyond weiser: from ubiquitous to collective computing. Computer **49**(1), 17–23 (2016)
7. Cook, A., et al.: Internet of cloud: Security and privacy issues. In: Shankar, B., et al. (eds.) Cloud Computing for Optimization: Foundations, Applications, and Challenges, pp. 271–301. Springer (2018)
8. Knijnenburg, B.: Privacy in social information access. In: Brusilovsky, P., He, D. (eds.) Social Information Access, pp. 19–74. Springer, Cham (2018)
9. Omoronyia, I.: Reasoning with imprecise privacy preferences. In: Proceedings of the 24th International Symposium on Foundations of Software Engineering, pp. 920–923. ACM, Seattle (2016)
10. Taddicken, M.: The 'privacy paradox in the social web: the impact of privacy concerns, individual characteristics, and the perceived social relevance on different forms of self disclosure. J. Comput.-Med. Commun. **19**(2), 248–273 (2014)
11. Poller, A., Ilyes, P., Kramm, A.: Designing privacy-aware online social networks-a reflective socio-technical approach. In: Proceedings of the Conference on Computer-Supported Cooperative Work and Social Computing, pp. 23–27. ACM, Texas (2013)

12. Belk, M., et al.: Adaptive & personalized privacy & security workshop chairs' welcome and organization. In: 27th Conference on User Modeling, Adaptation and Personalization, pp. 191–192. ACM, Cyprus (2019)
13. De Wolf, R., Pierson, J.: Researching social privacy on SNS through developing and evaluating alternative privacy technologies. In: Proceedings of the Conference on Computer-Supported Cooperative Work and Social Computing. ACM, Texas (2013)
14. Nissenbaum, H.: Privacy in Context: Technology, Policy and the Integrity of Social Life. Stanford University Press, California (2009)
15. Tikkinen-Piri, C., Rohunen, A., Markkula, J.: EU general data protection regulation: changes and implications for personal data collecting companies. Comput. Law Secur. Rev. 34(1), 134–153 (2018)
16. Pearson, S.: Taking account of privacy when designing cloud computing services. In: Proceedings of the Workshop on Software Engineering Challenges of Cloud Computing, pp. 44–52. IEEE Computer Society, Canada (2009)
17. Liu, Y., Sun, Y., Ryoo, J., Rizvi, S., Vasilakos, A.V.: A survey of security and privacy challenges in cloud computing: solutions and future directions. J. Comput. Sci. Eng. 9(3), 119–133 (2015)
18. Takabi, H., Joshi, J.B., Ahn, G.J.: Security and privacy challenges in cloud computing environments. IEEE Secur. Priv. 8(6), 24–31 (2010)
19. Toch, E., Wang, Y., Cranor, L.F.: Personalization and privacy: a survey of privacy risks and remedies in personalization-based systems. User Model. User-Adap. Inter. 22(1–2), 203–220 (2012)
20. Lahlou, S.: Identity, social status, privacy and face-keeping in digital society. Soc. Sci. Inform. 47(3), 299–330 (2008)
21. Solove, D.J.: Understanding Privacy. Harvard University Press, Cambridge (2008)
22. Acquisti, A., Brandimarte, L., Loewenstein, G.: Privacy and human behavior in the age of information. Science 347(6221), 509–514 (2015)
23. Nissim, K., Wood, A.: Is privacy privacy?. Philos. Trans. Roy. Soc. A: Math. Phys. Eng. Sci. 376(2128) (2018)
24. Bennaceur, A., et al.: Feed me, feed me: an exemplar for engineering adaptive software. In: Proceedings of 11th International Symposium on Software Engineering for Adaptive and Self-Managing Systems, pp. 89–95. ACM, Texas (2016)
25. Cerf, V.G: Prospects for the internet of things. XRDS: crossroads. The ACM Mag. Stud. 22(2), 28–31 (2015)
26. Poslad, S., Hamdi, M., Abie, H.: Adaptive security and privacy management for the internet of things. In: Proceedings of International Joint Conference on Pervasive and Ubiquitous Computing, pp. 373–378. ACM, Switzerland (2013)
27. Schaub, F., Könings, B., Dietzel, S., Weber, M., Kargl, F.: Privacy context model for dynamic privacy adaptation in ubiquitous computing. In: Proceedings of the 2012 ACM Conference on Ubiquitous Computing, UbiComp, pp. 752–757. ACM, Pittsburgh (2012)
28. Schaub, F., Könings, B., Weber, M.: Context-adaptive privacy: leveraging context aware-ness to support privacy decision making. IEEE Pervasive Comput. 14(1), 34–43 (2015)
29. Phan, N., Wu, X., Hu, H., Dou, D.: Adaptive laplace mechanism: differential privacy preser-vation in deep learning. In: International Conference on Data Mining, pp. 385–394. IEEE, New Orleans, USA (2017)
30. Schaub, F., et al.: PriCal: context-adaptive privacy in ambient calendar displays. In: International Joint Conference on Pervasive and Ubiquitous Computing, pp. 499–510. ACM, USA (2014)
31. Pallapa, G., et al.: Adaptive and context-aware privacy preservation exploiting user interac-tions in smart environments. Pervasive Mob. Comput. 12, 232–243 (2014)

32. Agir, B., Papaioannou, T.G., Narendula, R., Aberer, K., Hubaux, J.-P.: User-side adaptive protection of location privacy in participatory sensing. GeoInformatica **18**(1), 165–191 (2013). https://doi.org/10.1007/s10707-013-0193-z
33. Kumar, R., Naik, M.V.: Adaptive privacy policy prediction system for user-uploaded images on content sharing sites. Int. Res. J. Eng. Technol. **5**(7), 148–154 (2018)
34. Calikli, G., et al.: Privacy dynamics: learning privacy norms for social software. In: Proceedings of 11th International Symposium on Software Engineering for Adaptive and Self-Managing Systems, pp. 47–56. ACM, Texas (2016)
35. Hoang, L.N., Jung, J.J.: Privacy-aware framework for matching online social identities in multiple social networking services. Cybern. Syst. **46**(1–2), 69–83 (2015)
36. Bilogrevic, I., Huguenin, K., Agir, B., Jadliwala, M., Hubaux, J.P.: Adaptive information-sharing for privacy-aware mobile social networks. In: Proceedings of International Joint Conference on Pervasive and Ubiquitous Computing, pp. 657–666. ACM, Switzerland (2013)
37. Stutzman, F., Vitak, J., Ellison, N. B., Gray, R., Lampe, C.: Privacy in interaction: exploring disclosure and social capital in facebook. In: Proceedings of 6th Annual International Conference on Weblogs and Social Media, pp. 330–337. AAAI Publications, Ireland (2012)
38. Patkos, T., et al.: Privacy-by-norms privacy expectations in online interactions. In: Proceedings of 2015 IEEE International Conference on Self-Adaptive and Self-Organizing Systems Workshops, pp. 1–6. IEEE Computer Science, USA (2015)
39. Shane-Simpson, C., Manago, A., Gaggi, N., Gillespie-Lynch, K.: Why do college students prefer Facebook, Twitter, or Instagram? Site affordances, tensions between privacy and self-expression, and implications for social capital. Comput. Hum. Behav. **86**, 276–288 (2018)
40. Shafie, L., Nayan, S., Osman, N.: Constructing identity through Facebook profiles: online identity and visual impression management of university students in Malaysia. Soc. Behav. Sci. **65**, 134–140 (2012)
41. Hogg, M., Abrams, D., Brewer, M.: Social identity: the role of self in group processes and intergroup relations. Group Processes Intergroup Relat. **20**(5), 570–581 (2017)
42. Kramer, R.M.: Social identity and social capital: the collective self at work. Int. Public Manage. J. **9**(1), 25–45 (2006)
43. Wessels, B.: Identification and the practices of identity and privacy in everyday digital communication. New Media Soc. **14**(8), 1251–1268 (2012)
44. Hadar, I., et al.: Privacy by designers: software developers' privacy mindset. Empirical Softw. Eng. **23**(1), 259–289 (2017). https://doi.org/10.1007/s10664-017-9517-1
45. Kalloniatis, C.: Increasing internet users trust in the cloud computing era: the role of privacy. J. Mass Commun. J. **6**(3) (2016)
46. Kalloniatis, C.: Incorporating privacy in the design of cloud-based systems: a conceptual meta-model. Inform. Comput. Secur. **25**(5), 614–633 (2017)
47. Kalloniatis, C., Mouratidis, H., Vassilis, M., Islam, S., Gritzalis, S., Kavakli, E.: Towards the design of secure and privacy-oriented information systems in the cloud: identifying the major concepts. Comput. Stand. Interfaces **36**(4), 759–775 (2014)
48. Islam, S., Mouratidis, H., Weippl, E.R.: A goal-driven risk management approach to support security and privacy analysis of cloud-based system. In: Security Engineering for Cloud Computing: Approaches and Tools, pp. 97–122. IGI Global (2013)
49. Poisel, R., Tjoa, S.: Discussion on the challenges and opportunities of cloud forensics. In: Quirchmayr, G., Basl, J., You, I., Xu, L., Weippl, E. (eds.) CD-ARES 2012. LNCS, vol. 7465, pp. 593–608. Springer, Heidelberg (2012). https://doi.org/10.1007/978-3-642-32498-7_45
50. Romanou, A.: The necessity of the implementation of privacy by design in sectors where data protection concerns arise. Comput. Law Secur. Rev. **34**(1), 99–110 (2018)
51. Notario, N., et al.: PRIPARE: Integrating privacy best practices into a privacy engineering methodology. In: Proceedings of the Security and Privacy Workshops,, pp. 151–158. ACM, California (2015)

52. Pattakou, A., Mavroeidi, A.G., Diamantopoulou, V., Kalloniatis, C., Gritzalis, S.: Towards the design of usable privacy by design methodologies. In: Proceedings of the 5th International Workshop on Evolving Security & Privacy Requirements Engineering, pp. 1–8. IEEE, Canada (2018)
53. Li, T., Horkoff, J., Mylopoulos, J.: Holistic security requirements analysis for socio-technical systems. Softw. Syst. Model. **17**(4), 1253–1285 (2016). https://doi.org/10.1007/s10270-016-0560-y
54. Anthonysamy, P., Rashid, A., Chitchyan, R.: Privacy requirements: present & future. In: Proceedings of the 39th International Conference on Software Engineering: Software Engineering in Society Track, pp 13–22. IEEE Press, Piscataway (2017)
55. Hassan, M.U., Rehmani, M.H., Chen, J.: Differential privacy techniques for cyber physical systems: a survey. IEEE Commun. Surv. Tutorials **22**(1), 746–789 (2020)

SECPRE Workshop

Definition and Verification of Security Configurations of Cyber-Physical Systems

Ángel Jesús Varela-Vaca[1]($\boxtimes$), David G. Rosado[2], Luis Enrique Sánchez[2],
María Teresa Gómez-López[1], Rafael M. Gasca[1],
and Eduardo Fernández-Medina[2]

[1] Dpto. Lenguajes y Sistemas de Informóticos, IDEA Research Group, Universidad de Sevilla, Seville, Spain
{ajvarela,maytegomez,gasca}@us.es
[2] Dpto. Tecnologías y Sistemas de Información, GSyA Research Group, Universidad Castilla-La Mancha, Ciudad Real, Spain
{david.grosado,luise.sanchez,eduardo.fdezmedina}@uclm.es

Abstract. The proliferation of Cyber-Physical Systems (CPSs) is raising serious security challenges. These are complex systems, integrating physical elements into automated networked systems, often containing a variety of devices, such as sensors and actuators, and requiring complex management and data storage. This makes the construction of secure CPSs a challenge, requiring not only an adequate specification of security requirements and needs related to the business domain but also an adaptation and concretion of these requirements to define a security configuration of the CPS where all its components are related. Derived from the complexity of the CPS, their configurations can be incorrect according to the requirements, and must be verified. In this paper, we propose a grammar for specifying business domain security requirements based on the CPS components. This will allow the definition of security requirements that, through a defined security feature model, will result in a configuration of services and security properties of the CPS, whose correctness can be verified. For this last stage, we have created a catalogue of feature models supported by a tool that allows the automatic verification of security configurations. To illustrate the results, the proposal has been applied to automated verification of requirements in a hydroponic system scenario.

Keywords: Cyber-physical system · CPS · Security · Requirement · Feature model · Configuration · Verification

1 Introduction

Cyber-physical systems (CPS) can be defined as systems that collect information from the physical environment via sensors and communication channels, analyse it via controllers and affect the physical environment and relevant processes

S. Katsikas et al. (Eds.): CyberICPS 2020/SECPRE 2020/ADIoT 2020, LNCS 12501, pp. 135–155, 2020.
https://doi.org/10.1007/978-3-030-64330-0_9

via actuators to achieve a specific goal during operation [20]. The use of CPSs facilitates the interaction between the cyberworld and the physical world, but it increases the complexity of the systems derived from the heterogeneity of the CPS components, such as sensors, actuators, embedded systems, controllers, etc.

The correlation between physical and cyber systems brings out new difficulties, that have introduced significant challenges related to security and privacy protection of CPS [15]. In particular, with the complex cyber-physical interactions, threats and vulnerabilities become difficult to assess, and new security issues arise [21], where numerous security threats appear in addition to the traditional cyberattacks [16]. This is the reason why the analysis of the cybersecurity is a key feature in the CPS architecture, to ensure that CPS capabilities are not compromised by malicious agents. Moreover, it is relevant to analyse that the information used (i.e., processed, stored or transferred) has its integrity preserved and the confidentiality is kept where needed [19].

An important lesson should be learned from the way information systems had been engineered in the past is that security often came as an afterthought [13]. If security is not taken into account very early in the development lifecycle, it is nearly impossible to engineer security requirements properly into any complex system. One of the main reasons is that security requirements are often scattered and tangled throughout system functional requirements. Therefore, the security of CPSs should be engineered "by design" early in the development of the CPSs [28,32]. Different studies show that cyber threats have increased in the CPS environment, and there is a need to research how the security requirements can be systematically handled [24,38,42].

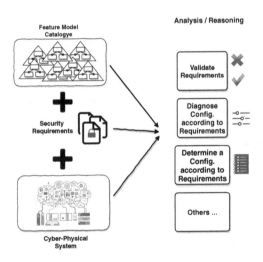

Fig. 1. Overview of the proposal.

The security requirements must include the correct configurations for the CPSs. However, the different types of components, both software and hardware, involve a high number of possible features that can participate in a CPS. Features about devices, users, platforms, and so on, can provoke a huge number of configurations, both incorrect or correct. Thereby, the description of the security requirements must restrict the incorrect configurations of the features. It implies the analysis of a very high number of possible configurations of the features, to validate if a specific CPS satisfies the defined requirements. Feature models are a well-known technique, belonged to Software Product Lines (SPLs) [8], that provide a mechanism to model and study the satisfiability of the requirements represented by a set of characteristics that can take a set of values restricted by a set of constraints. Derived from the high configurability, and that the features can be shared for various CPSs, we propose the creation of a catalogue of feature models to facilitate the automatic analysis of the security requirements in the context of CPSs. As shown in Fig. 1, the combination of these three elements (cf., Catalogue of Feature Models, Security Requirements and CPSs) will provide a mechanism for reasoning about: the validation of the requirements according to the possible configurations; the diagnosis of misconfigurations, how to ascertain the non-satisfied configurations; the creation of configurations according to the requirements and the feature models, and; other operations such as, in the case of incorrect configurations, the misconfiguration diagnosis by identifying the configuration faults.

To detail the proposal, the paper is organised as follows: Sect. 2 presents an overview of the related work. Section 3 includes a case study of CPS to introduce our proposal. Section 4 tackles the introduction of the main elements of the security requirements for a CPS, using the case study to exemplify the security requirements. Section 5 presents the second part of our proposal, where feature models are introduced as a mechanism to describe the possible correct configurations, that can be stored in a catalogue of Feature Models, and validated automatically concerning the security requirements. Finally, conclusions are drawn and future work is proposed.

2   Related Work

Currently, there is little research associated with software product lines, and security requirements, oriented to cyber-physical systems. Therefore, in this section, some of the main related researches are analyzed.

Related works have been divided into the two areas of research addressed in the article: how feature model analysis have been used in the security and software product lines fields, and; how security requirements and ontologies can be used for the modelling of risk scenarios.

2.1   Cybersecurity and Feature Model Analysis

Feature-Oriented Domain Analysis (FODA) have become mature fields in the Software Product Line (SPL) arena in the last decades [8]. Several are the scenarios where SPLs based on feature model analysis have been applied [18,40], and different researchers highlight the advantages of these systems since the use of Model-Driven Engineering (MDE) methodology and the Software Product Line (SPL) paradigm is becoming increasingly important [22]. The complexity and the high variability of a CPS, and how SPL can help were analysed in [4,7], detecting the points of variability using feature model analysis. The analysis of the variability of CPS can also support the testing [5].

Security is an understudied field in SPL area. Different approaches have been presented to manage the variability and specify security requirements from the early stages of the product line development [25–27]. Similarly, other approaches addressed the idea of including the security variability into an SPL [36]. In [17], the authors established a software architecture as a reference to develop SPL, dealing with information security aspects. SPLs are currently being targeted for application in CPS, as for some researchers, no standard provides a structured co-engineering process to facilitate the communication between safety and security engineers [11]. For other researches, the information security must be a top priority when engineering C-CPSs as the engineering artefacts represent assets of high value, and the research is focused on the generation of new security requirements stemming from risks introduced by CPSs [10].

On the other hand, there are approaches focused on the security as a use case, such as in [3] and the methodology SecPL [29], where is highlighted the importance of specifying the security requirements and product-line variability. These are annotated in the design model of any system. Other researches developed a security requirements engineering framework for CPSs, that is an extension of SREP [31]. The capacity to support the high variability in the security context though Feature Models appeared in previous papers [23], where the authors study the possible vulnerabilities to create attack scenarios, but not it does not apply to a complex scenario as the CPSs need.

2.2 Ontologies and Security Requirements for Cybersecurity

As seen in the introduction, today's cyber-physical systems require an adequate security configuration. Therefore, some researchers are focusing their research on the development of ontologies and security requirements. Some researchers have developed security tools based on ontologies capable of being integrated with the initial stages of the development process of critical systems, detecting threats and applying the appropriate security requirements to deal with these threats [35]. For other researchers, the use of tools is not enough, since, in this type of system, requirements analysis must consider the details not only of the software but also of the hardware perspective, including sensors and network security. Therefore they propose the development of a security requirements framework for CPSs, analysing the existing ones, and concluding that currently there is no suitable requirement framework for this type of systems. Therefore, they focus on proposing a security requirements engineering framework for CPSs that overcomes the problem of obtaining security requirements for heterogeneous CPS components [33,34]. Other researchers consider that CPSs have unique characteristics that limit the applicability and suitability of traditional cyber-security techniques and strategies, and therefore propose the development of a methodology of cyber-security requirements oriented to weapons systems [12]. This methodology allows us to discover solutions that improve dimensions (such as security, efficiency, safety, performance, reliability, fault tolerance and extensibility), being possible to use automated coding tools [43]. Additionally, it is also possible to take a more effective approach to understand early the security requirements, during the development of such systems, by using the STPA-Sec [37].

Therefore, we can conclude that at present different researchers have found the need to develop requirement grammars to control the security risks associated with CPSs. Moreover, derived from the complexity of the CPSs, Feature Models have been previously used in the context of the cyber-security.

3   Case Study of a Cyber-Physical System

The case study presented here, which can be seen in Fig. 2, is a CPS system for hydroponic farming, in which different components are involved, both hardware (sensors and actuators) and software (system for storage, monitoring and decision making with Big Data technology).

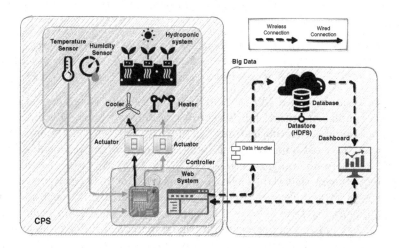

Fig. 2. CPS schema for a hydroponic farming.

The hydroponic farming is controlled by the following physical elements:

- **Temperature and humidity sensors.** They measure the existing temperature and humidity in the environment.
- **Heater and Cooler actuators.** The heater emits heat to increase the ambient temperature and the cooler moves the air to cool the environment. Both actuators are activated or deactivated from the controller.

- **Controller.** It is an Arduino device that receives the data from all the sensors and sends it (via wireless connections) from a web system to the Big Data system.

In addition to the physical part, the controller is connected to a visualisation and control system with Big Data technologies where we have deployed the following components:

- **Dashboard.** It allows the user to control the hydroponic farming in real-time and to consult statistics, as well as to interact (by switching actuators on or off) with the farming, through HTTP requests to the controller.
- **Data handler.** It is responsible for processing the sensor data, received from the controller, and storing it in the database.
- **Datastore.** It contains a Hadoop file system (HDFS) and an HBASE database where all the values coming from the sensors are saved.

4   Security Requirements for Cyber-Physical Systems

CPSs have physical, control and communication requirements, in addition to software security requirements, which make the task of identifying security requirements and translating them into the configuration of our CPS even more complicated. The security requirements represent security features of all types of assets in the system.

Definition 1. *Security Requirement*. *Let SR be a security requirement which consists of a tuple $\langle AT, SR \rangle$, where AT is a set of n assets types $\{at_1, at_2, \cdots, at_n\}$, and SF is a set of security features $\{sf_1, sf_2, \cdots, sf_m\}$.*

The set of assets types (AT) is based on the security recommendations for IoT in the context of critical infrastructures formulated by the ENISA agency [1]. Many of possible security features (SF) for CPS are obtained from OWASP [2] to extract the most important concepts (keys, encryption, protocol, network, AES, SSL, Bluetooth, range, lifetime, etc.). For instance, we can define as a security requirement that the Bluetooth communication between a sensor and a controller is encrypted using the HTTPS protocol, with AES128 encryption and a high confidentiality level. This requirement will generate certain security configurations that must be implemented in the system to ensure compliance with the requirement. This configuration will be verified as valid if the communication, protocol, encryption and confidentiality level defined in the requirement are compatible and correct.

Thereby, the elements that have been considered to define a security requirement (SR) for CPSs are mainly two, "AssetType" (AT) and "SecurityFeature" (SF). The possible values that both AT and SF can take are schematised in Fig. 3, and which are described below:

- **AssetType:** We have classified the types of assets into: "Device", "User", "Platform", "Infrastructure", "Applications and Services", and "Information and Data". Some are divided into other assets as can be seen in Fig. 3.

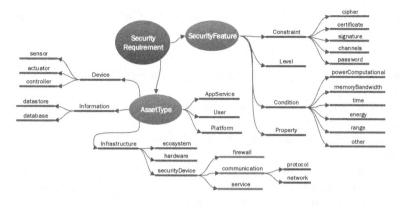

Fig. 3. Elements of a Security Requirement for CPS.

- **SecurityFeature**: This element defines the security features and needs for a security requirement, such as the associated property, the security level, or the conditions and constraints to be taken into account in a CPS.
  - **securityProperty** defines the relationship between a requirement and the security property according to the purpose and context of the requirement. For example, the protection of transmitted information is associated with the property of "Confidentiality" and "Integrity".
  - **securityLevel** indicates the level of security of the requirement and serve to prioritise the requirements during the development, which can range from a high to a low value.
  - **securityConstraint** indicates all possible security-related constraints on the system, such as the strength of passwords, what type of cryptographic or secure communication protocol is used, etc.
  - **securityCondition** indicates the limitations of a CPS that can influence the decision of how to protect the system; for example, if the device has little memory because it will not be able to support certain cryptographic algorithms, or its lifetime to properly define a correct availability service, etc.

4.1   Representation of Security Requirements in JSON

JSON claims to be a useful format for data publication and exchange in many different fields of application and many different purposes. It can be used to exchange information between different technologies, which makes it very useful and attractive to be used to represent the security requirements of a system and to be understood by any language and technology involved. We have proposed a JSON schema to represent the security requirements most easily, and that can be understood by the different applications easily. Part of the syntax of the proposed JSON schema to represent security requirements can be seen in Listings 1.1 and 1.2. This schema represents the properties indicated in Fig. 3. In

Listing 1.1 the schema for "AssetType" is shown, which is an object type with
the elements "user", "platform", "device", "infrastructure", "information" and
"appservice":

- **User** describes the possible users of the system, which are "consumer",
  "provider", "process", and "third-party".
- **Platform** includes values of "web-based services" and "Cloud infrastructure
  and services".
- **Device** contains all the devices of a CPS that are "sensor", "actuator" and
  "controller".
- **Infrastructure** defines the assets such as "ecosystem", "hardware", "security
  device" and "communication".
- **Information** determines whether the information is stored in a datastore
  and/or a database, in transit or in use.
- **AppService** defines all assets related to "analytics and visualization",
  "device and network management" and "device usage".

Listing 1.1: JSON Schema proposed. Tag: assetType

```
"AssetType": {"type":"object", "properties": {
 "user": {"type":"string",
   "enum": ["consumer","provider","process","third-party"]},
 "platform": {"type":"string",
   "enum": ["web-basedService", "CloudInfrastructure"]},
 "device": {"type":"object","minProperties":1, "maxProperties":3, "properties": {
   "sensor": {"type":"string", "enum": ["humidity","temperature", "accoustic",
         "presure","motion", "chemical","luminosity","flowmeter"]},
   "actuator": {"type":"string", "enum":["hydraulic","mechanical", "electric",
         "pneumatic","magnetic","thermal","TCP/SCP"]},
   "controller":{"type":"string","enum":["microController","microProcessor","FPGA"]}},
 "infrastructure": {"type": "object", "properties": {
   "ecosystem":{"type":"string","enum":["interface","deviceManage","embeddedSystems"]},
   "hardware": {"type": "string", "enum": ["router", "gateway", "powerSupply"] },
   "securityDevice": {"type": "object",  "properties": {
     "service": {"type": "string",
         "enum": ["CloudAuthentication", "AuthenticationSystem","IDS/IPS"]},
     "firewall": {"type": "string",  "enum": ["software", "hardware"]},
     "communication": {"type": "object",  "properties": {
       "protocol": {"type": "string", "enum": ["BLE","RFID","Wifi","ZigBee","ZWave",
           "CoAPP","MQTT","LoRaWAN"]},
       "network": {"type": "string", "enum": ["PAN","WPAN","WAN","VPN","LAN","WLAN"]}},
 "information": {"type": "object",  "properties": {
   "datastore": {"type": "string",  "enum": ["NFS","GPFS","HDFS"]},
   "database": {"type": "string",  "enum": ["SQL","NoSQL","GraphDB"]} },
 "appService": {"type": "string", "enum": ["data analytics and visualization",
     "device and network management", "device usage"]} },
```

In adittion to "AssetType" tag, in Listing 1.2 we can see the "SecurityFeature" tag with the elements '"securityProperty", '"securityLevel", "securityConstraint" and '"securityCondition":

```
Listing 1.2: JSON Schema proposed. Tag: securityFeature

"SecurityFeature": {"type": "object",  "properties": {
   "securityProperty": {"type": "array",  "items": [{"type": "string", "enum":
     ["Identification","Authentication", "Authorization","Confidentiality","Integrity",
     "Non-repudiation","Availability","Privacy","Trust","Audit","Detection"] }],
     "additionalItems": true },
   "securityLevel": {"type": "string",
     "enum": ["Very High","High", "Medium","Low","Very Low"] },
   "securityConstraint": {"type": "object", "properties": {
     "password": {"type": "string", "enum": ["strong", "weak", "multi-factor"]},
     "cipher": {"type": "string", "enum": ["AES128GCM","Camelia","ChaCha20"]},
     "channels": {"type": "string", "enum": ["SSL/TLS", "HTTPS", "Tunneling"]},
     "signature": {"type": "string", "enum": ["SRP","PSK"]},
     "certificate": {"type":"string","enum":["x509","openPGP","openSSL","SAML"]}}},
   "SecurityCondition": {"type": "object", "properties": {
     "powerComputational": {"type": "string", "enum": ["low","medium","high"]},
     "memoryBandwidth": {"type": "string", "enum": ["low","medium","high"]},
     "range": {"type": "string", "enum": ["low","medium","high"]},
     "time": {"type": "string", "enum": ["low","medium","high"]},
     "energy": {"type": "string", "enum": ["low","medium","high"]},
     "other": {"type": "string"}}
       }}}}
 "required": ["assetType","securityFeature"]
```

- **securityProperty** includes the values: "AccessControl", "Audit", "Authentication", "Authorization", "Availability", "Confidentiality", "Detection", "Identification", "Integrity", "Non-repudiation", "Privacy" and "Trust".
- **securityLevel** considers only a range of values, from a very high level of importance to a very low level of importance.
- **securityConstraint**: the elements are:
  - **password** can take the values: "strong", "weak", or "multi factor".
  - **cipher** describes the type of encryption algorithm, that can be: "Camelia", "AES128GCM" or "ChaCha20".
  - **channels** restricts the communication channels: "SSL/TLS", "HTTPS", or "Tunneling".
  - **signature** indicates if the system supports digital signature: "SRP" or "PSK".
  - **certificate** indicates the formats for the certificates managed: "x509", "openPGP", "openSSL", or "SAML".
- **securityCondition**: some features for the system, such as powerComputational, memoryBandwidth, range, time, energy, etc. They can take three possible values: "low", "medium" and "high".

4.2 Security Requirements for the Case Study

Using the notation we have presented in Sect. 4.1, we show below some examples of security requirements for our case study of the hydroponic farming. To see their expressive capacity, several requirements are defined at different levels of abstraction, which will give rise to different security configurations, which will later be verified with the features model defined in Sect. 5.3.

- **High level.** The wireless communication between the sensors and/or actuators, of the hydroponic farming, and the Arduino system must be encrypted, ensuring confidentiality. This requirement is defined in our JSON schema as is shown in Listing 1.3.

Listing 1.3: High level security requirement in JSON

```
assetType: {
  device: { sensor: "ALL",
            actuator: "ALL",
            controller: "microController" },
  information: {intransit: true}
  infrastructure: {communications:{protocol:["BLE","RFID"],network:"WPAN"}} },
securityFeature: {
  securityProperty: ["Confidentiality"],
  securityLevel: "high",
  securityContraint: {channel: "HTTPS" } }
```

- **Medium level.** The user who wants to visualise the data of the sensors of temperature and humidity of the hydroponic farming from any place must be authorised by the system of authentication. To activate an actuator like the cooler and/or the heater, the user must authenticate with a 2FA system. This requirement is defined in our JSON schema as is shown in Listing 1.4.

Listing 1.4: Medium level security requirement in JSON

```
assetType: {
    user: "consumer",
    device: { sensor: ["temperature","humidity"],
              actuator: "electric",
              controller: "microController"  },
    infrastructure: {
        securityDevice: {
            service: "AuthenticationSystem" },
            communication: { protocol: "Wifi", network: "WAN"} },
        appService: "analytics&visualization" },
securityFeature: {
    securityProperty: ["Authorization", "Authentication"],
    securityLevel: "high",
    securityContraint: { password: "multi-factor"},
    securityCondition: {other: "access authorised"} }
```

- **Low Level.** The short-range sensors of temperature and humidity are connected to an Arduino controller via Bluetooth. The transmitted information acts under the HTTP client/server protocol but the transmitted information must be secured by applying the SSL/TLS cryptographic protocol over HTTP, ensuring confidentiality. This information is stored encrypted in a local webserver with HDFS and HBASE, ensuring integrity. This requirement is defined in our JSON schema as is shown in Listing 1.5.

```
Listing 1.5: Low level security requirement in JSON

assetType: {
    platform: "web-basedService",
    device: { sensor: ["temperature","humidity"],
              controller: "microController" },
    infrastructure: { communication: {

                          protocol: ["BLE","Wifi"],
                          network: "WLAN"     } },
    information: { datastore: "HDFS", database: "NoSQL"     } },
securityFeature:
    { securityProperty: "Confidentiality",
      securityLevel: "high",
      securityContraint: { channels: "HTTPS"}
    },
    { securityProperty: "Integrity",
      securityLevel: "very high",
      securityContraint: { channels: "SSL/TLS", cipher: "AES128GCM"}
    }
}
```

5 Verification of CPS Security Requirements by Using Feature Models

The high variability of the configurations that can be included in the security requirements that involve CPSs, can generate a high number of configurations, whose verification can be very complex. Feature Models (FMs) represent a mechanism that facilitates the representation and treatment of the possible configurations. In this section, we describe how FMs can be used for automatic analysis of the configurations described and how the creation of a catalogue of feature models can be used for verifying the compliance of the security requirements described in the previous section.

5.1 Feature Models

As aforementioned, the use of Feature Models is a broad technique for analysing Feature-Oriented Domain Analysis (FODA) [8] in Software Product Lines (SPLs). Feature Models (FMs) involve a model that defines the features and their relationships.

Definition 2 Feature Model. *Let FM be a feature model which consists of a tuple (F,R), where F is a set of n features $\{f_1, f_2, \cdots, f_n\}$, and R is a set of relations $\{r_1, r_2, \cdots, r_m\}$.*

There are several notations and formalism to define FMs [6], although the most widely used is that proposed by Czarnecki [8], illustrated in Fig. 4. In general, FM diagrams are composed of six types of relations between a parent feature and its child features, although there exist extensions that enable attributes and extra-functionalities for features:

- *Mandatory* relation when child features are required (cf., Root is mandatory sub-feature of A, Root $\leftrightarrow$ A).
- *Optional* relation when child features are optional (cf., Root optional sub-feature of B, Root $\rightarrow$ B).
- *Alternative* relation when one of the sub-features must be selected (i.e., in general $a_1, a_2, \cdots, a_n$ alternative sub-feature of b, $a_1 \vee a_2 \wedge \cdots \wedge a_n \leftrightarrow \bigvee_{i<j}(a_i \vee \cdots \vee a_j))$.
- *Or-relation* when at least one of the sub-features must be selected (i.e., in general $a_1, a_2, \cdots, a_n$ or sub-feature of b, $a_1 \wedge a_2 \wedge \cdots \wedge a_n \leftrightarrow b$, in the figure $C \leftrightarrow C1 \wedge C2$).
- *Require relation*, when a feature requires the existence of other features with non-direct family relation (cf., in the figure A1 $\rightarrow$ B2).
- *Exclude relation*, when a feature excludes the existence of other features with non-direct family relation (cf., in the figure $\neg(D \wedge E)$).
- *Attributes* associated to features, such as B_{Cost} in the example, that is an Integer attribute attached to feature B.

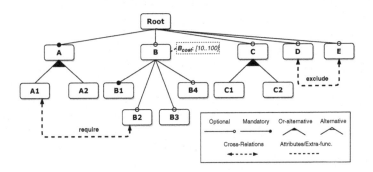

Fig. 4. Toy feature model.

The automated analysis of FMs can be achieved by formal methods [8] based on propositional logic, description logic or constraint programming. Most of the approaches in the literature make a transformation from the FMs to a formalisation, for instance, Constraint Satisfaction Problems (CSPs) or Constraint Optimisation Problems (COPs) [14]. In this work, the tools used to automated the analysis are FaMa and CyberSPL [9,39], both based on the Constraint Programming paradigm.

The automated analysis of FMs enable to perform different reasoning operations on them, for instance, to determine whether the model is valid or not, to obtain the number of all possible configurations, to obtain all possible configurations, even we can ascertain whether it is correct or not concerning the model and based on a configuration. Thus, we can verify a configuration according to the model.

The verification of the security requirement is based on the definition of a valid configuration [39]. Thus, a configuration, c_i, represents an assignment of features for certain FM. For instance, $c_i = \{Root=true,\ A=true,\ A1=true,\ A2=false,\ \dots\ \}$ represents an assignment for the model in Fig. 4, where missed features are assigned to *false* value. The configuration can be represented without the Boolean values but the same semantic, thus, $c_i = \{Root,\ A,\ A1,\ A2,\ \dots\ \}$.

The configurations can be *valid* (i.e., correct) whether the selection of assigned features satisfies all the relations, *invalid* otherwise. We revisited the definition of valid configuration [39] to adapt it for the context of the verification of a security requirement (SR) by considering it as a configuration to be checked. Thus, the security requirement represents an assignment according to the features of the model as aforementioned.

Definition 3 Verification of Security Requirements. *Let $\langle FM, SR \rangle$ be the tuple that represents the feature model, FM, and the security requirement, SR, respectively. Let SR be an configuration assignment of n asset type and security features $\{f_1, f_2, \cdots, f_n\}$ according to FM. Thereby, the SR is verified as valid when all the within features of the requirement satisfies the relation of FM.*

$$verify(FM, SR) = \textbf{valid} \iff \{\forall r_i \in FM.R | r_i(SR) \equiv true\} \tag{1}$$

For instance, the configuration assignment $c = \{Root, B\}$ which represent $Root = true$ and $B = true$ is *invalid* due to the relations between B and $B1$ is unsatisfied. This configuration can be seen as a security requirement which represents asset types and security constraints. In our approach, we will formalise a set of FMs that enables the reasoning for the verification of the security requirements presented in previous sections.

5.2   Catalogue of Feature Models for CPS

FM as a formalisation for the definition of security patterns has been also used in [41]. In our approach, FMs are used to formalised the security requirements specified in Sect. 4. To do that, we have formalised a catalogue of FMs that align the security requirements with the recommendation of ENISA [1] for the definition of a security CPS environment. The FMs explained in this section are accessible through the public catalogue of the tool CyberSPL[1].

The FM depicted in Fig. 5 is the result of this synthesis of the ENISA and our proposal for security requirement definition. To bear born in mind, the FM is just an overview since several parts have been hidden for clarity as some require relations and sub-models. As can be seen, the FM is encompassed of two main parts: (1) the assets (cf., Asset) involved in the security requirement, and; (2) the security requirement (cf., Security) specification where properties, conditions, and constraints can be defined.

---

[1] https://estigia.lsi.us.es/cyberspl/featureModels/publicFeatureModels/.

Regarding the relations, there is a set of requires relations that have been included to explain the relation between asset features and the security requirement aspects. For instance, the data stored into a database may require integrity, hence, the integrity property requires the application of a certain security constraint related to the encryption, e.g., ciphering.

Regarding sub-models, Fig. 6 represents the *Infrastructure* sub-model. The communications at least the specification of used protocols are mandatory but most of the part are optional such as gateways, routers, firewalls, authentication systems, etc.

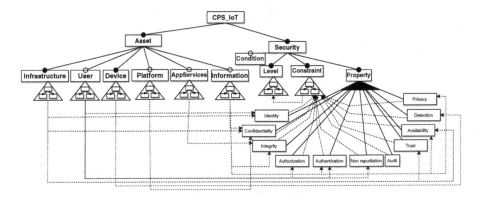

Fig. 5. Feature model for CPS and security requirements.

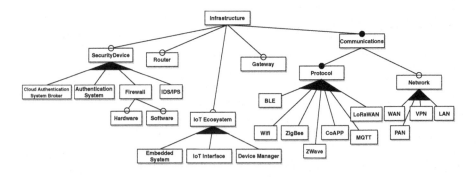

Fig. 6. Sub-model for Infrastructure of CPS.

From the general overview in Fig. 5, we provide different security configuration viewpoints [30] to illustrate some use cases. The first security configuration viewpoint in Fig. 7 is concerning the data-in-transit and confidentiality property. On the one hand, the in-transit data requires a type of network and confidentiality. On the other hand, any communication channel requires confidentiality properties. The confidentiality can be achieved by the enforcement of the communications using a security protocol such as SSL/TLS. However, the SSL/TLS requires the specification of any cipher methods. To illustrate, we have included three supported by the TLS 1.3 Camelia, AES128GCM, and ChaCha20; these have been matched to three security levels Medium, High, and Very High respectively.

The second security configuration viewpoint in Fig. 8 is concerning data storage and customers. The web-based services can require storage such as databases and users need to be authenticated and authorised to access the sensor data. Thereby, users need authentication and authorisation properties and data storage requires data integrity. On the one hand, integrity can be achieved by the enforcement of cipher methods on the data. These methods Camelia, AES128GCM, and ChaCha20 have been linked to three security levels Medium, High, and Very High respectively. On the other hand, the authentication can require some constraints for the password-based authentication system such as multi-factor. The multi-factor, the length and constraint policy, and the avoid-history based password policy are considered as high level, low level, and a medium level of security respectively.

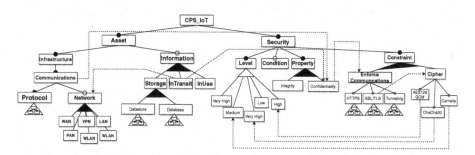

Fig. 7. Feature Model for the security configuration viewpoint of Confidentiality and Data in-transit.

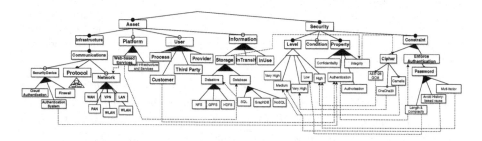

Fig. 8. Feature Model for the security configuration viewpoint of Integrity and Data storage.

To illustrate a running example regarding the security requirements, a security requirement that specifies data-in-transit without protocol and network or a bad combination of SSL/TLS version and the cipher methods concerning the level can provoke an incorrect configuration, therefore, an invalid security requirement. For instance, the data-in-transit through wifi channels requires to the medium level of confidentiality using 3DES or RC4. Both methods have been not considered in our viewpoint because they are deprecated, unrecommended and incompatible with recent versions of the TLS cipher suites.

5.3   Verification Examples for the Case Study

In this section, we show the results for the verification of the three requirements presented in Sect. 3. To do that, we define the configurations for each requirement and subsequently, we verify it against the FMs presented in the previous section.

I. High level Security Requirement

The security requirement establishes that the wireless communication (i.e., WPAN) in transit between the actuators (i.e., ALL), Arduino (i.e., microcontroller), and sensors (i.e., ALL) must be encrypted (i.e., HTTPS), ensuring confidentiality with a high level of security. Based on this specification, we have composed the next security configuration to verify the requirement:

$$
\begin{aligned}
\text{conf}_{\textbf{HighLevel}} = \{ & CPS\_IoT, Asset, Device, Sensor, Humidity, Temperature, \\
& Controller, microController, Actuator, Electric, Magnetic, Infrastructure, \\
& Communications, Protocol, BLE, RFID, Network, WPAN, Information, \\
& Intransit, Security, Enforce\ Communications, Property, Confidentiality, \\
& Level, High, Constraint, HTTPS\} \quad (2)
\end{aligned}
$$

The $conf_{HighLevel}$ configuration is correctly verified. Thus, it is *valid* since all the features chosen are correct and comply with all the relations in the model. Therefore, we can conclude that *High-Level Security Requirement* of the case study is correct.

II. Medium Level Security Requirement

The security requirement establishes that the users (i.e., Customer) who want to visualise the data (i.e., Data Analytic & Visualisation) of sensors and activate the actuators must be authorised and authenticate (i.e., Authorisation and Authenticate property) by authentication system (i.e., Authentication System) with a 2FA system (i.e., enforce Multi-factor Password).

$$
\begin{aligned}
\text{conf}_{\textbf{MediumLevel}} = \{ & CPS\_IoT, Asset, User, Customer, Device, \\
& Sensor, Humidity, Temperature, Actuator, Electric, Magnetic, Infrastructure, \\
& SecurityDevice, AuthenticationSystem, Communications, Protocol, Wifi, \\
& Network, WAN, AppServices, AnalyticVisualisation, Security, Property, \\
& Authorisation, Authentication, EnforceAuthentication,, Level, High, \\
& Constraint, Password, Multifactor, Condition\} \\
& \quad (3)
\end{aligned}
$$

The $conf_{MedimLevel}$ configuration is verified as *invalid*. The use of communication will require enforcement of the communication to comply with confidentiality properties that are not specified. Therefore, we can conclude that *Medium Level Security Requirement* of the case study is incorrect.

III. Low Level Security Requirement

The security requirement establishes that the sensors connected to the Arduino (i.e, microController) via Bluetooth (i.e., BLE protocol) send information through HTTP protocol but using an SSL/TLS cryptographic protocol to ensure Confidentiality properties. The information is located in encrypted HDFS and HBASE systems to ensure Integrity property. In this case, the requirement specified complementary security properties with two different levels of security, therefore, we need to verify the two configurations one for each security level with the security properties:

$$
\begin{aligned}
\mathbf{conf^{High}_{LowLevel}} = \{ & CPS\_IoT, Asset, Device, Sensor, Humidity, Temperature, \\
& Controller, microController, Infrastructure, Communications, \\
& Information, Storage, Datastore, HDFS, Database, NoSQL, Protocol, \\
& BLE, Wifi, Network, WPAN, Security, EnforceCommunications, Property, \\
& Integrity, Confidentiality, Level, High, Constraint, SSLTLS, Cipher, \\
& AES128GCM \} \quad (4)
\end{aligned}
$$

$$
\begin{aligned}
\mathbf{conf^{VeryHigh}_{LowLevel}} = \{ & CPS\_IoT, Asset, Device, Sensor, Humidity, Temperature, \\
& Controller, microController, Infrastructure, Communications, \\
& Information, Storage, Datastore, HDFS, Database, NoSQL, Protocol, \\
& BLE, Wifi, Network, WPAN, Security, EnforceCommunications, Property, \\
& Integrity, Confidentiality, Level, VeryHigh, Constraint, SSLTLS, Cipher, \\
& AES128GCM \} \quad (5)
\end{aligned}
$$

The $conf^{High}_{LowLevel}$ configuration is verified as *valid* but the $conf^{VeryHigh}_{LowLevel}$ configuration is verified as *invalid* due to the cipher chosen. The AES128GCM cipher method is unsupported for the very high level of security. Thereby, we can conclude that the *Low Level Security Requirement* is incorrect.

Summarising, we demonstrate the reasoning capabilities of the model by verifying the security requirement in which two of the three, i.e, Medium and Low have been verified as *invalid* due to problems in the specification, and just one, i.e, the High level is verified as *valid*.

6 Conclusion and Future Work

The high features that can be configurable in a CPS make difficult the evaluation of the requirements that involve security aspects. To facilitate the validation of the security requirements for CPSs, we propose the use of Feature Models to support the description of the possible configuration. To formalise the security requirement description, we have defined a common grammar to define security requirements for CPSs by using JSON that gathering the possible involved elements. For an automatic verification of the requirements, Feature Models are used to validate a configuration according to the requirements. Moreover, a catalogue of FMs for CPS has been created and stored in a special repository to be reused for any set of requirement to be validated. The feasibility of the solution, both the description capacity of the requirements and the catalogue of configurations in CPS has been evaluated through a case study of a hydroponic farming CPS. For the future, we plan to extend the types of reasoning that can be applied over the combination of the feature models and the security requirements for CPSs, such as the diagnosis of the configurations that do not satisfy the requirement, or the generation of correct configurations according to a set of requirements specified.

Acknowledgement. This research is partially supported by Ministry of Science and Technology of Spain with projects ECLIPSE (RTI2018-094283-B-C33), by Junta de Andalucía with METAMORFOSIS projects, and Junta de Comunidades de Castilla-La Mancha with the GENESIS project (SBPLY-17-180501-000202); and by European Regional Development Fund (ERDF/FEDER).

References

1. Baseline security recommendations for IoT (2018). https://www.enisa.europa.eu/publications/baseline-security-recommendations-for-iot
2. OWASP Top Ten. Available from OWASP (2020). https://owasp.org/www-project-top-ten/
3. Arciniegas, J.L., Dueñas, J.C., Ruiz, J.L., Cerón, R., Bermejo, J., Oltra, M.A.: Architecture reasoning for supporting product line evolution: an example on security. In: Kakola, T., Duenas, J.C. (eds.) Software Product Lines, pp. 327–372. Springer, Heidelberg (2006). https://doi.org/10.1007/978-3-540-33253-4_9
4. Arrieta, A., Sagardui, G., Etxeberria, L.: Cyber-physical systems product lines: variability analysis and challenges (2015)
5. Arrieta, A., Wang, S., Sagardui, G., Etxeberria, L.: Search-based test case selection of cyber-physical system product lines for simulation-based validation. In: Mei, H. (ed.) Proceedings of the 20th International Systems and Software Product Line Conference, SPLC 2016, Beijing, China, 16–23 September 2016, pp. 297–306. ACM (2016). https://doi.org/10.1145/2934466.2946046
6. Batory, D.: Feature models, grammars, and propositional formulas. In: Obbink, H., Pohl, K. (eds.) SPLC 2005. LNCS, vol. 3714, pp. 7–20. Springer, Heidelberg (2005). https://doi.org/10.1007/11554844_3
7. Beek, M.H.T., Fantechi, A., Gnesi, S.: Product line models of large cyber-physical systems: the case of ertms/etcs. In: Proceedings of the 22nd International Systems and Software Product Line Conference, SPLC '18, vol. 1, pp. 208–214. Association for Computing Machinery, New York (2018). https://doi.org/10.1145/3233027.3233046
8. Benavides, D., Segura, S., Ruiz-Cortés, A.: Automated analysis of feature models 20 years later: a literature review. Inf. Syst. **35**(6), 615–636 (2010). https://doi.org/10.1016/j.is.2010.01.001
9. Benavides, D., Segura, S., Trinidad, P., Cortés, A.R.: Fama: tooling a framework for the automated analysis of feature models. VaMoS **2007**, 01 (2007)

10. Biffl, S., Eckhart, M., Lüder, A., Weippl, E.: Introduction to security and quality improvement in complex cyber-physical systems engineering. Security and Quality in Cyber-Physical Systems Engineering, pp. 1–29. Springer, Cham (2019). https://doi.org/10.1007/978-3-030-25312-7_1

11. Bramberger, R., Martin, H., Gallina, B., Schmittner, C.: Co-engineering of safety and security life cycles for engineering of automotive systems. ACM SIGAda Ada Lett. **39**(2), 41–48 (2020)

12. Carter, B., Adams, S., Bakirtzis, G., Sherburne, T., Beling, P., Horowitz, B., Fleming, C.: A preliminary design-phase security methodology for cyber-physical systems. Systems **7**(2), 21 (2019)

13. Cysneiros, L.M., Leite, J.C.S.D.P.: Nonfunctional requirements: from elicitation to conceptual models. IEEE Trans. Softw. Eng. **30**(5), 328–350 (2004). https://doi.org/10.1109/TSE.2004.10

14. Dechter, R.: Constraint Processing. Morgan Kaufmann Publishers Inc, San Francisco (2003)

15. Ding, J.: Intrusion detection, prevention, and response system (IDPRS) for cyber-physical systems (CPSs). In: Securing Cyber-Physical Systems, pp. 371–392. CRC Press, Boca Raton (2015). https://doi.org/10.1201/b19311-16

16. Dorbala, S., Bhadoria, R.: Analysis for security attacks in cyber-physical systems. In: Cyber-Physical Systems, pp. 395–414. Chapman and Hall/CRC, Baco Raton (2015). https://doi.org/10.1201/b19206-23

17. Fægri, T.E., Hallsteinsen, S.: A software product line reference architecture for security. In: Kakola, T., Duenas, J.C. (eds.) Software Product Lines, pp. 275–326. Springer, Heidelberg (2006). https://doi.org/10.1007/978-3-540-33253-4_8

18. Galindo, J.A., Benavides, D., Trinidad, P., Gutiérrez-Fernández, A.-M., Ruiz-Cortés, A.: Automated analysis of feature models: Quo vadis? Computing **101**(5), 387–433 (2018). https://doi.org/10.1007/s00607-018-0646-1

19. Griffor, E., Wollman, D., Greer, C.: Framework for Cyber-Physical Systems: Volume 1, Overview. Technical Report, June, National Institute of Standards and Technology, Gaithersburg, MD (2017). https://doi.org/10.6028/NIST.SP.1500-201

20. Gunes, V., Peter, S., Givargis, T., Vahid, F.: A survey on concepts, applications, and challenges in cyber-physical systems. KSII Trans. Internet Inf. Syst. **8**(12), 4242–4268 (2014). https://doi.org/10.3837/tiis.2014.12.001

21. Humayed, A., Lin, J., Li, F., Luo, B.: Cyber-physical systems security - a survey. IEEE Internet Things J. **4**(6), 1802–1831 (2017). https://doi.org/10.1109/JIOT.2017.2703172

22. Iglesias, A., Iglesias-Urkia, M., López-Davalillo, B., Charramendieta, S., Urbieta, A.: Trilateral: software product line based multidomain IoT artifact generation for industrial CPS. In: Proceedings of the 7th International Conference on Model-Driven Engineering and Software Development, vol. 1, pp. 64–73. SCITEPRESS-Science and Technology Publications, Lda (2019)

23. Kenner, A., Dassow, S., Lausberger, C., Krüger, J., Leich, T.: Using variability modeling to support security evaluations: virtualizing the right attack scenarios. In: VaMoS '20: 14th International Working Conference on Variability Modelling of Software-Intensive Systems, Magdeburg, Germany, 5–7 February 2020, pp. 10:1–10:9 (2020). https://doi.org/10.1145/3377024.3377026

24. Liu, Y., Peng, Y., Wang, B., Yao, S., Liu, Z.: Review on cyber-physical systems. IEEE/CAA J. Automatica Sinica **4**(1), 27–40 (2017). https://doi.org/10.1109/JAS.2017.7510349

25. Mellado, D., Fernández-Medina, E., Piattini, M.: Security requirements management in software product line engineering. In: Filipe, J., Obaidat, M.S. (eds.) ICETE 2008. CCIS, vol. 48, pp. 250–263. Springer, Heidelberg (2009). https://doi.org/10.1007/978-3-642-05197-5_18

26. Mellado, D., Fernández-Medina, E., Piattini, M.: Towards security requirements management for software product lines: a security domain requirements engineering process. Comput. Stand. Interfaces **30**(6), 361–371 (2008)

27. Mellado, D., Mouratidis, H., Fernández-Medina, E.: Secure tropos framework for software product lines requirements engineering. Comput. Stand. Interfaces **36**(4), 711–722 (2014)

28. Nguyen, P.H., Ali, S., Yue, T.: Model-based security engineering for cyber-physical systems: a systematic mapping study (2017). https://doi.org/10.1016/j.infsof.2016.11.004

29. Peldszus, S., Strüber, D., Jürjens, J.: Model-based security analysis of feature-oriented software product lines. In: Proceedings of the 17th ACM SIGPLAN International Conference on Generative Programming: Concepts and Experiences, pp. 93–106 (2018)

30. Publishing, V.H.: The TOGAF Standard, Version 9.2. TOGAF series, Van Haren Publishing (2018). https://books.google.es/books?id=XQ6DtgEACAAJ

31. ur Rehman, S., Allgaier, C., Gruhn, V.: Security requirements engineering: a framework for cyber-physical systems. In: 2018 International Conference on Frontiers of Information Technology (FIT), pp. 315–320. IEEE (2018)

32. Rehman, S., Gruhn, V.: An effective security requirements engineering framework for cyber-physical systems. Technologies **6**(3), 65 (2018). https://doi.org/10.3390/technologies6030065

33. Rehman, S., Gruhn, V., Shafiq, S., Inayat, I.: A systematic mapping study on security requirements engineering frameworks for cyber-physical systems. In: Wang, G., Chen, J., Yang, L.T. (eds.) SpaCCS 2018. LNCS, vol. 11342, pp. 428–442. Springer, Cham (2018). https://doi.org/10.1007/978-3-030-05345-1_37

34. Rehman, S.U., Gruhn, V.: An effective security requirements engineering framework for cyber-physical systems. Technologies **6**(3), 65 (2018)

35. Shaaban, A.M., Gruber, T., Schmittner, C.: Ontology-based security tool for critical cyber-physical systems. In: Proceedings of the 23rd International Systems and Software Product Line Conference, vol. B, pp. 207–210 (2019)

36. Sion, L., Van Landuyt, D., Yskout, K., Joosen, W.: Towards systematically addressing security variability in software product lines. In: Proceedings of the 20th International Systems and Software Product Line Conference, pp. 342–343 (2016)

37. Span, M., Mailloux, L.O., Mills, R.F., Young, W.: Conceptual systems security requirements analysis: aerial refueling case study. IEEE Access **6**, 46668–46682 (2018)

38. Subramanian, N., Zalewski, J.: Quantitative assessment of safety and security of system architectures for cyberphysical systems using the NFR approach. IEEE Syst. J. **10**(2), 397–409 (2016). https://doi.org/10.1109/JSYST.2013.2294628

39. Varela-Vaca, A.J., Gasca, R.M., Ceballos, R., Gómez-López, M.T., Bernáldez Torres, P.: CyberSPL: a framework for the verification of cybersecurity policy compliance of system configurations using software product lines. Appl. Sci. **9**(24) (2019). https://doi.org/10.3390/app9245364

40. Varela-Vaca, Á.J., Galindo, J.A., Ramos-Gutiérrez, B., Gómez-López, M.T., Benavides, D.: Process mining to unleash variability management: discovering configuration workflows using logs. In: Proceedings of the 23rd International Systems and Software Product Line Conference, vol. A, pp. 265–276 (2019)
41. Varela-Vaca, Á.J., Gasca, R.M.: Formalization of security patterns as a means to infer security controls in business processes. Logic J. IGPL **23**(1), 57–72 (2015). https://doi.org/10.1093/jigpal/jzu042
42. Yoo, H., Shon, T.: Challenges and research directions for heterogeneous cyber-physical system based on IEC 61850: Vulnerabilities, security requirements, and security architecture. Fut. Gener. Comput. Syst. **61**, 128–136 (2016). https://doi.org/10.1016/j.future.2015.09.026
43. Zhu, Q., Sangiovanni-Vincentelli, A.: Codesign methodologies and tools for cyber-physical systems. Proc. IEEE **106**(9), 1484–1500 (2018)

GDPR Compliance: Proposed Guidelines for Cloud-Based Health Organizations

Dimitra Georgiou(✉) and Costas Lambrinoudakis

Systems Security Laboratory, Department of Digital Systems, School of Information
and Communication Technologies, University of Piraeus, 150, Odyssea Androutsou Str.,
18532 Piraeus, Greece
dimitrageorgiou@ssl-unipi.gr, clam@unipi.gr

Abstract. In this paper, we investigate the implications of the General Data Protection Regulation (GDPR) on the design of a Cloud-based Health System. Keeping secure healthcare information and protecting patients' privacy is a major responsibility of all healthcare providers. On May 25th 2018, when the GDPR has become mandatory within the European Union, this responsibility has been increased. Failure to comply with GDPR can result in huge fines. For this reason, it is of vital importance any health care organization to explore ways for achieving protection of the data subjects and ensuring GDPR compliance.

GDPR introduces the 'special category of personal data', that includes health data and is subject to special conditions regarding treatment and access by third parties. The focus of this research work is to provide guidelines for Cloud-based health Organizations in order to comply with GDPR and ensure patients' privacy and rights. In this paper, we demonstrate, in a practical way, how a Cloud provider may handle the difficulties of the legal framework by summarizing the legal text, identifying the GDPR requirements, highlighting the obligations that are specific for health data and providing guidelines for satisfying the GDPR requirements for a Cloud-based Health provider.

Keywords: GDPR · Cloud Computing · Data protection · Security · Privacy · Health data · SaaS

1 Introduction

Digitization plays an important role in today's life. New technologies are offering a variety of prospects to gather, use and share health data with efficiency, to empower patients in managing their diseases and to improve the quality, safety and efficiency of healthcare systems. Cloud computing is a new technology that has been spread in many ICT areas, significantly affecting the way in which personal data are processed and, subsequently, being protected. Over the past years, a lot of research has been conducted on security and privacy of Cloud environments and especially on Cloud-based Health systems. The GDPR [1] outlines rigorous new policies for collecting, processing and securing personal data and affects almost all industries but in the health care sector,

© Springer Nature Switzerland AG 2020
S. Katsikas et al. (Eds.): CyberICPS 2020/SECPRE 2020/ADIoT 2020, LNCS 12501, pp. 156–169, 2020.
https://doi.org/10.1007/978-3-030-64330-0_10

the new Regulation gives every patient enhanced control over the way his/her personal data are collected and processed. Today, complying with GDPR is a challenging and demanding task for organizations, highlighting the need for a process that could guide them in order to satisfy the requirements and build a GDPR compliant system.

The General Data Protection Regulation [1] was approved on April 2016 and came into force on May 2018, bringing along several challenges for citizens, institutions and other private and public organizations. GDPR has a direct impact on all 28 Member States of the EU and is the European Union's attempt to create an allied approach to online privacy. Unfortunately, even today, many Health-care businesses and Providers have not yet realized the huge fines that they are facing if they do not comply with GDPR, something which is also the case for those that provide their services through cloud infrastructures [2].

It is worthwhile to mention that the GDPR, applies to all companies that hold or process EU residents' data, including Cloud Computing users, Providers and their subcontractors. GDPR creates a uniform data privacy law across all 28 EU member nations to be enforced wherever data processing and management practices affect EU citizens. In other words, unless one Organization deals with non-Europeans, it is subject to the regulation. For Cloud Providers, that act either as Processors or Data Controllers the new obligations are extensive and challenging. Since the compliance of companies with the regulation is obligatory, it is relevant to declare companies' level of preparation for the new GDPR requirements. This requirement must be met regardless of the means used to process the personal data and it also covers Cloud services used to process the personal data. Numerous industry sectors could have been chosen, but this research work focused on the health sector. The objective of this paper is to give a brief advice on what a cloud Health Organizations and Providers should consider and what further actions to take in order to comply with GDPR.

In terms of its structure, this paper is divided in five sections, starting with an introduction and continuing with Sect. 2 that presents the challenges in Personal Data Protection in the GDPR era. Section 3 describes analytically the GDPR requirements while Sect. 4 focuses on the key aspects of the GDPR for health. Section 5 proposes the basic countermeasures for satisfying the aforementioned requirements. Finally Sect. 6 concludes the paper.

2 Challenges Faced by Organizations During GDPR Compliance

The GDPR introduces a new set of rules for the processing and protection of personal data and the privacy of the users. In the Cloud Computing era, users enjoy several gains, but concurrently, they are facing increased risks regarding the protection of their personal data.

Although organizations should comply with GDPR by May 25, 2018, this is not yet the case. One of the main reasons for the slow compliance uptake is the complexity of GDPR and the various challenges that organizations have to overcome in order to achieve compliance. The GDPR indeed introduces strict rules and obligations and recognizes a small quantity of rights to individuals that must be expected by organizations.

Apart from the mandate for GDPR compliance—and the non-neglectable financial fines, organizations have an extra reason to adopt the underlying principles and the appropriate measures for data protection: growing people awareness of data breaches and their growing demand that companies protect their information. In other words, compliance is driven also by the market needs. Organizations subject to GDPR compliance claim difficulties in provisions' implementation, despite the money spent, although specific problems are encountered with regard to the new requirements GDPR introduces. This is due to various reasons, either technical or organizational. Challenges include:

- **GDPR requirements' interpretation:** Since the Regulation introduces principles rather than concrete rules, several organizations struggle to put them in practice into their technical and operational context.
- **Operational adaptation:** GDPR implementation requires significant planning and review about people, roles, systems, processes and transformation of business practices to privacy friendly processes. However, it is often hard to identify the flaws of business practices against GDPR requirements, in some cases even have a clear view on the precise practices themselves and to appropriately re-engineer processes for becoming privacy-aware by design.
- **Unified data view:** Organizations must have a clear view on data subjects' information structure, semantics, and storage patterns. Currently, data is typically scattered across different systems and databases, thus hardening control over them, as well as responding to access, rectification, erasure and portability requests. Further, they should maintain a comprehensive record of processing actions and the associated context and make it readily available to data subjects and regulators.
- **Security means enforcement:** The GDPR requires, explicitly or implicitly, the application of various security mechanisms for the protection of data. Organizations have to identify and "plug" suitable mechanisms to their operations, new and re-engineered processes, data records and customer and third parties' relations.
- **Customer relationship management:** The GDPR provides data subjects with control over their data, while granting various other rights that level up the requirements as regards management of customer relations, along with the means that should be maintained by organizations for their implementation.
- **Management of third parties:** In the complex service provision ecosystem, organizations should provide for privacy-aware data exchange and operations' outsourcing. This is hardened by the increasing use of Cloud and as-a-service technologies, where data and operations are entrusted to third parties, thus creating implications for both service providers and consumers.
- **Accountability:** The GDPR provides very little guidance as to what measures processors and controllers should adopt in order to meet their accountability obligations. Article 24 [1] introduces the concept of accountability, which requires controllers to perform all of their data processing operations in compliance with the GDPR and to be able to demonstrate such compliance, without providing any guidance on how to do that.
- **Lack of resources and capabilities:** In order for the above to be implemented, significant resources and now-how are required. While big companies may have money

to invest, this does not essentially apply for small organizations that typically operate with few employees and make heavy use of cloud resources.

In addition to the aforementioned challenges, organizations have to carefully consider the GDPR principles in relation to the processing of personal data.

2.1 Principles Relating to Processing of Personal Data in GDPR

One of the major GDPR achievements is the clear refinement of data processing principles in a way that they guarantee that any personal data processing is fair, lawful, limited to the purposes of processing. These principles are listed under Article 5 [1] and are presented in Fig. 1. Therefore, all exceptions to the processing principles must be provided by law in order to be acceptable.

Fig. 1. Principles of GDPR

Lawfulness, Fairness and Transparency

Personal data should be processed in such a way "*lawfully, fairly and in a transparent manner in relation to the data subject*" Article 5(1) (a) and Articles 37-40 [1]. These principles guarantee that data will be processed in accordance with the law, proportionally to the aim foreseen and with transparent means for the natural persons who should be informed of the collection of their personal data, usage and consultancy and the extent to which such operations go. Any processing must comply with the law which implies not only data protection related law but also other legislations applying to the specific sector such as automotive services or energy providers. The principle of fairness brings a balance test that needs to be carried out for each processing activity, since the right to the protection of personal data must be balanced with other potentially conflicting rights. Such balance can be achieved through strict compliance with the general principles underpinning the processing of personal data, but also when ensuring the respect of data subjects' rights from the controller. Hence, processing can be lawful but still considered unfair with regard to the means foreseen. It is therefore essential that the processing entailed is always clear to the data subject and that the latter is aware of its rights under the GDPR.

Purpose Limitation

The collection of data should be limited to *"specified, explicit and legitimate purposes"* Article 5(1)(b) [1]. The purpose must be specific: a controller cannot collect data without knowing how and when these data will be used. When the purpose of data collection is determined then, the appropriate data will be collected and stored, only on condition that is necessary. Whether further processing is compatible with the original purposes of processing can be assessed by analyzing a number of factors, the nature of the data, the impact such further processing would have on the data subject, as well as the safeguards adopted by the controller in order to ensure that subject's rights are respected.

Data Minimization

Data minimization requests whether the same purpose can be achieved with a narrower collection of data and is one of the principles that is linked with data protection by design under the Regulation. The data gathered should be suitable and restricted to what is essential for the purpose foreseen. In reality, it can be more complicated to access since the added value of minimization depends on a multitude of criteria and the purposes of processing [3]. In some cases, such as police profiling, quality data is essential in order to ensure non-discrimination and acquiring more data ensures more accurate and fair results. For what concerns business purposes, collectors tend to acquire more data than what they actually need and this can be problematic.

Accuracy

In consequence, controllers should ensure accuracy at all stages of collecting and processing personal data, taking every step to guarantee that inaccurate data are deleted or rectified without delay. Thus, controllers should make sure that outdated data are eliminated or that data are correctly interpreted. The importance of this step varies according to the type of data collected and the sector to which these safeguards apply. The system should notify data subjects of their right to object or change personal data, as well as provide a communication channel where the user can inform about data disputation. Data should be analyzed for its quality and inaccurate or incomplete data should be erased either manually or automatically [4].

Storage Limitation

The data should only be stored for as long as necessary and the retention period should be decided at the moment of collection. However, in case of a new purpose that respects the legal requirements of the GDPR, the data retained for a longer period should again be limited to what is necessary to accomplish the new cause. Traceability is once again essential for this principle. Being able to trace personal data to different locations is crucial when personal data has been backed up or distributed to different locations [4]. Attaching metadata makes it easier to identify the specific purpose and defined storage duration of personal data, allowing an (automatic) erasure procedure.

Integrity and Confidentiality
The processing of personal data should be as secure as possible, *"including protection against unauthorized or unlawful processing and against accidental loss, destruction or damage, using appropriate technical or organizational measures"* [5]. For data protection by design purposes, it is important to limit unauthorized access, as well as implement systemic quality controls in order to ensure that an appropriate level of security is reached. Personal data contained in the system should be encrypted end-to-end, where the level of encryption depends on the risks of processing this personal data. Backups and distributed copies must also be taken into account. In order to ensure its integrity, personal data should be validated (e.g. using hashes), which also contributes to the accuracy of that data. Additionally, a suitable authentication mechanism should be implemented, taking into consideration the sensitivity of personal data. Lastly, access rights must be managed in order to prevent unauthorized access.

Accountability
The principle of accountability [6] in Article 5(2) [1] does not ensure that potential security problems will be avoided but guarantees the data subject that its rights will be lawfully respected. The significant fines under the new legislation illustrate the importance of ensuring that processing activities are well thought through, explained to the data subject and respectful of privacy principles. Accountability is an overarching principle that is reflected in several provisions of the Regulation. According to the GDPR, the controller is responsible for the processing and must be able to prove that processing operations are lawful. Additionally, he is responsible of mitigating the risks of violation of the rights of the data subject throughout the entire software development life cycle. Accountability is fulfilled through demonstration of legal compliance.

2.2 Other Security Aspects

In addition to the previous challenges, other security aspects are: the special categories of personal data, the anonymization/pseudonymization of data and the encryption that must be conducted by organizations.

Special Categories of Data
It is vital to bear in mind that not all data is of the same importance and that safeguards can vary with respect to the "sensitivity" of the data collected. The GDPR defines personal data broadly in order to increase the protection of the individuals. Hence, personal data is "any information relating to an identified or identifiable natural person", i.e. the data subject, *"who can be identified, directly or indirectly, in particular by reference to*

*an identifier such as a name, an identification number, location data, an online iden-
tifier or to one or more factors specific to the physical, physiological, genetic, mental,
economic, cultural or social identity of that natural person*" Article 4 [1]. Furthermore,
"*data revealing racial or ethnic origin, political opinions, religious or philosophical
beliefs, or trade union membership, [as well as] genetic data, biometric data [1], data
concerning health or data concerning a natural's person sex life or sexual orientation*"
are considered "*sensitive*" Article 9 [1]. Controllers can only process this data if they
respond to the requirements listed under Article 9(2) [1], otherwise the explicit consent
of the data subject is required or an issue of public interest is raised for the need to process
that data. Consideration of the risks is actually one of the most important changes of
the new legislation which wishes to ensure that data controllers evaluate, through every
operation, how a person's rights are affected by the processing.

Pseudonymization
According to Article 4(5) of GDPR [1], pseudonymization is a method of processing
personal data in a way that it can no longer be attributed to a specific data subject albeit
the use of additional information, if that information is kept separately with appropriate
technical and organizational measures.

Encryption
Encryption is mentioned several times in Articles 6, 32 and 34 by the GDPR [1] as
an example of a privacy friendly measure, since it guarantees that data is protected and
raises the trust of the data subject to the data controller. Strong and efficient encryption is
necessary in order to guarantee integrity of data as well as a secure flow of information.
As it was stated by the former Article 29 Working Party, "*encryption must remain
standardized, strong and efficient, which would no longer be the case if providers were
compelled to include backdoors or provide master keys*" [7, 8]. Personal data should be
encrypted when stored (including creation of backups) and in transition.

3   Changes Introduced by the GDPR

During the process of conforming with GDPR requirements, cloud-based health
organizations should carefully address the following points (Table 1).

3.1   Records of Processing Activities

The controller should keep records of all processing activities [8] including information
on the name and contact details of the controller, the Data Protection Officer (DPO), when
applicable, the processor if any, the purpose of processing, a description of the categories
of persons involved and which data about them will be processed, the categories of
recipients to whom the data will be disclosed, possible transfers in third countries or
international organizations, planned time limits for erasure of the different categories of
data, and where possible, a general description of the security measures adopted.

Table 1. EU-GDPR: Key Changes to the previous data protection framework

EU -GDPR: Key Changes to the previous data protection framework	
Records of processing activities	3.1
Territorial Scope	3.2
Data Protection Impact Assessment	3.3
Subjects' Rights	3.4
Data Breach Notification	3.5
Data Protection Officer	3.6
Penalties	3.7
Controllers and Processors	3.8
Consent	3.9
Data Protection by Design and by Default	3.10

3.2 Territorial Scope-Third Country Data Transfers

The GDPR also sets restrictions on how personal data is transferred outside EU. Data may only be transferred if certain criteria are met – for example, the third country or international organization offers "*an adequate*" level of data protection.

3.3 Data Protection Impact Assessment (DPIA)

Under the GDPR, companies should conduct formal Data Protection Impact Assessment regarding any processing that would result in "high risk" for individuals' rights and freedoms. The notion of high risk is not distinct in the GDPR, but there are three examples of high risk processing: (i) the large scale processing of sensitive personal data; (ii) automated decision taking; and (iii) systematic and large scale monitoring of publicly accessible areas.

3.4 Subjects' Rights

According to the provisions of the GDPR, citizens should regain control of their data. Therefore, companies in possession of personal data are obliged to inform the users of ways in which they use their data, provide them insight into their data, provide a copy of data or change incorrect data. Especially, the data subjects' right to data portability may challenge entities as they will have to provide datasets to their customers upon request. Other rights that are presented are: Right to information, Right to access, Right to rectification, Right to withdraw consent, Right to object, Right to object to automated processing, Right to be forgotten [1].

3.5 Data Breach Notification

Organizations must report data breaches to supervisory authorities and individuals affected by a breach within 72 h Article 33 [1] of the detection. According to Article 34, [1] a data subject should be also notified in cases where security breaches result in a risk to their rights and freedoms.

3.6 Data Protection Officer

The GDPR introduces the role and the duties of the Data Protection Officer in Articles 37–40 [1]. Specific tasks of the DPO and corresponding obligations of the employers are presented there. In addition, it is stated that the contact details of the Data Protection Officer should be made available to the public for ensuring continuous communication with data subjects. It is a responsibility of the controller and the processor to report to the supervisory authority the appointment of the Data Protection Officer.

3.7 Penalties

The GDPR significantly increases the fines that can be imposed for breaches of the data protection rules. At their highest, the fines can reach up to 4% of an organization's annual worldwide turnover or up to €20 million. The GDPR sets out a number of factors that would need to be taken into account by national Data Protection Authorities.

3.8 Controllers and Processors

The GDPR applies to both controllers (those who say how and why personal data is processed) and processors (those acting on the controllers' behalf). The obligations for processors – for example, being required to maintain records of personal data and processing activities – are new under the GDPR.

3.9 Consent

A person's consent for processing of their personal data is valid only if it is given in a voluntary, specific, conscious and unequivocal way, in a form of a statement, confirmation or other consent-expressing deed.

3.10 Data Protection by Design and by Default

These two principles place an obligation on organizations to ensure that all processing of personal data throughout the organization protects the privacy rights of individuals. Essentially, the principles require that an organization's practices and policies are privacy friendly. The GDPR requires the data controller to adopt internal policies and implement measures which comply with the principles of "data protection by design" and "data protection by default".

The GDPR suggests that data controllers should take the following measures:

- Minimize the processing of personal data
- Pseudonymize personal data as soon as possible
- Have complete transparency with regard to the functions and processing of personal data
- Enable the data subject to monitor data processing. The GDPR requires that in the design and creation of new products or services the data protection and privacy rights of individuals are considered throughout the design stage. Similarly, the principles of data protection by design and default should also be taken into consideration in the context of public tenders.

4 Key Aspects of the GDPR of Particular Relevance to Healthcare

After the analysis of GDPR key changes, we need to explore how these changes will influence the interaction of the user with the Cloud-based Health Provider. It is worthwhile to mention that our analysis provides a summary of the requirements that should be addressed by a cloud provider, in a private Cloud, acting as data Controller, categorized on the type of service.

4.1 Security

At this time that personal data protection is more than imperative, the question arises as to what the right way to process visitor data in health care units is (e.g. hospitalized patients or clinics, visitors to diagnostic laboratories, etc.) and which their rights, in accordance with European Regulation 679/2016 and current National legislation, are. Given that in this case "*specific categories of data*" are circulated, such as health data, genetic data and/or biometric data of the recipient of health services, the way in which the data is processed by the service provider is crucial. From their initial collection to their subsequent management and keeping in the medical file. According to the principle of integrity and confidentiality of data, the patient of a health care unit will expect the unit to protect his personal data through appropriate organizational and technical protection measures. The above obligation of the health unit, in the capacity of *"data controller"*, arises from Article 32 [1] of the GDPR, regarding the confidentiality and the security of the processing of personal data. Appropriate organizational and technical measures concern the overall organization and operation of the unit on data protection issues, such as the existence of relevant procedures, the existence of confidentiality clauses and its training, the overall compliance of the health unit with GDPR etc. In this way, the chances of an *"unauthorized access or accidental disclosure"*, as well as of an "unauthorized or accidental alteration" of data, according to Article 5 [1], are minimized.

4.2   Request (Explicit) Consent

The GDPR strengthens citizen's rights as regards the process of consent for the collection, use and sharing of their personal data. Article 9 [1] reflects that "consent" is the main legal base to process this type of data, which should be explicit and unambiguous, freely given, specific, informed and signified. It is clear that "explicit consent" for healthcare purposes will need the strongest forms of agreement, with explicit use(s) of data listed when getting such consent. Healthcare consent will also need to cover the case of many potential transfers of health data, including international data transfers and cloud storage. Users need to make a decision about whether to give consent to the collection of their personal information, they must have a button or a ticking box complemented with clear, specific and targeted information. Line (32) Article. 4 (11) Article. 22-2 (c) [1]. In addition, patients should be informed on how to withdraw consent prior to giving it Article 7 paragraph 3 [1].

4.3   Change in the Way Medical Results Are Obtained

The GDPR is particularly strict on the processing of sensitive personal data, i.e. health data, and points out that their processing is prohibited in the first place and that it is permitted only in exceptional cases, for reasons limited by law. This has practically changed the way health care providers operate. They are called upon to pay special attention on how they handle the communication of medical results to patients. For example, it is forbidden to provide medical results over the phone except in exceptional cases where this method of communication could not be avoided. In addition, the results of the examinations must be received by the patient in person and, in case he is unable to do so, by an authorized third party. If the patient chooses to receive his/her results via email, this should be done with encrypted email.

4.4   Strengthening of Data Subjects' Rights

The GDPR strengthens subjects' rights over their personal data. Although the rights of data subjects have been present in the former legal texts or case-law, GDPR's accomplishment is to list them in clear terms within other data protection rights and obligations. In fact, GDPR's focus on the data subjects aims to strengthen their protection by all means. Each patient, as a subject of personal data, has the right to be informed of his medical record and also to receive copies of it and, accordingly, the health care provider, as the controller, is obliged to satisfy this right-Article 15 [1]. On the contrast, the right to deletion, as enshrined in the provisions of Article 17 [26] of the GDPR, does not apply to the processing of data in the field of health care, taking into account the provisions of (3) of Article 17 [1]. Data controllers will be more accountable for what they do with personal data and how they protect it.

4.5 GDPR Roles

Cloud participants, in GDPR terms, can be separated into two main roles: the data processors and the data controllers. Most of the times, cloud providers act as data processors on behalf of their customers/users who are the data controllers. The Data Controller is obliged to ensure that there are appropriate technical and security measures implemented within the organization.

4.6 Security and Privacy Policies

Cloud providers that collect/process such special categories should take further actions in order to satisfy GDPR requirements. To this extend, the types of sensitive data that are processed should be identified and analytically described in the security policy of the cloud, providing also the reasoning for their necessity. The Privacy Policy should be freely available to patients in short format with basic information and clear pointers on how to access the full Privacy Policy.

5 Basis Tasks that Health Organizations Should Do for the Compliance with GDPR

The satisfaction of the requirements has been always the most critical and also most challenging aspect to achieve compliance with the GDPR. Health Organizations, in particular, require the highest possible security due to the sensitivity of the processed.

Starting with the data processors and taking into account the previous analysis, we summarize the principles and provide tips that Health Organizations should take into account:

5.1 Identify Categories of Subjects and Personal Data

Taking into account the basic definitions of Article 4 [1] of the GDPR, as well as the provisions of Articles 6, 9 and 10 of the GDPR [1], they should identify and classify the categories of subjects (e.g. patients, medical and nursing staff, blood donors, participants in scientific research, clinical trials, etc.) and personal data, which health Organizations collect and maintain per processing activity (e.g. collection and registration of patient data upon arrival for outpatient clinics) - whether this processing is paperwork (or/and) electronic - and ultimately by filing system (e.g. medical patient data file). Data subjects are not only the beneficiaries of the services provided by law (patients, citizens) but also the employees within the institution, for which the institution collects and processes personal data.

5.2 Identification of Personal Data Sources and of Purpose of Processing

Health Organizations should identify each specific category of personal data - whether it is special categories of personal data according to Article 9 provision 1 and Article 10 of the GDPR [1] or whether it is simple personal data and specify precisely each data category, with its subcategories of personal data that are being processed.

Health Organizations should identify the sources of personal data. e.g. data collected directly from their subjects (patients, employees, etc.), as well as those collected by third parties (e.g. other nursing institutions, insurance companies, etc.). In the event that personal data is collected from other sources and not directly from the data subject, the information obligations of Article 14 [1] of the GDPR shall be applied.

Furthermore, the purpose of processing for which the personal data is collected should be clearly described.

5.3 Selection and Determination of the Legal Basis for Each Processing of Personal Data

Health Organization should identify for each category of personal data that is being processed, the legal basis for the processing according to Article 6, Articles 9 paragraphs 2 and Article 10 of the GDPR [1]. The consent of the subject is the necessary legal basis for the processing of personal data in the field of health service provision. The obligation to offer written information to the subjects in Articles 12, 13, 14 of the GDPR [1] must not be confused with obtaining consent for the processing of their personal data.

The most suitable legal bases for the processing of personal data concerning health (special categories) are:

- the provision of medical services according to Article 9 [1]
- the fulfillment of public interest in the sector of public health according to Article 9 [1]
- the need to fulfill archiving purposes in the public interest, for research or for statistical purposes in accordance with Article 89 [1]

5.4 Determining the Period Personal Data Are Maintained

For each category of personal data, Health Organizations should determine the period for which the data should be maintained, ensuring compliance with formal law provisions.

5.5 Special Actions for Compliance with the GDPR

Health Organizations should identify step-by-step, following the structure of the GDPR provisions, all the necessary actions to ensure compliance with the GDPR requirements and any other arrangements for the protection of the individual against the processing of personal data.

6 Conclusions

Organizations have to be prepared to comply with GDPR now in order to avoid risks and heavy consequences. In this paper, we have analyzed the security requirements for a GPDR compliant *Software as a Service* Health system and proposed specific measures that could be engaged in the process of GDPR compliance in cloud computing-based health environments. Understanding these implications has high practical relevance to Health providers as significant amounts of time, planning and money are typically needed to satisfy the requirements. The aim of our research is to assist the Cloud-based Health organizations to the hard road of GDPR compliance and to provide them with a compliance guide with a security perspective and, thus, to select the appropriate security measures for the protection of the data that they collect, process and store. Thus, this work is a necessary step to start dealing with required legal transformations. Future work comprises the development and test of proposed methods and features within real Health scenarios.

Acknowledgment. This research is co-financed by Greece and the European Union (European Social Fund-ESF) through the Operational Programme «Human Resources Development, Education and Lifelong Learning» in the context of the project "Reinforcement of Postdoctoral Researchers - 2nd Cycle" (MIS-5033021), implemented by the State Scholarships Foundation (IKΥ).

References

1. European Union: Regulation (EU) 2016/679 of the European Parliament and of the Council L 119. Official Journal of the European Union (2016)
2. GDPR: GDPR key changes (2017). https://www.eugdpr.org/the-regulation.html
3. Berendt, B.: 'Better Data Protection by Design Through Multicriteria Decision Making: On False Trade-offs Between Privacy and Utility', Privacy Technologies and Policy. Springer, Cham (2017)
4. ElShekeil, S.A., Laoyookhong, S.: GDPR Privacy by Design: From Legal Requirements to Technical Solutions. Department of Computer and Systems Sciences Stockholm University (2017)
5. Mohassel, R.R., Fung, A., Mohammadi, F., Raahemifar, K.: A survey on advanced metering infrastructure. Int. J. Electr. Power Energy Syst. **63**, 473–484 (2014). https://doi.org/10.1016/j.ijepes.2014.06.025
6. Newborough, M., Augoud, P.: Demand-side management opportunities for the UK domestic sector. IET Proc. Gener. Trans. Distrib. **146**(3), 283–293 (1999)
7. TACIT Project 2016: Threat Assessment framework for Critical Infrastructures proTection (2016). https://www.tacit-project.eu
8. WP29 Opinion 1/2009 on e-Privacy Directive, 10 February 2009

Aligning the Concepts of Risk, Security and Privacy Towards the Design of Secure Intelligent Transport Systems

Vasiliki Diamantopoulou[1]([✉]), Christos Kalloniatis[2], Christos Lyvas[1],
Konstantinos Maliatsos[1], Matthieu Gay[3], Athanasios Kanatas[1],
and Costas Lambrinoudakis[1]

[1] Department of Digital Systems, University of Piraeus, 150 Androutsou Street,
18532 Piraeus, Greece
{vdiamant,clyvas,kmaliat,kanatas,clam}@unipi.gr
[2] Department of Cultural Technology and Communication, University of the Aegean,
University Hill, 81100 Lesvos, Greece
chkallon@aegean.gr
[3] Airbus CyberSecurity, Metapole, 1 Boulevard Jean Moulin, Elancourt 78996,
France
matthieu.gay@airbus.com

Abstract. Intelligent Transport Systems (ITS) play a key role in our daily activities. ITS development over the last decades has been based on the rapid evolution of information technologies, which include processing capabilities, availability of hardware and communication technologies. Moreover, ITS use Information and Communication Technologies (ICT) to improve sustainability, efficiency, innovation and safety of transportation networks helping towards better management of transportation networks with the use of advanced technologies, which facilitate monitoring, and management of information. However, as the development of ITS services increases so does the users' awareness regarding the degree of trust that they show on adopting this kind of services. The later has brought light to several security and privacy concerns that ITS analysts should consider when implementing various IT related services. This paper moves into this direction by identifying how risk analysis can interact with security and privacy requirements engineering world, in order to provide a holistic approach for reasoning about security and privacy in such complex environments like ITS systems. The key contribution of the paper is the conceptual alignment of three well-known methods (EBIOS, Secure Tropos and PriS) as the first step towards the design of a complete assurance framework that will assist analysts in designing safe and trustworthy ITS services.

Keywords: Intelligent Transport Systems · Risk analysis methodologies · Security requirements engineering methodologies · Privacy requirements engineering methodologies

© Springer Nature Switzerland AG 2020
S. Katsikas et al. (Eds.): CyberICPS 2020/SECPRE 2020/ADIoT 2020, LNCS 12501, pp. 170–184, 2020.
https://doi.org/10.1007/978-3-030-64330-0_11

1 Introduction

The way humans, smart things and engineered systems interact and exchange information has dramatically changed due to the recent advances in communications, computation, networking, software, and hardware technologies. The paradigm of *Connected Vehicles* constitutes a major technology and paradigm shift in the automotive industry, where enabling technologies and concepts of networked ICT, Internet-of-Things (IoT) and Cyber-Physical Systems (CPS) introduce new services and applications that will dramatically change driver-vehicle interaction. Based on a report that EC published [3], in the near future, the self-driving vehicles' market is expected to grow exponentially, developing profits of up to €620 billion by 2025 for the EU automotive industry. The benefits from these technological achievements are quite many [30], such as the transformation of roads to safer ones, the protection of the environment, the improvement of accessibility for disable people, the creation of new job positions and, consequently, the economic growth, to name a few.

However, autonomous driving rises a number of challenges that the scientific community, in cooperation with industry, has to overcome. Road safety, liability issues, data processing, and the necessary infrastructure are some that have been already identified in the early stages of the progression to the full automation of connected vehicles. Staying in the direction of the identification of challenges, a recent report of the European Commission [10] highlights the importance of finding the right balance in sharing only the appropriate amount of public and private data. As the market of the driverless vehicles increases [23], security research in this field will play a key role. Connected vehicles offer enormous opportunities for innovative features and services that in turn increase vehicles' cyber attack surface. Research in this area [21,31,39] has revealed that connected vehicles are prone to attacks due to the increased trend of high connected ICT, IoT and cloud services introduced.

Towards the direction of filling the aforementioned gaps, the ultimate goal of our work is to build a security assurance framework able to support connected vehicular technology, by addressing the safety, security and privacy of the handled data. This framework will be based on three well-established methodologies, each one focusing on addressing specific requirements, namely EBIOS [1], Secure Tropos [27], and PriS [18]. For this reason, in this study we present the first step towards the development of this framework, which is about the identification of the concepts shared in these three methodologies. In order to provide a more efficient design of the unified framework, an alignment of the EBIOS concepts with the concepts of Secure Tropos and PriS is important in order to identify any conceptual conflicts or any similarities in the terms used. Since Secure Tropos and PriS have their origins in the Software Engineering world [15], there was no need to align their concepts as well.

The rest of this paper is organised as follows: Sect. 2 presents related work regarding the three research areas that we examine. Section 3 presents the baseline of our work, by analysing all three methodologies that will allow us to align the concepts of the examined methodologies. Section 4 describes the outcome of this analysis, focusing on the common concepts of the analysed methodologies. Finally, Sect. 5 concludes the paper by raising issues for further research.

2   Literature Review

One of the novel aspects of the security assurance framework that we aim to develop, is that it integrates three different research areas, i.e. risk analysis, security requirements engineering, and the area of privacy requirements engineering. For this reason, since, to the best of our knowledge, there is no other integrated method that combines these three areas, in this section, we focus our literature review on these three areas separately.

Risk Analysis. In the area of risk analysis, OCTAVE methodology [2] focuses on activities, threats, and vulnerabilities. Its main concept is self-direction, which means that people within the organisation must practice information security risk assessment [22]. The OCTAVE approach has three stages, each of which is divided into processes. Each process has certain activities that must be completed, and within each of these activities, the different phases must be taken to achieve the desired results.

CORAS [35] was developed using information society technologies. One of its main objectives is to develop a structure that uses the methods of risk analysis, semi-formal methods for object-oriented modelling, and computer tools for an accurate and unambiguous assessment of risk, and efficient critical safety systems [13]. The methodology is based on Unified Modelling Language (UML), a language that uses diagrams to illustrate relationships and dependencies between users and the environment in which they work.

The CCTA Risk Analysis and Management Method (CRAMM) [37] is a qualitative risk analysis and management tool. It calculates/estimates risk for each group of assets versus the threats to which it is vulnerable on a scale of 1 to 7, utilizing a risk matrix with the default values, by comparing it with the activity level of threat and vulnerability.

Compared to the review conducted in risk analysis area, EBIOS is an adequate and industrially validated tool to start the study since it assists analysts by guiding them in the early steps of the system design, especially for defining system's security objectives [29].

Security Requirements Engineering. In the area of security requirements engineering, the authors of [33] propose Model Oriented Security Requirements Engineering (MOSRE) framework for Web Applications which considers security requirements at the early stages of the development process. It covers all phases of requirements engineering and suggests the specification of the security requirements in addition to the specification of systems requirements. The objectives, stakeholders, and assets of the Web application are identified during the inception phase. The final security requirements are elicited after a sequence of actions that include the identification - categorisation - prioritisation of threats and system vulnerabilities the risk assessment process, the analysis and modelling, and finally the categorisation - prioritisation - validation of the final security requirements.

SQUARE (Security Quality Requirements Engineering) methodology [24] is a risk-driven method that supports the elicitation, categorisation, prioritisation and inspection of the security requirements through a number of specific steps. It also supports the performance of risk assessment to assess the tolerance of a system against possible threats. The method outputs all the necessary security requirements that are essential for the satisfaction of the security goals of a system. The methodology introduces the concepts of security goal, threat, and risk, but does not consider the assets and the vulnerabilities of a system. All the required security requirements should be identified by the requirements engineering team and the relevant stakeholders.

Another approach is the Security Requirements Engineering Framework (SREF) [14] which enables the elicitation and analysis of security requirements. This framework includes four stages. Firstly, it identifies functional requirements and afterwards, the security goals. Continuing, it identifies the security requirements of the functional requirements. Each security requirement satisfies one or more security goals. After these steps, the framework decides if the system satisfies the security requirements. The authors introduced an asset-based approach for the elicitation of security goals from business process models which are then translated into security requirements.

In [11,12] the authors propose the Problem-based Security Requirements Elicitation (PresSuRE) Methodology that facilitates the identification of security needs during requirements analysis of software systems. More specifically, it provides a computer security threat recognition and then the development of security requirements. This methodology uses problem diagrams to support the modelling of functional requirements. Firstly, based on its contents, this methodology identifies system's assets and the rights of authorised entities. Then, it determines possible attackers and their abilities. Based on these steps, PresSuRE generates graphs which depict threats on system's assets. Every functional requirement of each asset is related with possible threats and security requirements.

Compared to the methodologies presented in this sub-section, Secure Tropos offers a more advanced tool for modelling, while the programming language used for the development of the tool is easily extended. Moreover, the methodological approach can be easily aligned with a risk-based approach. Finally, it combines actor and goal-based modelling, which is very important for the alignment of the common concepts of the three examined areas.

Privacy Requirements Engineering. In the area of privacy requirements engineering, in [7] the authors present LINDDUN, a privacy threat analysis framework which, in its first release, aimed at the elicitation and fulfilment of privacy requirements in software-based systems. The process that LINDDUN follows is that a data flow diagram (DFD) of the system is designed and then the identified privacy threats are related to DFD elements. Privacy threat trees and misuse cases are used for the collection of threat scenarios that might affect the system. Moreover, this methodology supports the elicitation of the final privacy requirements and the selection of appropriate privacy enhancing technologies. The final stage of this methodology is the prioritisation and validation of privacy threat through risk assessment.

Next, in [34] the authors adopt the concepts of privacy-by-policy and privacy-by-architecture, and propose a three-sphere model of user privacy concerns, relating it to system operations (i.e. data transfer, storage and processing). Additionally, the Modelling and Analysis of Privacy-aware Systems (MAPaS) framework [6] is a framework for modelling requirements for privacy-aware systems. The ABC4Trust project [32] protects privacy in identity management systems.

Compared to the methodologies presented in this sub-section, the PriS method is one of the oldest and mostly evaluated privacy-by-design methodologies, while it is successfully used for the elicitation and modelling of privacy requirements in traditional and cloud-based systems.

Finally, on a conceptual level the Secure Tropos and PriS methods are already successfully tested under a unified framework [28].

3   Background Analysis

This section presents the methodologies that we will rely upon, in order to develop an enhanced security assurance framework, able to support connected vehicular technology, by addressing safety, security and privacy of the handled data. More specifically, the methodology for the risk analysis is EBIOS, for the identification of security requirements, we present Secure Tropos methodology and finally, for the identification of privacy requirements, we present PriS methodology.

3.1   Risk Analysis

EBIOS (English: Expression of needs and identification of security objectives) is the risk analysis methodology created by the french Agence Nationale de la Sécurité des Systèmes d' Information (ANSSI) (English: National Cybersecurity Agency of France). A risk analysis method identifies the critical part of the system and their corresponding threats in order to evaluate the risk for these assets and then the proper security objectives regarding the evaluated risks. EBIOS is composed of five steps and offers many advantages, particularly the flexibility, quickness besides the fact that it is a proven methodology that has been used in several risk assessments and that it is compatible with the ISO 27005 risk analysis phase.

During the first step, *Circumstantial study*, the analyst can define the perimeter (boundaries) of the study. A global vision of the components and communications between components will be clarified. At this step, the following data will be collected and formalised (non-exhaustive list):

- Essentials assets in a connected vehicle system

- Functional description of components and relations between components
- Security issues that need to be addressed by the study
- Assumptions made if appropriate
- Existing security rules (law and regulation, existing rules in other studies)
- Potential constraints (internal or external) that might be imposed from the specific under examination system

At the end of this step, a clear vision of the components and the links between them will be formalised.

The second step, namely *Expression of security needs*, contributes to risk estimation and definition of risk criteria. The expression of security needs will be performed based on scale of needs. Security criteria and hypothetic impacts will be stated. Security needs will be associated with each essential component by taking into account the security criteria. A security needs report will be the output of this step. Next, the *Threat study and modelling* step follows, where the threats affecting the connected vehicle systems are studied. The threats are specific to the connected vehicles. There will be no dependencies between these threats and the security needs collected in the previous step. The list of the pertinent threats and the type of attacks will be the main outputs of this step.

Step 4 follows, entitled *Identification of security objectives*. The purpose of this step is to evaluate the risks affecting the connected vehicle environment. The security objective is highlighted by comparing the threats with security needs. The security objectives will contain the security requirements fulfilled in the development of secure connected vehicle system (or component).

The final step, Step 5 *Determination of security requirements*, brings an answer to the question how the security objectives will be achieved.

3.2   Security Requirements Engineering Analysis

Secure Tropos [27] is a security requirements engineering methodology that supports elicitation and analysis of security requirements. It is based on the principle that security should be analysed and considered from the early stages of the software system development process, and not added as an afterthought. To support that approach, the methodology provides a modelling language, a security-aware process, and a set of automated processes to support the analysis and consideration of security from the early stages of the development process. The Secure Tropos language consists of a set of concepts from the requirements engineering domain, and in particular Goal-Oriented Requirements Engineering [4,36], such as actor, goal, plan, and dependency, which are enriched with concepts from security engineering, such as security constraint, secure plan, and attacks. This methodology closely follows the software development life-cycle, i.e. capturing of early requirements, late requirements, architectural design, detailed design, and finally, implementation. Thus, it allows the developer to create and refine models, starting from the system-as-it-is, in order to finally develop the system-to-be, during the analysis and design stage [9].

Concepts Description

Secure Tropos combines concepts from requirements engineering for representing general concepts and security engineering for representing security-oriented concepts [25].

A (hard) *Goal* [38] represents a condition in the world that an actor would like to achieve. In other words, goals represent actors' strategic interests. In Tropos, the concept of a hard-goal (simply goal hereafter) is differentiated from the concept of soft-goal.

A *Soft-Goal* is used to capture non-functional requirements of the system, and unlike a (hard) goal, it does not have clear criteria for deciding whether it is satisfied or not and therefore it is subject to interpretation [38]. For instance, an example of a soft-goal is the "system should be scalable". According to Chung et al. [5], the difference between a goal and a soft-goal is underlined by saying that goals are satisfied whereas soft-goals are satisfied under specific circumstances.

An *Actor* represents an entity that has intentionality and strategic goals within the multi-agent system or within its organisational setting. An actor can be human, a system, or an organisation.

A *Plan* [4] represents, at an abstract level, a way of doing something. The fulfillment of a task can be a mean for satisfying a goal, or for contributing towards the satisfying of a soft-goal. In Tropos different (alternative) tasks, that actors might employ to achieve their goals, are modelled. Therefore, developers can reason about the different ways that actors can achieve their goals and choose the best one.

A *Resource* [4] presents a physical or informational entity that one of the actors requires. The main concern when dealing with resources is whether the resource is available and who is responsible for its delivery.

A *Dependency* [38] between two actors represents that one actor depends on the other to attain some goal, execute a task, or deliver a resource. The depending actor is called the depender and the actor who is depended upon is called the dependee. The type of the dependency describes the nature of an agreement (called dependum) between dependee and depender. Goal dependencies represent delegation of responsibility for fulfilling a goal. Soft-goal dependencies are similar to goal dependencies, but their fulfilment cannot be defined precisely whereas task dependencies are used in situations where the dependee is required to perform a given activity. By depending on the dependee for the dependum, the depender is able to achieve goals that it is otherwise unable to achieve on their own, or not as easily or not as well [38]. On the other hand, the depender becomes vulnerable, since if the dependee fails to deliver the dependum, the depender is affected in their aim to achieve their goals.

A *Secure Dependency* [28] introduces one or more Security Constraint(s) that must be fulfilled for the dependency to be valid. In the Secure Tropos methodology we distinguish among three types of secure dependencies: dependee secure dependency, depender secure dependency, and double secure dependency. In terms of the modelling language, different Secure Dependency types are defined using depender and dependee attributes of Security Constraints.

A *Security Constraint* is used to represent security requirements. A Security Constraint is a specialisation of the concept of constraint. In the context of software engineering, a constraint is usually defined as a restriction that can influence the analysis and design of a software system under development by restricting some alternative design solutions, by conflicting with some of the requirements of the system, or by refining some of the systems objectives. In other words, constraints can represent a set of restrictions that do not permit specific actions to be taken or prevent certain objectives from being achieved. Constraints are often integrated in the specification of existing textual descriptions. However, this approach can often lead to misunderstandings and an unclear definition of a constraint and its role in the development process. Consequently, this results in errors in the very early development stages that propagate to the later stages of the development process, causing many problems when discovered; if they are discovered. Therefore, in the Secure Tropos modelling language, security constraints are handled as a separate concept. To this end, the concept of security constraint has been defined within the context of Secure Tropos as: A security condition imposed to an actor that restricts achievement of an actor's goals, execution of plans or availability of resources. Security constraints are outside the control of an actor. This means that, differently than goals, security constraints are not conditions that an actor wishes to introduce but it is forced to introduce.

A *Vulnerability* [28] is defined as a weakness, in terms of security and privacy, that exists in a resource, an actor and/or a goal. Vulnerabilities are exploited by threats, as an attack or incident within a specific context.

A *Threat* [28] represents circumstances that have the potential to cause loss; or a problem that can put in danger the security features of the system.

Threats can be operationalised by different attack methods, each exploiting a number of system vulnerabilities. An *Attack Method* [26] in Secure Tropos is an action aiming to cause a potential violation of security in the system.

Security Mechanisms [26] represent security methods for helping towards the satisfaction of the security objectives. Some of these methods are able to prevent security attacks, whereas others are able only to detect security breaches. It must be noted that further analysis of some security mechanisms is required to allow developers to identify possible security sub-mechanisms. A security sub-mechanism represents a specific way of achieving a security mechanism. For instance, authentication denotes a security mechanism for the fulfilment of a protection objective such as authorisation. However, authentication can be achieved by sub-mechanisms such as passwords, digital signatures and biometrics.

3.3 Privacy Requirements Engineering Analysis

PriS (Privacy Safeguard) is a privacy requirements engineering methodology, which provides a set of concepts for modelling privacy requirements in the organisation domain and a systematic way-of-working for translating these requirements into system models.

PriS, initially introduced in [18–20], is a privacy requirements engineering methodology, developed for assisting designers on eliciting, modelling, designing privacy requirements of the system to be and also providing guidance to the developers on selecting the appropriate implementation techniques that best fit the organisation's privacy requirements. In a recent work [8], privacy process patterns have been integrated to PriS, in order to facilitate system developers to bridge the gap between design and implementation. PriS provides a set of concepts for modelling privacy requirements in the organisation domain and a systematic way-of-working for translating these requirements into system models. This methodology identifies privacy as a multifaceted concept and defines it in the context of eight technical privacy requirements (such as anonymity and unlinkability) and adopts the use of process patterns as a way to:

– describe the effect of privacy requirements on business processes; and
– facilitate the identification of the system architecture that best supports the privacy-related business processes.

PriS was designed for supporting the realisation of privacy-aware information systems on traditional environments and not for the cloud. Cloud environments introduced a number of new privacy related concepts that along with the ones already stated form a new set of concepts that need to be considered when designing privacy-aware services over the cloud. Thus, extended versions of PriS were introduced [16,17] for assisting designers to reason about privacy concerns in cloud environments as well.

PriS Conceptual Model
The conceptual model of PriS uses the concept of *goal* as the central and most important concept. Goals are desired state of affairs that need to be attained. Goals concern stakeholders, i.e. anyone that has as interest in the system design and usage. Also, goals are generated because of *issues*. An issue is a statement of a *strength, weakness, opportunity* or *threat* that leads to the formation of the goal. *Cloud Service Providers* (CSPs) constraint the functionality of the developed system or service due to the technologies they use, the policies they follow, the contractual requirements with third parties, etc. Thus, the CSP may provide requirements that designers need to take under consideration during the realisation of the system. Protection of users' privacy is stated in many European and national *legislations* through the form of laws, policies, directives, best practices, etc. All these sources need to be taken under consideration during the identification of functional and non-functional requirements for traditional and cloud-based systems. Thus, goal identification needs to take under consideration all these elements before further analysis is conducted.

PriS distinguishes two types of goals, namely *organisational goals* and *privacy goals*. Organisational goals express the main organisation objectives that need to be satisfied by the system into consideration. Organisational goals will lead to the realisation of system's functional requirements. In parallel, privacy goals are introduced because of specific cloud based privacy related concepts namely *anonymity, pseudonymity, unlinkability, undetectability* and *data protection*. *Unobservability* is realised if the system sufficiently realises undetectability among the respective assets and anonymity of the user accessing them. Thus it is

Table 1. EBIOS Concepts and Alignment with Secure Tropos and PriS

Concept	Meaning	Example	Concept Alignment with Secure Tropos and PriS
Entities	Main organisation elements	Hardware, Software, Network, etc.	Resources (Assets), Actors
Essential Elements	Functions and information providing added value to the entities. They are linked to the Entities	A computational parameter is an essential element that is linked with the computer A and Software Process B	–
Sensitivity	Security criteria that constraint an essential element. Avoiding the coverage of a security criterion there will be an impact on the organisation through the linked entity	Integrity, Availability, Confidentiality	Security Constraint, Privacy Constraint
Threat Agents	Natural, human, environmental threats, either accidental or deliberate	Earthquake, loss of password	Threat
Attack Methods	The knowledge derived by the combination of the sensitivity of the organization and the respective threat agents	Availability and denial of service attack	Attack method
Vulnerability	Each entity has a number of vulnerabilities that can be exploited by threat agents using attack methods	A denial of service attack (attack method) exploited by a malicious actor (threat agent) on the web server (entity) due to lack of cryptographic protocol usage (vulnerability)	Vulnerability
Security Objectives	The way that vulnerabilities are reduced thus reducing the potential risk on the entities	Protect the integrity of users' data in order to avoid unauthorized alterations from malicious parties	Security Objectives, Privacy Objectives
Security Requirements	The transformation of security objectives into security functionalities that are translated into functional requirements	–	Security Process patterns and plans, Privacy Process patterns and plans
Assurance Requirements	Specific requirements that will guarantee the required level of confidence for the realization of the security requirements expressed as Functional requirements	–	Security mechanisms

not accomplished directly but indirectly through the realisation of the respective two concepts. Finally, the concepts of *isolation, provenanceability, traceability, interveanability* and *accountability* are related to data protection of user's or systems data over the cloud, as it was explained previously. Thus, all these concepts are grouped under the data protection class. Privacy goals may have an impact on organisational goals. In general, a privacy goal may cause the improvement/adaptation of organisational goals or the introduction of new ones. In this way, privacy issues are incorporated into the system's design.

Goals are realised by *processes*. The transition process from goals to processes includes the causal transformation of general goals into one or more subgoals that form the means for achieving desired ends. During this process, in every step, new goals are introduced and linked to the original one through causal relations, thus forming a hierarchy of goals. Every subgoal may contribute to the achievement to more than one goals.

As it was mentioned previously, goals are realised by processes. PriS uses a set of *privacy process patterns* [8] as a more robust way of bringing the gap between the design and the implementation phase. Privacy process patterns are usually generalised process models, which include activities and flows connecting them, presenting how a business should be run in a specific domain. Privacy process patterns are applied on privacy related processes in order to specify the way that the respective privacy issues will be realised through a specific number of steps. This assists also the developer who can understand in a better and specific way, how to implement the aforementioned privacy concepts. Privacy process patterns are also used for identifying a number of *Privacy Enhancing Technologies* (PETs) already available for implementing the system's privacy requirements. In this way, the developer can choose the most appropriate technology based on the privacy process patterns applied on every privacy-related process.

4   Concept Alignment

For proposing a generic approach that combines risk analysis with security and privacy requirements elicitation and modelling approaches, it is important to examine if a correlation between the aforementioned methodologies can occur from a conceptual point of view. The goal is to design a methodology that facilitates analysts and software engineers to get from the system description and threats knowledge a detailed, clearly justified, and well-structured set of security and privacy requirements, covering these threats. EBIOS is an adequate and industrially validated tool to start the study since it assists analysts by guiding them in the early steps of the system design, especially for defining system's security objectives. Secure Tropos, a well-known security requirements engineering methodology can use the EBIOS output as input for deriving "formally" the adequate security requirements for the various elements of the system. Finally, PriS provides an extra focus on privacy, which is a very important topic in the field of ITS security, aiming to increase users' trust, by providing privacy-aware services.

Thus, in order to provide a more efficient design of the unified methodology, an alignment of the EBIOS concepts with the concepts of Secure Tropos and PriS was important in order to identify any conceptual conflicts or any similarities in the terms used. The alignment of the concepts is presented in Table 1. Since Secure Tropos and PriS have their origins from the Software Engineering world, there was no need to align their concepts as well. The necessary alignment was between EBIOS and the two other methods.

5   Conclusions

This work comprises the first step towards the development of a methodology for a security assurance framework, able to support connected vehicular technology, by addressing safety, security and privacy of the handled data. The first step of this work, presented in this paper, focuses on the identification of the common concepts of three already existing methodologies, namely EBIOS, Secure Tropos, and PriS. In order to provide a more efficient design of the unified methodology, an alignment of the EBIOS concepts with the concepts of Secure Tropos and PriS was important in order to identify any conceptual conflicts or any similarities in the terms used. This output will be the basis for the development of the methodology that facilitates the transition from a system description and threats knowledge, to a detailed, clearly justified and well-structured set of security requirements.

Assurance security evaluation methods always rely on the definition of a proper security target. Thus, it is an important aspect of the evaluation process to define a meaningful security target. It is often one of the most criticised parts of an evaluation, since there is no universal way to assess the relevance of such a document. But one thing that helps gain confidence in this part of the evaluation is the existence of elements of proof that the system and the real threats associated to it, are properly understood and justified. With this work, we aim to overcome the aforementioned limitations, by providing a methodology which will be able to facilitate the design process of the relevant security target, representing real-world security objectives for Intelligent Transportation Systems (ITS).

In the next steps of this work, the aim is to develop a new tool that will be able to make assurance of security, safety and privacy aspects for Connected Vehicles, measurable, visible and controllable by stakeholders, and thus, enhancing confidence and trust in Connected Vehicles.

Acknowledgment. This work is a part of the SAFERtec project. SAFERtec has received funding from the European Union's Horizon 2020 research & innovation programme under grant agreement no 732319. Content reflects only the authors' view and European Commission is not responsible for any use that may be made of the information it contains.

References

1. Ebios – expression des besoins et identification des objectifs de sécurité (2019). https://www.ssi.gouv.fr/guide/ebios-2010-expression-des-besoins-et-identifica tion-des-objectifs-de-securite/
2. Alberts, C., Dorofee, A., Stevens, J., Woody, C.: Introduction to the octave approach. Carnegie-Mellon Univ Pittsburgh PA Software Engineering Inst., Technical report (2003)
3. Després, J., et al.: An analysis of possible socio-economic effects of a cooperative, connected and automated mobility (CCAM) in Europe. EUR - Scientific and Technical Research Reports, Publications Office of the European Union (2018)
4. Bresciani, P., Perini, A., Giorgini, P., Giunchiglia, F., Mylopoulos, J.: Tropos: an agent-oriented software development methodology. Auton. Agent. Multi-Agent Syst. **8**(3), 203–236 (2004)
5. Chung, L., Nixon, B.A.: Dealing with non-functional requirements: three experimental studies of a process-oriented approach. In: Proceedings of the 17th International Conference on Software Engineering, pp. 25–37. ACM (1995)
6. Colombo, P., Ferrari, E.: Towards a modeling and analysis framework for privacy-aware systems. In: Privacy, Security, Risk and Trust (PASSAT), 2012 International Conference on and 2012 International Conference on Social Computing (Social-Com), pp. 81–90. IEEE (2012)
7. Deng, M., Wuyts, K., Scandariato, R., Preneel, B., Joosen, W.: A privacy threat analysis framework: supporting the elicitation and fulfillment of privacy requirements. Requir. Eng. **16**(1), 3–32 (2011)
8. Diamantopoulou, V., Kalloniatis, C., Gritzalis, S., Mouratidis, H.: Supporting privacy by design using privacy process patterns. In: De Capitani di Vimercati, S., Martinelli, F. (eds.) SEC 2017. IAICT, vol. 502, pp. 491–505. Springer, Cham (2017). https://doi.org/10.1007/978-3-319-58469-0_33
9. Diamantopoulou, V., Pavlidis, M., Mouratidis, H.: Evaluation of a security and privacy requirements methodology using the physics of notation. In: Katsikas, S.K., Cuppens, F., Cuppens, N., Lambrinoudakis, C., Kalloniatis, C., Mylopoulos, J., Antón, A., Gritzalis, S. (eds.) CyberICPS/SECPRE -2017. LNCS, vol. 10683, pp. 210–225. Springer, Cham (2018). https://doi.org/10.1007/978-3-319-72817-9_14
10. European Commission: Communication from the commission to the european parliament, the council, the european economic and social committee, the committee of the regions, on the road to automated mobility: An eu strategy for mobility of the future (2018)
11. Faßbender, S., Heisel, M., Meis, R.: Functional requirements under security pressure. In: 2014 9th International Conference on Software Paradigm Trends (ICSOFT-PT), pp. 5–16. IEEE (2014)
12. Faßbender, S., Heisel, M., Meis, R.: Problem-based security requirements elicitation and refinement with PresSuRE. In: Holzinger, A., Cardoso, J., Cordeiro, J., Libourel, T., Maciaszek, L.A., van Sinderen, M. (eds.) ICSOFT 2014. CCIS, vol. 555, pp. 311–330. Springer, Cham (2015). https://doi.org/10.1007/978-3-319-25579-8_18
13. Fredriksen, R., Kristiansen, M., Gran, B.A., Stølen, K., Opperud, T.A., Dimitrakos, T.: The coras framework for a model-based risk management process. In: International Conference on Computer Safety, Reliability, and Security, pp. 94–105. Springer, Boston (2002)

14. Haley, C., Laney, R., Moffett, J., Nuseibeh, B.: Security requirements engineering: a framework for representation and analysis. IEEE Trans. Softw. Eng. **34**(1), 133–153 (2008)

15. Islam, S., Ouedraogo, M., Kalloniatis, C., Mouratidis, H., Gritzalis, S.: Assurance of security and privacy requirements for cloud deployment models. IEEE Trans. Cloud Comput. **6**(2), 387–400 (2015)

16. Kalloniatis, C.: Designing privacy-aware systems in the cloud. In: Fischer-Hübner, S., Lambrinoudakis, C., Lopez, J. (eds.) TrustBus 2015. LNCS, vol. 9264, pp. 113–123. Springer, Cham (2015). https://doi.org/10.1007/978-3-319-22906-5_9

17. Kalloniatis, C.: Incorporating privacy in the design of cloud-based systems: a conceptual meta-model. Inf. Comput. Secur. **25**(5), 614–633 (2017)

18. Kalloniatis, C., Kavakli, E., Gritzalis, S.: Pris methodology: incorporating privacy requirements into the system design process. In: Mylopoulos, J., Spafford, G., (eds.) Proceedings of the SREIS 2005 13th IEEE International Requirements Engineering Conference-Symposium on Requirements Engineering for Information Security (2005)

19. Kalloniatis, C., Kavakli, E., Gritzalis, S.: Addressing privacy requirements in system design: the PriS method. Requir. Eng. **13**(3), 241–255 (2008)

20. Kalloniatis, C., Kavakli, E., Kontellis, E.: PRIS tool: A case tool for privacy-oriented requirements engineering. In: MCIS, p. 71 (2009)

21. Kleberger, P., Olovsson, T., Jonsson, E.: Security aspects of the in-vehicle network in the connected car. In: 2011 IEEE Intelligent Vehicles Symposium (IV), pp. 528–533. IEEE (2011)

22. Labuschagne, W.B.L., et al.: A comparative framework for evaluating information security risk management methods. Rand Afrikaans University, Standard Bank Academy for Information Technology (2004)

23. McKeefry, H.L.: Consumers get on board with connected cars (2016)

24. Mead, N.R., Stehney, T.: Security Quality Requirements Engineering (SQUARE) Methodology, vol. 30. ACM (2005)

25. Mouratidis, H.: A security oriented approach in the development of multiagent systems: applied to the management of the health and social care needs of older people in England. Ph.D. thesis, University of Sheffield (2004)

26. Mouratidis, H.: Secure software systems engineering: the secure tropos approach. JSW **6**(3), 331–339 (2011)

27. Mouratidis, H., Giorgini, P.: Secure tropos: a security-oriented extension of the tropos methodology. Int. J. Softw. Eng. Knowl. Eng. **17**(02), 285–309 (2007)

28. Mouratidis, H., Islam, S., Kalloniatis, C., Gritzalis, S.: A framework to support selection of cloud providers based on security and privacy requirements. J. Syst. Softw. **86**(9), 2276–2293 (2013)

29. général de la défense nationale Direction centrale de la sécurité des systèmes d'information, P.M.S.: The ebios method, expression of needs and identification of security objectives

30. Parliament, E.: Self-driving cars in the EU: from science fiction to reality (2019)

31. Petit, J., Shladover, S.E.: Potential cyberattacks on automated vehicles. IEEE Trans. Intell. Transp. Syst. **16**(2), 546–556 (2015)

32. Sabouri, A., Rannenberg, K.: ABC4Trust: protecting privacy in identity management by bringing privacy-ABCs into real-life. In: Camenisch, J., Fischer-Hübner, S., Hansen, M. (eds.) Privacy and Identity 2014. IAICT, vol. 457, pp. 3–16. Springer, Cham (2015). https://doi.org/10.1007/978-3-319-18621-4_1

33. Salini, P., Kanmani, S.: Application of model oriented security requirements engineering framework for secure e-voting. In: 2012 CSI Sixth International Conference on Software Engineering (CONSEG), pp. 1–6. IEEE (2012)

34. Spiekermann, S., Cranor, L.F.: Engineering privacy. IEEE Trans. Softw. Eng. **35**(1), 67–82 (2009)

35. Stolen, K., den Braber, F., Dimitrakos, T., Fredriksen, R., Gran, B.A., Houmb, S.H., Lund, M.S., Stamatiou, Y., Aagedal, J.: Model-based risk assessment-the CORAS approach. In: iTrust Workshop (2002)

36. Van Lamsweerde, A.: Goal-oriented requirements engineering: A guided tour. In: Fifth IEEE International Symposium on Requirements Engineering, 2001, Proceedings, pp. 249–262. IEEE (2001)

37. Yazar, Z.: A qualitative risk analysis and management tool-CRAMM. SANS InfoSec Read. Room White Paper **11**, 12–32 (2002)

38. Yu, E.: Modelling strategic relationships for process reengineering. Soc. Model. Requir. Eng. **11**, 2011 (2011)

39. Zhang, T., Antunes, H., Aggarwal, S.: Defending connected vehicles against malware: challenges and a solution framework. IEEE IoT J. **1**(1), 10–21 (2014)

Identifying Implicit Vulnerabilities
Through Personas as Goal Models

Shamal Faily[1]([⊠]) [ID], Claudia Iacob[2] [ID], Raian Ali[3] [ID], and Duncan Ki-Aries[1] [ID]

[1] Department of Computing and Informatics, Bournemouth University, Poole, UK
{sfaily,dkiaries}@bournemouth.ac.uk
[2] School of Computing, University of Portsmouth, Portsmouth, UK
claudia.iacob@port.ac.uk
[3] Hamid Bin Khalifa University, Doha, Qatar
raali2@hbku.edu.qa

Abstract. When used in requirements processes and tools, personas have the potential to identify vulnerabilities resulting from misalignment between user expectations and system goals. Typically, however, this potential is unfulfilled as personas and system goals are captured with different mindsets, by different teams, and for different purposes. If personas are visualised as goal models, it may be easier for stakeholders to see implications of their goals being satisfied or denied, and designers to incorporate the creation and analysis of such models into the broader RE tool-chain. This paper outlines a tool-supported approach for finding implicit vulnerabilities from user and system goals by reframing personas as social goal models. We illustrate this approach with a case study where previously hidden vulnerabilities based on human behaviour were identified.

1 Introduction

Personas are fictional characters that represent archetypal users, and embody their needs and goals [4]. Personas are the product of research with representative end-users, so designing for a single persona means designing for the user community he or she represents. By facilitating design for one customer voice rather than many, personas have become a popular User Experience (UX) technique for eliciting and validating user requirements.

Personas can be a useful addition to requirements processes and tools when 'building security in'. If we identify that a persona experiences physical or cognitive burden while completing a task then its performance might not be as intended. Steps might be omitted or the task altered to achieve an end more conducive to the persona's own goals, irrespective of whether or not the intent is malicious.

Personas can inspire the identification of security vulnerabilities. In practice, they usually do not. Design processes prioritising agility provide little time for using personas for anything besides validating stakeholder value has been

© Springer Nature Switzerland AG 2020
S. Katsikas et al. (Eds.): CyberICPS 2020/SECPRE 2020/ADIoT 2020, LNCS 12501, pp. 185–202, 2020.
https://doi.org/10.1007/978-3-030-64330-0_12

achieved. Even if we assume UX and security engineers collaborate, personas are not always used in the ways envisaged by designers [12], while security engineers might primarily focus on requirements for security mechanisms. Given their differing concerns and perspectives, problems may not be found even when these are indicated during the collection or analysis of user research data.

Personas, as user models, can be integrated into Security Requirements Engineering (RE) practices and tools, but they need to be built and presented differently. This may make it easier for stakeholders to identify the security implications of user goals being satisfied or denied. Goal models in languages like i^* [29] and the Goal-oriented Requirements Language (GRL) [1] provide a foundation for this improved integration; they represent the intentions and rationale of social and technical actors, their inter-relations, and alternative strategies giving a space for variability accommodation, including that of user types. Approaches like Secure Tropos [21] and STS-ml [23] show how goal models can be used in the early stage of design to find vulnerabilities. However, they are role-focused whereas people are expected to align to one or more ways to achieve predefined goals.

To integrate personas into Goal-oriented Security Requirements Engineering, we need to answer two research questions. First, how can persona creation be leveraged to construct goal models (RQ1)? Second, how can existing goal modelling approaches and RE tools, with minimal changes, be constructed to reveal *implicit* vulnerabilities – vulnerabilities that may be present when dependees fall short of their responsibility to deliver dependums [16] – without burdening designers with additional conceptual knowledge (RQ2)? User research and threat modelling can be time-consuming and cognitively intensive activities that might happen separately or in parallel before, during, or after other Requirements Engineering activities. It is, therefore, necessary to loosely couple these goal models such that other design models can evolve orthogonally with minimum disruption to existing processes and tools.

In this paper, we present a tool-supported approach for finding implicit vulnerabilities by reframing personas as social goal models. The remainder of this paper is structured as follows. In Sect. 2, we consider related work in social goal modelling and security, personas, and usable & secure Requirements Engineering upon which our approach is based. In Sect. 3, we present the processes and tool-support algorithms that underpin our approach before describing its application to an industrial control systems case study example in Sect. 4. We discuss the implications of our work and potential limitations in Sect. 5, before concluding in Sect. 6 by summarising the contributions of our work to date, and directions for future work.

2   Related Work

2.1   Finding Vulnerabilities Using Social Goal Modelling

Social goal modelling languages like i^* capture the modelling of dependencies, where a *depender* actor depends on *dependee* actor for some resource *depen-*

dum. Actors become vulnerable when they rely on dependees for dependums. Analysing chains of these dependencies can help us understand how vulnerable these actors are [28]. Moreover, when such models capture a socio-technical system of actors and resources, they can also highlight potential system vulnerabilities resulting from inconsistencies between an organisation's policies and working practices [17].

In previous work examining the use of social goal modelling to support Security Requirements Engineering, Liu et al. [16] considered how legitimate actors might use their intentions, capabilities and social relationships to attack the system, and how dependency relationships form the basis of exploitable vulnerabilities. The idea of dependencies as implicit vulnerabilities was further elaborated by Giorgini et al. [13], who indicated that dependency relationships can also capture trust relationships where dependers believe dependees will not misuse a goal, task or resource (Trust of permission), or a trustee believes dependees will achieve a goal, execute a task, or deliver a resource (Trust of execution).

Elahi et al. [5] incorporated vulnerabilities into goal models to link knowledge about threats, vulnerabilities, and countermeasures to stakeholder goals and security requirements. Vulnerabilities are considered as weaknesses in the structure of goals and activities of intentional agents, which can be propagated via decomposition and dependency links. The introduction of vulnerabilities was added on the basis that including security and non-security elements on a single model makes models clearer and facilitates model discussion [27]. However, while this approach supports the *specification* of vulnerabilities, it provides little support for *eliciting* them. This still requires a priori knowledge of potential system weaknesses or threat models that could take advantage of them. Moreover, Moody et al. [20] found that the graphical complexity of i^* is several times greater than a human's standard limit for distinguishing alternatives. As such, approaches that increase the complexity of the i^* language are likely to hinder rather than improve the understandability of social goal models, particularly for novices.

2.2   Personas for Security

UX professionals have long used personas to bring user requirements to life, and there has been some been work within the Requirements Engineering community on using personas to add contextual variability to social goal models, e.g. [22].

The merits of using personas to explicitly elicit security requirements was identified by Faily et al. [8], who showed how the use of personas could show the human impact of security to stakeholders who have never met user communities represented by personas. In recent years, there has also been additional interest in the RE community on the use of personas to engage stakeholders when validating requirements [3], and how data used to construct personas can have some security value. For example, Mead et al. [19] demonstrated how the text from personas built on assumptions about attackers (Personae Non Gratae) could be mined to identify potential threat models and identify gaps between a designer's and attacker's model of a system. However, Mead et al. focuses on the identification of threats to a system rather than vulnerabilities that might arise from interactions between personas and the system.

2.3   IRIS and CAIRIS

IRIS (Integrating Requirements and Information Security) is a process framework for designing usable and secure software [7]. The framework incorporates a methodology agnostic meta-model for usable and secure requirements engineering that supports the complementary use of different Security, Usability, and Requirements Engineering techniques. Personas are integrated into this framework, which uses the KAOS language for modelling system goals [15], obstacles that obstruct the satisfaction of these goals, dependency associations between roles, and relationships between tasks, system goals, and the roles responsible for them. The framework is complemented by CAIRIS (Computer-Aided Integration of Requirements and Information Security): a software platform for eliciting, specifying, automatically visualising, and validating secure and usable systems that is built on the IRIS meta-model. By making explicit the links between different security, usability, and software models using IRIS, and providing tool-support for automating generating and validating these models, IRIS and CAIRIS can put one model in context with another. For example, we recently demonstrated how data flow *taint* could be identified in data flow diagrams within CAIRIS by putting these diagrams in context with other software and usability models [11].

Previous work has shown that, if personas are constructed using qualitative data analysis, the results of this analysis can be framed as argumentation models [9], and the elements of these models can be re-framed as goals and soft goals in social goal models [6]. Not only does this make it possible to automatically generate goal models from argumentation models, some assurance is also provided for both the basis of user goals and the broader impact of satisfying these goals on other system elements. Subsequent work has demonstrated how these concepts can lead to generation of elaborate GRL compatible goal models [10]. However, a weakness of this approach is its reliance on additional tool-support (jUCMNav), and the limited support of traceability links between the goal modelling platform and its originating data should the GRL model evolve; such evolution is likely as different stakeholders make sense of this model. Subsequent refinement of the jUCMNav model could lead to additional effort by analysts to ensure the goal model and its foundational CAIRIS models are synchronised.

3   Approach

3.1   Conceptual Model

To reframe a persona as a social goal model, our approach relies on aligning concepts from IRIS with concepts from social goal modelling. A review of the complete conceptual model, which is described in more detail in [7], is beyond the scope of this paper. We do, however, summarise this model concept alignment in Fig. 1, which we provide further rationale for in the sub-sections below.

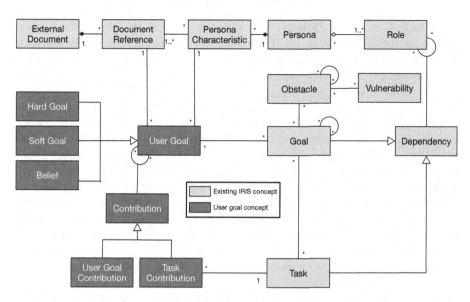

Fig. 1. UML class diagram of IRIS and user goal concepts

Personas and Persona Characteristics. Our approach has only a minimal impact on existing IRIS concepts. We assume personas consist of multiple persona characteristics. These characteristics are attributes of persona behaviour; they can be considered as arguments for persona behaviour, and are grounded in one or more grounds, warrants, and rebuttal elements. These elements (document references) are *factoids* that can be drawn from a variety of primary and secondary data sources (external documents) such as interview transcripts, observational notes, and web sites. Further details on these concepts can be found in [7].

User Goals. User goals represent the intentional desires of actors, where actors are personas. This definition is inline with the definition used for goals by the social goal modelling community, e.g. [28]. In our approach, user goals are factoids expressed intentionally. Yu et al. [30] states that intentional properties can only be inferred based on information obtained by indirect means, and that the validity of these attributions can never be certain. However, a premise of earlier work in the HCI community [9] is that the qualitative underpinnings of personas *can* be validated, in the same way that qualitative models in general can be validated. So, although validity can never be certain, our model provides some level of assurance. Based on the satisfaction levels proposed by Amyot et al. [1], user goals can be assigned a qualitative satisfaction level associated with a quantitative score; these values are Satisfied (100), Weakly Satisfied (50), Weakly Denied (−50), and Denied (−100).

Hard/Soft Goals and Beliefs. Our approach inherits the idea of hard goals, soft goals, and beliefs from *i**. Hard goals are goals that can be measurably satisfied, whereas soft goals are goals with less well-defined success criteria that can be satisficed [26]. Beliefs capture facts important to stakeholders [1]; we use these to capture beliefs held by personas. Beliefs are used irregularly in goal models, and while it has been suggested these are used to capture the rationale of designers during modelling rather than stakeholders [25], it has also been accepted that further exploration on the semantics of beliefs is needed [31]. The grounding of personas and IRIS' support for KAOS domain properties – that can capture this form of rationale – means we need not explicitly incorporate rationale meta-data into visual models. Therefore, beliefs can be safely used to represent stakeholder beliefs without confusion. User goals are elicited from persona characteristic elements based on the trust characteristic elicitation process described in [10], where implied goal, soft goal or belief intentions form the basis of user goals associated with the characteristic and its grounds, warrants and rebuttal elements. These user goals are expressed as persona intentions.

Aligning System and User Goals. As Fig. 1 shows, IRIS supports the concept of system goal, i.e. prescriptive statements of intent that the system should satisfy throughout the co-operation of its intended roles in a particular environment; this definition is based on the KAOS definition of goal [15]. Obstacles obstructing these goals may be associated with vulnerabilities, thereby connecting a goal view of a system with a risk view. IRIS also supports dependency modelling of system goals, where a *depender* role depends on *dependee* role for a goal or task *dependum*.

Until now, IRIS has not incorporated the notion of user goal because, as a methodologically agnostic meta-model, discretion on how to map user goals and expectations to system functionality is left to designers. However, in the case of a goal dependum, we should be able to capture the need for user goals to be satisfied to satisfy system goals. Consequently, our approach now adds an explicit traceability link between user goals that personas might have, and KAOS goals that a system needs to satisfy. This traceability link could be bi-directional, as we do not prescribe the elicitation of one type of goal before the other. For example, an analyst may capture system goals to satisfy a persona's goals, so may wish to indicate the system goals that address these user goals. Conversely, in a pre-existing system model, an analyst may wish to examine the implication of system requirements on the value a persona wishes to achieve. Our approach precludes neither possibility, and facilitates subsequent model validation checks.

3.2   Modelling User Goal Contributions

To visualise personas as goal models, our approach extends the *i** Strategic Rationale model [28] in two ways. First, we align persona characteristic elements with *contribution* links. Contribution links indicate the desired impact that one system element has on another [1]. As user goals are part of the broader socio-technical system being modelled, it is reasonable to assume that one user goal can contribute to another. In our approach, argumentation elements form the basis of means/end contribution links between user goals, i.e. where one user goal is the *means* for another user goal's *end*. Links are annotated with two additional pieces of information: (i) whether a link is a 'means' or an 'end' with respect to the characteristic's goal, soft goal or belief, (ii) an optional initial satisfaction level, based on the qualitative values and quantitative scores specified in [1], i.e. Satisfied (100) Weakly Satisfied (50), Weakly Denied (−50), and Denied (−100); this is analogous to the setting of *strategies* in jUCMNav [1]. Second, as tasks can have a security impact [5], completion of a task contributes to one or more user goals.

Algorithm 1: calculateGoalContribution

    Input : *goalName* - the goal name
    Data: *evaluatedGoals* - set of previously evaluated goals and their contribution scores, *cts*
          - names of tasks contributing to user goal *goalName*, *cgs* - names of user goals
          contributing to user goal *goalName*, *linkScore* - quantitative score for the
          contribution of user goal *cgName* to user goal *goalName*, *contScore* - product of
          linkScore and the goal contribution score for user goal *cgName*
    Output: *score* - contribution score

```
 1  Function calculateGoalContribution(goalName) is
 2      score ← initialSatisfactionScore goalName;
 3      if score = 0 then
 4          isObstructed ← systemGoalObstructed goalName;
 5          if isObstructed then
 6              score ← -100;
 7          else
 8              if goalName ∉ domain evaluatedGoals then
 9                  cts ← taskLinks goalName;
10                  while taskName ← cts do
11                      score ← score + taskContributionScore taskName;
12                  end
13                  cgs ← goalContributions goalName;
14                  while cgName ← cgs do
15                      linkScore ← contributionLinkScore goalName cgName;
16                      cgScore ← calculateGoalContribution cgName;
17                      contScore ← linkScore × cgScore ;
18                      score ← score + contScore;
19                  end
20                  score ← score / 100;
21                  if score < -100 then
22                      score ← -100;
23                  else if score > 100 then
24                      score ← 100;
25                  end
26                  evaluatedGoals ← evaluatedGoals ∪ {goalName → score};
27              else
28                  score ← evaluatedGoals goalName;
29              end
30          end
31      end
32      return score;
33  end
```

Like other goal modelling languages, contributions have a qualitative value corresponding to a quantitative score. We base these values on those used by GRL: Make (100), SomePositive (50), Help (25), Hurts (−25), SomeNegative (−50), and Break (−100). Make and Break contributions lead to the satisfaction or denial of user goals respectively; similarly, Help and Hurt contributions help or hinder satisfaction of user goals. SomePositive and SomeNegative values indicate some indeterminate level of positive or negative contribution that exceeds helping or hindering.

The approach for calculating contributions is similar to Giorgini et al.'s label propagation algorithm [14]. We implemented a recursive, forward propagation *calculateGoalContribution* (Algorithm 1) based on the *CalculateContribution* algorithm described in [1].

The setting of an initial satisfaction score (Line 2) based on the previously described satisfaction level is permitted; this can override the calculated goal score from related task and goal contributions. If the initial satisfaction score has not been overridden and no system goals associated with a user goal have not been obstructed (Lines 4–6), a contribution score is calculated. To handle goal contribution loops, i.e. where user goal x is a means to goal y, which is a means to goal x, or situations where the user goal x contributes to several user goals that eventually contribute to user goal y, a persistent set of visited goals and their contribution scores, *evaluatedGoals*, is retained. Propagation occurs if a goal's name is not in this set (Lines 9–26), otherwise the previously retained contribution for that goal is reused (Line 28). The contribution score is calculated based on the tasks contributing to it (Lines 9–12), and the product of each contributing goal and the contribution link strength (Lines 13–19). If the score calculated is greater than 100 or less than −100 then the score is normalised to a value within this range (Lines 21–25).

3.3 Identifying Implicit Vulnerabilities

Our approach for identifying implicit vulnerabilities, which is concerned with dependencies between system rather than user goals, identifies two situations where dependums might not be delivered. First, if a system goal dependum or its refinements are obstructed and not resolved. Second, if the dependum or its refinements are linked with denied user goals.

Algorithm 2: isGoalObstructed check

```
Input   : g - the goal name
Data: ugs - names of user goals linked to system goal g, goals - names of system goals
        refinements of g, obs - names of obstacles obstructing system goal g
Output: isObstructed - indicates if goal g is obstructed
```
1 **Function** *isGoalObstructed(g)* **is**
2   *isObstructed* ← false;
3   *ugs* ← linkedUserGoals *g*;
4   **while** *ug* ← *ugs* **do**
5   *score* ← calculateGoalContribution *ug* [];
6   **if** *score* < *0* **then**
7   *isObstructed* ← true;
8   break;
9   **end**
10   **end**
11   **if** *isObstructed* = *false* **then**
12   *goals* ← refinedGoals *g*;
13   **if** *goals* = ∅ **then**
14   *obs* ← obstructingGoals *g*;
15   **if** *obs* ≠ ∅ **then**
16   *isObstructed* ← true;
17   **else**
18   **while** *o* ← *obs* **do**
19   *isObstructed* ← isObstacleObstructed *o*;
20   **end**
21   **end**
22   **else**
23   **while** *g* ← *goals* **do**
24   *isObstructed* ← isGoalObstructed *g*;
25   **end**
26   **end**
27   **end**
28   **return** *isObstructed*;
29 **end**

Algorithm 2 specifies how the presence of such implicit vulnerabilities might be identified within a typical recursive system goal satisfaction algorithm. The algorithm returns a value of true if the system goal g is obstructed.

The algorithm navigates the operationalising tree-based KAOS goal refinements (Lines 11–27) to determine if there are *obstruct* associations between refined goals and obstacles, and these obstacles have not been resolved, i.e. there are no *resolve* relationships between obstacles and goals which address them. However, this check can be shortcut should a linked user goal associated with system goal g be denied, i.e. has a score less than 0. (Lines 3–10). Should this check not be shortcut then the *isObstacleObstructed* algorithm (Line 19) determines whether a goal is obstructed. This algorithm returns a value of true should one or more of the following conditions hold: (i) the obstacle or one of its obstacle refinements are not resolved by a [mitigating] system goal, (ii) an obstacle or one of its obstacle refinements are resolved, but the resolved goal has one or more linked user goals which are denied. The *isObstacleObstructed* algorithm is formally specified in [11].

Vulnerabilities within IRIS are defined as system weaknesses [7], but an implicit vulnerability may not always be a system weakness. It may indicate some inconsistency between what system roles and humans fulfilling might want and need, or – as suggested by [24] – some level of human fallibility resulting from roles that participate in too many dependencies as a depender. However, implicit vulnerabilities can help make sense of different system models and, in doing so, provide rationale for vulnerabilities feeding into risk models.

3.4   Tool-Support

To show how this approach might be implemented in Requirements Management tools more generally, we incorporated a new model type and supporting tools into CAIRIS release 2.3.6.

We tool-supported the additional concepts and algorithms by introducing a *User goal* visual model. This is based on the visual semantics of GRL, where a rounded box represents a hard goal, a polygon with rounded corners represents a soft goal, an ellipse represents a belief, and a dashed rectangle models the actor boundary. In this model, actors are represented by personas. Further drawing from the semantics used by GRL and jUCMNav, these nodes are coloured from dark green to dark red corresponding with satisfaction values of Satisfied (100) and Denied (−100); nodes with a value of None (0) are coloured yellow.

User goal models are generated automatically by CAIRIS using the same pipeline process used to visualise other CAIRIS models. A declarative model of graph edges is generated by CAIRIS; this is processed and annotated by graphviz [2] before being subsequently rendered as SVG. This annotation stage includes applying Algorithm 1 to user goal nodes to determine its score, and subsequent colour. The CAIRIS model generation process is described in more detail in [7]. The algorithms described were incorporated into a *Implied vulnerability* model validation check, which is applied to all KAOS goal dependency relationships in a CAIRIS model. CAIRIS model validation checks are implemented internally within the relational database used by a CAIRIS model as SQL stored procedures.

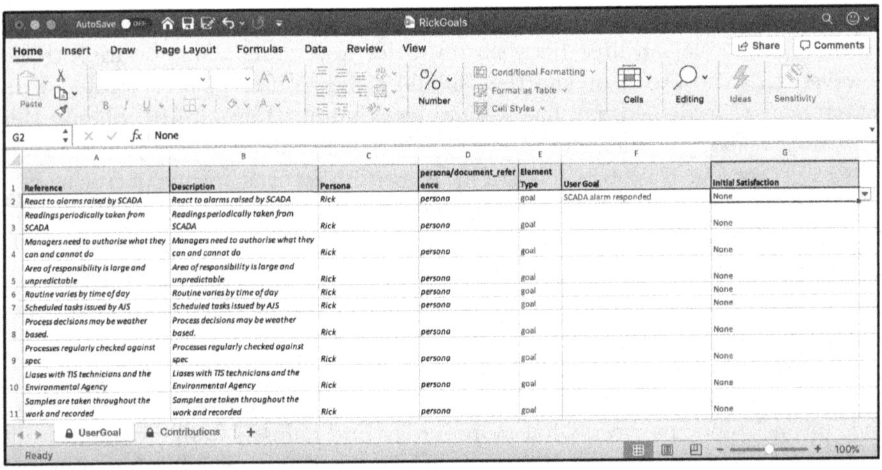

Fig. 2. Generated Excel workbook for entering user goals and contributions

As shown in Fig. 2, we also extended CAIRIS to generate Excel workbooks for capturing user goals and contribution links. Such workbooks are useful for analysts wishing to contribute to user goal modelling via more familiar office automation tools.

The generated Excel workbook contains UserGoal and UserContribution spreadsheets, where edited cells for both are coloured green. The UserGoal worksheet is pre-populated with read-only data on the persona characteristic or document reference name, its description, the persona it is associated with, and an indicator to whether the reference corresponds to a persona [characteristic] or document reference. When completing the worksheet, analysts should indicate the intentional elements associated with the persona characteristics or document references providing their grounds, warrants, or rebuttals. Analysts should also indicate the element type (goal, softgoal, or belief), and the initial satisfaction level using the dropdown lists provided. The source and destination cells in the ContributionsSheet are pre-populated once user goals have been added in the UserGoal sheet, so only the means/end and contribution links need to be set.

We further extended CAIRIS to allow the contents of these workbooks to be imported into a pre-existing CAIRIS model.

4   Case Study

4.1   ACME Water Security Policy

We evaluated our approach by using it to identify implicit vulnerabilities associated with the security policy of *ACME Water*: an anonymised UK water company responsible for providing clean and waste water services to several million people in a particular UK region. The infrastructure needed to support such a large customer base was substantial, amounting to over 60 water treatment works, 800 waste water treatment works, 550 service reservoirs, 27,000 km of water mains, 19,000 km of sewer networks, with over 1,900 pumping stations, and 3,200 combined sewer outflows. This policy was modelled as a KAOS goal model where each system goal represented a policy goal.

Four in-situ interviews were held with 6 plant operators, SCADA engineers and plant operation managers at two clean water and two waste water treatment plants. These interviews were recorded, and the transcripts analysed using Grounded Theory. The results of this analysis are a qualitative model of plant operations security perceptions. Using the persona case technique [9], we analysed the Grounded Theory model to derive a single persona of a water-treatment plant operator, Rick, incorporating 32 persona characteristics, and backed up by 82 argumentation elements (grounds, warrants, or rebuttals).

Fig. 3. High-level ACME Water security policy goals

The security policy goals were created by analysing existing documentation about ACME's existing information security policy and agreeing the scope of the policy to be modelled with ACME's IT security manager. Existing policy documentation was analysed to elicit and specify a KAOS goal model of 82 policy goals, with a single high level goal (*Secure operating environment*) and, as shown in Fig. 3, 11 refined sub-goals representing the different policy areas. These goals and other security and usability elements of the operating environment were specified in a CAIRIS model; these included 2 personas, 11 roles, 21 obstacles, 9 vulnerabilities, 5 tasks, and 6 role-goal-role dependencies.[1]

4.2   User Goal Model Creation

To generate a user goal model based on Rick, we initially derived 104 user goals and beliefs from both the persona characteristics and argumentation elements, and 165 contribution links. The first two authors then reviewed the model to de-duplicate synonymous user goals. For example, a *Site protected* user goal was associated with a *Copper theft* document reference, as the intention implied was that the site needed to be protected from this threat. However, we identified a *Site secured* user goal associated with *Physical and login security* document reference. As a result, we deleted the former user goal, and contribution linked its user goals to *Site secure*. In parallel with the de-duplication of user goals, we also added additional contribution links between user goals based on our understanding of the persona and his intentions, where these contribution links cross-cut persona characteristics. For example, on reviewing the persona characteristics and their underpinning data, we noted that the *Thieves ignore impact* user goal, which was associated with the *Thieves do not care about their impact* characteristic, helped foster the belief that *Personal safety is a hygiene factor*; this belief was associated with the *Personal safety is an infosec hygiene factor* persona characteristic. Following this analysis, the final model resulted in 93 user goals and beliefs, and 205 contribution links.

Figure 4 shows the goal model generated by CAIRIS for Rick.

---

[1] The case study CAIRIS model is available from https://doi.org/10.5281/zenodo.3979236.

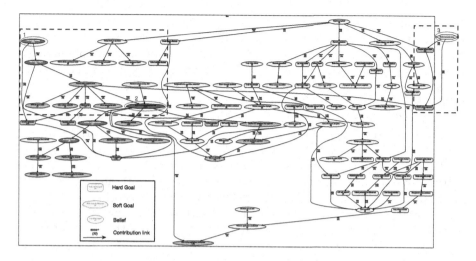

Fig. 4. Annotated CAIRIS User Goal model based on Rick persona

4.3 ICT Awareness Implicit Vulnerabilities

From Fig. 5, we identified a link between the *InfoSec communications perceived* user goal (annotated as 2) and the *ICT awareness* system goal, which is a refinement of the high-level *Secure Site* system goal.

The *ICT awareness* system goal indicates ICT partners should know how to maintain equipment hosted in the secure areas and, as Fig. 5 (inset) shows, this

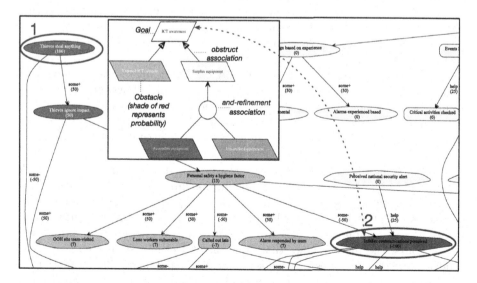

Fig. 5. Alignment between *ICT awareness* system goal in KAOS goal model (inset) and *InfoSec communications perceived* user goal in user goal model

system goal is already obstructed due to exposed and surplus equipment which should not be present. Unfortunately, as Fig. 5 also indicates, the related user goal is also denied. The negative impact affects not only the perception of site security, but also the perception the site is run efficiently; this corroborates the obstacles found to be present in the system goal model. To reinforce this, the belief *Thieves steal anything* (annotated as 1) was set to satisfied, which weakly denied *InfoSec communications perceived*, further validating negative perception. This highlighted the need for a new dependency where an IT security manager depends on ICT partner to achieve the *ICT awareness* goal.

The limited security awareness means operators fail to see the connection between misunderstanding authorisation, and wifi insecurity and site security, due to their belief than an air-gap exists between wireless networks and industrial control systems. Access controls on pump actions further supports the belief that unknown applications are unauthorised. To explore this further, we associated the *Pump action restricted* user goal with the *Access Control* system goal, and added a dependency to indicate that plant operators depend on Information Security managers for this goal. CAIRIS subsequently flagged a model validation warning because a refined goal *Vendor passwords* was obstructed, due to evidence that vendors were using easily guessed default passwords for certain critical components.

4.4   Validating Vulnerabilities with Implicit Vulnerabilities

As indicated in Fig. 1, obstacles can be associated with vulnerabilities to capture the rationale for including vulnerabilities in subsequent risk analysis activities. In the ACME Water model, an *Exposed ICT Cabinets* obstacle was already associated with an *Exposed cabinet* vulnerability, but - given how divisive resolving obstacles might be due to the architectural implications of their resolution – we wanted to see if the user goal model of Rick provided a human rationale for the obstacle's presence.

Information Security Managers depend on Plant operators for a related *Industrialised secure cabinet* system goal to ensure control systems are kept in secure cabinets. On reviewing the user goal model and the tasks in the ACME Water model, we noted that no-one was explicitly required to check these cabinets; instead, ACME Water trusted Rick to do this while discharging other duties.

As Fig. 6 shows, as part of a pre-existing *Broken Instrument alarm* task (annotated as 3), we introduced help contribution links to *Complex failure callout* and *SCADA alarm responded* because Rick completes the task to satisfy these user goals. The task entails Rick being away from the safety of the control room to respond to equipment alarms from these cabinets. Should these alarms fire out of hours, the model shows that Rick might feel uneasy, particularly if he thinks the alarm indicates intruders are stealing equipment. The potential for Rick to skip the steps necessary to check these cabinets was corroborated in the user goal model due the *SCADA alarm responded* being very weakly satisfied.

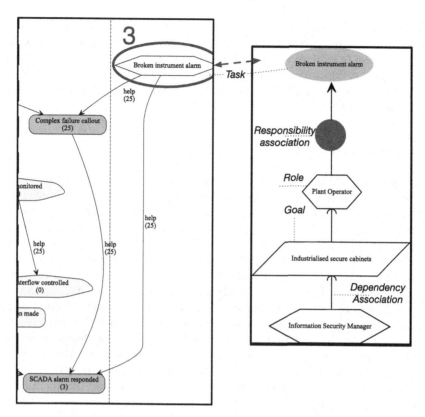

Fig. 6. Contribution of *Broken Instrument alarm* task to user goals (left) and related responsibility and dependency associations (right)

5   Discussion and Limitations

While important for validating requirements, traceability is a weakness of languages like *i** due to lack of guidelines for working with complementary models [24]. Our approach addresses this traceability problem by drawing user goal relationships from the qualitative data analysis underpinning personas. However, a limitation of our approach is the restricted expressiveness of the generated user goal models, particularly the lack of support for *strategic dependencies* between user goals. Supporting dependencies between user goals may appear trivial from a modelling perspective, but retaining traceability would necessitate changes to how the qualitative data grounding personas is elicited and analysed to ensure both personas and their collaborative aspects are encapsulated. Approaches for creating such personas already exist, e.g. [18], and could provide a grounding for subsequent modelling of user goal dependencies.

Another limitation of our work is that our case study considers only a single persona. However, our initial results developing and evaluating the changes to CAIRIS indicate that user goal models place little additional performance burden to model validation checks. Because CAIRIS can incrementally import models that overlay existing models, it is possible to incrementally add personas to a baseline system to explore the impact of different personas interacting with each other. Based on the process and performance of the tool-support, we believe our approach scales to multiple personas too, but a more thorough performance evaluation will be the subject of future work.

6   Conclusion

This paper presented an approach for reframing personas as social goal models and, in doing so, using both the reframed and related models to find implicit vulnerabilities. As a result, we have made two contributions addressing our research questions in Sect. 1. First, we addressed RQ1 by demonstrating how the user research used to construct personas can be leveraged to partially automate construction of social goal models. Such user goals could be elicited either while constructing personas, or afterwards - in which case the process of constructing the user goal models helps further validate the personas and the data upon which they are based. Second, we addressed RQ2 by illustrating how minimal contributions to existing tool-support facilitate automation for both the identification of implicit vulnerabilities from user goal models, and the validation of existing system goal obstructions based on user goals and user goal contributions. Our intention is not to replace traditional RE approaches to system and social goal modelling, but to show how applying them in a different way can identify and confirm potential security problems that might have otherwise remained hidden.

Future work will further examine persona characteristics and goal and task attributes to evaluate fitness between persona and actors in goal models. For example, some goals might require long-term attention span while others require different social skills. The user model associated with these attributes will be then used to simulate how different personas interact, and whether this leads to insecurity. We will also investigate collaborative information gathering techniques to capture goal models and their personas, e.g. through an interactive algorithm driven by representative users providing satisfaction and denial weights, and propagation options.

References

1. Amyot, D., Ghanavati, S., Horkoff, J., Mussbacher, G., Peyton, L., Yu, E.: Evaluating goal models within the goal-oriented requirement language. Int. J. Intell. Syst. **25**(8), 841–877 (2010)
2. AT&T: Graphviz Web Site (2020). http://www.graphviz.org
3. Cleland-Huang, J.: Meet elaine: a persona-driven approach to exploring architecturally significant requirements. IEEE Softw. **30**(4), 18–21 (2013)
4. Cooper, A., Reimann, R., Cronin, D., Noessel, C.: About Face: The Essentials of Interaction Design. Wiley, Hoboken (2014)

5. Elahi, G., Yu, E., Zannone, N.: A vulnerability-centric requirements engineering framework: analyzing security attacks, countermeasures, and requirements based on vulnerabilities. Requir. Eng. **15**(1), 41–62 (2010). https://doi.org/10.1007/s00766-009-0090-z

6. Faily, S.: Bridging user-centered design and requirements engineering with GRL and persona cases. In: Proceedings of the 5th International i* Workshop, pp. 114–119. CEUR Workshop Proceedings (2011)

7. Faily, S.: Designing Usable and Secure Software with IRIS and CAIRIS. Springer, Cham (2018). https://doi.org/10.1007/978-3-319-75493-2_9

8. Faily, S., Fléchais, I.: Barry is not the weakest link: eliciting secure system requirements with personas. In: Proceedings of the 24th BCS Interaction Specialist Group Conference, pp. 124–132. BCS (2010)

9. Faily, S., Fléchais, I.: Persona cases: a technique for grounding personas. In: Proceedings of the 29th ACM CHI Conference on Human Factors in Computing Systems, pp. 2267–2270. ACM (2011)

10. Faily, S., Fléchais, I.: Eliciting and visualising trust expectations using persona trust characteristics and goal models. In: Proceedings of the 6th International Workshop on Social Software Engineering, pp. 17–24. ACM (2014)

11. Faily, S., Scandariato, R., Shostack, A., Sion, L., Ki-Aries, D.: Contextualisation of data flow diagrams for security analysis. In: Eades III, H., Gadyatskaya, O. (eds.) GraMSec 2020. LNCS, vol. 12419, pp. 186–197. Springer, Cham (2020). https://doi.org/10.1007/978-3-030-62230-5_10

12. Friess, E.: Personas and decision making in the design process: an ethnographic case study. In: Proceedings of the 30th ACM CHI Conference on Human Factors in Computing Systems, pp. 1209–1218. ACM (2012)

13. Giorgini, P., Massacci, F., Mylopoulos, J., Zannone, N.: Modeling security requirements through ownership, permission and delegation. In: 13th IEEE International Conference on Requirements Engineering, pp. 167–176 (2005)

14. Giorgini, P., Mylopoulos, J., Nicchiarelli, E., Sebastiani, R.: Reasoning with goal models. In: Spaccapietra, S., March, S.T., Kambayashi, Y. (eds.) ER 2002. LNCS, vol. 2503, pp. 167–181. Springer, Heidelberg (2002). https://doi.org/10.1007/3-540-45816-6_22

15. van Lamsweerde, A.: Requirements Engineering: From System Goals to UML Models to Software Specifications. Wiley, Hoboken (2009)

16. Liu, L., Yu, E., Mylopoulos, J.: Security and privacy requirements analysis within a social setting. In: Proceedings of the 11th IEEE International Requirements Engineering Conference, pp. 151–161 (2003)

17. Massacci, F., Zannone, N.: Detecting conflicts between functional and security requirements with Secure Tropos: John Rusnak and the Allied Irish Bank. In: Yu, E., Giorgini, P., Maiden, N., Mylopoulos, J. (eds.) Social Modeling for Requirements Engineering, pp. 337–362. MIT Press, Cambridge (2011)

18. Matthews, T., Whittaker, S., Moran, T.P., Yuen, S.: Collaboration personas: a new approach to designing workplace collaboration tools. In: Proceedings of the 29th ACM CHI Conference on Human Factors in Computing Systems, pp. 2247–2256 (2011)

19. Mead, N., Shull, F., Spears, J., Heibl, S., Weber, S., Cleland-Huang, J.: Crowd sourcing the creation of personae non gratae for requirements-phase threat modeling. In: Proceedings of the 25th International Requirements Engineering Conference, pp. 412–417 (2017)

20. Moody, D.L., Heymans, P., Matulevicius, R.: Improving the effectiveness of visual representations in requirements engineering: an evaluation of i* visual syntax. In: Proceedings of the 17th IEEE International Requirements Engineering Conference, pp. 171–180. IEEE (2009)

21. Mouratidis, H., Giorgini, P.: Secure Tropos: a security-oriented extension of the Tropos methodology. Int. J. Softw. Eng. Knowl. Eng. **17**(2), 285–309 (2007)

22. Nunes Rodrigues, G., Joel Tavares, C., Watanabe, N., Alves, C., Ali, R.: A persona-based modelling for contextual requirements. In: Kamsties, E., Horkoff, J., Dalpiaz, F. (eds.) REFSQ 2018. LNCS, vol. 10753, pp. 352–368. Springer, Cham (2018). https://doi.org/10.1007/978-3-319-77243-1_23

23. Paja, E., Dalpiaz, F., Giorgini, P.: Designing secure socio-technical systems with STS-ml. In: Proceedings of the 6th International i* Workshop 2013, pp. 79–84 (2013)

24. Pastor, O., Estrada, H., Martínez, A.: Strengths and weaknesses of the i* framework: an empirical evaluation. In: Yu, E., Giorgini, P., Maiden, N., Mylopoulos, J. (eds.) Social Modeling for Requirements Engineering, pp. 607–643. MIT Press, Cambridge (2011)

25. Regev, G., Wegmann, A.: Where do goals come from: the underlying principles of goal-oriented requirements engineering. In: 13th IEEE International Conference on Requirements Engineering, pp. 353–362 (2005)

26. Simon, H.A.: Rational decision making in business organizations. Am. Econ. Rev. **69**(4), 493–513 (1979)

27. Sindre, G., Opdahl, A.L.: Capturing dependability threats in conceptual modelling. In: Krogstie, J., Opdahl, A.L., Brinkkemper, S. (eds.) Conceptual Modelling in Information Systems Engineering, pp. 247–260. Springer, Heidelberg (2007). https://doi.org/10.1007/978-3-540-72677-7_15

28. Yu, E.: Modeling strategic relationships for process reengineering. Ph.D. thesis, University of Toronto (1995)

29. Yu, E.: Towards modeling and reasoning support for early-phase requirements engineering. In: Proceedings of the 3rd IEEE International Symposium on Requirements Engineering, pp. 226–235. IEEE (1997)

30. Yu, E., Giorgini, P., Maiden, N., Mylopoulos, J.: Social modeling for requirements engineering: an introduction. In: Yu, E. (ed.) Social Modeling for Requirements Engineering. MIT Press, Cambridge (2011)

31. Yu, E.S.: Social modeling and i*. In: Borgida, A.T., Chaudhri, V.K., Giorgini, P., Yu, E.S. (eds.) Conceptual Modeling: Foundations and Applications. LNCS, vol. 5600, pp. 99–121. Springer, Heidelberg (2009). https://doi.org/10.1007/978-3-642-02463-4_7

ADIoT Workshop

Cooperative Speed Estimation of an RF Jammer in Wireless Vehicular Networks

Dimitrios Kosmanos[1], Savvas Chatzisavvas[1], Antonios Argyriou[1],
and Leandros Maglaras[2(✉)]

[1] Department of Electrical and Computer Engineering, University of Thessaly,
Volos, Greece
{dikosman,savchatz,anargyr}@uth.gr
[2] Faculty of Computing, Engineering and Media, De Montfort University,
Leicester, UK
leandrosmag@gmail.com

Abstract. In this paper, we are concerned with the problem of estimating the speed of an RF jammer that moves towards a group/platoon of moving wireless communicating nodes. In our system model, the group of nodes receives an information signal from a master node, that they want to decode, while the Radio Frequency (RF) jammer desires to disrupt this communication as it approaches them. For this system model, we propose first a transmission scheme where the master node remains silent for a time period while it transmits in a subsequent slot. Second, we develop a joint data and jamming estimation algorithm that uses Linear Minimum Mean Square Error (LMMSE) estimation. We develop analytical closed-form expressions that characterize the Mean Square Error (MSE) of the data and jamming signal estimates. Third, we propose a cooperative jammer speed estimation algorithm based on the jamming signal estimates at each node of the network. Our numerical and simulation results for different system configurations prove the ability of our overall system to estimate with high accuracy and the RF jamming signals and the speed of the jammer.

Keywords: Platoon of vehicles · RF jamming attack · RF jammer speed

1 Introduction

Wireless communication has constraints in terms of power, bandwidth, reliability, and communication range. As the utility and usefulness of these networks increase every day, more and more malicious competitors appear and target these networks with different types of security attacks. Radio frequency (RF) jamming is one method that a malicious node can use to disrupt the transmission between the nodes of a wireless network [19,23]. In this type of attack a signal is used to disrupt the communication via the broadcast medium, as most nodes use

© Springer Nature Switzerland AG 2020
S. Katsikas et al. (Eds.): CyberICPS 2020/SECPRE 2020/ADIoT 2020, LNCS 12501, pp. 205–223, 2020.
https://doi.org/10.1007/978-3-030-64330-0_13

one single frequency band. In certain application domains where groups of wireless nodes must communicate reliably in broadcast mode, like drone swarms or platoons of autonomous vehicles [17] and applications for dynamic charging of electric vehicles through inter-vehicle communication [13,16], an RF jammer can have a profound effect in the operation of the system if it can disrupt wireless communication [11,18]. There are methods to defend against a jamming attack such as spread spectrum communication or increase of transmission power, but they typically incur a high cost (power, bandwidth, or complexity). Another way to defend against an RF jamming attack is for the whole group of nodes to move away from the jammer in a flying ad hoc networks (FANETs) environment [8,26] or in a platoon that forms a wireless vehicular network [26]. But to do so the group of nodes, especially in a platoon of vehicles, must be able to estimate the behavior of the jammer [3,14]. Of particular interest is its speed relative to the platoon since it reveals whether the jammer is approaching or moving away. The focus of this paper is to derive accurate estimates of the speed of the jammer in a group of wireless moving nodes.

Motivation: Contrary to seeing RF jamming interference as a problem of an individual node, we propose to address it at the group level since the applications of interest fall into the category of a platoon of vehicles that its movement is coordinated using Cooperative Adaptive Cruise Control (CACC). The estimated jammer speed value has been proved as a crucial feature for detecting and classifying a RF jamming attack in a cross-layer Machine Learning (ML) jamming detection scheme combined with other features from the PHY layer or the network layer [15,17]. In particular, by improving the speed of the jammer estimation at the group level, we suggest that the proposed estimated metric can further improve the performance of an intrusion detection system. Last, the estimated speed of the jammer is particularly important for a future model of predicting the future position of the jammer.

Contributions: The contributions of this work are described below. Firstly, we propose to use jointly the data from wireless receivers in platoon nodes for the purpose of estimating the jamming signal and eventually the speed of the jammer. To achieve our goal we design a transmission protocol for the platoon and an associated estimation algorithm. With our protocol in the first time slot the master node does not transmit any useful information so we obtain a clear observation of just the jamming signal and the receiver noise, while in the second time slot where the information signal is transmitted we observe an additive form the information signal, the jamming signal, and the noise. Our approach ensures that we have a clean interfering signal. Under this protocol, we use the Linear Minimum Mean Square Error Estimator (LMMSE) to estimate both the information signal u and the jamming signal z_i for every node i in the platoon. Our main result is a closed-form expression of the Mean Square Error (MSE) of the signal u and the jamming signal z_i. The second contribution is a new algorithm that combines the jamming signal estimates received at the nodes of the platoon, so as to achieve an accurate estimate of the jammer speed.

The rest of the paper is organised as follows: in Sect. 2 we present related work while in Sect. 3 we describe our system model and the assumptions. In Sects. 4 and 5, we present the proposed joint data, jamming signal, and speed estimation algorithms including all the analytical results. In Sects. 6 and 7 we present numerical and simulation results. Finally in Sect. 8 we conclude this paper.

2   Related Work

Speed Estimation. Our literature survey indicates that active vehicle safety systems have not benefited sufficiently from the additional information received from a connected vehicle network so as to design more reliable vehicle speed estimation algorithms [12,29,31]. Pirani et al [22] introduce distributed algorithms for speed estimation where each vehicle can gather information from other vehicles in the network to be used for speed fault detection and reconstruction. This procedure is used as a bank of information for a single vehicle to diagnose and correct a possible fault in its own speed estimation/measurements. The same approach is also considered in [6] for a platoon of connected vehicles equipped with CACC. Without using a distributed system, the authors in [14] proposed a method for speed estimation between one transmitter and one receiver. However, none of these approaches take into account the possible RF jamming in the area and are not concerned with the speed of the jammer. In contrast, there is considerable work regarding distributed jamming attack detection, but only a few methods exploit distributed jamming signal estimation.

Jamming Detection. Several works cover the problem of distributed jamming detection (but not estimation) in Multiple-Input-Multiple-Output (MIMO) systems. The majority of these works proposed jamming detection methods with a Generalized Likelihood Ratio Test (GLRT) in MIMO systems [2,10]. The authors in [30] in order to secure the legitimate communication, proposed a jamming detection method in non-coherent Single-Input-Multiple-Output (SIMO) systems, in which channel statistics are not required. It was shown that the probability of detection initially grows with the number of receive antennas but converges quickly, while the channel statistics from the jammer to the receiver always influence the performance. All of these works use additional hardware (e.g. more antennas) on the transmitter and receiver to detect a jamming attack. More recent works like [11] proposed methods for jamming detection in Vehicular Networks (VANETs) with Machine Learning (ML) methods like clustering. The authors proposed new algorithms that can differentiate intentional from unintentional jamming as well as extract specific features of the RF jamming signal. In contrast, our proposed method desires to exploit the distributed environment of multiple receivers to effectively estimate the jamming signal and the jammer speed.

Jamming Estimation. Distributed estimation (DES) is a topic that has been investigated considerably in the literature. However, to the best of our knowledge no works have considered using DES in a setting where a jamming signal and the jammer speed need to be simultaneously estimated. The most closely related work where DES is used for jamming estimation can be found in [4] where the authors implemented a joint Successive Interference Cancellation (SIC) decoder and LMMSE estimator for an interfering (jamming) signal. Similarly, the authors in [9] investigate the problem of distributed decoding under a white noise jamming attack. However, the aforementioned methods have as prime goal the correct decoding of the valuable data sent by the transmitter under an interference source.

Our Work. In contrast to all the aforementioned works, this paper proposes a two-stage transmission scheme in which the master node remains silent for one slot out of the two time slots. This method is superior in estimating jointly the data and jamming signal using an LMMSE estimation compared to a baseline system. Subsequently, using this jamming signal estimate, the speed of the jammer is also estimated. All the above are accomplished without any extra hardware such as multiple antennas on the transmitter and the receiver.

3   System Model and Assumptions

Topology: We consider a wireless Vehicle-to-Vehicle (V2V) communication network that consists of a set of N nodes. The first node is the master node who sends the same information messages to the other nodes. Also there is a Jammer (J) who uses his jamming signals to thwart the communication between the master node and the other nodes of the network. In our topology the $N-1$ receivers move as a realistic application of platoon of vehicles with approximately the same speed (u_r), using the CACC technology [25] and with a constant distance (d) between the members of the platoon (fixed to $5m$ in our experiments). Also there is a jammer who moves on a parallel road in relation to the platoon with speed u_j and when approaching the platoon within a relatively short distance on the x-axis (at about x_{dist}) starts its jamming attack. Observing the topology of the investigated scenario, $N-1$ orthogonal triangles are formed between the jammer, the specific receiver and the vertical projection (v_{dist}) of the position of the jammer on the road that the platoon is located. So, for every vertical triangle the Angle of Departure (AOD) values between the jammer and each one from the receivers can be defined using the geometry of the proposed topology as:

$$(1): \cos \phi_1 = \frac{x_{dist}}{dist_1},$$

$$(2): \cos \phi_2 = \frac{x_{dist} + d}{dist_2},$$

$$...$$

$$(N-1): \cos \phi_{N-1} = \frac{x_{dist} + (N-2) * d}{dist_{N-1}} \tag{1}$$

where $dist_i$ is the actual distance between the jammer and the i-th receiver.

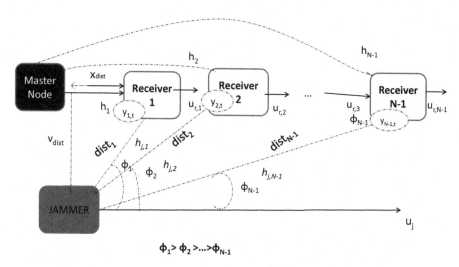

Fig. 1. Wireless communication network for DES of the speed of the jammer.

Observation Model: Each node i during slot t observes $y_{i,t}$ as illustrated in Fig. 1. In the first time slot, when the master node does not transmit anything, each node observers only the jamming signal z_i. In the second time slot when the master node transmits a signal u, each node receives two interfering signals: one from the master node, u through a channel h_i, and the aggregate signal z_i from the jammer (which is the result of what the jammer transmitted through an unknown channel $h_{j,i}$) that takes into account the relative speed between jammer-receiver and AOD of the transmitted jamming signal. The noise $w_{i,t}$ for each time slot is Additive White Gaussian Noise (AWGN) with zero mean and variance σ_w^2 and is uncorrelated across the nodes. So in two different time slots we have two observations in every node:

$$y_{i,t} = z_i + w_{i,t} \quad \text{(master node does not transmit)} \tag{2}$$

$$y_{i,t} = h_i * u + z_i + w_{i,t} \quad \text{(master node transmits)} \tag{3}$$

In the above i indicates the node and t indicates the time slot. Hence, the observations form the random vector $\boldsymbol{y} = [y_{1,1}\ y_{1,2}\ y_{2,1}\ y_{2,2}\ \cdots\ y_{N-1,1}\ y_{N-1,2}]^T$ that has $2(N-1)$ elements. We now define the vectors

$$\boldsymbol{u} = [z_1\ z_2\ z_3\ z_4\ \dots\ z_{N-1}\ u]^T$$

which is a $N \times 1$ vector and

$$\boldsymbol{w} = [w_{1,1}\ w_{1,2}\ w_{2,1}\ w_{2,2}\ \dots\ w_{N-1,1}\ w_{N-1,2}]^T$$

which is also a $2(N-1) \times 1$. The final signal model for our system becomes:

$$y = Hu + w \tag{4}$$

where H is the following matrix:

$$\begin{bmatrix} 1 & 0 & 0 & \dots & 0 \\ 1 & 0 & 0 & \dots & h_1 \\ 0 & 1 & 0 & \dots & 0 \\ 0 & 1 & 0 & \dots & h_2 \\ \dots\dots\dots\dots & \dots \\ 0 & 0 & \dots & 1 & 0 \\ 0 & 0 & \dots & 1 & h_{N-1} \end{bmatrix}$$

3.1 Considered Channel Models

We progressively investigate our idea in the context of more complex channel models and we describe them next.

Rayleigh Channel: For the wireless link we assume flat Rayleigh fading, while the channel remains the same for two consecutive time slots (quasi-static). Hence for every time slot during the transmission of a packet we have $|h_i| \sim Ray(E[|h_i|^2])$ [21]. The average received power is $E[|h_i|^2] = 1/dist_{M(i)}^{po}$ where $dist_{M(i)}$ is the node's distance from the master node and po is the path loss exponent set to 3. We assume that the channel between the master node and the remaining ones is known since it can be easily calculated from packet preambles.

V2V Stochastic Channel: With this more advanced model, the received signal at the $i \in [1, ..., N-1]$ receiver nodes that is received from the jammer through a stochastic wireless V2V channel using the proposed two-stage transmission protocol can be modeled as follows [14]:

$$y_{i,1} = \gamma_i po_{j,i} e^{j\frac{2\pi}{\lambda}f_{D,i}\tau_i} * z_i + w_{i,1} \tag{5}$$

$$y_{i,2} = \gamma_i po_{M,i} e^{j\frac{2\pi}{\lambda}f_{DM,i}\tau_{i,M}} * u + \gamma_i po_{j,i} e^{j\frac{2\pi}{\lambda}f_{D,i}\tau_i} * z_i + w_{i,2} \tag{6}$$

All the wireless links between the jammer and the multiple receivers and the links between the master node and the multiple receivers are assumed Line of Sight (LOS). However, the proposed method can be easily applied in a multipath scenario in which in addition to the specular LOS component there are several other Non Line of Sight (NLOS) diffuse components due to multipath reflections [14]. In the above equations, γ_i is the amplitude associated with the LOS path, $po_{M,i}$, $po_{j,i}$ represents the corresponding free space propagation losses from the master node and the jammer to the i-th receiver. The λ is the wavelength. The complex coefficient γ_i is assumed to be constant over the observation interval. The variables $\tau_{i,M}$, τ_i

and $f_{DM,i}, f_{D,i}$ represent the time delays and Doppler shifts of the transmitted signal from the master node and the jammer, respectively. Finally, Δu_i is the relative speed between the jammer and the specific receiver and $w_{i,1}, w_{i,2}$ represents the AWGN with zero mean. Note that (5) corresponds to the first time slot in which only the jammer transmits its symbol (as in (2)) and (6) corresponds to the second time slot in which the master node transmits its signal and the jammer interferes too (as in (3)). The channel model can be modeled exactly as the relation (11) in [14]. Since we want to include the relative speed between the jammer and the receiver in the last equations (5), (6) we write the Doppler frequency $f_{D,i}$ from the transmitted signal by the jammer as:

$$f_{D,i} = \frac{\Delta u_i f_c \cos \phi_i}{c} \qquad (7)$$

where f_c the carrier frequency with value 5.9 Ghz (which is the band dedicated to V2V communication). Also $\cos \phi_i$ is the incidence AOD between the jammer and the i-th receiver and c is the speed of light. All parameters used in this paper are summarised in Table 1.

3.2   Jammer Behavior

We consider jammers that aim to block completely the communication over a link by emitting interference reactively when they detect packets over the air, thus causing a Denial of Service (DoS) attack. The jammers minimize their activity to only a few symbols per packet and use minimal, but sufficient power, to remain undetected. We assume that the jammer is pretty capable and is able to sniff any symbol of the over the air transmissions in real-time and react with a jamming signal that flips selected symbols at the receiver with high probability (see [28]). This type of reactive jammer is designed to start transmitting upon sensing energy above a certain threshold in order for a reactive jamming attack to succeed. We set the latter to -75 dBm as it is empirically determined to be a good tradeoff between jammer sensitivity and false transmission detection rate, when an ongoing 802.11p transmission is assumed [24]. For the jamming signal we don't have any information for its variance. We assume that the reactive jammer transmits after its being triggered for two consecutive time slots and this has the result that the jamming signal is the same. Also we assume that the channel conditions between the jammer and the multiple receivers remain the same through two consecutive time slots.

4   Joint Data and Jamming Signal Estimation

For estimating the information and the jamming signal in this paper we adopt the LMMSE [4,21]. An LMMSE estimator is an estimation method which minimizes the MSE which is a common measure of estimator quality. The LMMSE estimator ensures the minimum MSE from all linear estimators. For our general linear model $\boldsymbol{y} = H\boldsymbol{u} + \boldsymbol{w}$, the estimator of $\boldsymbol{u}$ is given as:

$$\hat{\boldsymbol{u}} = (H^H C_w^{-1} H + C_u^{-1})^{-1} H^H C_w^{-1} \boldsymbol{y} \qquad (8)$$

Table 1. Mathematical symbols used in this paper.

Symbol	Description
N	Actual number of nodes
$dist_i$	Actual distance between jammer- receiver i
x_{dist}	Distance between jammer- receiver i in x-axis
v_{dist}	Vertical distance between jammer- receiver i in y-axis
$dist_{M(i)}$	The node's i distance from the master node
M	Master node
$\cos \phi_i$	AOD between jammer - receiver i
d	Distance between platoon members
u	Information signal
z_i	Jamming signal transmitted in receiver i
h_i	Channel between master node and receiver i
$h_{j,i}$	Channel between jammer and receiver i
$w_{i,t}$	AWGN at the receiver i at time t
$y_{i,t}$	The overall signal received at the receiver i at time t
σ_w^2	AWGN variance
γ_i	The amplitude associated with the LOS path
$po_{M,i}$	Free space propagation losses from M to receiver i
$po_{j,i}$	Free space propagation losses from jammer to receiver i
λ	The wavelength
$\tau_{i,M}$	Time delay from the M to receiver i
τ_i	Time delay from the jammer to receiver i
$f_{DM,i}$	The doopler shift of the transmitted signal from M to receiver i
$f_{D,i}$	The doopler shift of the transmitted signal from the jammer to receiver i
Δu_i	The relative speed between the jammer and the receiver i
f_c	Carrier frequency
c	Speed of light
C_w	The auto-covariance matrix of w
C_u	The auto-covariance matrix of u
$u_{r,i}$	The speed of the receiver i
u_j	The speed of the jammer
σ_w^2	The variations of the power of the jamming signal
α	The smoothing parameter of the filter
Δt	The time interval for updating the estimation procedure

where C_w and C_u are the auto-covariance matrices of w and u respectively. The MSE of this estimator is the trace of C_e, that is the covariance matrix or the estimation error:

$$MSE = \text{Tr}(C_e) = \text{Tr}((H^H C_w^{-1} H + C_u^{-1})^{-1})) \tag{9}$$

4.1   MSE Derivation

As the literature has shown, a very challenging task is to produce a closed-form expression for the desired estimator and signal model [4,5,20]. In this subsection we outline the process that has led to the desired expression that will help us study the behavior of the proposed system.

Recall that in our model we assume that the noise is AWGN with zero mean and variance σ_w^2 and is uncorrelated across the nodes. We have no information about the jamming signal and so we assume that its mean is zero. Under these assumptions and with the use of the general LMMSE estimator, the MSE for the information u and jamming signal z_i for nodes is given in (10), and (11) respectively.

$$MSE_u = \frac{1}{\sum_{n=2}^{N}\left(\frac{h_n^2}{\sigma_{wn,2}^2}\right) + \frac{1}{s_u^2} - \sum_{n=2}^{N}\left(\frac{h_n^2}{\sigma_{wn,2}^4 * \left(\frac{1}{\sigma_{wn,1}^2} + \frac{1}{\sigma_{wn,2}^2} + \frac{1}{\sigma_{zn}^2}\right)}\right)} \tag{10}$$

$$MSE_{zi} = \frac{\prod_{n=2,n\neq i}^{N}\left(\frac{1}{\sigma_{wn,1}^2} + \frac{1}{\sigma_{wn,2}^2} + \frac{1}{\sigma_{zn}^2}\right) * \left(\sum_{k=2}^{N}\left(\frac{h_n^2}{\sigma_{wn,2}^2}\right) + \frac{1}{s_u^2}\right) - \sum_{k=2}^{N}\left(\frac{h_n^2}{\sigma_{wn,2}^4}\right) * \prod_{n=2,n\neq i,k}^{N}\left(\frac{1}{\sigma_{wn,1}^2} + \frac{1}{\sigma_{wn,2}^2} + \frac{1}{\sigma_{zn}^2}\right)}{\prod_{n=2}^{N}\left(\frac{1}{\sigma_{wn,1}^2} + \frac{1}{\sigma_{wn,2}^2} + \frac{1}{\sigma_{zn}^2}\right) * \left(\sum_{n=2}^{N}\left(\frac{h_n^2}{\sigma_{wn,2}^2}\right) + \frac{1}{s_u^2}\right) - \sum_{k=2}^{N}\left(\frac{h_n^2}{\sigma_{wn,2}^4}\right) * \prod_{n=2,n\neq i}^{N}\left(\frac{1}{\sigma_{wn,1}^2} + \frac{1}{\sigma_{wn,2}^2} + \frac{1}{\sigma_{zn}^2}\right)} \tag{11}$$

In order to understand better the implications of the produced expression we present results for the case of $N = 4$ where we have that

$$MSE_u = \frac{1}{s - \frac{h_2^2}{\sigma_{w2,2}^4 * \alpha} - \frac{h_3^2}{\sigma_{w3,2}^4 * \beta} - \frac{h_4^2}{\sigma_{w4,2}^4 * \gamma}} \tag{12}$$

Also MSE_{z2} is equal to

$$\frac{\beta * \gamma * s - \frac{h_3^2}{\sigma_{w3,2}^4} * \gamma - \frac{h_4^2}{\sigma_{w4,2}^4} * \beta}{\alpha * \beta * \gamma * s - \frac{h_2^2}{\sigma_{w2,2}^4} * \beta * \gamma - \frac{h_3^2}{\sigma_{w3,2}^4} * \alpha * \gamma - \frac{h_4^2}{\sigma_{w4,2}^4} * \alpha * \beta} \tag{13}$$

where:

$$s = \frac{h_2^2}{\sigma_{w2,2}^2} + \frac{h_3^2}{\sigma_{w3,2}^2} + \frac{h_4^2}{\sigma_{w4,2}^2} + \frac{1}{s_u^2}, \quad \alpha = \frac{1}{\sigma_{w2,1}^2} + \frac{1}{\sigma_{w2,2}^2} + \frac{1}{\sigma_{z2}^2}$$

$$\beta = \frac{1}{\sigma_{w3,1}^2} + \frac{1}{\sigma_{w3,2}^2} + \frac{1}{\sigma_{z3}^2}, \quad \gamma = \frac{1}{\sigma_{w4,1}^2} + \frac{1}{\sigma_{w4,2}^2} + \frac{1}{\sigma_{z4}^2}$$

The first thing we notice from these expressions is that the MSE of the information signal u is inversely proportional to the number of nodes, that is we have benefits in the accuracy of bit detection (MSE can be easily converted to Signal-to-Noise Ratio (SNR) and Bit Error Rate (BER)) when more nodes assist in the estimation process. Regarding the MSE of the estimated jamming signal it is also increased with a higher number of nodes but this is not obvious from the expression (11) that is more involved. The precise quantification of these gains is presented in the respective performance evaluation section where we will delve into the performance of this estimator in isolation first.

5   Jammer Speed Estimation

Our ultimate goal is to estimate the jammer speed based on jamming signal estimates that we obtained from the previous section. Figure 1 indicates that between the jammer and each receiver there is different AOD and a different distance ($dist_i$). Using again the estimator in (8) we propose to combine the values in the $N \times 1$ estimated vector u (that contains the joint data and the jamming signal) by diving them pairwise and taking then the absolute value:

$$|\frac{\hat{u}_1}{\hat{u}_2}| = |\frac{\hat{z}_1}{\hat{z}_2}| = |\frac{h_{j,1}z}{h_{j,2}z}| = |\frac{\gamma_1 po_{j,1}e^{j\frac{2\pi}{\lambda}f_{D,1}\tau_1}}{\gamma_2 po_{j,2}e^{j\frac{2\pi}{\lambda}f_{D,2}\tau_2}}|$$

$$\cdots$$

$$|\frac{\hat{u}_{N-2}}{\hat{u}_{N-1}}| = |\frac{\hat{z}_{N-2}}{\hat{z}_{N-1}}| = |\frac{\gamma_{N-2} po_{j,N-2}e^{j\frac{2\pi}{\lambda}f_{D,N-2}\tau_{N-2}}}{\gamma_{N-1} po_{j,N-1}e^{j\frac{2\pi}{\lambda}f_{D,N-1}\tau_{N-1}}}| \qquad (14)$$

Under specific assumptions and mathematical manipulations presented in the Appendix A taking into account the equations for the stochastic V2V channel (5), (6), (7) and the set of Eq. (1) with the geometry of the considered topology, the above equations can be simplified and solved for the speed of the jammer:

$$(1): \hat{u}_j = \frac{\hat{b}_1 * \lambda * c^2}{d * 2\pi * f_c} + u_r$$

$$(2): \hat{u}_j = \frac{\hat{b}_2 * \lambda * c^2}{d * 2\pi * f_c} + u_r$$

$$\cdots$$

$$(N-2): \hat{u}_j = \frac{\hat{b}_{N-2} * \lambda * c^2}{d * 2\pi * f_c} + u_r$$

This means that we have $N - 2$ equations that involve the speed of the jammer and the known value of d which is the distance between the members of the platoon. We observe that the only factor that differentiates these equations are the $(\hat{b}_1, \hat{b}_2, ..., \hat{b}_{N-2})$ which are the imaginary parts of the estimated complex numbers $(\ln(\frac{\hat{z}_1}{\hat{z}_2}), \ln(\frac{\hat{z}_2}{\hat{z}_2}), ..., \ln(\frac{\hat{z}_{N-2}}{\hat{z}_{N-1}}))$. Consequently, these values are only related to the estimated jamming signals $\hat{z}_i$. Obtaining the unbiased sample mean estimator of the above point estimates for the speed of the jammer we have:

$$\hat{\bar{u}}_j = \sum_{l=1}^{N-2} \frac{1}{N-2} \left(\frac{\hat{b}_l * \lambda * c^2}{d * 2\pi * f_c} + u_r \right) \tag{15}$$

Hence, if we increase the number of receivers we obtain a better estimate of the speed of the jammer. Now in the case that the jammer approaches the i-th receiver at a speed lower than the relative speed between the jammer and the receiver, it has positive sign if $|u_r - u_j| = u_j - u_r$. Repeating the above procedure results in something analogous to (15), namely:

$$\hat{\bar{u}}_j = \sum_{l=1}^{N-2} \frac{1}{N-2} \left(u_r - \frac{\hat{b}_l * \lambda * c^2}{d * 2\pi * f_c} \right) \tag{16}$$

We must note that we do not need to know a-priori the correct sign of the relationship $|u_r - u_j|$ since one of the two (15), (16) will have a negative sign and consequently this estimated jammer speed value must be rejected. In this case, the alternative equation must be used to estimate the speed of the jammer.

6   Numerical and Simulation Results for AWGN and Rayleigh Channels

For our simulations we assume that the master node together with the other nodes form a platoon of vehicles that move together in a specific direction with approximately a constant velocity. The jammer is in a specific distance and moves in parallel with them but we do not have any information for its position and channel condition between itself and the nodes in the platoon. We gradually present results for the AWGN channel, a Rayleigh fading channel, and finally a realistic vehicular channel that includes LOS and shadowing from obstacles in the next section. In this way we can offer a full exploration of all the aspects of our system.

For the AWGN and Rayleigh channels our purpose is to evaluate the ability of the estimator in (10) and (11) to accurately estimate the jamming signal. Consequently, we also test a baseline system where the master node transmits data continuously without stopping its transmission as with the proposed scheme. In our analytical model this result can be obtained by setting the noise variance to infinity in (2). Furthermore, we assume σ_w^2 to be equal to 0.1. The information signal u is a random binary sequence with power equal to $\sigma_u^2 = 1$ leading thus to a transmit SNR of 10dB. Higher SNRs would lead to higher gains. For the jamming signal note that its variance σ_{zi}^2 at every node takes different values because of channel fading. We implemented our algorithm in Matlab and we executed 50000 iterations for every different system configuration. For our results we present the MSE for the transmitted information u and for the jamming signal z_i.

6.1 Results for an AWGN Channel

In Fig. 2a we present the results for the MSE_u and MSE_{zi} for the proposed
and baseline systems. We observe that in the baseline system the MSE_u and
the MSE_{zi} for $N = 2$ nodes start at the same value. This is what we expect
to observe because only (3) is available for u and z_i (and $h_i = 1$). As we add
nodes the two MSE's improve and the MSE of the information u enjoys higher
improvements with every new node. For the proposed system our results are
much better as we have also the observations from the first time slot for every
node and we can estimate and isolate better the jamming signal that eventually
results in a better estimation of the information u. Specifically, the MSE of the
estimated jamming signal using the proposed transmission protocol is about
0.19 lower as compared to the baseline protocol for $N = 6$. The above result
proves that using the proposed transmission protocol we achieve a significant
increase in accuracy of the estimated jamming signal. Although we have better
MSE's for both estimated parameters we observe a behavior that requires some
further explanation. As we observe in Fig. 2a for the proposed system for a

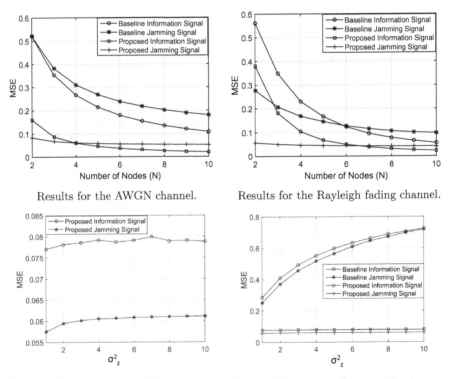

Results for the AWGN channel.   Results for the Rayleigh fading channel.

Power of the jamming signal increases in Power of the jamming signal increases in
the proposed system for N=5.   both systems for N=5.

Fig. 2. Information and jamming signal estimation

number nodes $N = 2, 3$, the MSE_{zi} is better than the MSE_u. This indicates that one can estimate better the different jamming signals for every node than the common information u for all nodes but this is not the case. The reason for this behavior is that the information signal that we are trying to estimate is common for all nodes but the jamming signal z_i is different for every node and contains the unknown channel h_{ji} and the real jamming term z. So it is easier for us to estimate a range of values z_i than a discrete value u.

6.2   Results for Rayleigh Fading Channel

When the channels between the master node and the other nodes are Rayleigh fading h_i takes random values. We adopt the same assumptions for the variance of the information signal and the noise. In Fig. 2b we present the results for MSE_u and MSE_{zi}. We observe that in the baseline system the MSE is greater than the proposed system because in the baseline system we have only the observations of the second time slot for every node so we do not have the ability to estimate the jamming signal. The MSE of the estimated jamming signal using the proposed transmission protocol is about 0.07 lower as compared to the baseline protocol for $N = 6$. In both systems the MSE_u that is achieved for $N \geq 4$ is adequate for a communication system. The final thing that we observe is that for a small number of nodes the estimation of the jamming signal seems to be better than that of the information. The information signal u that we want to estimate is common for all nodes but the jamming signal is just a different term z_i which contains also the unknown channel $h_{j,i}$ for every node. That means that with the same two observations for every node we are estimating from a set of two possible discrete BPSK values for u (effectively detecting the signal), and simultaneously we estimate $z_i = h_{j,i}z$ (and not z which might also be a discrete modulated signal). The MSE_{zi} has low values even for small N. As the number of nodes increases the observations from the different nodes for the information signal u increase leading to a MSE_u that is lower than MSE_{zi}. This is achieved for $N \geq 6$.

6.3   Results for MSE Vs σ_z^2

In our next set of results we assume a constant number of nodes $N = 5$ and we vary σ_z^2 between 1 to 10. In Fig. 2c we observe that in the proposed system that we have two observations for every node, as σ_z^2 increases, both MSE_u, MSE_{zi} remain practically in the same low desirable value below 0.1. That means that our system is not vulnerable to jamming, and as the power of the jamming signal σ_z^2 increases the system responds and estimates the information signal u in a very efficient way. In Fig. 2d we observe the difference between the baseline and the proposed system. Here as σ_z^2 increases (power of jamming increases) we observe a massive increase in MSE_u and MSE_{zi}. These results illustrate the importance of the observations in (2) for every node. In the baseline system that we practically cannot use these observations we have only (3) for every node. That means that we have no more information for every z_i and when this jamming signal has higher power than the information signal we cannot isolate and estimate the later.

7   Simulation Results for Vehicular Channel

In this section we seek to evaluate the performance of the speed estimation algorithm in conjunction with the jamming signal estimation algorithm. For this purpose, we used the Simulation of Urban Mobility (SUMO) tool and OMNET++/VEINS [27]. SUMO is adopted as our traffic simulator and OMNET++ is used to simulate wireless communication. Furthermore, the GEMV (a geometry-based efficient propagation model for V2V) [7] tool was integrated into the VEINS network simulator for a more realistic simulation of the PHY layer [18]. Specifically, the experiments are conducted in a rural area at the outskirts of the city of Aachen.

7.1   Cooperative Jammer Speed Estimation Results

We present our results in terms of the Mean Absolute Error (MAE) between the real value of the speed u_j and the estimated mean of the jammer speed in (15), (16) using the estimated results from multiple receivers $\hat{\hat{u}}_j$:

$$MAE = |\hat{\hat{u}}_j - u_j| \qquad (17)$$

The MAE is calculated for both baseline and the proposed two-stage transmission scheme. These estimated MAE values are presented in Fig. 3a for both baseline and the proposed two-stage transmission scheme with a different number of receivers in the interval [0, 50] in a realistic vehicular channel. In this experiment we also assume that the jammer approaches the platoon of vehicles with a maximum speed of 28 km/h and the receivers move with random speeds that belong in the interval [30] km/h. By setting the number of receivers to $N = 50$ nodes, we observed that the jammer can effectively communicate with only 25 out of 50 nodes based on the GEMV simulator [7]. It can be seen in Fig. 3b that after a number of 25 receivers the MAE of the estimated jammer speed converges to a stable value for both systems under comparison. This is because beyond 25, there are no other effective communication pairs between the jammer and the receivers. Moreover, the MAE of the estimated speed of the jammer under realistic vehicular communication channel using the proposed transmission protocol is about 0.5 lower as compared to the baseline protocol for $N = 20$. The above results indicate the significance of the proposed transmission protocol in terms of increasing the accuracy of the estimated speed of the jammer. Because of its superior performance we use the proposed two-stage transmission scheme for the rest of the experiments.

But in reality, the members of a platoon of vehicles never moves at exactly the same speed. So, when we change slightly the range where the speed of the receivers can vary, we observe in Fig. 3b that as this range is narrower, the MAE decreases. This is because in this case the speed deviation of all the receivers will

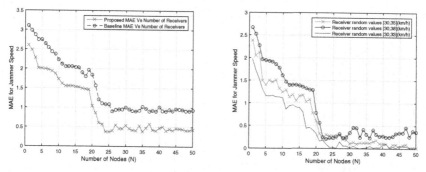

Comparing the proposed with the baseline method.   Different ranges for the speed of the receivers.

Fig. 3. MAE of the jammer speed estimation using the proposed transmission protocol for a different number of receivers

be present as an additional condition in (15), (16). This result is very encouraging since it states that when it is used in vehicle formations that all have the same approximate speed (e.g. platoons), the speed of the jammer can be estimated with improved accuracy.

For our next experiment we check the robustness of the proposed distributed system with 20 multiple receivers but over time. We update the jamming signal z_i estimate using (8) every $\Delta t = 20$ s, while in the intermediate time instants we use the last estimated jamming signal as our current estimate of the jammer speed. The jammer speed estimate that takes place in the time interval $[1, 100]$ s is presented in Fig. 4a. During $[1,75]$ s the jammer moves with a speed of 25 km/h, while from time 75 s onwards a sharp increase in the speed of the jammer to 50 km/h is observed. Therefore, for the specific time interval $[75, 90]$ s the MAE value increases significantly. This is happening because of the jammer speed in the subsequent time instants between 75 and 90 s is actually the old estimate made at 70 s. This is clearly an approach that may create a stale value for the estimated speed when we have changes.

To solve the previous problem we apply a smoothing filter for combining the jammer speed estimates across time. In particular we combine the last estimate with the estimated jammer speed at the present time instant $\hat{\bar{u}}_j(t)$ as follows:

$$\hat{\bar{u}}_{j(filtered)}(t) = (1 - a)\hat{\bar{u}}_j(t) + a * \hat{\bar{u}}_{j(filtered)}(t - 1) \tag{18}$$

We explored for two extreme values $a = [0.8, 0.2]$ and the results can be seen in Fig. 4b. Observing these results, it is obvious that giving parameter a large values such as 0.8, results in a sharp changes in filtered speed estimate over the entire duration of this specific experiment and especially in the specific time interval $[75, 90]$ s. This is because the speed of the jammer is mainly estimated using the last estimate of its speed. This results in the smoothing filter being unable to estimate the actual instantaneous changes in the speed of the jammer. On the contrary, by giving lower values to parameter a around 0.3 or 0.2, all abrupt changes are absorbed by the smoothing filter and so the MAE does not vary significantly over time.

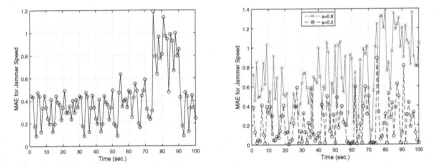

Updating the jamming signal estimation every $\Delta t = 20$ sec.

Using a smoothing filter with different values for parameter a.

Fig. 4. Jammer speed estimation over the time for 100 s.

8   Conclusions

In this paper, we considered a network when a swarm of nodes that receive an information signal from a master node and a signal from an RF jammer. We proposed both a transmission scheme where the master node remains silent for a slot, and a joint data and jamming signal estimation algorithm using LMMSE estimation. We derived analytical closed-form expressions for the MSE of our system. Our results indicate that as the number of nodes in the swarm increases, the estimation of both the jamming and information signals is improved significantly. Our results also showed that our proposed transmission scheme is robust against RF jamming attacks since, although the power of the jamming signal (σ_z^2) increases, the MSE_u and MSE_{zi} remains constant. Finally, we proposed a method for combining the jamming signal estimates from the multiple receivers so as to improve the accuracy of the jammer speed estimate in a realistic vehicular channel. To the best of our knowledge, our proposed scheme is the first distributed estimation scheme for the speed of an RF jammer. The experimental results prove that the speed estimate of the jammer is improved by increasing the number of receivers and the proposed method is particularly suitable for a platoon of vehicles since they use approximately the same speed. An accurate estimation of the speed of the jammer and its use as an extra feature in a ML approach [17], increases the accuracy of an RF jamming attack detection.

However, a "smart" jammer can overhear the transmissions of the master node to swarm nodes, learn the proposed transmission protocol and act accordingly. For this reason, we could further improve the security of the proposed transmission protocol turning it into a pseudo-random time hopping protocol so that the master node only transmits at specific times slots which are selected pseudo-randomly according to a private key pre-sharing procedure [1] between the master node and the receivers. This proposed "smart" communication protocol can further confuse the jammer and is an area of future research.

A   Appendix

Recall that the $N-1$ receivers are assumed to be close to each other, resulting in a constant value for the free space propagation loss $po_{j,i}$ and the random variable γ_i for the observation interval in the above equations. Under these assumptions the set of Eq. (14) is simplified to:

$$\frac{\hat{z}_1}{\hat{z}_2} = \frac{e^{j\frac{2\pi}{\lambda}\Delta u_1 \frac{f_c}{c}\cos\phi_1\tau_1}}{e^{j\frac{2\pi}{\lambda}\Delta u_2 \frac{f_c}{c}\cos\phi_2\tau_2}}$$

$$...$$

$$\frac{\hat{z}_{N-2}}{\hat{z}_{N-1}} = \frac{e^{j\frac{2\pi}{\lambda}\Delta u_{N-2} \frac{f_c}{c}\cos\phi_{N-2}\tau_{N-2}}}{e^{j\frac{2\pi}{\lambda}\Delta u_{N-1} \frac{f_c}{c}\cos\phi_{N-1}\tau_{N-1}}}$$

By taking the natural logarithm of the expressions on the left and right we have:

$$\ln\left(\frac{\hat{z}_1}{\hat{z}_2}\right) = \ln\left(\frac{e^{\omega|u_{r,1}-u_j|\cos\phi_1\tau_1}}{e^{\omega|u_{r,2}-u_j|\cos\phi_2\tau_2}}\right)$$

$$...$$

$$\ln\left(\frac{\hat{z}_{N-2}}{\hat{z}_{N-1}}\right) = \ln\left(\frac{e^{\omega|u_{r,N-2}-u_j|\cos\phi_{N-2}\tau_{N-2}}}{e^{\omega|u_{r,N-1}-u_j|\cos\phi_{N-1}\tau_{N-1}}}\right)$$

where $u_{r,i}$ is the speed of every receiver, u_j the speed of the jammer in the area and the variables $f_{cx} = \frac{f_c}{c}$, $\omega = j\frac{2\pi}{\lambda}f_{cx}$. If we assume that the jammer approaches the i-th receiver at a speed lower than its own speed the relative speed between jammer and receiver is positive and so $|u_{r,i} - u_j| = u_{r,i} - u_j$. By simplifying the previous logarithmic equations we have:

$$\ln\left(\frac{\hat{z}_1}{\hat{z}_2}\right) = \omega[(u_{r,1} - u_j)\cos\phi_1\tau_1 - (u_{r,2} - u_j)\cos\phi_2\tau_2]$$

$$...$$

$$\ln\left(\frac{\hat{z}_{N-2}}{\hat{z}_{N-1}}\right) = \omega[(u_{r,N-2} - u_j)\cos\phi_{N-2}\tau_{N-2} - (u_{r,N-1} - u_j)\cos\phi_{N-1}\tau_{N-1}]$$

In the above equations the estimated jamming signal values on the left-hand side are complex numbers of the form: $(\hat{a}_1 + \hat{b}_1j), ..., \hat{a}_{N-2} + \hat{b}_{N-2}j$. We observe that the real part of the above equations on the right side is equal to zero. So all the real parts, that is the $\hat{a}$'s, are equal to zero. We also assume that the receivers move at similar speeds ($u_{r,1} \simeq u_{r,2} \simeq ... \simeq u_{r,N-1} = u_r$) as they are members of the platoon. By replacing the AOD values with the order of Eq. (1) and the time delays as $\tau_1 = \frac{dist_1}{c}, \tau_2 = \frac{dist_2}{c}, ..., \tau_{N-1} = \frac{dist_{N-1}}{c}$ we have:

$$\hat{b}_1 = \omega[(u_r - u_j)\frac{x_{dist}}{dist_1} * \frac{dist_1}{c} - (u_r - u_j)\frac{x_{dist} + d}{dist_2} * \frac{dist_2}{c}]$$

...

$$\hat{b}_{N-2} = \omega[(u_r - u_j)\frac{x_{dist} + (N-3)*d}{dist_{N-2}} * \frac{dist_{N-2}}{c} - (u_r - u_j)\frac{x_{dist} + (N-2)*d}{dist_{N-1}} * \frac{dist_{N-1}}{c}]$$

References

1. Adem, N., Hamdaoui, B., Yavuz, A.: Pseudorandom time-hopping anti-jamming technique for mobile cognitive users. In: 2015 IEEE Globecom Workshops (GC Wkshps), pp. 1–6 (2015)
2. Akhlaghpasand, H., Razavizadeh, S.M., Bjornson, E., Do, T.T.: Jamming detection in massive MIMO systems. IEEE Wirel. Commun. Lett. **7**, 242–245 (2018)
3. Alipour-Fanid, A., Dabaghchian, M., Zhang, H., Zeng, K.: String stability analysis of cooperative adaptive cruise control under jamming attacks. In: 2017 IEEE 18th International Symposium on High Assurance Systems Engineering (HASE), January 2017
4. Argyriou, A., Alay, O.: Distributed estimation in wireless sensor networks with an interference canceling fusion center. IEEE Trans. Wirel. Commun. **15**(3), 2205–2214 (2016)
5. Bahceci, I., Khandani, A.: Linear estimation of correlated data in wireless sensor networks with optimum power allocation and analog modulation. IEEE Tran. Commun. **56**(7), 1146–1156 (2008)
6. Biron, Z.A., Pisu, P.: Distributed fault detection and estimation for cooperative adaptive cruise control system in a platoon. In: PHM 2015 Conference (2015)
7. Boban, M., Barros, J., Tonguz, O.K.: Geometry-based vehicle-to-vehicle channel modeling for large-scale simulation. IEEE Trans. Veh. Technol. **63**, 4146–4164 (2016)
8. Duan, B., Yin, D., Cong, Y., Zhou, H., Xiang, X., Shen, L.: Anti-jamming path planning for unmanned aerial vehicles with imperfect jammer information. In: 2018 IEEE International Conference on Robotics and Biomimetics (ROBIO), December 2018
9. Farahmand, S., Cano, A., Giannakis, G.B.: Anti-jam distributed MIMO decoding using wireless sensor networks. IEEE Trans. Signal Process. **58**, 3661–3680 (2010)
10. He, Q., Blum, R.S., Haimovich, A.M.: Noncoherent MIMO radar for location and velocity estimation: more antennas means better performance. IEEE Trans. Signal Process. **58**, 3661–3680 (2010)
11. Karagiannis, D., Argyriou, A.: Jamming attack detection in a pair of RF communicating vehicles using unsupervised machine learning. Veh. Commun. **13**, 56–63 (2018)
12. Kassem, N., Kosba, A.E., Youssef, M.: RF-based vehicle detection and speed estimation. In: 2012 IEEE 75th Vehicular Technology Conference (VTC Spring) (2012)
13. Kosmanos, D., et al.: A novel intrusion detection system against spoofing attacks in connected electric vehicles. In: Array. Elsevier, December 2019

14. Kosmanos, D., Argyriou, A., Maglaras, L.: Estimating the relative speed of RF jammers in VANETs. Secur. Commun. Netw. **2019**, 18 (2019). Article ID 2064348
15. Kosmanos, D., Karagiannis, D., Argyriou, A., Lalis, S., Maglaras, L.: RF jamming classification using relative speed estimation in vehicular wireless networks (2018)
16. Kosmanos, D., et al.: Route optimization of electric vehicles based on dynamic wireless charging. IEEE Access **6**, 42551–42565 (2018)
17. Kosmanos, D.,et al.: Intrusion detection system for platooning connected autonomous vehicles. In: SEEDA-CECNSM Conference (2019)
18. Kosmanos, D., Prodromou, N., Argyriou, A., Maglaras, L.A., Janicke, H.: MIMO techniques for jamming threat suppression in vehicular networks. Mob. Inf. Syst. **2016**, 1–9 (2016)
19. Malebary, S., Xu, W., Huang, C.T.: Jamming mobility in 802.11 p networks: modeling, evaluation, and detection. In: 2016 IEEE 35th International on Performance Computing and Communications Conference (IPCCC), pp. 1–7 (2016)
20. Mukherjee, J.C., Gupta, A.: A review of charge scheduling of electric vehicles in smart grid. IEEE Syst. J. **9**(4), 1541–1553 (2015). https://doi.org/10.1109/JSYST. 2014.2356559
21. Neely, M.J.: Stochastic Network Optimization with Application to Communication and Queueing Systems. Morgan & Claypool (2010)
22. Pirani, M., Hashemi, E., Khajepour, A., Fidan, B., Litkouhi, B., Chen, S.K.: Cooperative vehicle speed fault diagnosis and correction. IEEE Trans. Intell. Transp. Syst. **20**, 783–789 (2018)
23. Puñal, O., Aktaş, I., Schnelke, C.J., Abidin, G., Wehrle, K., Gross, J.: Machine learning-based jamming detection for IEEE 802.11: design and experimental evaluation. In: 2014 IEEE 15th International Symposium on a World of Wireless, Mobile and Multimedia Networks (WoWMoM), pp. 1–10 (2014)
24. Punal, O., Pereira, C., Aguiar, A., Gross, J.: Experimental characterization and modeling of RF jamming attacks on VANETs. IEEE Trans. Veh. Technol. **64**, 524–540 (2015)
25. Santini, S., Salvi, A., Valente, A.S., Pescape, A., Segata, M., Cigno, R.L.: Platooning maneuvers in vehicular networks: a distributed and consensus-based approach. EEE Trans. Intell. Veh. **4**(1), 59–72 (2019)
26. Sheikholeslami, A., Ghaderi, M., Pishro-Nik, H., Goeckel, D.: Jamming-aware minimum energy routing in wireless networks. IEEE Access **6**, 2313–2318 (2018)
27. Sommer, C., German, R., Dressler, F.: Bidirectionally coupled network and road traffic simulation for improved IVC analysis. IEEE Trans. Mob. Comput. **10**(1), 3–15 (2015)
28. Spuhler, M., Lenders, V., Wilhelm, M.: Detection of reactive jamming in DSSS-based wireless communications. IEEE Trans. Wirel. Commun. **13**, 165–171 (2014)
29. Wang, J., Tong, J., Gao, Q., Wu, Z., Bi, S., Wang, H.: Device-free vehicle speed estimation with wifi. IEEE Trans. Veh. Technol. **67**, 8205–8214 (2018)
30. Xu, S., Xu, W., Pan, C., Elkashlan, M.: Detection of jamming attack in non-coherent massive SIMO systems. IEEE Trans. Inf. Forensics Secur. **14**, 2387–2399 (2019)
31. Zheng, Y.R., Xiao, C.: Mobile speed estimation for broadband wireless communications over rician fading channels. IEEE Trans. Wirel. Commun. **8**, 1–8 (2009)

Extended Abstract: Towards Physical-Layer Authentication for Backscatter Devices

Thiemo Voigt[1,2](✉) ⓘ, Carlos Pérez-Penichet[1] ⓘ, and Christian Rohner[1] ⓘ

[1] Uppsala University Sweden, Uppsala, Sweden
{thiemo.voigt,carlos.perez-penichet,christian.rohner}@it.uu.se
[2] RISE Computer Science, Kista, Sweden

Abstract. Backscatter communications relieves sensor tags from the energy-intensive task of generating their own radio waves. This enables sensor tags to transmit their sensor readings at an energy consumption that is several orders of magnitude lower than that of conventional low-power radios. The resource-constraints of typical backscatter tags, however, make it challenging to provide security for them. In this extended abstract, we take a first step towards authentication of backscatter transmissions. We propose to add authentication information in the chip sequences of the physical layer. We discuss design issues and in particular the trade-off between security and reliability and propose mechanisms to enable low-power authentication suitable for backscatter tags.

Keywords: Backscatter · Authentication · Security

1 Introduction

Backscatter communications enable data transmissions while avoiding the need to generate a radio wave at the backscatter device, which is one of the most energy-consuming tasks for low-power Internet of Things (IoT) devices. Instead, an external device generates the carrier wave on which the backscatter tags modulate their sensed data values. Recent progress in backscatter communications enables IoT sensors and actuators to transmit physical-layer protocols such as Bluetooth [2], WiFi [8,23], IEEE 802.15.4 (often called ZigBee) [15,16] and LoRa [14,18] with a power consumption below one milliwatt, several orders of magnitude lower than with conventional low-power radios and, in some cases, at distances in the range of kilometers [18]. This dramatic reduction of power consumption makes it increasingly feasible to power devices by energy harvested from the environment. At the same time, using commodity physical-layer protocols removes the need for an expensive dedicated device (RFID reader) to generate the required carrier wave on which the devices modulate their data. Backscatter promises large-scale data collection from battery-free IoT devices that run on harvested energy. We are, however, not aware of any security-related efforts in backscatter, other than for RFID [20].

© Springer Nature Switzerland AG 2020
S. Katsikas et al. (Eds.): CyberICPS 2020/SECPRE 2020/ADIoT 2020, LNCS 12501, pp. 224–234, 2020.
https://doi.org/10.1007/978-3-030-64330-0_14

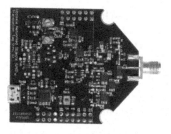

Fig. 1. Backscatter transceiver prototype

While security based on Public Key Infrastructure (PKI) systems are becoming possible for resource-constrained, battery-powered devices [5], the resources on backscatter tags are usually too limited for dealing with, for example, certificates required for device authentication. In this paper, we propose an alternative physical-layer authentication mechanism for backscatter devices that employs watermarking to authenticate packets. Watermarking here refers to embedding secret information in the packets [7]. Several IoT physical layers such as IEEE 802.15.4 and IEEE 802.11b (WiFi) use Direct-Sequence Spread Spectrum (DSSS), a spread-spectrum modulation technique used to better handle interference. In the case of 802.15.4, the transmitter maps one 4-bit symbol to one out of 16 32-chip pseudonoise codes (PN-code). The receiver maps the received code to the best matching 4-bit symbol. The 16 codes are chosen so that this matching process is robust against chip flips. Our key idea is that backscatter tags, upon transmission, could intentionally flip one or more chips to enable the receiver to identify the transmitter, without altering the original data. This is similar to recent efforts in using the 802.15.4 chip sequence as steganographic channel [9,12,24] or watermarking [11] but with a focus on authentication for ultra-low-power backscatter devices. Similar mechanisms could be implemented in other parts of the packets as we discuss in Sect. 6.

Contributions. Our main contribution is the design of a physical-layer authentication scheme for backscatter-based IoT devices. We discuss several design trade-offs such as the one between security and reliability. To the best of our knowledge, this is the first paper that addresses security for backscatter with IoT physical layer protocols.

2   Background

In this section we present a brief background on backscatter transmissions and DSSS, both with a focus on IEEE 802.15.4.

Backscatter. Backscatter transmitters selectively reflect an external Radio Frequency (RF) signal to convey information such as their sensor readings [8,23]. By offloading the carrier generation to an external device, backscatter tags avoid the energy-consuming task of generating their own radio wave, which reduces their power consumption by up to three orders of magnitude compared to traditional low-power radios. The backscatter transmitter controls how the carrier wave is reflected by changing the load attached to its antenna to create a specific impedance mismatch. This enables the tags to control the amplitude, phase and frequency of the reflected signal. Therefore, the tags can backscatter almost any standard physical layer protocol including packets conforming to the IEEE 802.15.4 standard [15,16]. A backscatter prototype is shown in Fig. 1.

DSSS. Physical layer protocols such as those employed by IEEE 802.15.4 and IEEE 802.11b use DSSS, a spread-spectrum modulation technique used to better handle interference. Using DSSS, this is achieved by widening (spreading) the bandwidth of the transmitted signal. When despreading at the receiver, unintentional and intentional interference is reduced. In IEEE 802.15.4 each symbol (consisting of 4 bits) is mapped to a 32-chip long pseudonoise code (PN-code). There are 16 of these PN-codes as defined in the standard. These 16 PN-codes have been selected to maximize the number of chip positions in which the two PN-codes are different (Hamming distance). In 802.15.4, the minimum distance between two PN-codes is 12 and the maximum 20. A receiver takes the received PN-code and matches it to the symbol whose PN-code has the minimum Hamming distance to the received PN-code.

3   Related Work

There are a number of studies that discuss steganography and watermarking for IEEE 802.15.4. Ko proposes a first system using a steganographic channel that is based on the 802.15.4 chip sequence [9]. The main contribution of the paper is to show that this channel enables the transmission of additional data to save energy. Along the same lines, Metha et al. also propose to use this channel to communicate with a specialized receiver while sending data to a conventional one [12]. Towards this end, they expand the original 802.15.4 chip sequences with additional chip sequences that still resolve to the original ones for a conventional 802.15.4 receiver. Zielinska and Szczypiorski add additional scrambling to the modified chip sequences to complicate detection of the steganographic channel [24]. They demonstrate the possibility of creating a covert channel with the same data rate as 802.15.4, with a low impact on the bit error rate and only a slight decrease in receiver sensitivity. Li et al. study the same issues for watermarking in 802.15.4 and also implement a prototype system to gain experimental results [11]. Nain et al. extend the channel with acknowledgements to make it reliable [13]. In contrast to these approaches, we aim at exploiting the 802.15.4 PN-codes for authentication of extremely resource-constrained backscatter devices.

Ureten and Serinken are among the first to propose to use RF fingerprints for identifying individual nodes in wireless networks by means of their RF fingerprints [19]. Xu et al. differentiate between the conventional passive approaches for fingerprinting and active approaches [21]. The latter approaches do not only observe ongoing communication but also try to trigger responses from devices to make them transmit useful features. Oracle [17] goes beyond the previous approaches by using transmitter-side modifications to increase the chances of correct identification at the receiver. In contrast to our approach, Oracle requires machine learning methods to differentiate between different nodes whereas our approach relies on much simpler methods at the receiver as we discuss in the next section. Some studies have shown that RF fingerprinting is feasible also for RFID tags [1, 22].

4 Design Issues

4.1 Overview

On a high level, we devise a backscatter communications authentication system that works as follows: A carrier generator that could be a software-defined radio, a WiFi or an IEEE 802.15.4 device, generates an unmodulated carrier. One or more backscatter tags transmit their collected sensor data by modulating their sensed data in 802.15.4 frames on top of the unmodulated carrier. In order to enable authentication, the tags embed authentication information by flipping selected chips in the PN-code. We call these chips authentication chips. The chips are flipped according to the tag's individual random sequence that is known by both the receiver and the backscatter tags. In our case, the receiver needs to be able to detect the flipped chips. Current 802.15.4 radios do not offer access to such low-level information and hence we would need a specialized receiver that we implement with a software-defined radio, similar to related work. Note that low-power software-defined radios exist [4].

Using the 802.15.4 PN-code for authentication by watermarking is interesting for backscatter devices as it allows us to add information without increasing the packet size. On the other hand, it needs to be done with care since it reduces the robustness of the backscattered signals which are particularly weak and vulnerable. We discuss these and other issues in the sequel of this section.

4.2 Message Authentication Code

We use a Message Authentication Code (MAC) to provide authenticity. To that end, we split the MAC into 5-bit chunks to identify one of the 32 PN-code positions to be flipped. Given the maximum IEEE 802.15.4 packet size of 127 bytes and the fact that there are 4 bits per DSSS symbol we can encode up to 254 bits in one packet by flipping one chip per DSSS symbol. Knowing the message and the tag's random sequence (key) the receiver can decode and verify the MAC.

4.3 Preliminary Reliability Analysis

The goal of this section is to provide a preliminary analysis about the impact of flipping chips of the PN-code on the reliability of packet transmissions and outline ways of improving reliability. We implement a Monte Carlo simulation

Table 1. The results show that under worse channel conditions there is an increase in symbols and authentication chips that cannot be detected. Using two instead of one authentication chips per chip PN-code improves the situation.

Number Auth. chips	Number RX chip errors	Symbol correct	Auth. chips correct	Symbol and Auth. correct
1	0	1.0	1.0	1.0
1	1	1.0	0.97	0.97
1	2	1.0	0.94	0.94
1	4	1.0	0.88	0.88
1	6	0.99	0.81	0.8
1	8	0.88	0.75	0.64
2	0	1.0	1.0	1.0
2	1	1.0	1.0	1.0
2	2	1.0	0.997	0.998
2	4	0.998	0.99	0.99
2	6	0.96	0.97	0.93
2	8	0.78	0.94	0.73

in Python. In the simulation, we take one of the 16 PN-codes and first flip one or more chips of the code before transmission. The first chip is flipped as part of the authentication, the other chips are flipped to increase security by adding additional chip flips. We flip an additional number of chips to simulate errors at the receiver where interference actually occurs. Note that such a chip flip during reception could undo the transmitter's chip flip. After the reception of a packet, the receiver decodes the PN-code and retrieves the authentication chips.

Basic Reliability. The goal of our first simulation is to evaluate if the correct PN-code and hence symbol is detected. Further, we evaluate if the authentication chip is correctly detected, i.e., if it has not been flipped again which could happen because of interference at the receiver.

Table 1 depicts the simulation results. The table shows how the number of authentication chips and the number of chip errors at the receiver impact the correctness of the received symbol (i.e., the receiver selects the correct symbol out of the 16 possible ones), if the authentication chip is still valid (i.e., it has not been flipped again during reception) and finally in the right-most column if both the PN-code and the authentication chip are still correct. The table shows that with only one authentication chip, there is a high chance that interference (additional chip flips) prevents that both the correct symbol and the correct authentication chip can be detected. Therefore, we opt for using two authentication chips in each symbol. With two authentication chips, we consider the authentication chips also correctly received if only one of them is correct.

The results in the table show that under worse channel conditions, i.e., when we flip more chips at the receiver, there is an increase in symbols and authenti-

Table 2. While flipping additional chips before transmission increases security, it leads to a further decrease in the correct detection of symbols and authentication chips

Number Auth. chips	Number RX chip errors	Symbol correct	Auth. chips correct	Symbol and Auth. correct
$2+1$	0	1.0	1.0	1.0
$2+1$	1	1.0	1.0	1.0
$2+1$	2	1.0	0.998	0.998
$2+1$	4	0.99	0.99	0.98
$2+1$	6	0.91	0.97	0.87
$2+1$	8	0.66	0.94	0.61
$2+2$	0	1.0	1.0	1.0
$2+2$	1	1.0	1.0	1.0
$2+2$	2	0.998	0.998	0.996
$2+2$	4	0.97	0.99	0.96
$2+2$	6	0.83	0.97	0.8
$2+2$	8	0.56	0.94	0.51

cation chips that cannot be detected. The table also shows that only less than in total six chip flips per symbol can be corrected. As Zielinska and Szczypiorski denote [24], the maximum error correcting capability in 802.15.4 is $\lfloor \frac{d_{min}-1}{2} \rfloor$ where d_{min} is the minimum Hamming distance between two PN-codes (12 in 802.15.4).

Since we require that only one out of the two authentication chips needs to be correct, we increase the risk that an attacker that sends faked packets and tries to guess the authentication chips succeeds. With only one authentication chip per symbol the probability that the attacker flips the correct chip is $\frac{1}{32}$ since there are 32 chips per symbol. Using two authentication chips and requiring that only one of them is correct increases this probability to $\frac{1}{32} + 2 \cdot \frac{1}{32} \cdot \frac{30}{32}$, i.e., from 0.03125 to 0.0596. If we assume that the attacker needs to guess 10 symbols correctly, the probability of a correct guess decreases beyond 5.63e-13. We make two assumptions here: First, we assume that we have two distinct authentication chips in the (manipulated) PN-code of a symbol. Second, since chips may be flipped at the receiver due to interference, the receiver does not require that all symbols have the expected authentication chips but a subset is sufficient for successful authentication.

Additional Chip Flips. One possibility to make it more difficult for the attacker to identify the random sequence based on observed chip flips is to create additional chip flips. While this increases security the chances increase that the receiver cannot decode the transmitted symbol correctly. We quantify this risk with additional simulations that we depict in Table 2.

The table shows that as expected the risk of symbol mismatch increases. Assuming that during reception eight chips are flipped because of interference,

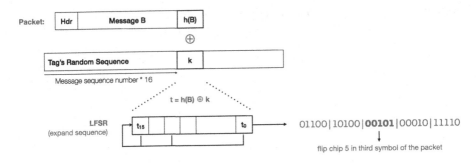

Fig. 2. MAC implementation

the ability to decode the right symbol decreases from 78% (Table 1) to 68% with one additional chip flip before transmission to 56% with two additional chip flips.

These results demonstrate that adding additional chip flips in order to increase the security has as expected a negative impact on the symbol detection ability of the receiver when there is radio interference. Therefore, the decision if and how many additional chip flips should be performed depends on the state of the radio channel. If the channel conditions are good and there is a low risk for interference and hence chip flips during reception, additional chip flips seem an attractive idea. If, however, the radio channel conditions are bad adding additional chip flips may cause symbol errors at the receiver. As in such scenarios we may expect additional chip flips caused by interference, it is not necessary to add artificial chip flips for security reasons.

Conventional low-power radios have mechanisms such as CCA (Clear Channel Assessment) checks to get an understanding of the state of the radio channel. There are, however, currently no similar mechanisms for backscatter tags. Therefore, we expect that we need to measure the channel conditions at the receiver (where interference actually takes place) and inform the backscatter tags about the channel conditions.

4.4   MAC Implementation

As illustrated in Fig. 2, we base our MAC on a CRC-based MAC $t = h(B) \oplus k$ [10], where B is the b-bit message to be sent, $h(B) = \mathrm{coef}(B(x) \cdot x^m \bmod p(x))$ a function of the (b, m) hash-family with polynomial $p(x)$ of degree m, and k is a one-time key. We use the 16-bit CRC (polynomial) of IEEE 802.15.4 because it has to be calculated and concatenated to the packets for error detection purposes anyway. The one-time key is derived from the tag's random sequence. For each packet we use another 16-bit sub-sequence with an offset depending on the message sequence number times 16 (modulo the sequence length).

We finally use a linear-feedback shift register to extend the $m = 16$ bit MAC t (used as initial value) into a longer pseudo-random sequence. For this purpose we use the feedback polynomial $x^{16} + x^{15} + x^{13} + x^4 + 1$ to achieve a maximum-

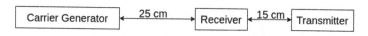

Fig. 3. Experimental setup

length period of $2^{16} - 1$, which is plenty for practical packet lengths. An LFSR is easy to implement in both soft- and hardware.

The success probability of an adversary that tries to modify a single message that results in the same MAC is at most ϵ for ϵ-opt-secure hash families [10]. For the (b, m) hash-family: $\epsilon = (b + m)/(2^{m-1})$. This shows that the message length m has a significant impact on ϵ, and hence on the security of the system. Short messages reduce the search space for brute force attacks, long messages increase ϵ. The hash function $h()$ (in our case the CRC) can be reused if for each new message a different one-time key k is used. It is therefore important to chose a sufficiently long random sequence for each tag to derive unique keys.

5   First Prototype

In order to demonstrate the basic feasibility of our approach, i.e., that we can flip chips even on our resource-constrained prototype, we implement chip flipping in our backscatter tag [15]. The modifications are implemented in the FPGA that features the baseband logic to generate 802.15.4 frames. As a carrier generator, we use a USRP B200 software-defined radio and as a receiver a Zolertia Firefly IoT development platform. We place the devices at close distances as shown in Fig. 3 to avoid undesired chip flips due to weak communication links. We flip a specific number of chips and evaluate whether the Zolertia node is still able to receive the packets. In order to consider a worst case, we flip the chips so that the minimum Hamming distance is minimized. For example, when flipping two chips, the minimum Hamming distance that is 12 without any chip flips, becomes 10, 12 or 14 dependent on which chips are flipped. For the purpose of this experiment, we flip the chips that lead to a minimum Hamming distance of 10. We send 160 packets with the same number of flipped chips, 10 with each of the different PN-codes.

Our results show that the Zolertia node receives almost all packets correctly when we flip up to four chips in each PN-code. In fact, we see one error (out of 640 packets) in these scenarios which we attribute to external interference since the experiments are conducted in an office environment. If we flip five or more chips in one chip sequence, however, we see an increasing rate of symbols that are wrongly detected. When we flip 8 chips in each PN-code, roughly half of the packets can still be correctly received.

6   Discussion

While our first prototype has been implemented in the physical layer, we could also implement the same algorithms in other places in the packet, for example, in the application layer. The main disadvantage of implementations at higher layers is that the packets increase in size due to the additional bytes required for authentication. Note that while the smallest unit we can manipulate in the physical layer is a chip, in higher layers it is a bit which corresponds to eight chips. Hence, implementing the same approach in a higher layer may lead to a non-negligible increase of the size of the packets and larger packets have a higher risk of being corrupted [6]. On the other hand, our approach of flipping chips in the 802.15.4 frames has a negative impact on the packet reliability. Furthermore, the implementation of our approach requires a gateway that is capable of dealing with physical layer information. Note, however, that there is a current trend of more capable gateways for the Internet of Things [3]. In the long run, we intend to combine our approach with RF fingerprinting which also requires information from the physical layer and hence gateways that are able and need to handle physical layer information.

7   Conclusions

In this extended abstract, we have taken the first steps towards authentication for extremely resource-constrained sensor devices using backscatter communication. In particular, we target backscatter devices that use IEEE 802.15.4 as their physical layer protocol where we embed the authentication information as chip flips. We have discussed several design options that highlight the trade-off between security and reliability and have shown that chip flipping is feasible also in those resource-constrained backscatter devices. Towards the best of our knowledge, this is the first paper that targets security for backscatter with standard IoT protocols.

Acknowledgments. This project is financially supported by the Swedish Foundation for Strategic Research and the Swedish Research Council (grants 2017-045989 and 2018-05480).

References

1. Danev, B., Heydt-Benjamin, T.S., Capkun, S.: Physical-layer identification of RFID devices. In: USENIX Security Symposium, pp. 199–214 (2009)
2. Ensworth, J.F., Reynolds, M.S.: Every smart phone is a backscatter reader: modulated backscatter compatibility with bluetooth 4.0 low energy (BLE) devices. In: IEEE International Conference on RFID, pp. 78–85. IEEE (2015)
3. Hazra, S., Duquennoy, S., P., Wang, S., Voigt, T., Lu, C., Cederholm, D.: Handling inherent delays in virtual IoT gateways. In: International Conference on Distributed Computing in Sensor Systems (2019)
4. Hessar, M., Najafi, A., Iyer, V., Gollakota, S.: TinySDR, a software-defined radio platform for internet of things. In: The 25th Annual International Conference on Mobile Computing and Networking, pp. 1–3 (2019)
5. Höglund, J., Lindemer, S., Furuhed, M., Raza, S.: Pki4iot: towards public key infrastructure for the internet of things. Comput. Secur. **89**, 101658 (2020)

6. Jacobsson, M., Rohner, C.: Estimating packet delivery ratio for arbitrary packet sizes over wireless links. IEEE Commun. Lett. **19**(4), 609–612 (2015)
7. Kang, T., Li, X., Chansu, Yu., Kim, J.: A survey of security mechanisms with direct sequence spread spectrum signals. J. Computi. Sci. Eng. **7**(3), 187–197 (2013)
8. Kellogg, B., Talla, V., Gollakota, S., Smith, J.R.: Passive wi-fi: Bringing low power to wi-fi transmissions. In: 13th USENIX Symposium on Networked Systems Design and Implementation (NSDI) (2016)
9. Kho, T.: Steganography in the 802.15.4 physical layer. UC Berkeley (2007)
10. Krawczyk, H.: LFSR-based hashing and authentication. In: Desmedt, Y.G. (ed.) CRYPTO 1994. LNCS, vol. 839, pp. 129–139. Springer, Heidelberg (1994). https:// doi.org/10.1007/3-540-48658-5_15
11. Li, X., Yu, C., Hizlan, M., Kim, W.-T., Park, S.: Physical layer watermarking of direct sequence spread spectrum signals. In: IEEE Military Communications Conference. IEEE (2013)
12. Mehta, A.M., Lanzisera, S., Pister, K.S.J.: Steganography in 802.15.4 wireless communication. In: 2008 2nd International Symposium on Advanced Networks and Telecommunication Systems, pp. 1–3. IEEE (2008)
13. Nain, A.K., Rajalakshmi, P.: A reliable covert channel over IEEE 802.15.4 using steganography. In: 2016 IEEE 3rd World Forum on Internet of Things (WF-IoT), pp. 711–716. IEEE (2016)
14. Peng, Y., et al.: PLoRa: a passive long-range data network from ambient LoRa transmissions. In: Proceedings of the 2018 Conference of the ACM Special Interest Group on Data Communication, pp. 147–160 (2018)
15. Pérez-Penichet, C., Hermans, F., Varshney, A., Voigt, T.: Augmenting IoT networks with backscatter-enabled passive sensor tags. In: Proceedings of the 3rd Workshop on Hot Topics in Wireless, pp. 23–27 (2016)
16. Pérez-Penichet, C., Piumwardane, D., Rohner, C., Voigt, T.: TagAlong: efficient integration of battery-free sensor tags in standard wireless networks. In: 2020 19th ACM/IEEE International Conference on Information Processing in Sensor Networks (IPSN), pp. 169–180. IEEE (2020)
17. Sankhe, K., Belgiovine, M., Zhou, F., Riyaz, S., Ioannidis, S., Chowdhury, K.: Oracle: optimized radio classification through convolutional neural networks. In: IEEE INFOCOM 2019-IEEE Conference on Computer Communications, pp. 370–378. IEEE (2019)
18. Talla, V., Hessar, M., Kellogg, B., Najafi, A., Smith, J.R., Gollakota, S.: LoRa backscatter: enabling the vision of ubiquitous connectivity. Proc. ACM Interact. Mob. Wearable Ubiquit. Technol. **1**(3), 1–24 (2017)
19. Ureten, O., Serinken, N.: Wireless security through RF fingerprinting. Can. J. Electr. Comput. Eng. **32**(1), 27–33 (2007)
20. Van Huynh, N., Hoang, D.T., Lu, X., Niyato, D., Wang, P., Kim, D.I.: Ambient backscatter communications: a contemporary survey. IEEE Commun. Surv. Tutor. **20**(4), 2889–2922 (2018)
21. Qiang, X., Zheng, R., Saad, W., Han, Z.: Device fingerprinting in wireless networks: challenges and opportunities. IEEE Commun. Surv. Tutor. **18**(1), 94–104 (2015)
22. Zanetti, D., Danev, B., Capkun, S.: Physical-layer identification of UHF RFID tags. In: Proceedings of the Sixteenth Annual International Conference on Mobile Computing and Networking, pp. 353–364 (2010)

23. Zhang, P., Bharadia, D., Joshi, K., Katti, S.: Hitchhike: practical backscatter using commodity wifi. In: Proceedings of the 14th ACM Conference on Embedded Network Sensor Systems CD-ROM, pp. 259–271 (2016)
24. Zielinska, E., Szczypiorski, K.: Direct sequence spread spectrum steganographic scheme for IEEE 802.15.4. In: 2011 Third International Conference on Multimedia Information Networking and Security, pp. 586–590. IEEE (2011)

P2Onto: Making Privacy Policies Transparent

Evgenia Novikova[1,2] 🆔, Elena Doynikova[1,2(✉)] 🆔, and Igor Kotenko[1,2] 🆔

[1] HUAWEI Research Center, Marata str. 69-71, St. Petersburg, Russia
{novikova,doynikova,ivkote}@comsec.spb.ru
[2] SPC RAS, SPIIRAS, 39, 14 Line, St. Petersburg 199178, Russia

Abstract. The privacy issue is highly relevant for modern information systems. Both particular users and organizations usually do not understand risks related with personal data processing. The ways an organization gathers, uses, discloses, and manages a customer's or client's data should be described by privacy policy, but in major cases such policies are confusing for the customer. The goal of this research is making privacy policy transparent for the users via automation of the privacy risks assessment process based on the privacy policy. The paper introduces the developed common approach to privacy risks assessment based on analysis of privacy policies and ontology for privacy policies. The approach includes construction of an ontology for a privacy policy, and generation of rules for privacy risks assessment based on the proposed ontology. The applicability of the proposed approach and ontology is demonstrated on the case study for IoT device.

Keywords: Privacy policy · Privacy risks · Personal data · Ontology · Semantic analysis · Natural language processing · Risk assessment

1 Introduction

The privacy issue is not novel for modern society. From the moment the various processes began moving into the information space, a large amount of personal information moved there. Personal data is data that identifiably describe a living individual person [1]. This information may be of financial interest, and it is used by different companies for a variety of purposes. In addition to using with so-called legal purposes, i.e. the purposes that have legal basis, this information can be stolen if information security requirements are not satisfied. It should be noticed that though the privacy issue is under discussion for the many years, the individuals, generally, do not understand what is personal data, how and when they provide legal basis for using their personal data while interacting with systems, products, and services, how and when their personal data can be stolen, as well as how personal data can be used against the individuals (e.g. annoying advertising, black PR (Public Relations), black market, damage to reputation, etc.). At the same time, the organizations that provide the systems, products, and services, may not completely realize the consequences of the personal data leakage both for their customers, and the organizations themselves. These consequences can include the financial losses, damage to reputation, and negative impact for the organization's development.

© Springer Nature Switzerland AG 2020
S. Katsikas et al. (Eds.): CyberICPS 2020/SECPRE 2020/ADIoT 2020, LNCS 12501, pp. 235–252, 2020.
https://doi.org/10.1007/978-3-030-64330-0_15

A number of incidents involving the personal data leakage led to the development of the EU General Data Protection Regulation (GDPR) [1] that emphasizes control over personal data and states that data subjects should be made aware of the risks related to personal data processing. This has forced the organizations to pay more attention to the privacy issues to avoid law and financial problems. The organizations should generate a privacy policy while providing various information products. Privacy policy is a statement or a legal document (in privacy law) that discloses some or all of the ways a party gathers, uses, discloses, and manages a customer or client's data. But most users accept such policies without even reading and understanding what kind of data and on what period they provide. A representative example is the application developed in Moscow to track the movements of individuals infected with COVID. All individuals that install the application and accept the privacy policy, give their consent to transfer all the data that application can get (from IP address to the passport ID and employer) to any third parties for almost any purposes including advertising for 10 years.

The goal of this research is making privacy policy transparent for the users by automation of the privacy risks assessment process based on the privacy policy. The approach based on the ontology is proposed.

As it is mentioned, the analysis of privacy policies is highly relevant and not novel issue. But to this moment there is no completed research related to the risk assessment based on the privacy policies analysis.

In this paper we propose an approach that incorporates analysis of the privacy policies written in natural language for the subsequent formal specification of the policies using an ontology and privacy risk assessment based on the constructed ontology.

The main contributions of the paper are as follows:

- a common approach to privacy risks assessment based on ontology constructed for a privacy policy;
- a privacy policy based ontology;
- an approach for constructing rules for privacy risks assessment based on the proposed ontology;
- a usage scenario.

The paper is organized as follows. Section 2 analyzes the main related works in the area of formal languages development for the privacy policies specification, application of natural language processing for the privacy policies analysis, existing privacy aware ontologies and privacy risks assessment. In Sect. 3 the developed methodology for privacy risks assessment is introduced, the developed ontology is provided, including the design and implementation processes, key concepts and application (Subsect. 3.1), converting privacy policy text to ontology (Subsect. 3.2), and privacy risks assessment procedure (Subsect. 3.3). In Sect. 4 the case study on application of the developed ontology to assess privacy risks is given, examples of the rules that can be used for privacy risks assessment are considered, and the discussion on advantages of the suggested ontology and the proposed privacy risks assessment procedure is provided. The paper ends with conclusion and future research directions.

2   Related Works

In this section we outline and analyze two main groups of researches related with ours.

The first group of the researches covers development of formal languages. The proposed languages can be used to specify the policies, while the developed policies can be used for the further analysis or privacy risk assessment. We consider this group of works as soon as in the scope of our approach we should develop a formal language for subsequent ontology specification.

The second group of the researches covers analysis of privacy policy texts represented using natural language. We consider this group of works as soon as privacy policies are usually generated using natural language. To develop formal language for ontology specification automatically we analyze the text of the privacy policy given in natural language first. In scope of this group of works we consider both the papers devoted to the natural language processing (NLP) and the papers devoted to the NLP application to analyze privacy policies and to assess the risks.

The formal languages are used for specification of the security policies, license agreements, access control policies, and privacy policies. The essence of approaches devoted to development of formal languages is specification of the language alphabet and of the rules for constructing the sequences using the characters of the alphabet (i.e. the language grammar). The text specified using such language can be processed using mathematical methods. There are a lot of application areas of this approach. As soon as this research is devoted to the privacy policies processing, we review in details the papers that consider development of formal languages for specification of privacy policies.

In [2] the authors propose the Platform for Enterprise Privacy Practices (E-P3P) to formalize a privacy policy into a machine-readable language that can be enforced automatically within the enterprise by the means of an authorization engine. The formalized policy specifies what types of the personally identifiable information (PII), for what purposes and by what users in the organization can be used. To formalize the policy the language that incorporates the terminology and the set of authorization rules is used. The terminology includes six elements, namely, data categories, purposes, data users, the set of actions, the set of obligations and the set of conditions. The authorization rules are used to allow or deny an action. Similar approach to authorization management and access control is introduced in [3]. The proposed model consists of users/groups, the accessed data, the purposes of access, and access modes. It is used to ensure that personal information is used only for authorization. Authors also proposed a privacy language based on the proposed model. This language is used for privacy and access control rules formalization and automated enforcement of these rules by the means of the access control system. The proposed model is limited only by the access control considering privacy aspects.

In [4] the language based approach is also used. The authors consider the privacy principle that states that the user's personal data can't be used for the purpose different from the one that they were collected for without consent of the concerned user. The authors assume that in major cases the users do not have any idea how and what purposes their personal information is used for. To resolve this issue the authors propose a data handling policy (DHP) showing users who and under what conditions can process their personal data. This policy can be developed by the service provider or by the user using the developed DHP language. The language incorporates the set of terms (namely, recipients, actions, purposes, PII, conditions, provisions and obligations) and rules. The DHP then enforced using policy decision points (make decision regarding the access request) and policy enforcement points (implement decision) of the access control system. The disadvantage is that such policy should be developed for each new product.

In [5] another language called PILOT for privacy policy specification is proposed. The authors also developed a tool that allows assessing privacy related risks if the policy is specified using the proposed language. The advantage of the approach is that it allows assessing the risks. The disadvantage is that this approach doesn't allow assessing them automatically if the policy is not specified using the developed formal language. The authors propose to users define the privacy policies themselves and then represent the risks of the developed policy. It is also not clear from the article how to define all possible risks that are required to get assessment for the specific risk.

In [6] the authors proposed the Layered Privacy Language (LPL) that fulfill the introduced requirements, namely, differentiation between the source and recipient of data, generating privacy policies considering the purposes of operations with data, guarantee of human-readability based on layering of privacy policies. The disadvantages of this work are as follows: the research is not completed and the proposed language does not cover all privacy aspects now; the company should define their privacy policy using LPL before analyzing it.

The privacy risks assessment approach is proposed in [7]. It is based on the harm trees. The trees are constructed based on information about the system, the personal data, the relevant risk sources, the relevant events and their impacts on privacy. The harm tree nodes are represented as triples incorporating personal data, system component, and risk source. The root node of the harm tree corresponds to a privacy harm. The leaf nodes correspond to the exploitation of data by the most likely risk source. The users' privacy settings are also considered while calculating the likelihood of the privacy harms.

The main difference between the papers of this group and our approach is that we propose generating and processing the ontology automatically for every policy specified in natural language using NLP.

The second group of the researches covers analysis of texts written in natural languages, including privacy policy texts. In [8] authors presented a pipeline for automatic privacy policy extraction and analysis of the Android applications. The main contribution is annotated corpus of the privacy policies APP-350 Corpus available by link: https://www.usableprivacy.org. The authors applied the TF-IDF (term frequency and inverse document frequency) approach to construct feature vector from text of the policies and the support vector machine (SVC) classifier to detect different data practices in policies. In [9] the authors applied machine learning approach to automated detection of opt-in/opt-out choices to control personal data visibility. They tested different machine learning techniques for policy text analysis, such as linear regression and neural networks and experimented with different set of features. However, application of the approach requires labeled data set. The authors implemented this procedure manually.

In [10] the authors propose a semantic framework PrivOnto to analyze privacy policies. The proposed framework uses as input the set of annotated privacy policies and developed an ontology representing a set of policies with identified privacy aware data practices. The key challenge here was related to the automated annotation of privacy policies to generate specific ontologies, for this goal crowdsourcing, machine learning and natural language processing were used. First, the experts analyzed the set of privacy policies and annotated them using outlined 11 categories of data practices (First Party Collection/Use:Privacy, Third Party Sharing/Collection:Privacy, User Choice/Control, User Access, Edit, & Deletion, Data Retention, Data Security, Policy Change, Do Not Track, International & Specific Audiences, Other). These categories served as main concepts to model privacy policies. Annotated set then was used to train the framework for automated annotation. The researches annotated over 23,000 data practices extracted from 115 privacy policies and made them publicly available by link: https://www.usable privacy.org. This research is the most closest to ours, but we focus not only on detection of data practices in text of policies, but on assessment of risks for personal data. To achieve this we focus on a particular privacy policy and develop a detailed semantic presentation of each privacy-aware data practice.

In this paper we introduce the proposed ontology that is the basis for our approach to the automated analysis of privacy risks based on the privacy policies. Though some aspects related to privacy policies analysis are covered in the related research, today there is no end-to-end approach to automated privacy risks assessment based on policies. Thus, the main contribution of our research is a new approach to privacy risks assessment based on analysis of privacy policies defined using natural language and ontology for privacy policies.

3 Methodology

In Fig. 1 the suggested risk assessment procedure based on analysis of privacy policies is shown.

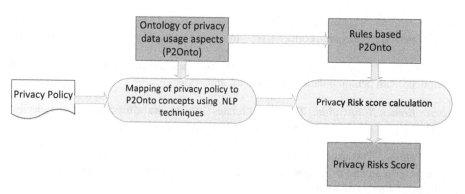

Fig. 1. General scheme of privacy risks calculation based on privacy policy analysis

The key element of the suggested approach is the P2Onto ontology that describes different aspects of personal data processing such as first party collection, third party sharing, etc. It serves as the basis for constructing an ontology for each particular privacy policy. The mapping of individuals to its concepts is implemented using natural language techniques. P2Onto ontology also serves as the basis for constructing rules for automated privacy risk calculation. All these steps with particular focus on P2Onto ontology are described below in detail.

3.1 P2Onto Ontology

The goal of P2Onto ontology is to describe possible data usage scenarios that involve personal data processing, and to provide formal basis for the risk assessment. To construct the ontology, we used the data usage practices and associated privacy aspects proposed in [10]. These aspects were identified by the domain experts who studied both existing privacy policies and corresponding legal regulations and requirements, such as COPPA [11], and the HIPAA Privacy Rule [12]. They are listed below.

First-Party Data Collection and Usage. This aspect characterizes what personal data are collected by the service provider, operating the device, web site or application, how they are collected, what legal basis and purposes of data collection are.

Third-Party Data Collection and Sharing. This aspect characterizes all issues concerning data sharing procedures, including form of data shared – aggregated, anonymized or raw.

Data Security. This aspect describes security mechanisms, both technical and organizational, used to protect data.

Data Retention. This aspect characterizes temporal issues of personal data processing and storage.

Data Aggregation. This aspect defines if service provider aggregate personal data.

Privacy Settings. This practice defines available tools and options to end user to limit scope of personal data being collected (opt-in/opt-out issues of personal data collection).

Data Control. This aspect relates to tools and mechanisms provided to user to manipulate with personal data – access, edit, and erase.

Privacy Breach Notification. This aspect relates to the tools and mechanisms the service provider uses to inform about breach of personal data privacy.

Policy Change. This aspect relates to what tools and mechanisms the service provider uses to inform an end user about changes in text of personal data privacy and possible reactions available to end user.

Do Not Track. This practice describes how tracking signals for online tracking and advertising are processed.

International and Special Audience. This aspect discusses different issues relating with processing personal data of special audience such as children, and citizens of certain states and regions.

According to the workflow for designing ontologies based on privacy policies proposed in [13], the definition of the competence questions for each privacy aspect is a key issue that specifies the goal and tasks of the ontology. We used this approach for constructing the P2Onto ontology and determined a set of competence questions specifying issues associated with them. These competence questions are based on guidelines and questionnaires provided by international security IoT assessment frameworks such as IoTF, GSMA in the field of privacy risk assessment [14, 15]. The examples of competence questions for some privacy aspects are given in Table 1.

Table 1. Some privacy aspects and corresponding competence questions

Privacy aspect	Competence questions	Examples
First-party data collection and usage	What data categories are collected?	Geo location, activity tracking, health status, financial info, contact info, etc.
	What is the data collection mode?	Automatically without user consent, automatically but with given consent every time when automatic collection performed, or given by user directly (i.e. financial data)
	What is the purpose of data collection?	Service provision including additional services, enhancement of service provision, analytics and research, marketing and advertising, personalization, security and support services, legal requirement, etc.
	What is the basis for data collection	User given consent, legal requirement, other
	Do you collect data from third party service providers?	No, public sources, third-party service providers, others
Privacy settings	Who provides privacy settings control?	First-party service provider, Third-party service provider (including web-browser privacy settings)
	How are they implemented?	Opt-in (user directly specifies what data to collect and share), opt-out using web-link or mailing, stop using services

These questions helped us to identify core concepts and properties of the P2Onto ontology. We outlined four core concepts – *Data, Activity, Agent* and *Mechanism* – that serve as the basis for describing all aspects of data processing including tools involved in this process. Let us consider them in detail.

Data is a generic concept, it is a super class for *Personal_Data* and *Non-Personal_Data*. The concept *Personal_Data* is defined in GDPR text as "any information relating to an identified or identifiable natural person ('data subject'); an identifiable natural person is one who can be identified, directly or indirectly, in particular by reference to an identifier such as a name, an identification number, location data, an online identifier or to one or more factors specific to the physical, physiological, genetic, mental, economic, cultural or social identity of that natural person" [1, Article 4].

This allowed us to determine *Sensitive_Data* concept and its subclasses to describe racial or ethnic origin (*Racial_Data*), political opinions, religious or philosophical beliefs (*Religion_Data*), genetic data (*Genetic Data*), biometric data for the purpose of uniquely identifying a natural person (*Biometric_Data*), data concerning person health (*Health_data*), data about crime records (*Crime_Data*). We also outlined *Tracking_Data* concept to have possibility to answer Do Not Track data usage aspect. Concept *Non-Personal_Data* is used to describe non-personal data such as statistical data and is valuable to understand how many types of data – identifiable and not – are collected about particular device user.

Figure 2 shows the hierarchy of *Data* subclasses.

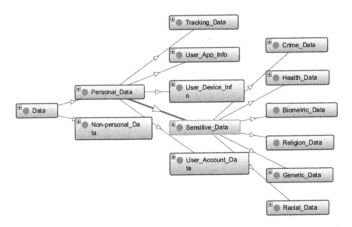

Fig. 2. Structure of data concept

Concept *Activity* (Fig. 3) is a generic concept that may be used to describe possible actions concerning data processing and data control activities. That is why we defined two different subclasses *Data_Activity* and *Control_Activity*. The first subclass is purposed to describe possible activities arising with data processing – collection, usage (or processing), storage and sharing with third parties, while the purpose of the second subclass is describe wide variety of activities associated with data privacy control and data access operations available to user, consent giving and withdrawal. It also includes activities of service provider concerning notifications in case of policy change and breach of data. Each individual or subclass of *Data_Activity* concept has property *hasLegal-Basis* that defines legal basis for data activity, including data collection. The legal basis is represented by a concept *Legal_Basis*. The purpose of data activity is described by Data_Activity_Purpose concept. We assume that there is a variety of data processing purposes but in general case they may fall into categories listed in Table 1.

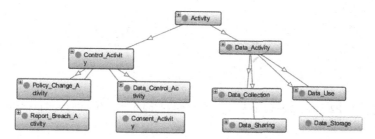

Fig. 3. Structure of activity concept

Two other important concepts are *Agent* and *Mechanism*. The concept *Agent* is used to describe service provider, end user, i.e. data subject, and third party participating in data processing. We currently suggest reusing this concept from PROV-O ontology that specifies a concept Agent as a subject that "bears some form of responsibility for an activity taking place, for the existence of an entity, or for another agent's activity" [16].

The *Mechanism* class is a generic class that is used to define different mechanisms, tools or interfaces for implementing different types of data activities. It serves as a super-class to describe tools and mechanisms to collect and share data, options available to user to access data and control their privacy. The *Mechanism* is a superclass for the *Notification_Mechanism* concept used to describe ways the server provider notifies the data subject in case of data breach or privacy policy change. These classes are linked to data subjects or activities using special object properties reflecting the relationship between corresponding classes. For example, to describe security mechanisms and tools used to secure data processing, we use the property *isSecuredBy* linking the *Data_Activity* concept with the *Security_Mechanism* concept.

Figure 4 shows main concepts and properties related to the First Party Collection aspect.

3.2 Mapping of the Policy Text into P2Oto Concepts

Mapping text of the privacy policy into the concepts of the P2Onto ontology is a critical process. In major cases, text policies are monolithic texts structured in paragraphs. Some policies present important information in the form of tables or lists. This allows us to make following assumptions:

- if policy is a text organized in paragraphs, then each paragraph represents a set of P2Onto concepts semantically linked to one privacy aspect and data usage scenario;

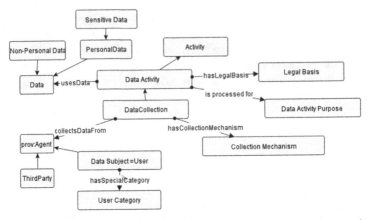

Fig. 4. P2Onto concepts and properties describing first party collection practice

- if paragraph contains a list, then each list item represent individuals of one concept or a set of P2Onto concepts semantically linked to one privacy aspect;
- if text contains a table then each row is treated as one data usage scenario, where columns contain individuals relating to different P2Onto concepts;
- if policy text is monolithic and does not contain paragraphs, then we treat it as one usage scenario, detecting individuals relating to P2Onto concepts, without linking them to one scenario.

P2Onto concepts are instantiated by words or phrases from a text policy based on simple matching them to a vocabulary that contains key words for each P2Onto concept, extended by generated synonyms.

As the result mapping each P2Onto concept will be assigned a set of individuals, if the P2Onto concept except the *Personal_Data* class and its subclasses was not detected in a given data usage scenario, then it is assigned the *NotDef* individual.

3.3 Privacy Rule Construction

The P2Onto ontology is constructed in such a way that one concept or subset of concepts may provide an answer to one competence question. Table 2 shows some examples of mapping between privacy aspects, competency questions and P2Onto concepts and properties.

Mapping one concept to one competency question allows us to propose the following privacy risk assessment procedure.

Let *PA* is a particular privacy aspect, and it includes n competence questions. Let CQ_i is i^{th} competence question, and then the risk score for *PA* privacy aspect is defined as follows.

Table 2. Privacy aspects and P2Onto concepts and properties

Privacy aspect	Competency questions	P2Onto concepts	P2Onto properties
First party collection/use	What data categories are collected?	Data and its subclasses (personal data, non-personal data)	usesData
	Do you collect data from third party service providers?	Third party	CollectsDataFrom
	What is the data collection mode?	Collection mechanism	hasCollectionMechanism
	What is the purpose of data collection?	Data activity purpose	isProcessedFor
	What is the legal basis of collection?	Legal basis	hasLegalBasis
Privacy settings	Who provides privacy settings control?	Agent	providedBy
	How are they implemented?	User_Control_mechanism	Implements
	What data types do they affect?	Data and its subclasses (personal data, non-personal data)	Involves

1. For each competence question CQ_i

   a) define a C_i concept or a set $\mathbf{C}_i$ of concepts (belonging to one superclass, i.e. class *Data*),

   b) calculate $RiskScore(CQ_i)$ risk score for competence question CQ_i as a $RiskScore(C_i)$ risk score of instances belonging to Ci concept, i.e. $RiskScore(CQ_i) = RiskScore(C_i)$. $RiskScore(\mathbf{C})$ for a set of concepts is defined as follows $RiskScore(\mathbf{C}) = \max\{RiskScore(C_i), C_i \in \mathbf{C}\}$.

2. Calculate privacy risk score for privacy aspect as a sum of risk scores for each competence question CQ_i:

$$RiskScore_{PA} = \sum_{i=1}^{n} RiskScore(CQ_i). \tag{1}$$

3. If $RiskScore_{PA} \geq$ High_Threshold, then privacy risks are High, if $RiskScore_{PA} <$ Low_Threshold, then privacy risks are Low, else they are Medium.

The values of threshold need to be determined during experiments after some statistical distribution of risks is obtained, but currently we suggest defining them as follows:

- High_Threshold $= 4/3 \cdot n$,
- Low_Threshold $= 2/3 \cdot n$,

where n is the number of competence questions defined for privacy aspect *PA*. The overall privacy risks are calculated as sum of $RiskScore_{PAi}$ determined for each privacy aspect PA_i.

To calculate $RiskScore(C)$ based on individuals of the concept C, we propose to rank them as *critical, generic* and *other*. The rank of individuals is determined for each concept individually. Let us consider the following example, the purposes of the data collection may be as follows: p1 – service provision including additional services, p2 – enhancement of service provision, p3 – analytics and research, p4 – marketing and advertising, p5 – personalization, p6 – security and support services, p7 – legal requirement. The purposes p1 and p2 are rather generic, it is rather difficult to judge whether the data collected are really necessary or not, we propose to rank them as *generic*; purposes p3, p4 and p5 assume data aggregation and possible user profiling that is why we suggest ranking them as *critical,* purposes p6 and p7 are clear and we rank them as *other*.

Let us define following functions:

- *Critical(C)* returns a number of individuals of the concept C that have critical rank;
- *Generic(C)* returns a number of individuals of the concept C that have generic rank;
- *Other(C)* returns a number of individuals of the concept C that have other rank;
- *Not_defined(C)* returns a number of *NotDef* individuals assigned to the concept C.

Then in general case we propose using the following rule to score the risks for each concept C:

If $Critical(C) > 0$, then $RiskScore(C) = 2$, else
If $Others(C) = 0$ or $\frac{Generic(C) + Not\_defined(C)}{Others(C)} \geq 1$, then $RiskScore(C) = 1$,
else $RiskScore(C) = 0$.

However, in some cases it is necessary to define individual rules for some concepts. The example of such concept is *Data*, as we consider that risks are getting higher with the amount of collected data, and that is why we suggest scoring this concept according to the following rule:

If (individuals of *Sensitive_Data* is not null) then $RiskScore(Data) = 2$, if individuals of *Personal_Data* or its subclasses is not null) then $RiskScore(Data) = 1$, else $RiskScore(Data) = 0$.

4   Usage Scenario and Discussion

To demonstrate our approach, we analyzed the privacy policy of the August company that produces smart lock, doorbell cameras and other accessories [17]. Their smart lock allows implementing a variety of convenient but privacy risky functions as remotely lock and unlock the door, logging exit/entrance activity of smart lock owners as well as their guests, supports biometrical identification and voice assistant. We constructed an ontology for the privacy policy concerning August services and products [17] and calculated privacy risks based on the information provided within it.

We examined the following data usage aspects: *first-party data collection and usage scenario, third-party data collection and sharing, data security, data retention, privacy settings, data control and policy change.* We omitted from the explicit risk analysis international and special audience scenario as special audience is usually represented by citizens of EU and California protected by a set of regulations such GDPR [1], CCPA [18].

These regulations require specifying explicitly the purpose of data processing including collection and third party sharing, and our analysis showed that these concepts are considered in first data collection and third party-sharing. Moreover, it is interesting to understand privacy risks in general but not for a specific audience, however, in future we are planning to include this scenario and analyze the difference in privacy risks for different type of audience. The August products are not purposed for the use by minors under 16, therefore privacy risks for this specific audience are not calculated. It also should be noted that the usage scenario describing *privacy breach notification* was not detected in the text at all.

The given privacy policy is represented by a text structured as a sequence of paragraphs, some of them contain bulleted lists, there was also a table. Currently the process of mapping privacy policy to P2Onto concepts is done manually, however, to detect P2Onto concepts and data usage scenarios in text of the policy we used assumptions defined in Sect. 3.2 and treated paragraph without bulleted list or item of a list as one data usage scenario.

Figure 5 shows a part of constructed P2Onto ontology describing collection activity constructed under following assumptions.

We used Graffoo OWL editor [19] for prototyping and visualizing ontology before moving it to OWL/XML format. We also used its capabilities to highlight different usage scenario for different type of data. The rectangles on Fig. 5 correspond to P2Onto concepts, labeled arrows – to object properties, while small circles – to the individuals. The individuals that belong to one usage scenario, i.e. were detected in one paragraph or bullet list item are marked by one color.

From Fig. 5 it is clearly seen that in major cases the privacy policy text did not contain individuals of all P2Onto classes referring to one data usage, this resulted in appearance of *NotDef* individuals in many data usage scenarios. In some cases these concepts were described separately. For example, the purposes of data usage and storage were given in separate paragraph, but there was no clear specification what type of the data they refer.

We detected similar case in data retention usage practice (Fig. 6).

The product manufactures first provide general description of how long all collected data is retained for, the purpose and legal basis for data retention (white circles in Fig. 6),

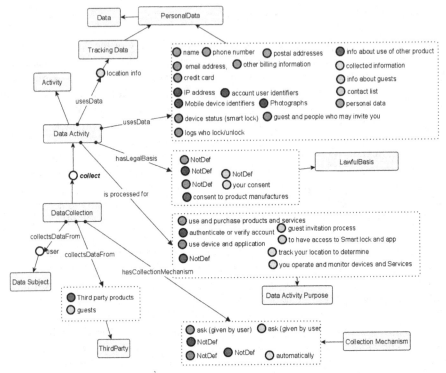

Fig. 5. Part of P2Onto ontology presenting first party collection data usage practice detected in August privacy policy (Color figure online)

and then specify some particular scenarios, for example, they inform that lock activity, including guest activity as well as account information is stored at least 90 days after account deletion (orange circles in the Fig. 6), however, they do not provide information how long the financial data of the smart lock user is stored (lilac circles in the Fig. 6).

Let us calculate privacy risks for first party collection and usage practice. It is described by five competence questions that are given in Table 2 alongside with corresponding P2Onto concepts. To calculate risk score associated with each competence question it is necessary to assign ranks to the individuals detected.

Table 3 contains suggested ranks for the individuals.

We assumed that collection information from the user's guests may pose high privacy risks both to user and his/her guests. The purposes of data processing concerning personalization and understanding of user behavior are also considered as critical as they highly related to user behavior profiling, and at last we refer to *not defined* legal basis of data collection and processing as critical, as personal data processing has to have clearly defined basis for this activity what is stated in many legislative regulations.

For the assigned ranks of the individuals we obtained the following risk scores for each competence question or corresponding P2Onto concept and risk score for the given data practice (see Eq. 1):

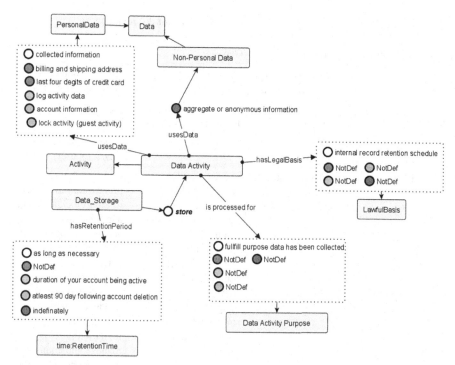

Fig. 6. Part of P2Onto ontology presenting data retention practice detected in August privacy policy (Color figure online)

- *RiskScore (Data)* = 1;
- *RiskScore (Third Party)* = 2;
- *RiskScore (Collection Mechanism)* = 0;
- *RiskScore (Data Activity Purpose)* = 2;
- *RiskScore (Legal Basis)* = 2;
- *RiskScore (First party collection and usage)* = 7.

The values of the risk thresholds for the given usage scenario are the following:

- High_Threshold = 4/3·5 = 6.67,
- Low_Threshold = 2/3·5 = 3.33,

Thus, The *RiskScore* equal to 7 corresponds to high privacy risks.

It should be noted that the procedure of assigning ranks to the individuals is a critical part in the risk assessment procedure. For example, changing rank of *not defined* legal basis to not critical results in RiskScore for *Legal_Basis* concept equal to 0, that in its turn results in medium privacy risks for this data practice (*RiskScore* = 5).

Table 3. Assigned ranks of P2Onto individuals for different concepts

P2Onto concepts	Critical	Generic	Others
Data	All individuals of Sensitive_Data class	All individuals of Personal_Data class	All individuals of Non_Personal Data
Third party	Guests	Third party products	
Collection mechanism			Automatically ask (given by user)
Data activity purpose	Personalized, understand your needs, interests	Use and purchase products and services; use device and application; provide, administer, improve app, services; provide service; product and communication; comply legal obligations; enforce agreements; provide further information and offers	Guest invitation process, to have access to Smart lock and app, authenticate or verify account, track your location to determine..., You operate and monitor devices and services conduct market research, guest invitation process, manage and administer our account, fulfill orders, respond to support requests; resolve disputes; protect, investigate, deter against fraudulent, illegal activity; administer promotional activity
Legal basis	NotDef		Your consent, consent to product manufactures, expressed consent, performance, our legitimate interest, legal obligation

Application of similar procedure to assess the rest of privacy policies allows obtaining following risk scores for them:

- *RiskScore(third-party data collection and sharing)* = Medium
- *RiskScore(data security)* = Medium
- *RiskScore(data retention)* = High
- *RiskScore(privacy settings)* = Medium

- *RiskScore(data control)* = Medium
- *RiskScore(policy change)* = Medium.

The overall risk score for the given policy is Medium, that it is expected privacy risks for this policy, as the device collects and stores a lot of personal information that relates not only to the end users but to their guests. However, the sharing process is described rather transparent, though the format of data sharing is not defined.

Interestingly that it is clearly stated only when data sharing is done in market research and other purposes. The retention data aspect received High risk score because it has indefinite period of retention, however this period is mentioned in the usage scenario of aggregated and anonymous data.

This made us to conclude that it is necessary to consider the type of the data (personal, sensitive or non-personal data) involved in each data scenario. The application of the ontology as a framework for constructing such rules allows these changes as all data scenarios are presented as linked ontology concepts. This ability of the ontology is also useful in explaining obtained results as it is clear how different types of personal data are collected, processed and shared, what tools and options to access, edit personal data or delete of them are available to end user, etc.

The authors consider that this ontology can serve as the basis for elaborating interactive graph-based visualization models targeted to explain the privacy risks to the end user in clear and readable manner.

5 Conclusions

The personal data protection is highly relevant task in the modern information systems due to their complexity and strong link with everyday life of people, on the one hand, and possible negative consequences of the personal data leakage, on the another hand. In some cases privacy polices are the only way for the end user to understand what types of personal data are processed by device or application, how they are processed and protected, what the goals of data collection and sharing are.

This paper proposed an approach for privacy risk assessment based on ontology constructed for a particular privacy policy. The risk assessment procedure uses rules that score privacy risks depending on the rank of ontology individuals detected in the text of privacy policy. The resulting scores can help end user to understand what privacy risks he/she accepts when accept privacy policy.

In the paper the authors demonstrated the proposed approach for assessing privacy policy of the smart lock that allows remote control. The usage scenario showed that proposed ontology is able to present main data usage aspects in clear and readable manner, it also allows explain the calculated risk score.

However, it also revealed that setting ranks for individuals is a critical aspect that requires additional research. Another important direction of the future research is related to the automation of ontology concepts detection in the policy text.

References

1. General Data Protection Regulation (GDPR). https://gdpr-info.eu/
2. Ashley, P., Hada, S., Karjoth, G., Schunter, M.: E-p 3p privacy policies and privacy authorization. In: Proceedings of the ACM workshop on Privacy in the Electronic Society (WPES 2002), Washington, DC, USA (2002)
3. Karjoth, G., Schunter, M.: Privacy policy model for enterprises. In: Proceedings of the 15th IEEE Computer Security Foundations Workshop, Cape Breton, Nova Scotia, Canada (2002)
4. Ardagna, C.A., De Capitani di Vimercati, S., Samarati, P.: Enhancing user privacy through data handling policies. In: Damiani, E., Liu, P. (eds.) DBSec 2006. LNCS, vol. 4127, pp. 224–236. Springer, Heidelberg (2006). https://doi.org/10.1007/11805588_16
5. Pardo, R., Le Métayer, D.: Analysis of privacy policies to enhance informed consent. In: Foley, Simon N. (ed.) DBSec 2019. LNCS, vol. 11559, pp. 177–198. Springer, Cham (2019). https://doi.org/10.1007/978-3-030-22479-0_10
6. Gerl, A., Bennani, N., Kosch, H., Brunie, L.: LPL, towards a GDPR-compliant privacy language: formal definition and usage. Trans. Large-Scale Data- Knowl.-Centered Syst. **37**, 41–80 (2018)
7. De, S.J., Le Metayer, D.: Privacy risk analysis to enable informed privacy settings. In: 2018 IEEE European Symposium on Security and Privacy Workshops (EuroS&PW), London, pp. 95–102 (2018)
8. Zimmeck, S., et al.: MAPS: scaling privacy compliance analysis to a million apps. In: Proceedings on Privacy Enhancing Technologies, vol. 66 (2019). https://ir.lawnet.fordham.edu/faculty_scholarship/1040
9. Kumar V.B., et al.: Finding a choice in a haystack: automatic extraction of opt-out statements from privacy policy text. In: Proceedings of the Web Conference 2020 (WWW 2020), p. 1943–1954. Association for Computing Machinery, New York (2020)
10. Oltramari, A., et al.: PrivOnto: a semantic framework for the analysis of privacy policies. Semant. Web **9**(2), 185–203 (2018)
11. Children's Online Privacy Protection Rule ("COPPA"). https://www.ftc.gov/enforcement/rules/rulemaking-regulatory-reform-proceedings/childrens-online-privacy-protection-rule. Accessed 05 July 2020
12. Health Information Privacy. https://www.hhs.gov/hipaa/index.html. Accessed 05 July 2020
13. Pandit, H.J., O'Sullivan D., Lewis, D.: An ontology design pattern for describing personal data in privacy policies. In: WOP@ISWC (2018)
14. IoT Security Compliance Framework. https://www.iotsecurityfoundation.org/best-practice-guidelines/. Accessed 05 July 2020
15. GSMA IoT Security Guidelines and Assessment. http://gsma.com/iot/iot-security/iot-security-guidelines/. Accessed 05 July 2020
16. PROV_O: The PROV Ontology. https://www.w3.org/TR/prov-o/#Agent. Accessed 05 July 2020
17. August Device and Service Privacy Policy. https://august.com/pages/privacy-policy#product. Accessed 05 July 2020
18. California Consumer Privacy Act 2018. https://oag.ca.gov/privacy/ccpa. Accessed 05 July 2020
19. Graffoo OWL Editor. https://essepuntato.it/graffoo/. Accessed 05 July 2020

Extended Abstract - Transformers: Intrusion Detection Data in Disguise

James Boorman⬥, Benjamin Green$^{(\boxtimes)}$, and Daniel Prince$^{(\boxtimes)}$

Lancaster University, Lancaster, UK
{j.boorman,b.green2,d.prince}@lancaster.ac.uk

Abstract. IoT cyber security deficiencies are an increasing concern for users, operators, and developers. With no immediate and holistic device-level fixes in sight, alternative wraparound defensive measures are required. Intrusion Detection Systems (IDS) present one such option, and represent an active field of research within the IoT space. IoT environments offer rich contextual and situational information from their interaction with the physical processes they control, which may be of use to such IDS. This paper uses a comprehensive analysis of the current state-of-the-art in context and situationally aware IoT IDS to define the often misunderstood concepts of context and situational awareness in relation to their use within IoT IDS. Building on this, a unified approach to transforming and exploiting such a rich additional data set is proposed to enhance the efficacy of current IDS approaches.

Keywords: Internet of Things · IoT · Intrusion detection · Context awareness · Situational awareness

1 Introduction

One of the largest computing platforms in the world, the Internet of Things (IoT) is a continually evolving paradigm that aims to permeate and interconnect every facet of society. Comprised of heterogeneous devices in growing numbers sensing and interacting with each other and the surrounding world, IoT brings significant benefits to its ever expanding set of application domains.

Computationally constrained when compared to traditional computing systems, IoT devices utilise varying technologies designed to support communication using limited resources. Consequently, this exposes them to cyber attacks through their inability to adopt traditional defensive techniques [15]. These issues are compounded through deficiencies in development practices, and contribute towards IoT devices being considered as promising targets of attack [15]. This ever increasing threat necessitates the use of alternative wraparound defensive measures, including intrusion detection systems (IDS).

IDS for IoT is an active field of research, with many solutions being created to overcome device-level resource limitations [5]. However, few IDS solutions incorporate the large swathe of context and situational information generated by IoT

© Springer Nature Switzerland AG 2020
S. Katsikas et al. (Eds.): CyberICPS 2020/SECPRE 2020/ADIoT 2020, LNCS 12501, pp. 253–263, 2020.
https://doi.org/10.1007/978-3-030-64330-0_16

devices. Even in micro deployments, there exists a large quantity of information that has the potential to provide any IDS with contextual and situational understanding, empowering decision making. Authors in this space have identified the potential for context and situational awareness in IoT IDS [3]. However, the difference between these two terms is often misunderstood, with context awareness and situational awareness being mislabelled and subsequently misused [14,22]. This presents a challenge to other researchers looking to incorporate context and situational awareness into their own IDS solutions.

In this paper we clarify the difference between context and situational awareness for IoT IDS through a comprehensive analysis of their current state-of-the-art within literature. We then offer a unified approach to generating situational awareness data for IoT IDS through a theoretical pathway, highlighting the necessary steps to take to transform raw data into situational awareness.

2   Background and Related Work

IDS for IoT is a varied and active research area, with a broad body of literature dedicated to detecting the ever increasing profile of attack techniques. While active, it is an area that faces unique challenges, with a vastly heterogeneous device base adding new concerns to long standing security issues inherited from traditional computing systems.

There exists 3 primary surveys that focus on IDS in IoT. Zarpelão et al. [31] present a taxonomy to classify IDS in IoT literature, alongside a critical analysis of future research directions in this space. The authors identify that research efforts should focus on investigating detection methods and placement strategies, increasing the range of detectable attacks, addressing more IoT technologies, improving validation strategies, and overcoming the unsuitability of traditional IDS for IoT networks. Santos et al. [25] provide a more recent literature review, corroborating Zarpelão et al.'s [31] proposed research directions, and highlight that IoT IDS is still in its infancy. Finally, Benkhelifa et al. [5] critically reviewed practices and challenges in IoT IDS, before proposing an architecture supporting IoT IDS that spans all three IoT layers (perception, network, and application).

While the aforementioned surveys identify key research issues currently affecting IoT IDS, they fail to discuss or identify the use of context and situational awareness as a suitable base for augmentation. This is to be expected when considering that although there are over 900 IoT IDS papers returned from cursory searches on SCOPUS, only 24 of these are focused towards context or situational awareness for IoT IDS. Although context and situational awareness IoT IDS constitutes a very small proportion of overall IoT IDS literature, there are authors who demonstrate that context information when considered in conjunction with network information offers improvement over non-context aware IDS [3]. Furthermore, Kouicem et al.'s [15] survey of IoT security advocates that to improve IoT device security there should be an increased effort towards utilising the environment in which they pervade.

As demonstrated across the following sections, efforts have been made to exploit context and situational awareness within IoT IDS literature. However, there is still much confusion surrounding the difference between these two distinct terms, and how one can transform raw data into usable context and situational awareness. Moreover, the initial attempts present in literature often claim to use context awareness, but in actuality are using situational awareness [22], and vice versa [14]. To alleviate this confusion, the following two sections outline what constitutes context and situational awareness, including the state-of-the-art for their use in IoT IDS.

3 Context and Context Awareness

3.1 Definitions

To successfully identify implementations of context awareness for IoT IDS, it is important to first understand what is meant by context and context awareness. Dey and Abowd [1], provide the following widely accepted definition of context, Definition 1, as:

> *"any information that can be used to characterize the situation of an entity. An entity is a person, place, or object that is considered relevant to the interaction between a user and an application, including the user and applications themselves"*

Once understood, it becomes possible to distinguish between raw data and context information. Sanchez et al. [24] posit that this distinction is simple; raw data is unprocessed and comes directly from the data source, while context information can only be generated through the processing of raw data. This distinction is important to keep in mind to ensure that the use of context information and raw data is kept separate to avoid confusion.

Following on from their definition of context, Dey and Abowd [1] provide the following widely accepted definition of context aware, Definition 2, as:

> *"A system is context aware if it uses context to provide relevant information and/or services to the user, where relevancy depends on the user's task"*

While both definitions are widely accepted, there are cases in which related works opt for alternative definitions [6,16]. However, IDS for IoT using context awareness requires definitions that are generically applicable due to the heterogeneous nature of IoT devices, and where the reshaping of situations can occur from the smallest of changes in environmental composition. For this reason, Dey and Abowd's [1] definitions are preferred, as they are more generically applicable when compared with those suggested in other works.

3.2 Context and Context Awareness for IoT IDS

Before discussing context and context awareness for IoT IDS, it is first important to identify the state of context and context awareness for IoT as a whole so that an appropriate basis can be formed. Perera et al. [23] provide the most comprehensive context aware IoT survey to date. In this work the authors identify factors necessary for context awareness formation, and introduce the context life cycle. This life cycle covers the movement of context in context aware systems, and consists of four stages: Acquisition, Modelling, Reasoning, and Dissemination. Following a discussion surrounding the overall context life cycle, the authors present a number of practical techniques applicable to each stage. Sezer et al. [26] build upon this to provide the most recent survey on IoT context awareness. Their work provides an overview of the state of the art in context aware IoT, and goes on to discuss new techniques supporting stages within the context life cycle, before defining context awareness as an essential part of IoT.

Anton et al. [3] present a context aware intrusion detection system for Industrial IoT that uses context information alongside network information. Their system is shown to offer an increase in performance over non-context aware IDS, with a lower false positive rate overall. The authors successfully demonstrate the value of context awareness for IoT IDS, and suggest that context awareness should be considered more widely to increase the reliability of IoT intrusion detection systems.

Sharma et al. [27] created a context aware system used for IoT-embedded Cyber Physical systems IDS, evaluated on an Unmanned Arial Vehicle. The system effectively uses context awareness to outperform similar systems in reliability and rates of false-positives, false-negatives, and true positives.

Sikder et al. [28] developed a context aware sensor based attack detector for smart devices. This attack detector demonstrates the use of machine learning techniques for context aware IDS, and is evaluated on a smart phone. The authors use context in a way consistent with previously highlighted definitions, and can be viewed as an accurate example of context awareness use for IoT IDS.

Park et al. [22] present a smart factory context aware IDS, however the authors introduce uncertainty as the work is identified as context aware, yet is also explicitly described as being based on situational awareness. This serves as an example of the confusion still present between context and situational awareness.

Pan et al. [21] and Gopal and Parthasarathy [12] utilise context awareness for IDS within building management systems and wireless sensor networks respectively. Both examples utilise context awareness to achieve the goals of intrusion detection in a manner consistent with definitions. As both application areas contain large overlaps with IoT, these two examples should be considered when attempting to utilise context awareness for IoT.

Finally, Choi et al. [8] implement context extraction to detect and identify faulty IoT devices. The author's use of context is not explicitly used for intrusion detection, however as the generated context information is used to provide services, the authors have successfully implemented context awareness according to definitions. While not designed for IDS, the approaches used within are easily adaptable for use in a different context.

While context awareness is a rich and varied area of research within IoT as a whole, literature surrounding its current use for IoT IDS is currently in its infancy. Understanding of context and its technical implementations within general literature is good, with the existence of artefacts such as the context life cycle serving to enable research within this space. Researchers are beginning to identify context awareness as a useful approach towards improving the capability of current IDS for IoT, with implementations showing enhancement of reliability, false-positives, false-negatives, and true positives over non-context aware solutions. However, some confusion still remains surrounding its use, and in some cases its fundamental construct. Overall, the use of context awareness within IoT IDS shows promise, although there is much work still to be done.

4   Situation and Situational Awareness

4.1   Definitions

Compared to context and context awareness, definitions of situation and situational awareness do not have as great a presence or understanding within existing literature. There are, however, common themes that pervade provided definitions and support in their understanding.

In their work on situation aware access control, Kayes et al. [13] propose that to specify a situation, it is required to capture the states of relevant context entities along with their relationships. Combining this with other information available within the environment, Kayes et al. [13] defined a situation as consisting of the set of elementary information. This view is corroborated by Goker et al. [11], who view context as a description of the aspects of a situation. While not necessarily a direct definition of situation, it can be taken from Kayes et al. [13] and Goker et al. [11] that a situation must, at the very least, contain context to be identified as such. This can then be substantiated further by Ye et al. [30], who state that a situation can be seen as an abstraction of the events occurring in the real world derived from context. Transforming this into a formal construct, Meissen et al. [19] define situation as $S = (t_{beg}, t_{end}, cs)$ where S is the situation, t_{beg} is the starting time of the situation, t_{end} is the end time of the situation, and cs is a set of characteristic features, with a characteristic feature viewed as a logical proposition about a context, or a subset of its components. From these examples we can conclude that for a situation to exist, it must implicitly contain context information. This information must be understood, processed, and combined to comprehend what the current situation at a specific point in time is. Rewording Meissen et al.'s [19] formal definition into Definition 3, a situation is therefore:

> "a set of characteristic features over an identified time that can uniquely describe the real world scenario that is of current interest"

Situational awareness is less prevalent than context awareness in existing literature, potentially due to its use as a synonym within context definitions. Endsley [9] can be considered an early adopter of situational awareness, provided a widely accepted definition, Definition 4, as:

"the perception of the elements in the environment within a volume of time and space, the comprehension of their meaning, and the projection of their status in the near future"

While Endsley's [9] original definition was created for military purposes, its applicability to the field of computing, and more specifically IoT, is valid. Achieving Endsley's [9] view of situational awareness would allow for improved user interaction, and the prediction of required services and resources before they are requested. Other definitions of situational awareness do exist within IoT focused literature [2], however, similarly to context and context awareness, our selected definitions are more generically applicable and thus better suited for IoT IDS.

4.2 Situation and Situational Awareness for IoT IDS

Of particular importance to situational awareness for IoT IDS is the conceptual model of Network Security Situation Awareness (NSSA) developed by Xu et al. [29], formed through a combination of Endsley's [9] situational awareness model and Bass' [4] JDL model. Consisting of three levels, security situation perception, situation evaluation, and situation prediction, the model was developed specifically with IoT in mind. Expanding on this, Xu et al. [29] focus on the first two levels and develop a situation reasoning framework, before demonstrating how it could detect attacks, worms, and evaluate IoT network vulnerabilities. The framework consists of 3 main components: a NSSA ontology, a reasoning engine, and user defined rules. Heterogeneous information, including context information, is formatted and fed into the ontology model, which models inputted information and the relationships existing between data points. Once the ontology is populated, the reasoning engine reasons out abnormalities using instances and user defined rules that identify different scenarios (e.g. attack scenarios). These three components combine to partially achieve the first two levels of NSSA, however Xu et al.'s approach [29] cannot monitor the overall security of IoT, as it does not contain the capabilities to handle all relevant information.

Utilising Xu et al.'s [29] conceptual model, Liu and Mu [17] present a network security situation awareness model using risk assessment methodologies. While the authors provide a starting point for this research area, the developed model simply scans a target network to obtain vulnerability information, assesses the risk value using their own custom formulas, then computes the network risk level based on the risks of all connected assets. As such, this model is limited and does not achieve true situational awareness.

McDermott et al. [18] correctly identify and utilise situational awareness, however from the perspective of a device owner's awareness of a cyber attack on their device. The authors make no mention of NSSA, and instead utilise Endsley's [9] original model. Casillo et al. [7] use situational awareness terminology, however the authors fail to demonstrate any implementation of situational awareness. Gendreau [10] demonstrates in depth understanding of situational awareness and its potential application to IoT IDS, however the author only suggests that their work is applicable to it from their given application of a

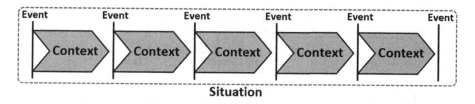

Fig. 1. Depiction of relation between events, context, and situation

self-reliant management and monitoring wireless sensor network cluster head selection algorithm.

Kirupakar and Shalinie [14] present a situation aware IDS design for industrial IoT gateways. The authors appear to have confused situation awareness with context awareness, as there is little to no mention of situational awareness within their work, instead they utilise a context analyser in their system and appear to be attempting to achieve context awareness.

Similar to context and context awareness, literature for situational awareness within IoT IDS is currently in its infancy. There are examples of models designed to achieve situational awareness for IoT IDS, such as NSSA, although there is no general adoption of one specific model. Furthermore, there are concrete examples of situational awareness for IoT IDS, albeit a small number. While this means that researchers are beginning to identify its use for improving IoT intrusion detection, there is still confusion surrounding the exact nature of situational awareness and the difference between it and context awareness, with works in this area confusing the two. Overall, the use of situational awareness within IoT intrusion detection shows promise, encompassing and expanding the previously shown benefits of context awareness due to it including context awareness in its creation. However,it is in a much earlier stage than that of context awareness from both a theoretical and technical perspective, and as such the potential benefits of situational awareness for IoT IDS remain largely unexplored.

5 Comparison

Context and situational awareness concepts can be difficult to separate, as shown by the aforementioned definitions, where context requires the acknowledgement of a situation. Within existing literature, there are works that understand and utilise context awareness, yet do not consider situational awareness. Moreover, as previously demonstrated, there is a degree of confusion within context and situational awareness literature surrounding the difference between the two distinct concepts, with authors claiming to implement one, while actually implementing the other. There exists further evidence of separation between context and situational awareness in the National Institute of Standards and Technology's (NIST) framework and roadmap for smart grid interoperability standards [20]. In this document, NIST identify situational awareness as one of the top eight priority areas to be considered when protecting critical infrastructure, with a focus on

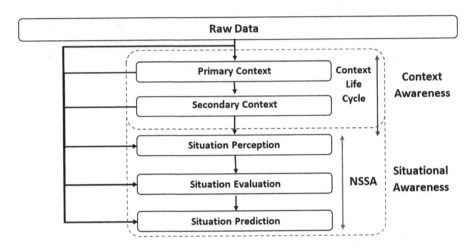

Fig. 2. Pathway from raw data through to situational awareness

smart grids. This example, and the previously described body of literature, form a basis towards the conclusion that context and situational awareness are two separate, yet interlinked entities, and not merely interchangeable concepts. This conclusion forms the basis for the following figures.

Figure 1 depicts the relationship between events, context, and a situation. As shown in Definition 3, a situation is a set of characteristic features over an identified time, that uniquely describes the real world scenario that is of current interest. Combined with Definition 1, which describes context as any information that can be used to characterise the situation of an entity, it is logical to reason that a situation's characteristic features must contain context. From Definition 4, it can be seen that context is a data source understood at a specific snapshot of time, while a situation develops and evolves over a period of time, thereby meaning that a situation is composed of context available within a specific window of time. Within a situation there can be many different contexts available and of use in understanding the situation, while context itself is implicitly tied to characterising the specific situation in question.

Expanding this relationship through to context and situational awareness, Definition 2 states that a system is context aware if it uses context to provide relevant information and/or services. According to Definition 4, situational awareness involves perceiving the situation, which as previously mentioned contains context within its set of characteristic features. Therefore, if a system implements situational awareness then it must intrinsically implement context awareness by default, as context is part of a situation and thereby used to provide relevant information. Figure 2 demonstrates this relationship and provides a theoretical pathway from raw data through to an understanding of a situation, based on the aforementioned conclusions and previously described differentiation between raw data, primary context, and secondary context. As context information is a building block in the understanding of a situation, the progression from both primary and secondary context towards understanding the current situation is natural. This viewpoint is partially substantiated by Perera et al. [23], who when discussing primary and secondary context note that secondary context without primary context could indicate a less than complete understanding of the situation. Finally, the figure also highlights where current aspects of literature, such as the context life cycle and NSSA reside.

With a situationally aware system inherently implementing context awareness, it stands to reason that previously highlighted benefits of context aware IDS for IoT such as improved reliability, false-positives, false-negatives, and true-positives would be present within such a system. Furthermore, as a situation requires the understanding of a much larger set of information than purely context, we believe that situationally aware IoT IDS would provide a more complete and holistic approach to IDS for IoT.

6   Conclusion

In this paper we have discussed the differences between context and situational awareness, identified by the current state of the art for both areas. This formed a basis to provide a discussion on how situational awareness implicitly utilises context awareness. Moreover, as situational awareness provides a more holistic and complete view of the security situation for an IoT environment, we suggest that future work implementing these concepts within IDS for IoT focus primarily on situational awareness and the use of context as a core constituent. We have identified that literature for context awareness in IoT is more developed than that of situational awareness, however common to both is a lack of literature surrounding their application towards IoT IDS, with both areas in their infancy. Although this area is in its early stages of development, authors are beginning to identify the benefits situational and context awareness can bring to IoT IDS. Finally, we have provided a pathway supporting the transformation of raw data towards situational awareness, including the use of context information as a core component. Our future work will focus on the practical implementation of this pathway to develop an IDS that is situationally aware, offering an enhanced viewpoint to further improve decision making processes and attack detection.

References

1. Abowd, G.D., Dey, A.K., Brown, P.J., Davies, N., Smith, M., Steggles, P.: Towards a better understanding of context and context-awareness. In: Gellersen, H.-W. (ed.) HUC 1999. LNCS, vol. 1707, pp. 304–307. Springer, Heidelberg (1999). https://doi.org/10.1007/3-540-48157-5_29

2. Alcaraz, C., Lopez, J.: Wide-area situational awareness for critical infrastructure protection. Computer **46**(4), 30–37 (2013). https://doi.org/10.1109/MC.2013.72

3. Anton, S.D., Fraunholz, D., Schotten, H.D., Teuber, S.: A question of context: enhancing intrusion detection by providing context information. In: Joint 13th CTTE and 10th CMI Conference on Internet of Things - Business Models, Users, and Networks, 1–8 January 2018 (2017). https://doi.org/10.1109/CTTE.2017. 8260938

4. Bass, T.: Intrusion detection systems and multisensor data fusion. Commun. ACM **43**(4), 99–105 (2000). https://doi.org/10.1145/332051.332079

5. Benkhelifa, E., Welsh, T., Hamouda, W.: A critical review of practices and challenges in intrusion detection systems for IoT: toward universal and resilient systems. IEEE Commun. Surv. Tutor. **20**(4), 3496–3509 (2018). https://doi.org/10. 1109/COMST.2018.2844742

6. Bricon-Souf, N., Newman, C.R.: Context awareness in health care: a review (2007). https://doi.org/10.1016/j.ijmedinf.2006.01.003

7. Casillo, M., Coppola, S., De Santo, M., Pascale, F., Santonicola, E.: Embedded intrusion detection system for detecting attacks over CAN-BUS. In: 2019 4th International Conference on System Reliability and Safety, ICSRS 2019, pp. 136–141 (2019). https://doi.org/10.1109/ICSRS48664.2019.8987605

8. Choi, J., et al.: Detecting and identifying faulty IoT devices in smart home with context extraction. In: Proceedings - 48th Annual IEEE/IFIP International Conference on Dependable Systems and Networks, DSN 2018, pp. 610–621 (2018). https://doi.org/10.1109/DSN.2018.00068

9. Endsley, M.R.: Toward a theory of situation awareness in dynamic systems (1995). https://doi.org/10.1518/001872095779049543

10. Gendreau, A.A.: Situation awareness measurement enhanced for efficient monitoring in the internet of things. In: Proceedings - 2015 IEEE Region 10 Symposium, TENSYMP 2015, pp. 82–85 (2015). https://doi.org/10.1109/TENSYMP.2015.13

11. Göker, A., Myrhaug, H., Bierig, R.: Context and Information Retrieval (chap. 7), pp. 131–157. Wiley, Hoboken (2009). https://doi.org/10.1002/9780470033647.ch7

12. Gopal, R., Parthasarathy, V.: CAND-IDS: a novel context aware intrusion detection system in cooperative wireless sensor networks by nodal node deployment. Circ. Syst. **07**(11), 3504–3521 (2016). https://doi.org/10.4236/cs.2016.711298

13. Kayes, A.S.M., Han, J., Colman, A.: PO-SAAC: a purpose-oriented situation-aware access control framework for software services. In: Jarke, M., et al. (eds.) CAiSE 2014. LNCS, vol. 8484, pp. 58–74. Springer, Cham (2014). https://doi.org/10.1007/ 978-3-319-07881-6_5

14. Kirupakar, J., Shalinie, S.M.: Situation aware intrusion detection system design for industrial IoT gateways. In: ICCIDS 2019–2nd International Conference on Computational Intelligence in Data Science, Proceedings (2019). https://doi.org/ 10.1109/ICCIDS.2019.8862038

15. Kouicem, D.E., Bouabdallah, A., Lakhlef, H.: Internet of things security: a topdown survey. Comput. Netw. **141**, 199–221 (2018). https://doi.org/10.1016/j. comnet.2018.03.012

16. Liu, Y., Seet, B.C., Al-Anbuky, A.: An ontology-based context model for wireless sensor network (WSN) management in the internet of things. J. Sens. Actuator Netw. **2**(4), 653–674 (2013). https://doi.org/10.3390/jsan2040653

17. Liu, Y., Mu, D.: A network security situation awareness model based on risk assessment. In: Krömer, P., Zhang, H., Liang, Y., Pan, J.-S. (eds.) ECC 2018. AISC, vol. 891, pp. 17–24. Springer, Cham (2019). https://doi.org/10.1007/978-3-030-03766-6_3

18. McDermott, C.D., Jeannelle, B., Isaacs, J.P.: Towards a conversational agent for threat detection in the internet of things. In: 2019 International Conference on Cyber Situational Awareness, Data Analytics and Assessment, Cyber SA 2019 (2019). https://doi.org/10.1109/CyberSA.2019.8899580

19. Meissen, U., Pfennigschmidt, S., Voisard, A., Wahnfried, T.: Context- and situation-awareness in information logistics. In: Lindner, W., Mesiti, M., Türker, C., Tzitzikas, Y., Vakali, A.I. (eds.) EDBT 2004. LNCS, vol. 3268, pp. 335–344. Springer, Heidelberg (2004). https://doi.org/10.1007/978-3-540-30192-9_33

20. National Institute of Standards and Technology: NIST Framework and Roadmap for Smart Grid Interoperability Standards, Release 3.0. Technical report (2014). https://doi.org/10.6028/NIST.SP.1108r3

21. Pan, Z., Hariri, S., Pacheco, J.: Context aware intrusion detection for building automation systems. Comput. Secur. 85, 181–201 (2019). https://doi.org/10.1016/j.cose.2019.04.011

22. Park, S.-T., Li, G., Hong, J.-C.: A study on smart factory-based ambient intelligence context-aware intrusion detection system using machine learning. J. Ambient Intell. Humaniz. Comput. 11(4), 1405–1412 (2018). https://doi.org/10.1007/s12652-018-0998-6

23. Perera, C., Zaslavsky, A., Christen, P., Georgakopoulos, D.: Context aware computing for the internet of things: a survey. IEEE Commun. Surv. Tutor. 16(1), 414–454 (2014). https://doi.org/10.1109/SURV.2013.042313.00197

24. Sanchez, L., Lanza, J., Olsen, R., Bauer, M., Girod-Genet, M.: A generic context management framework for personal networking environments. In: 2006 3rd Annual International Conference on Mobile and Ubiquitous Systems: Networking and Services, MobiQuitous (2006). https://doi.org/10.1109/MOBIQ.2006.340411

25. Santos, L., Rabadao, C., Goncalves, R.: Intrusion detection systems in internet of things: a literature review. In: Iberian Conference on Information Systems and Technologies, CISTI 2018, 1–7 June 2018 (2018). https://doi.org/10.23919/CISTI.2018.8399291

26. Sezer, O.B., Dogdu, E., Ozbayoglu, A.M.: Context-aware computing, learning, and big data in internet of things: a survey. IEEE Internet Things J. 5(1), 1–27 (2018). https://doi.org/10.1109/JIOT.2017.2773600

27. Sharma, V., You, I., Yim, K., Chen, I.R., Cho, J.H.: Briot: behavior rule specification-based misbehavior detection for IoT-embedded cyber-physical systems. IEEE Access 7, 1–25 (2019). https://doi.org/10.1109/ACCESS.2019.2917135

28. Sikder, A.K., Aksu, H., Uluagac, A.S.: A context-aware framework for detecting sensor-based threats on smart devices. IEEE Trans. Mob. Comput. 19(2), 245–261 (2020). https://doi.org/10.1109/TMC.2019.2893253

29. Xu, G., Cao, Y., Ren, Y., Li, X., Feng, Z.: Network security situation awareness based on semantic ontology and user-defined rules for internet of things. IEEE Access 5, 21046–21056 (2017). https://doi.org/10.1109/ACCESS.2017.2734681

30. Ye, J., Dobson, S., McKeever, S.: Situation identification techniques in pervasive computing: a review. Pervasive Mob. Comput. 8(1), 36–66 (2012). https://doi.org/10.1016/j.pmcj.2011.01.004

31. Zarpelão, B.B., Miani, R.S., Kawakani, C.T., de Alvarenga, S.C.: A survey of intrusion detection in Internet of Things. J. Netw. Comput. Appl. 84(September 2016), 25–37 (2017). https://doi.org/10.1016/j.jnca.2017.02.009

Author Index

Printed in the United States
By Bookmasters